Redneck Liberal

Redneck Liberal

Theodore G. Bilbo and the New Deal

Chester M. Morgan

Louisiana State University Press
Baton Rouge and London

For
Frances Davis Morgan

Manufactured in the United States of America

Designer: Marcy Fleming
Typeface: Linotron Sabon
Typesetter: G & S Typesetters, Inc.
Printer: Thomson-Shore, Inc.
Binder: John H. Dekker & Sons, Inc.

Library of Congress Cataloging in Publication Data

Morgan, Chester M.
Redneck liberal.

Bibliography: p.
Includes index.
1. Bilbo, Theodore Gilmore, 1877–1947.
2. Mississippi–Politics and government—1865–1950.
3. New Deal, 1933–1939. 4. United States—Politics and government—1933–1945. 5. Legislators—United States—Biography. 6. United States. Congress. Senate—Biography. I. Title.
E748.B5M67 1985 976.2′06′0924 [B] 85-11023
ISBN 0-8071-1243-7

Contents

Acknowledgments xi

Introduction 1

Chapter One
Redeemers, Rednecks, and Rotarian Reform 5

Chapter Two
Prince of the Peckerwoods 24

Chapter Three
New Deal Senator 58

Chapter Four
Hooey or Huey, It Means the Same Thing 78

Chapter Five
From Hell to Breakfast 107

Chapter Six
In the Market for a Colleague 117

Chapter Seven
Politics and Human Misery 132

Chapter Eight
Liberal New Dealer 161

Chapter Nine
Champion of the One-Horse Farmer 186

Chapter Ten
The Potentate of Mississippi Politics 216

Chapter Eleven
Still Redneck, Still Liberal 232

Epilogue 247

Bibliography 255

Index 269

Illustrations

following page 86

Governor Bilbo
James K. Vardaman
The "Pastemaster General" and his secretary
Pat Harrison and Senator-elect Bilbo
Martin Sennett "Mike" Conner
Hugh L. White
Paul B. Johnson
Dennis Murphree
A Bilbo campaign flyer from the 1934 Senate race
Senator Bilbo
"Competition!"
Bilbo campaign truck
Fred Sullens and Bilbo
Mississippi's "original third-termer" for Roosevelt
Bilbo campaigning for the national Democratic ticket in 1940
The Mississippi delegation to the 1941 presidential inauguration
Bilbo's Dream House
Mrs. Linda Bilbo
Bilbo and admirers
At the Dream House
Bilbo speaking in 1940
Bilbo addresses a crowd at a political rally
"The people loved him"

Table and Maps

Vardaman's Percentage of the Total Democratic Primary Vote in the White Counties in South Mississippi 53

Map 1: Bilbo's Strength in Mississippi's White Counties 54

Map 2: Bilbo's Weakness in Mississippi's Black Counties 55

Map 3: Bilbo's Strength in Mississippi's Low-Income White Counties in 1934 56

Acknowledgments

There are, naturally, countless people who have contributed valuable assistance in the making of this book: the staffs of the Mississippi Department of Archives and History, the Library of Congress, the Franklin D. Roosevelt Library, the National Archives, the University of Mississippi Library, Mississippi State University Library, Duke University Library, and the University of North Carolina Library. Grants from the Belle McWilliams Fund of Memphis State University and the Eleanor Roosevelt Institute enabled me to do important research at the National Archives in Washington, D.C., and at the Franklin D. Roosevelt Library in Hyde Park, New York. A grant from the University of Southern Mississippi aided in producing the maps and in securing permission to use the photographs. Dr. Claude Fike and Dr. William D. McCain of the University of Southern Mississippi made it possible for me to have access to the Bilbo Papers, and Terry Latour and Henry Simmons of the McCain Graduate Library offered great assistance in using the collection. Richard Baker and Donald Ritchie of the Senate Historical Office made several helpful sources available to me. Aloha South of the National Archives took special pains to enable me to see certain papers of the Work Projects Administration. Professors John E. Gonzales, John Ray Skates, Neil McMillen, and William Scarborough read portions of the manuscript and made valuable suggestions, and Professor Martha Swain offered useful hints regarding sources. I owe special thanks to typists Carrie Parrett and Mary Jane Morgan and to Betty Williams, who rendered valuable assistance in the preparation of the manuscript. My greatest debt is to Dr. Charles Crawford, whose patient guidance and sound advice aided my work from start to finish.

Redneck Liberal

Introduction

During the 1960s one would see frequently on Mississippi streets and highways those defensively arrogant bumper stickers that read: MISSISSIPPI, THE MOST LIED ABOUT STATE IN THE UNION. Beneath the bluster lay a truth beyond the sentiment intended by those who brandished the slogan as a badge of defiance. Almost everything written about the state in that era focused on race or politics or both. Those central aspects of Mississippi life were so volatile that few people approached them without their emotional and moral guns loaded. Those who wrote about Mississippi usually produced either blind and foolish apologies or smug indictments. In such an atmosphere, lies, or at least distortions, were inevitable and abundant.

What was true of the state at large during the era of civil rights was also true of the state's dominant political personality of the era of segregation. In that period one might have proclaimed: "Theodore Bilbo, the Most Lied About Politician in Mississippi." He was, in the words of his only biographer, "God or Satan. He dwelled—dwells—in heaven or hell, but never in limbo." Yet limbo is precisely where the truth about Bilbo seems to have taken up residence, the limbo of impassioned predilection. His tempestuous personality and extravagant style usually provoked instantaneous and passionate judgment, so that most observers admired or, more likely, condemned him with little knowledge of his substantive record. Thus, like the history of the state itself, Bilbo's career has been characterized, even by reputable scholars, in diametrically opposing terms.[1]

Such confusion between style and substance in the academic and public perception is not unique to Mississippi or to Bilbo. William Chafe recognized the same dichotomy at work in the struggle for black civil rights in Greensboro, North Carolina, wherein that state's "reputation for enlightenment"—the "progressive mystique," as Chafe terms it—in fact obscured a "social reality that was reactionary." This progressive mystique by which the respectable white leadership main-

1. A. Wigfall Green, *The Man Bilbo* (Baton Rouge, 1963), vii.

tained social and political supremacy, "far from being a contradiction to . . . conservatism . . . ultimately served as its cornerstone." At the heart of the progressive mystique was the notion of "civility . . . a way of dealing with people and problems that made good manners more important than substantial action." Respectable southerners were able to blame poor whites for the South's social problems, not because establishment whites were more amenable to substantive social justice than were the rednecks, but because the bigotry of the poor whites reflected bad manners; it was raw and socially distasteful. The difference between the peckerwoods and their social superiors over the issue of race was not so much a matter of substance as one of style.[2]

Civility is hardly the word to describe Bilbo's style. In fact it was his very lack of civility that became the basis of his notoriety, both within Mississippi and beyond, and that so distorted the common perception of who he was and what he really did in forty years of public life. While no one is likely to quibble with using the term *redneck* to describe Bilbo, some, perhaps many, will find the characterization of him as *liberal* surprising if not incredible. But both terms have been chosen with trepidation and with care: trepidation because the connotations of both words are elusive and have changed over time; care because when precisely qualified, they capture so perfectly the paradox of Bilbo's career, especially during the New Deal period.

Associating rednecks with liberalism is particularly ironic, since redneckism has become in some circles so clearly identified with conservatism. A recent sociological study suggests that the modern redneck "may soon feel himself less alienated" because of "the current trend in the United States toward the radical Right." Yet the term *redneck* had its very origin in political dissent against the southern status quo. It originated as an epithet hurled in derision at those agrarian spokesmen who soon after the turn of the century challenged the political supremacy of black-county Bourbonism in Mississippi. The redneck is often described as violent, uneducated, common, crude, vulgar, and visceral. He is Wilbur Cash's simple man at the center, shaped by the frontier heritage into a composite of individualism, romanticism, and hedonism, ultimately a man of temperament rather than thought. For him politics became, as Cash said, theater, "an arena wherein one great champion confronted another or a dozen and sought to outdo them in rhetoric and splendid gesturing. It swept back the loneliness of the land, it brought men together under torches, it filled them with the

2. William H. Chafe, *Civility and Civil Rights: Greensboro, North Carolina, and the Black Struggle for Freedom* (New York, 1980), 1–4, 353–54, 8.

contagious power of the crowd, it unleashed emotion and set it to leaping and dancing." Thus was redneck politics, and few ever mastered its style so thoroughly as did Theodore Bilbo.[3]

But if the style of Bilbo's politics was redneck, its substance was liberal, an expression that also demands some definition. The influence of the civil rights era has been so pervasive that today the notion of a liberalism devoid of active commitment to racial justice has become virtually unthinkable. But in the 1930s the very godfather of modern Democratic liberalism, Franklin Roosevelt, exercised at best a benevolent neutrality toward civil rights for blacks. As George Mowry notes, the image makers of the Northeast, where civil rights aroused such emotional intensity, have had "a predominant role in deciding what goes into the permanent national record." To illustrate, Mowry points to the varying reputations of James K. Vardaman and Robert La Follette, whose "ideological careers," excluding the race question, were "strikingly similar." Historians, however, by and large rate La Follette a statesman while ranking Vardaman among the rabble-rousers. Likewise, La Follette's son is hailed as a sincere liberal reformer while Vardaman's protégé, Bilbo, is seen as the quintessential demagogue.[4]

The standard of liberalism by which this study measures Bilbo—and the purpose is neither to commend or condemn Bilbo nor to defend or attack liberalism, but to understand both in historical terms—is the standard of the 1930s, that is, the standard of the New Deal. On the eve of Roosevelt's election, Virginius Dabney described the southern liberal as one who sought "a distinct improvement in the status of the average man," one who supported such laws "for the economic and social welfare of the masses" as "regulation of the trusts, improvement of working conditions in industry . . . better educational facilities, improved health regulations, and so on." By that measure Bilbo emerges as one of the most liberal southern senators of the New Deal period. His support for the Roosevelt administration went far beyond strictly local interests, such as agricultural policy. As the New Deal moved toward welfare liberalism after 1935, Bilbo's enthusiasm waxed rather

3. Julian B. Roebuck and Mark Hickson III, *The Southern Redneck: A Phenomenological Class Study* (New York, 1982), 188; Wilbur J. Cash, *The Mind of the South* (New York, 1941), 54–55.

4. Frank Freidel, *F.D.R. and the South* (Baton Rouge, 1965), 97; Raymond Wolters, "The New Deal and the Negro," in John Braeman, Robert H. Bremner, and David Brody (eds.), *The New Deal: The National Level* (Columbus, Ohio, 1975), 177–78, 200–202. Vol. I of Braeman, Bremner, and Brody (eds.), *The New Deal*, 2 vols.; George E. Mowry, *Another Look at the Twentieth-Century South* (Baton Rouge, 1973), 21–22; Patrick J. Maney, *"Young Bob" La Follette: A Biography of Robert M. La Follette, Jr., 1898–1953* (Columbia, Mo., 1978).

than waned, as he built a record on relief spending, labor legislation, and public housing that would have been the envy of any urban Democrat.[5]

So Bilbo the New Dealer was both redneck and liberal. What follows is an effort to describe and to explain that seemingly paradoxical combination as it existed both in Bilbo and in the sociopolitical environment that bred, nurtured, and sustained him.

5. Virginius Dabney, *Liberalism in the South* (Chapel Hill, 1932), xiii–xv.

Chapter One

Redeemers, Rednecks, and Rotarian Reform

He was "a pert little monster," said William Alexander Percy, "glib, and shameless, with that sort of cunning common to criminals that passes for intelligence. The people loved him." It was a trenchant appraisal of Theodore Bilbo. It was also a keen insight into Mississippi's political and social life during Bilbo's day, because the man was inseparable from the context in which he was born and by which he was molded and nurtured. But as a child forever redefines the pattern of his family's life, so this heir of Mississippi's cultural legacy profoundly altered the subsequent development of his political patrimony.[1]

Mississippians, said Percy, traced their lineage to three distinct and different social strains, "and only three": the old slaveholding gentry, the poor whites, and the slaves. The clash between the first two, fought beneath the vague and ominous shadow of the third, shaped the nature of Mississippi politics until well into the twentieth century. V. O. Key described it as "a battle between the Delta planters and the rednecks," an analysis that was oversimplified but true withal. The state's whites divided into two general groups for which the terms *planter* and *redneck* became identifying symbols. Both groups existed throughout the state, but each came to be associated with a geographical center: for the rednecks, the red clay hills of the northeast, and for the planters, the Delta, that fecund swath of alluvium between the Yazoo and Mississippi rivers that begins, according to David Cohn, "in the lobby of the Peabody Hotel in Memphis and ends on Catfish Row in Vicksburg." To be sure, not all planters lived in the Delta; nor were all who lived in the Delta planters. Nonetheless, the small-town bankers, businessmen, and professionals whose interests and, more important, whose manners coincided with those of the aristocrats of the black counties,

1. William Alexander Percy, *Lanterns on the Levee: Recollections of a Planter's Son* (New York, 1941), 148.

became identified with the term and ideal of the Delta planter—the Sartorises of Faulknerian legend.[2]

Likewise, not all rednecks dwelt in the white counties of the hills or even in the comparable piney woods of south Mississippi. Wherever there were poor, illiterate, debt-ridden souls scratching a meager existence from acreage so small or so poor that it yielded its paltry ration of cotton or foodstuffs only grudgingly, there one found rednecks. By the 1930s a significant number had spilled over into the Delta itself. Some were small landowners. Most were tenants or sharecroppers, swapping their labor for a few acres to work, a cabin to sleep in, and a modest share of their own crops. The owner extended credit for necessities until the crops came in. He also kept the books, those "ledgers," as Faulkner described them, that recorded the "slow outward trickle of food and supplies and equipment which returned each fall as cotton made and ginned and sold (two threads frail as truth and impalpable as equators yet cable-strong to bind for life them who made the cotton to the land their sweat fell on)." Rarely did the tenant's percentage of the crop earn enough to offset the exorbitant prices and interest that he paid for his "furnish," so he sank deeper and deeper into debt and despair.[3]

The political struggle that issued from this social arrangement fell into three fairly distinct periods. The first began at the close of Reconstruction in 1875 and was marked by planter ascendancy. It ended in 1903, not suddenly but after a decade of rising agrarian dissent that forced structural changes in the electoral machinery and ushered in an era of redneck reform. For two full decades Mississippi shared in the progressive movement that swept much of the nation. By the mid-1920s, however, planter-business conservatives were again in control, not by conquest so much as by subversion. Among the heirs of the Redeemer tradition were many who, having seen the light of reform and repented of the sins of intransigent conservatism, were now received into the household of progressive faith. But if they had got religion, it was not the true gospel, and most of the pure in heart viewed the converts as wolves in sheep's clothing. Their suspicions were not altogether groundless. In 1923, under the leadership largely of these Redeemers *cum* reformers, Mississippi launched its version of what

2. *Ibid.*, 19; V. O. Key, Jr., *Southern Politics: In State and Nation* (New York, 1949), 230–31; David L. Cohn, *God Shakes Creation* (New York, 1935), 14.

3. John Ray Skates, *Mississippi: A Bicentennial History* (New York, 1979), 120–27; Vincent A. Giroux, Jr., "The Rise of Theodore G. Bilbo (1908–1932)," *Journal of Mississippi History*, XLIII (1981), 180–88; William Faulkner, *Go Down Moses and Other Stories* (New York, 1942), 255–56.

George Tindall has called business progressivism, and while it might not have been the old planter-business heresy of Redeemer days, it was more business than progressive and was certainly not the old-time religion. This modified and muffled progressivism dominated state politics until the end of the New Deal period.[4]

Throughout the half century and more of conservative-redneck conflict, the antagonists' perceptions often outweighed reality in political importance. Whether Redeemer rule was in fact benevolent and enlightened, it seemed so to the Redeemers. Whether the system was, in fact, oppressive to the lower classes, it seemed so to the peckerwoods. Thus, the way in which the two white classes viewed themselves and their interests in relation to each other—and to the blacks—explains more about their political behavior than do the socioeconomic facts of the matter, notwithstanding a seemingly endless academic and popular debate over those facts.

The planters esteemed themselves the saviors of their state and its heritage from a Reconstruction that was little more than "one glorious orgy of graft, lawlessness, and terrorism." Having redeemed Mississippi from Republican Yankees and rapacious blacks, the gentry felt they possessed a proprietary interest in state government, which they now intended to administer as they saw fit. Theoretically, of course, fitness included the demands of noblesse oblige and equity. The "Delta sages" who had engineered redemption, men like L. Q. C. Lamar, J. Z. George, and E. C. Walthall, acquired the mantle of political leadership, said Percy, not by plebiscite or usurpation, but rather by divine call from a destiny that had fashioned them with "superior intellect, training, character, and opportunity. . . . Applause or aggrandizement played no part in their calculations. They knew leadership was a burden, they knew there was no such thing in the long run as public gratitude for public service, they also knew that unless the intelligent disinterested few fought for good government, government would be bad."[5]

But the planters' public service was the rednecks' poison. To the poor whites, good government all too often came in the guise of a con-

4. For the Redeemer and progressive periods in Mississippi, see James G. Revels, "Redeemers, Rednecks and Racial Integrity," in Richard Aubrey McLemore (ed.), *A History of Mississippi* (2 vols.; Hattiesburg, 1973), I, 590–621; Albert D. Kirwan, *Revolt of the Rednecks: Mississippi Politics, 1876–1925* (Lexington, Ky., 1951); William F. Holmes, *The White Chief: James Kimble Vardaman* (Baton Rouge, 1970); Charles G. Hamilton, "Mississippi Politics in the Progressive Era" (Ph.D. dissertation, Vanderbilt University, 1958); and Jon Richard Lewis, "Progressivism Revisited: A Re-evaluation of Mississippi Politics, 1920–1930" (Master's thesis, University of Southern Mississippi, 1977).

5. Percy, *Lanterns on the Levee*, 69.

servatism geared to the interests of the propertied and to the maintenance of the economic status quo. It seemed more oppressive than paternalistic. It meant undertaxed corporations and plantations; it meant laws granting the merchant a lien against the farmer's crop until he repaid his inflated debt; it meant a minimum of government services for the poor; it meant inadequate schools. In short it meant that from the grinding poverty that strangled the redneck, there would be no relief and no way out. Indeed, there was little public gratitude and a wealth of public grumbling.[6]

That grumbling spawned sporadic but largely ineffective independent political efforts during the last quarter of the nineteenth century. From the Greenbackers of the seventies to the Populists of the nineties, agrarian groups advocated a host of reforms including free schools, reapportionment, inflation, corporate regulation and taxation, and more democratic voting requirements.[7] Reform did not come, however, because power remained in the hands of senators like Lamar and Walthall and governors like Robert Lowry and John M. Stone, men with sympathies more attuned to the interests of railroads, merchants, bankers, and eastern capitalists than to the desires of poor farmers. The administrations of Lowry and Stone cut, rather than extended, government services and reduced, rather than increased, corporate taxes. When the legislature forced a railroad commission upon Lowry in 1884, he appointed to head it ex-Governor Stone, who had earlier vetoed a similar commission bill and was himself a railroad agent. When Senator Lamar opposed a free-silver bill in 1878, he suffered the ignominy of being censured by the public press while the state legislature passed a resolution commending his black colleague, Blanche K. Bruce, for supporting the measure.[8]

More generally, blacks found themselves crushed between the upper and nether millstones of white class politics, exploited on the one hand and resented on the other. Both the exploitation and the resentment

6. Dewey W. Grantham, Jr., *The Democratic South* (New York, 1963), 23–24; T. Harry Williams, *Romance and Realism in Southern Politics* (Athens, Ga., 1961), 44–48.

7. See the following articles by Willie D. Halsell: "The Bourbon Period in Mississippi Politics, 1875–1890," *Journal of Southern History*, XI (1945), 519–37; "James R. Chalmers and 'Mahoneism' in Mississippi," *Journal of Southern History*, X (1944), 37–58; "Democratic Dissensions in Mississippi, 1878–1882," *Journal of Mississippi History*, II (1940), 123–36; and "Republican Factionalism in Mississippi, 1882-1884," *Journal of Southern History*, VII (1941), 84–101.

8. Halsell, "The Bourbon Period," 522–29; Revels, "Redeemers, Rednecks and Racial Integrity," 591–606; Charles G. Hamilton, *Progressive Mississippi* (Aberdeen, Miss., 1978), 20–21.

were part of redemption's legacy.[9] Republican Reconstruction had thrust into the political arena, said Percy, "hordes of Negroes," whose cultural heritage consisted of "a thousand years and more in tribal barbarism [and] a hundred and more in slavery." The essence of redemption had been to reinstitute white supremacy, and the task had "required courage, tact, intelligence, patience; it also required vote-buying, the stuffing of ballot-boxes, chicanery, intimidation. Heart-breaking business and degrading, but in the end successful. At terrific cost white supremacy was re-established. Some of us still remember what we were told of those times, and what we were told inclines us to guard the ballot as something precious, something to be withheld unless the fitness of the recipient be patent."[10]

So the planters and their allies became the guardians of the redeemed ballot. But after the "revolution of 1875," the danger of "black rule" diminished rapidly. Lacking both land and money, most ex-slaves became sharecroppers and remained in virtual economic bondage to the landowning and mercantile classes, who now preferred to control and use black voting rather than end it. The efficacy of electoral fraud and intimidation sufficiently inured the Redeemers to the heartbreak and degradation of these essential instruments of "good government."[11]

After 1875, carpetbag and scalawag whites abandoned Republicanism in droves, leaving the party in the hands of the freedmen. Subsequent threats to Redeemer control thus came, not from the cowed black Republicans, but from dissident white Democrats. At the grass-roots level, the dissension centered among the increasingly hostile poor farmers. Within the Democratic leadership, it came from disgruntled individuals who, for whatever reasons, felt themselves denied their proper place among the political elite. Fortunately for the Redeemers, none of the maverick Democrats was willing or able to tap the rednecks' frustration sufficiently to galvanize it into a potent political force. It became obvious that if the poor whites were to improve their lot, it would come largely from their own efforts. As Willie Stark, fictional champion of the latter-day redneck, told his followers: "Nobody ever helped a hick but the hick himself. Up there in town they won't help you. It's up to you and God, and God helps those who help themselves."[12]

9. See Vernon L. Wharton, *The Negro in Mississippi, 1865–1890* (Chapel Hill, 1947).

10. Percy, *Lanterns on the Levee*, 273–74.

11. Skates, *Mississippi*, 120–22; Kirwan, *Revolt of the Rednecks*, 3–17.

12. Halsell, "James R. Chalmers and 'Mahoneism,'" 56–58; Robert Penn Warren, *All the King's Men* (New York, 1946), 102.

But the guardians' grip on the ballot made it very difficult for the rednecks to help themselves. The race issue and Mississippi's election machinery combined to make the ballot well-nigh meaningless anyway. As the hill farmers became restive under an increasingly unresponsive government, conservatives used black votes to offset the defections of those who dared to challenge the political hierarchy. When that failed, Redeemers resorted to intimidation, warning that any political divisions among white voters would usher in another era of government by blacks and Republicans. In defending their political hegemony, then, the conservatives relied upon weapons related in paradoxical fashion to black voting: enlistment of its strength on their own behalf and dire warnings against its dangers.[13]

As race reduced the threat from outside the Democratic party, so the state election laws allowed more effective control within. The state Democratic convention held absolute power in the party, and when not in session yielded its authority to the state executive committee. Apportionment in the convention was proportional to representation in the state house of representatives, which was based on total population, giving whites in the black counties much more power than their counterparts in white counties. The planters of the Delta, where black population was heaviest, thus dominated the state convention and the executive committee. The same was true at the local level, where whites from black districts controlled county conventions and executive committees. As long as these conventions and committees controlled the party, Redeemer rule was secure. So it was, as C. Vann Woodward observed, the Bourbons from the black counties "who laid the lasting foundations in matters of race, politics, economics, and law for the modern South."[14]

However, two significant events near the turn of the century loosed the rednecks' political bonds. In 1890 the state adopted a new constitution designed to disfranchise blacks. Twelve years later the legislature enacted an open primary law that transferred the nomination of Democratic candidates for office (which in a one-party state was tantamount to election) from conservative-controlled conventions to the electorate. Black disfranchisement swept away the last obstacle that discouraged agrarian leaders from running for office, and the open primary removed the last barrier that kept them from winning.[15]

The new fundamental law proved something less than an unquali-

13. Skates, *Mississippi*, 121–22.

14. Kirwan, *Revolt of the Rednecks*, 27–39; C. Vann Woodward, *The Origins of the New South, 1877–1913* (Baton Rouge, 1951), 22.

15. Skates, *Mississippi*, 122–27; Kirwan, *Revolt of the Rednecks*, 122–35.

fied victory for the poor whites. For years farmers from the white counties had been clamoring for a constitutional convention, which they hoped would adopt a broad array of democratic reforms. Most conservatives and most spokesmen from the black counties had opposed the movement, but in the late eighties, when Senator George joined the convention bandwagon, its momentum became irresistible. Having seized the leadership of the convention movement from farmer leaders like Putnam Darden and Frank Burkitt, George was able largely to dictate the constitutional agenda. For George the convention had a single objective, to disfranchise the black man, and the senator hoped to do so in a manner as acceptable to his Redeemer friends as possible. Rednecks of the white counties wanted disfranchisement too, for it would deprive the Redeemer leaders of their most effective weapon in beating back agrarian challenges, the issue of white supremacy. Spokesmen for the black counties could hardly oppose disfranchisement after all their rantings about the danger of black voting, but as self-appointed guardians of the ballot, they were determined to supervise the disfranchisement process. Once the convention became a reality, conservatives dominated it as they dominated every other political institution in the state.[16]

The convention debate over new voter qualifications became a struggle between black counties and white counties with the conservatives insisting upon educational and property requirements. After all, fitness for the ballot was, to the guardians, the only proper index for voting, and they had grave reservations about the fitness of most poor whites, perhaps even more so than about the blacks. Like Percy, most of the "Delta sages" saw the redneck as "intellectually and spiritually inferior to the Negro" anyway. The poll tax and the literacy test, which the delegates eventually adopted, seemed perfectly suited to the task, since, as Percy put it, the poor whites "were not blest with worldly goods or mental attainments." In fact "the present breed," he noted, was "probably the most unprepossessing on the broad face of the ill-populated earth." Percy's summary judgment on the rednecks was probably shared by most in his class: "I can forgive them as the Lord forgives, but admire them, trust them, love them—never."[17]

It is little wonder, then, that Percy's social forbears, while they were disfranchising, did all they could to disfranchise as many poor whites as possible, despite the clamor, as one black-county delegate described

16. Kirwan, *Revolt of the Rednecks*, 58–68; Holmes, *The White Chief*, 44–45; James P. Coleman, "The Mississippi Constitution of 1890 and the Final Decade of the Nineteenth Century," in McLemore (ed.), *History of Mississippi*, II, 5–10.

17. Percy, *Lanterns on the Levee*, 19–20.

it, "of a lot of white ignoramuses . . . who have no property." The best that the agrarian delegates could achieve was the addition of an "understanding clause" that provided a means to circumvent the literacy requirement. But even that loophole was dependent on its administration by election officials who would most likely be part of the ruling faction. Besides, the poll tax became the real instrument of effective disfranchisement, and for that there was no loophole. The rest of the democratic reforms proposed by leaders from the white counties were virtually ignored by the convention. The new constitution, then, left control of Mississippi's government safely in the hands of the black-county "oligarchs" and their political allies throughout the state. The new arrangement did not even eliminate the white-supremacy issue completely. Because the franchise restriction did not specifically exclude any social group, election officials could as easily allow blacks to vote as they could exclude poor whites. In fact throughout the 1890s blacks continued to vote in substantial numbers, especially in black counties where their votes were easily controlled by white leaders. And the conservatives continued to preach on the dangers of black rule and the necessity of white unity, which in practice left lower-class whites little choice but to acquiesce in continued Redeemer dominance.[18]

In fact the conservatives used the race issue to great effect against the valiant but futile Populist movement that flickered briefly in Mississippi in the nineties. The strength of that third-party effort demonstrated the incipient class consciousness of the state's agrarian masses. It likewise reflected the conflict between white counties and black counties, Redeemers and rednecks, and conservatives and liberals that had dominated the constitutional debate and would continue to shape Mississippi politics well into the twentieth century. Although Populism failed to crack Democratic solidarity, it did rouse the rednecks politically and did energize liberal elements within the Democratic party. Enough poor whites came to believe that their problems were tied to politics that by the end of the decade, the Democracy's leaders felt it necessary at least to pay lip service to agrarian interests. This awakening of lower-class political consciousness and the growing stench of fraud in the convention system, even in the nostrils of many conservatives, paved the way for the primary law that was finally enacted in 1902.[19]

It was the statewide primary that truly revolutionized Mississippi politics. By placing party nominations in the hands of rank-and-file

18. Kirwan, *Revolt of the Rednecks*, 66–84.

19. *Ibid.*, 122–27. For Populism in Mississippi see William D. McCain, "The Populist Party in Mississippi" (Master's thesis, University of Mississippi, 1931).

Democrats, the new system thrust an entirely new complex of demands upon officeseekers. No longer were courthouse rings and other cliques of legislators, executive committeemen, and party potentates the kingmakers of state government. Instead, the mass of white voters who could and would participate in the primaries became the decisive factor, and those who aspired to statewide office would henceforth have to accommodate themselves to the electorate. Also, it was the primary that finally eliminated the black vote. In 1903 the state executive committee resolved that the Democratic primary would be a white primary, and the rule soon became a fixture of party politics. To be sure, the Delta, which had led the opposition to the primary law, and conservatives statewide still held some good cards: the poll tax still disfranchised many poor whites; conventions still controlled the election officials; black counties still dominated the legislature; the organizational and fund-raising demands of the new system were more easily met by conservative than agrarian factions. But the black-county monopoly of nominations for statewide office was gone forever. Whoever could best do those things necessary to arouse mass support would win state office, and few among the Redeemers were temperamentally suited to do those things very well.[20]

There soon emerged, however, a new breed of politician whose temperament was more than suited to the demands of mass politics. During the first decade of the new century, Mississippi entered the era of the "southern demagogue," a political genre to which the state made two prime contributions, James K. Vardaman and Theodore Bilbo. The precise nature of the demagogue and those attributes that distinguish him from other political champions of similar constituencies have remained somewhat undefined, partly because of the popularity of the label as an epithet to fling at enemies. Nonetheless, long-standing practice makes it difficult to dispense with the term, and it is, after all, an accurate designation in a literal if not a connotative sense. However sincere such leaders as Vardaman and Bilbo were, and however flamboyant was the style of their appeal, that appeal was assuredly aimed at the *demos*. It was the style, more than anything else, that "set the demagogues apart," says J. Morgan Kousser. It was their style, too, more than anything else, that elicited criticism and, hence, gave the term its negative connotations. Not that passionate rhetoric was anything new to Mississippi politics, for, as Wilbur Cash noted, the whole story of southern politics has in some sense been one of "continual progress in the personal and the extravagant." What the new breed

20. Kirwan, *Revolt of the Rednecks*, 128–35.

added was a remarkable ability to enlist "the high histrionic gifts to body forth the whole bold, dashing, hell-of-a-fellow complex precisely in terms of the generality themselves." But the demagogue offered the rednecks more than style. The substantive element of his appeal was the bold acknowledgement of what the rednecks themselves were already beginning to sense, that their economic plight was invariably linked to politics and that the existing political leadership was not giving them a fair shake. "The time came when they realized," as Andrew Nelson Lytle put it, that with all the talk about "chivalry and pure womanhood . . . the generals and colonels and lawyer-statesmen . . . did not put sow-belly in the pantry, nor meal in the barrel." The Populists had said as much in the nineties, but their efforts had foundered on the shoals of one-party politics and the race issue. Now the primary law had cracked the wall that Redeemers had built around state government, and in 1903 Vardaman led the rednecks through the breach.[21]

In some ways Vardaman hardly seemed a logical choice to command the offensive by the poor whites. He was a Delta man. He had been a successful newspaper editor, a civic leader, a holder of minor offices, a county Democratic chairman, and a two-term legislator, all in Leflore County in the heart of the Delta. Such prominence hardly suggests a maverick spirit at war with the conservative establishment. In fact Vardaman's political training had come at the hands of J. Z. George and George's protégé, H. D. Money, who was Vardaman's own cousin. Both were Redeemer stalwarts, and Vardaman's legislative record reflected their tutorial handiwork. The young lawmaker had supported tax exemptions for banks and railroads and defended corporate interests generally. He had opposed a state income tax, an elective judiciary, and a primary law, and had endorsed the poll tax and literacy test for voting. He had voted for the conservative senatorial incumbents, George and Walthall, and had helped torpedo the efforts of agrarian leaders in the legislature. The Delta Democrats were pleased enough to return him to office without opposition in 1893, and he appeared anything but the rednecks' rising star.[22]

But that is precisely what Vardaman became in the gubernatorial

21. J. Morgan Kousser, *The Shaping of Southern Politics: Suffrage Restriction and the Establishment of the One-Party South, 1880–1910* (New Haven, 1974), 236; Cash, *The Mind of the South*, 252–53; J. Wayne Flynt, *Dixie's Forgotten People: The South's Poor Whites* (Bloomington, 1979), 2–3; Andrew Nelson Lytle, "The Hind Tit," in Twelve Southerners, *I'll Take My Stand: The South and the Agrarian Tradition* (New York, 1930), 215.

22. Holmes, *The White Chief*, 43–53.

race in 1903. The shift was more the result of a complex of circumstances than a single cause. Vardaman had already betrayed latent democratic tendencies in some of his early editorials, tendencies that had perhaps remained dormant while ambition led him into conformity with the prevailing political climate. Then in the 1890s he had carried the banner of Democracy against Populism into white counties, where he must have discovered both the intensity of the rising farmer discontent and his own ability to ignite that intensity into political consciousness from the stump. At the same time, his editorials began to reflect an awareness of Benjamin Tillman, who was, with similar rhetorical magic, leading a successful poor-white assault on the political establishment in South Carolina. Finally, there was the race issue. Through the influence of Benjamin Ward of Winona, Vardaman had early absorbed a passionate commitment to white supremacy that profoundly affected his entire career. By the mid-1890s he was demanding an end to black education, an idea for which he found great enthusiasm in the white counties. There, total education expenditure lagged far behind that of black counties because funds were allocated on the basis of total population. By spending a bare minimum on black schools, black counties were able to spend much more per white child on education than could white counties. Bitterness over this inequity fused with general racial prejudice among poor whites to make Vardaman's race-baiting especially effective in the white counties.[23]

The primary law completed Vardaman's transformation. Twice in the 1890s he had sought the nomination for governor, and twice the Redeemer establishment had denied him. Now matters were out of the hands of the convention cliques, and the open primary unleashed Vardaman's oratorical endowments. In town after town, often atop a lumber wagon drawn by scores of oxen, he stirred the poor whites with assaults on entrenched privilege and demands for an impressive list of reforms: uniform textbooks, an elective judiciary, better roads, and an end to the convict lease system. Resplendent in white linen suit, white boots, and a large black Stetson hat, he appeared a demigod to the entertainment-starved farmers, a tribune come to judgment for the people. And they flocked to cheer his fulminations. The harshest invective was reserved for the dangers of the "black menace" and the necessity of white supremacy. With raven hair flowing over massive shoulders, the White Chief warned his rapt listeners that the presence of the black man constituted America's greatest danger. Assailing black edu-

23. *Ibid.*, 49–60, 85–93, 102–103.

cation, he vowed to abolish it along with the Fourteenth and Fifteenth Amendments to the federal Constitution.[24]

This combination of race-baiting and economic realism swept Vardaman to the governor's chair and carried numerous allies to legislative seats. His administration launched Mississippi's progressive era, as the legislature under his leadership improved the prison system and ended convict leasing, increased appropriations for education and teachers' pay, created a textbook commission, and regulated railroads, businesses, and utilities. Even then it left undone much of what the governor had requested.[25]

The state's venture in reform continued through the next four administrations: Edmund F. Noel (1908–1912), Earl Brewer (1912–1916), Bilbo (1916–1920), and Lee Russell (1920–1924). During those sixteen years, Mississippi restricted child labor; outlawed blacklisting of union members; increased employer liability; set safety standards for railroads; increased appropriations for education; consolidated rural schools; created a junior college system; established a normal college; made school attendance compulsory; restricted lobbyists; stiffened antitrust regulations; restricted corporate land ownership; regulated stock sales; established a highway commission, a tax commission, a bank board, and a pardon board; strengthened the railroad commission; adopted the initiative, the referendum, and a presidential primary; built a tuberculosis hospital, a school for the feebleminded, a juvenile reformatory, and charity hospitals; allowed cities to adopt the commission system; ratified the federal income tax amendment and enacted a state income tax; outlawed usury, interlocking directorates, and bank holding companies; ended the fee system, county convict leasing, and public hanging; enacted a food and drug law and a tick eradication program; and made the state judiciary elective. It was an impressive record that thrust Mississippi into the mainstream of American progressivism.[26]

By the early twenties, however, the face of progressivism was changing in the South. In Mississippi, reform had heretofore come largely at the hands of agrarian leaders who, like progressives elsewhere, had sought to transform state government into an instrument of efficiency and public service, one that was more democratic, more wary of corporate power, and more interested in social justice. By the twenties,

24. Ibid., vii–x, 97–115.

25. Kirwan, *Revolt of the Rednecks*, 175–77.

26. Hamilton, *Progressive Mississippi*, 62–69, 81–82, 126–30, 162–68, 172–80; Charles G. Hamilton, *Mississippi, Mirror of the 1920s* (Aberdeen, Miss., 1979), 14–24, 30–32.

however, an emerging business class was beginning to infiltrate the reform movement, transforming it into "business progressivism." This hybrid accented the efficiency and public-service aspects of earlier progressivism at the expense of the objectives of increased democracy, social justice, and regulation. Reform became more fashionable among respectable society, but it lost a good deal of its sweep and militancy.[27]

From the mid-1920s to the end of the 1930s, business progressivism was a potent force in Mississippi politics. William Allen White suggested that progressivism was merely Populism that had "shaved its whiskers, washed its shirt, put on a derby, and moved up into the middle class." One might similarly caricature the business progressive as a Redeemer who had taken Henry Grady to heart, kissed the Old South a fond farewell, moved to town, and joined the business class. The new sophisticated reform was the fruition of the New South creed. It would build good roads and improve public health and education, eliminate waste and streamline administration, rationalize the tax system and root out corruption; in short, it would industrialize and modernize the South. It was to be a New South of "good government, great churches, improved schools, industry, business, real estate booms." Its advocates claimed the heritage of reform, but theirs was the reform of the Rotary Club.[28]

But Rotarianism in Mississippi was hardly a broad enough constituency to support a successful political movement, a truth not lost on a man of Bilbo's political acumen. "Never speak to a Rotary club," he advised, for "you speak to twenty on the inside and a hundred on the outside looking in are against you for being with the twenty." Mississippi's urban middle class was simply too frail to exert much political clout by itself. As late as 1940 Mississippi could boast but 438,882 urban dwellers, less than 20 percent of the state's population. To make headway, business progressives would have to form expedient alliances with segments of the older factions. But both the black-county Bourbons and the agrarians were suspicious of middle-class reform. For the Delta gentry noblesse oblige was fully sufficient to care for the welfare of "their people," so the Bourbons saw little need for a government of public service, however restrained and conservative. The old probusiness posture of Redeemer rule had been a safeguard to protect private investment by men of means, not a commitment to industrial

27. For business progressivism in the South, see George B. Tindall's *The Emergence of the New South, 1913–1945* (Baton Rouge, 1967), 219–53, and his "Business Progressivism: Southern Politics in the Twenties," *South Atlantic Quarterly*, LXII (1963), 92–106. For business progressivism in Mississippi, see Lewis, "Progressivism Revisited."

28. Tindall, "Business Progressivism," 92–95.

capitalism. However much the Bourbons might applaud middle-class taming of redneck radicalism, they cast suspicious eyes on a state-sponsored industrialism that sought basic changes in Mississippi's social and economic structure. Leaders from the black counties remained vigilant in defense of the plantation system and its interests.[29]

The rednecks were also ambivalent toward business-style reform. They, too, wanted good roads, good schools, and good public health, but they entertained grave doubts that businessmen with business methods would tax business property and profits sufficiently to provide adequate public services. As for good government, the peckerwoods had heard it acclaimed before, but good government had too often meant simply government without their participation.

The era of business reform dawned in Mississippi in 1923 with the election of Governor Henry L. Whitfield, and his administration exemplified how the changes in progressivism had intensified factionalism and blurred what had been relatively clear ideological lines. The middle-class reformers allied themselves with the reactionaries on some issues and with the agrarians on others to inch the state toward New South industrialism.

Whitfield was the son of a Baptist minister and had served as state superintendent of education and as president of the state women's college in Columbus. Under his leadership the legislature extended some reforms of the earlier progressives: higher income and inheritance taxes, new privilege taxes, a new teachers college, a library commission, a textbook commission, a new school code, a timber severance tax, a reforestation program, a forestry commission, a road program, a new mental hospital, and a rural credits system. At the same time, however, the lawmakers exempted certain businesses from taxation, abolished limitations on corporate landholding, legalized utility holding companies, encouraged railroad mergers, and eased antitrust regulations. To some the result was an environment more conducive to economic progress and a more equitable relationship between capital and labor. To others the changes made Mississippi a "happy hunting ground for corporations" and left the people in worse condition than they had been under governors less moral but more democratic.[30]

Under Whitfield, then, emerged the various factions that composed

29. Hamilton, *Progressive Mississippi*, 150; John N. Burrus, "Urbanization in Mississippi, 1890–1970," in McLemore (ed.), *History of Mississippi*, II, 348, 358–60; Lewis, "Progressivism Revisited," 3–9.

30. Lewis, "Progressivism Revisited," 69–82; Bill R. Baker, *Catch the Vision: The Life of Henry L. Whitfield of Mississippi* (Jackson, Miss., 1974), 116–45; Hamilton, *Mississippi, Mirror of the 1920s*, 33–44.

the loosely tripartite structure that dominated Mississippi politics during the depression and the New Deal. The seat of Bourbon power remained where it had been since the advent of the primary—in the legislature, particularly the lower house. There black-county interests were managed by the Big Four: Speaker Thomas L. Bailey of Lauderdale, Ways and Means Chairman Joseph W. George of Leflore, Appropriations Chairman Laurens Kennedy of Adams, and Judiciary Chairman Walter Sillers, Jr., of Bolivar. All were lawyers, and all but George had entered the legislature during Bilbo's first administration (1916–1920). Only Bailey did not represent a black county; George and Sillers were from the heart of the Delta, and Kennedy represented the old river county that included Natchez. The group's collective credentials were impressive. Sillers' father had sat on the state Democratic executive committee, had chaired the most powerful Delta political institution, the levee board, and had even participated in the most hallowed event of the Redeemer heritage, the revolution of 1875. George's father was J. Z. George, who had been the chief strategist of that revolution and a member of the original Redeemer triumvirate with Lamar and Walthall. Before they were finished, the Big Four would amass over a hundred years of legislative experience, thirty-three of those as Speaker (Sillers and Bailey), and almost all of them as chairmen of powerful committees. Bailey would become governor, and Sillers would serve longer as a member of the house (forty-nine years) and as its Speaker (twenty-one years) than anyone else in Mississippi history. These men were the heirs of a Redeemer legacy whose resilience they themselves manifested. Determined to defend Bourbon interests, they shaped one administration (Whitfield's, 1924–1928) and destroyed another (Bilbo's, 1928–1932), and no administration could hope to succeed without accommodating itself to their power.[31]

The remaining factions that dotted the political landscape were divided between business and agrarian progressives. All of them paid homage to the principle of reform, and all traced their ideological heritage, however tenuously, to Vardaman. Bilbo, of course, claimed direct descent, a pedigree that endeared him to the rednecks but blunted his appeal to "respectable" reformers. Still, his constituency, centered in the white counties of the hills and the piney woods, had been the heart and soul of earlier progressivism, and its support would be necessary for any further reform. Middle-class progressives might find the poor

31. Laurie Drago, "The Second Bilbo Administration, 1928–1932" (MS in possession of the author), 49–95; Dunbar Rowland (comp.), *The Official and Statistical Register of the State of Mississippi, 1924–1928* (New York, 1928), 183, 190–92, 231–32, 236–37; Hamilton, *Mississippi, Mirror of the 1920s*, 33–61.

farmer's logic embarrassingly primitive, his tone frighteningly strident, and his manners unbearably crude, but they also found his vote absolutely indispensable in overcoming intransigent black-county resistance to significant social and economic change. The urban reformers would have to find some allies in the hills.[32]

Fortunately for middle-class sensibilities, Bilbo was not the only agrarian spokesman. Lester Franklin, Albert Anderson, and Ross Collins all vied with him for leadership of the poor farmers, particularly in northeast Mississippi. Franklin was born in Webster County and reared in Choctaw, both hotbeds of Populism in the 1890s. He had been a Vardaman stalwart in the legislature, and in 1928 Bilbo chose him to chair the state tax commission. Four times Franklin sought the governorship without ever making the second primary. Anderson, a Tippah County editor, also began as a Vardaman legislative leader and also ran unsuccessfully for governor. Collins came to prominence in 1911 as the Vardaman candidate for attorney general. Following two terms in that post, he, too, made a futile bid for governor, after which he was elected to Congress. There he served with distinction for ten terms, though he was three times denied a promotion to the Senate. None of the three could match Bilbo's statewide appeal, but all could and did appreciably erode his strength in the hills when they challenged his supremacy. More significant, they provided the middle class a bridge to the rednecks that bypassed Bilbo.[33]

But The Man's most serious challenge for hegemony among the poor farmers came from south Mississippi. Paul Johnson was, like Bilbo, one of ten children. Born in Scott County near Hillsboro, he earned a degree from Millsaps College and in 1903 opened a law office in Hattiesburg. Following terms on the city and circuit benches, he was elected to Congress in 1918 in a surprising victory over Bilbo, who was then governor. In 1931 he ran for governor but was defeated. After another loss in 1935, he buried the hatchet and formed a powerful alliance with his old enemy, who was by then Senator Bilbo. The alliance was a natural one ideologically, and only a violent personality clash and the quirks of factional politics had prevented its earlier emergence. Johnson was the only south Mississippi politician who rivaled Bilbo's popularity among "the runt pigs," as Johnson termed them. Bilbo would have been quite comfortable with Johnson's platform of free

32. Lewis, "Progressivism Revisited," 3–9.

33. Dunbar Rowland (comp.), *The Official and Statistical Register of the State of Mississippi, Centennial Edition, 1917* (Madison, Wis., 1917), 798–99; Rowland (comp.), *Statistical Register of Mississippi, 1924–1928*, pp. 125–26, 296–97.

textbooks, cheap car tags, homestead exemption from property taxes, a universal eight-month school term, and higher teacher pay.[34]

Support for business progressivism was spread among three factions in the thirties. One was led by Dennis Murphree of Calhoun County, who succeeded Whitfield upon the latter's death in 1927. Murphree was elected lieutenant governor a total of three times and again succeeded to the top office in 1943 upon the death of Paul Johnson. Three other times Murphree sought the governorship in his own right, without success. One of those was a loss in 1927 to Bilbo. Murphree had begun his career as something of a reform legislator during the Vardaman era, but he was basically business-minded and continued the policies of Whitfield, his most visible contribution being the "Know Mississippi Better Train." For several years this rolling exhibition of Mississippi boosterism annually rumbled across the nation's rails carrying two representatives of each Mississippi county and a smorgasbord of state products. Bilbo scorned the notion that 164 political hacks, handpicked by county supervisors and touring the nation at the state's expense, would do much to persuade outsiders that Mississippi was, after all, a paradise of enlightened modernism. He deemed the venture an expensive boondoggle and dubbed it the "Mississippi Knows Better Train."[35]

The two other business progressive leaders were Martin Sennett Conner and Hugh L. White, both sons of wealthy lumbermen. Oscar Weir Conner of Covington County meticulously groomed young "Mike," as he became known, for public service: a private tutor, undergraduate and law degrees from Ole Miss, and an additional law degree from Yale. The scholar-politician found himself more comfortable discussing the intricacies of finance and economics with bankers and businessmen than swilling Nehi and swapping lies with the general-store crowd. He projected a cold aloofness that became a severe liability in a political environment that placed a premium on personality. Conner first became prominent in 1916 when Governor Bilbo helped him become Mississippi's youngest ever Speaker of the house. The partnership dissolved into deep hostility, however, and the two men opposed each other for governor in 1923 and 1927. Conner fi-

34. John Ray Skates, "World War II and Its Effects," in McLemore (ed.), *History of Mississippi*, II, 129.

35. William D. McCain, "The Life and Labor of Dennis Murphree," *Journal of Mississippi History*, XII (1950), 183–91; Ralph J. Rogers, "The Effort to Industrialize," in McLemore (ed.), *History of Mississippi*, II, 240–41; Hamilton, *Mississippi, Mirror of the 1920s*, 36.

nally became chief executive on his third try and in 1932 succeeded a Bilbo now discredited by recalcitrant lawmakers and relentless depression. Governor Conner's most noted achievement was a retail sales tax that he wrung from a reluctant legislature but that saved the state's fiscal integrity. His administration was marred, however, by a bitter feud with the elected highway commission, whose jobs the governor wanted to make appointive. Ironically, Conner spent much of his administration managing a flood of desperately needed federal relief money dispensed under a president whose nomination he had opposed in 1932 and whose policies he frequently criticized.[36]

Hugh White was a third-generation lumber baron who in 1909 inherited from his father, John James White, an empire that included seventy thousand acres of south Mississippi land, a small railroad, several sawmills, and a textile mill. The young heir added a veneer plant, a container factory, and numerous lumber yards, so that by the early 1920s the J. J. White Company employed more than a thousand Mississippians. White graduated from Soule's Business College in New Orleans and St. Thomas' Hall, an Episcopal school in Marshall County. He attended the University of Mississippi but never earned a degree, a fact that lent credence to his enemies' persistent suggestions that he was something less than nimble intellectually. Moreover, his physical appearance—he was a corpulent man of some three hundred pounds—did little to vindicate his mental prowess.[37]

Nevertheless, White forged quite a career for himself in business and politics. In 1926 he was elected to the first of three terms as mayor of Columbia, where he launched a successful program to attract industry. By persuading Marion County to construct an $85,000 factory building, White was able to convince the Reliance Manufacturing Company, a Chicago clothing firm, to open a plant in Columbia. He justified the local contribution as an investment that would pay rich dividends in jobs and economic expansion, both for the city and its rural neighbors. Other industries followed Reliance, and Columbia's experiment in public-sponsored industrial development became the prototype of a proposed statewide Balance Agriculture With Industry (BAWI) program, which thrust White into Mississippi's political limelight. After an unsuccessful race for governor in 1931, he was elected

36. Dudley Conner, personal interview with the author, June 8, 1982; J. Oliver Emmerich, "Collapse and Recovery," in McLemore (ed.), *History of Mississippi*, II, 100–109. See also Frank Wallace, "A History of the Conner Administration" (Master's thesis, Mississippi College, 1960).

37. Emmerich, "Collapse and Recovery," 110–12; Charles G. Hamilton, personal interview with the author, March 3, 1983.

in 1935 with the backing of Bilbo. The following year the legislature enacted a BAWI program whereby local governments, if approved by a state industrial commission, were allowed to issue bonds to pay for construction of manufacturing facilities to lure outside industry. The ultimate value of BAWI has been debated, but there is no doubt that it became a model for business progressives throughout the South.[38]

This "progressivism of expansion and efficiency," said George Tindall, "became by and large the norm of southern statecraft in the decades that followed." Yet it was a political philosophy whose limitations included a relative indifference to "the larger economic problems of the underprivileged." For Mississippi, that was a striking anomaly, especially when one considers V. O. Key's quip that in a region with the nation's greatest gap between rich and poor, "every other southern state finds some reason to fall back on the soul-satisfying exclamation, 'Thank God for Mississippi!'" Low per-capita income and high infant mortality, a low level of literacy and a high level of tenancy, staggering public debt and deficient public services, all were characteristic of Mississippi in the thirties, and all were severely aggravated by the depression. Even the New Deal, which restructured the party of the Solid South in the interests of the forgotten man, could not "in any fundamental way," said Tindall, "reshape the amorphous factionalism below the Potomac." Nonetheless, for the first time since Reconstruction, the federal government, under the emergent welfare liberalism of Franklin Roosevelt's refashioned Democratic party, tried to remake the South after its own image. In Mississippi, New Deal liberalism found its most ardent disciple and its most effective missionary in Theodore Bilbo.[39]

38. James C. Cobb, *The Selling of the South: The Southern Crusade for Industrial Development, 1936–1980* (Baton Rouge, 1982), 8–16, 21–25, 33–36.

39. Tindall, "Business Progressivism," 105–106; Key, *Southern Politics*, 229; Tindall, *Emergence of the New South*, 649.

Chapter Two

Prince of the Peckerwoods

In the highly acclaimed *Origins of the New South*, C. Vann Woodward notes that "by some obscure rule of succession," Vardamans tended to beget Bilbos. The observation is by no means one of approbation. Even Vardaman's most severe critics have found the White Chief more palatable than his political protégé. Perhaps the most eloquent and penetrating comparison of the two men comes again from the pen of William Alexander Percy. Vardaman was "a kindly vain demagogue unable to think, and given to emotions he considered noble. . . . He did love the common man after a fashion," and his infectious inability to reason made it difficult to separate his idealism from his demagoguery. "He stood for the poor white against the 'nigger'—those were his qualifications as a statesman." But despite his sympathy for the poor whites, Vardaman had the pretensions of aristocracy, at least in manners and demeanor. It was otherwise with Bilbo. The masses adored him, "not because they were deceived in him, but because they understood him thoroughly; they said of him proudly, 'He's a slick little bastard.' He was one of them and he had risen from obscurity to the fame of glittering infamy—it was as if they themselves had crashed the headlines. Vardaman's glamour waned and this man rode to power."[1]

Here Percy fingered the key to Bilbo's success and also to his failure, his strength among the rednecks and his weakness elsewhere. In explaining the sense of identity between Bilbo and the poor whites he championed, Percy also revealed, unwittingly perhaps, the source of the deep animosity that Bilbo aroused in men of more refined sensibilities. Vardaman had seized the redneck imagination from without, having moved with political adroitness and reasoned conviction from

1. Woodward, *Origins of the New South*, 392; Percy, *Lanterns on the Levee*, 143–44, 148.

conservatism to agrarian progressivism. Bilbo captivated the commons from within, through a communion of beliefs, of manners, of taste. Both men were politically committed to the same ideals, but one was a reformer by choice, the other a reformer by nature. Vardaman's progressivism was learned, Bilbo's was innate. The difference between them was primarily one of class, not in the Marxian economic sense but in cultural terms, and that difference does much to explain the political distinction between them in its effect on both their friends and their enemies.

For Percy and his type, Vardaman was the "kindly, vain demagogue," an amusing but powerful political force that had to be defeated. Bilbo was more; he was the "pert little monster," a dangerous and loathsome vermin that had to be destroyed. Bilbo was, after all, the true political embodiment of the poor whites, the hordes who thronged political rallies, turning them into profane camp meetings where justice was promised and entertainment guaranteed, where the rednecks came to revel in the very extravagance of Bilbo's personality and rhetoric. Surveying the Bilbo mob at one such gathering at Black Hawk, Percy described them as "ill-dressed, surly . . . unintelligent and slinking . . . the sort of people that lynch Negroes, that mistake hoodlumism for wit, and cunning for intelligence, that attend revivals and fight and fornicate in the bushes afterwards. They were undiluted Anglo-Saxons. They were the sovereign voter." It was Vardaman who awakened this royal horde to their political power, but it was Bilbo who became the stark expression of their will.[2]

Democracy in some sense, then, made Theodore Bilbo a political force. For the very reasons Percy detailed, Bilbo was perfectly equipped to tap the newborn power of the redneck masses. The irony is that the very excesses that made him their darling—his crudeness, his passion for their cause, his flamboyance—made him contemptible in the eyes of others more educated and more refined. Even liberals, especially those outside the South, who worked to improve the lot of the kinds of people for whom Bilbo spoke, found it more palatable to deal with urbane conservatives than with a liberal redneck. That paradox haunted Bilbo and his constituency throughout their political rise, but nowhere more than in Washington, where as a senator he would be so dependent on sophisticated liberal academics who were unable or unwilling to understand him or those he represented.

2. Percy, *Lanterns on the Levee*, 149.

Bilbo's origins were ordinary enough. He was born in a log house on an autumn Saturday, October 13, 1877. His father, James Oliver Bilbo, raised ten children and a few cattle on 240 acres of farmland near Juniper Grove in rural Pearl River County. The country was poor, piney, predominantly white, and profoundly Baptist. During Bilbo's youth most families still scratched a modest existence from the sandy soil, but already lumbering was beginning to challenge agriculture as the region's primary economic force. As south Mississippi's sawmill boom shifted from the pioneering stage to large-scale production, northern and eastern companies purchased millions of acres of timberland at minimal prices. As Robert Penn Warren told it:

> They got in, and set up the mills and laid the narrow-gauge tracks and knocked together the company commissaries and paid a dollar a day and folks swarmed out of the bush for the dollar. . . . The saws sang soprano and the clerk in the commissary passed out the blackstrap molasses and the sowbelly and wrote in his big book . . . and all was merry as a marriage bell. Till, all of a sudden, there weren't any more pine trees. They stripped the mills. The narrow-gauge tracks got covered with grass. Folks tore down the commissaries for kindling wood. There wasn't any more dollar a day. The big boys were gone, with diamond rings on their fingers and broadcloth on their backs.

Warren could easily have been describing south Mississippi, where a single firm, the Edward Hines Company, at one time owned almost a quarter of a million acres in Pearl River and Hancock counties alone.[3]

With the multiplying mills came the railroads. By 1907 the Gulf and Ship Island (G. and S. I.) line, which did business in Pearl River County, hauled a tenth of all the yellow pine shipped in the entire South. As more and more acres came into the hands of a few major companies and as those companies came to wield more and more political power, piney-woods farmers, like their counterparts in the Midwest and elsewhere, began to clamor for regulation of the "monopolistic" corporations and railroads. It is likely that the young Bilbo absorbed much of the rhetoric and urgency of Populism, though the third-party movement made little headway in his home county. One of the early and favorite targets of Bilbo's political fire was the G. and S. I., and many of

3. Larry T. Balsamo, "Theodore G. Bilbo and Mississippi Politics, 1877–1932" (Ph.D. dissertation, University of Missouri, 1967), 1–6; Nollie W. Hickman, "The Lumber Industry in South Mississippi, 1890–1915," *Journal of Mississippi History*, XX (1958), 211–17; Nollie W. Hickman, *Mississippi Harvest: Lumbering in the Longleaf Pine Belt, 1840–1915* (Oxford, Miss., 1962), 153–66; Warren, *All the King's Men*, 4–5.

those who had imbibed the spirit of the People's party eventually found their way into his reform faction of Mississippi's Democracy.[4]

Information on Bilbo's early years is scant. At fifteen he began public school at nearby Poplarville in the third grade and received a diploma four years later in 1896. In the same year that he started public school, he was elected teacher of a local Sunday school, introducing him to another of his lifelong interests, Baptist church affairs. By graduation Bilbo had become a lay preacher, probably through the influence of W. W. Mitchell, a one-armed Baptist minister with whom he boarded in Poplarville. A few years later Mitchell would be involved in Bilbo's baptism into another and more notable passion, politics. Little more is known of Bilbo's schooling except that he was a voracious reader and a star debater, rarely able to resist an opportunity to speak. Once called upon to help bury a landlord's mule, he offered an unsolicited eulogy as the owner and friends lowered the animal to its final rest.[5]

In 1897 Bilbo enrolled at Peabody College in Nashville, Tennessee. There is some confusion about his college career. It appears that he carried a substantial academic load for more than two years but never earned a degree. When he returned to Mississippi in 1899, he brought with him a new bride, Lillian Herrington of Wiggins, Mississippi. Almost nothing is known of Bilbo's first wife except that she died suddenly in 1900, leaving her husband to care for an infant daughter, Jessie. For the next five years Bilbo taught in a succession of rural south Mississippi schools, at one of which he met a fellow teacher, Linda Gaddy Bedgood, who became the second Mrs. Bilbo in January of 1903.[6]

Later that year the financial pressures of family life nudged the fledgling pedagogue toward his first taste of politics. He decided to run for circuit clerk of Pearl River County, and his opponent was W. W. Mitchell, the same one-armed Baptist minister with whom he had boarded during high school in Poplarville. Mitchell, who had already served a term as county treasurer, proceeded to teach his young opponent a valuable political lesson. The old preacher had discovered the power of a sympathy vote, and he made certain that every elector knew he was lacking a full complement of usable upper appendages. Bilbo later told a friend, "I could see that damn empty sleeve myself when

4. Hickman, "The Lumber Industry," 212–17; McCain, "The Populist Party," 42–46, 105; Balsamo, "Bilbo and Mississippi Politics," 4–6.

5. Balsamo, "Bilbo and Mississippi Politics," 6–7; Picayune *Item*, March 12, 1964; Willard F. Bond, *I Had a Friend* (Kansas City, Mo., 1958), 41–42.

6. Green, *The Man Bilbo*, 12–15; Bobby Wade Saucier, "The Public Career of Theodore G. Bilbo" (Ph.D. dissertation, Tulane University, 1971), 4.

I went into the booth to vote." Playing the martyr soon became a standard element of Bilbonic politics, a campaign ploy that The Man refined to an art and that stood him in good stead throughout his career.[7]

Defeated but not discouraged, Bilbo returned to the classroom, this time in Wiggins under Willard F. Bond, whom he had known at Peabody. Bond later declared that Bilbo could do more mental and physical labor than anyone he had ever seen, but he was forced to dismiss the young teacher after only two years. In addition to their teaching duties, the Bilbos supervised the dormitory for boarding students, and it seems that during the second year Mr. Bilbo became quite friendly with a comely young orphan girl who occupied the room next door. Thus began the whispers that would plague Bilbo's entire career and the marital strain that would ultimately end in divorce in the 1930s. Mrs. Bilbo insisted that there was nothing between her husband and the student, but Bond later admitted that "Mrs. Bilbo had cause to be jealous." In any case, gossip forced the principal to dismiss teacher and student, and Bilbo found himself jobless.[8]

In 1905 he somehow acquired enough money to become partner in a Wiggins drugstore. The same year, he returned to Nashville and entered the Vanderbilt University School of Law, where after two academic years he entered the senior class but again failed to earn a degree. One possible explanation was a charge of cheating lodged against him by a fellow student. Since an Honor Committee jury acquitted him, it seems more likely that he left school for financial reasons. Nonetheless, the cheating episode directed his ethical standing along the same path the Wiggins scandal had already cast his moral reputation. Bilbo learned to handle the ethical muddles, beginning there in Nashville. Upon learning of the charge against him, "he created a rough-house and demanded a trial at once." The committee had no sooner exonerated him—by a two-to-two deadlock—than he assailed his accuser as a "damned son of a bitch" and restrained the urge to "whallop him" only because, Bilbo later said, his adversary seemed so indifferent to the insult. Here, as Wigfall Green has noted, Bilbo added another political technique to his growing repertoire: "When accused, to bluster; when barely vindicated, to denounce." He mastered the tactic thoroughly, perhaps simply from so much practice.[9]

7. Green, *The Man Bilbo*, 15; Bond, *I Had a Friend*, 64.

8. Saucier, "The Public Career of Bilbo," 6–7; Willard F. Bond to Wigfall Green, September 1, 1958, in A. Wigfall Green Papers, Williams Library, University of Mississippi, Oxford.

9. *Investigation by the Senate of the State of Mississippi of the Charges of Bribery in*

The increasing sordidness of Bilbo's reputation, which an almost universally hostile press later embellished and broadcast—this image of a lewd womanizer, of a sleazy shyster—eventually turned him into a personal pariah for a certain class of people, both within Mississippi and without. Yet it never seemed to corrode his popularity with the rednecks. Indeed, some of them apparently took a kind of perverse delight in inflicting an ulcer like Bilbo on the body politic just to spite the sensibilities of their social betters. Others simply refused to believe the rumors and rallied to him as one suffering unjustly for righteousness' sake. Whether Bilbo manufactured the later situations for political purposes or was in fact ethically bankrupt is not demonstrable from the record. In none of the notorious incidents is there conclusive evidence one way or the other. What is conclusive is that he turned each of them to his own political advantage by blustering and denouncing.

As for the question of sexual promiscuity, there seems little doubt that, as Bond put it, "Girl friends was his great weakness." But then, as Wilbur Cash so aptly argues, both hedonism and religiosity run deep in the southern soul: "God was stern, yes, but if one gave uncompromising allegiance to the Right, well, He knew the strength of the world and the Enemy, how sweet was profitless mirth; He would not be too hard on the sound in doctrine and the contrite." And to the unlettered tillers of the soil, Bilbo's orthodoxy was as solid as stone. More likely, the peckerwoods again simply chose to discredit the rumors and to believe Bilbo rather than his enemies. But the very bonds that tied him to the masses—his identity with them in their interests, their manners, their likes and dislikes, their passions and prejudices—ensnared him in his efforts to serve them. To those in positions of power in Mississippi but more particularly those in Washington, he would become not the rednecks' champion of the downtrodden but Percy's "slick little bastard."[10]

For the second time, then, financial pressures pushed Bilbo toward public office, and in April of 1907 he returned home to announce for senator from Mississippi's five-county Fourth District. His lone opponent was E. L. Dent, the county attorney of Covington County, and the two candidates agreed to stump the district together. Their platforms were similar, but Bilbo had several advantages. Since the creation of the district in 1890, only one man from Bilbo's county had held the seat, and most people acknowledged that it was time for a Pearl River

the Election of a United States Senator (Nashville, 1910), 14; Green, *The Man Bilbo*, 16–17.

10. Bond to Green, September 1, 1958, in Green Papers; Cash, *The Mind of the South*, 137.

man to go to Jackson. Almost every office holder in the county endorsed Bilbo, and his church activities gave him significant exposure throughout the district. Most important, though, was his growing mastery of the political stump. One morning Dent violated their tacit agreement to travel together and set out early for the day's first speech at a small country church. When Bilbo discovered his predicament, he headed his horse through the cutover timberlands, hoping to beat Dent's roadbound buggy to the rally. When the young prosecutor arrived, he found his lay-preacher adversary holding court from the old church's well-worn organ, on which he regaled the faithful with "Lord, Plant My Feet on Higher Ground." Dent was the first politician—though by no means the last—to discover that trying to outflank Bilbo was a precarious venture.[11]

When August came, Bilbo swamped Dent, 4,420 votes to 1,554, in the Democratic primary, polling over 80 percent of Pearl River's votes. With thirty-four other freshman senators, he entered the legislature just as Mississippi's progressive movement was beginning to blossom. His own platform had been one of reform, emphasizing regulation of railroads, equitable taxation, and a fair apportionment of both school funds and legislative seats. The apportionment issues were of special interest to his constituents. White counties in general chafed under the system of appropriating school funds, and south Mississippians particularly objected to what they considered discriminatory legislative apportionment. As the section's population increased after 1890, so did the clamor for additional seats. In 1900 the lawmakers established a fixed ratio among the delegations from northeast, west, and southeast Mississippi, which would have precluded any overall growth in the south's representation. Pearl River voters wanted both apportionment inequities rectified.[12]

Bilbo quickly emerged as a champion of his section and a stalwart of the Vardaman forces in the senate. He made the first motion, was appointed to the first committee, and nominated the president pro tempore. He personally sponsored bills to equalize school funds and to reapportion the legislature, both unsuccessfully. His position on other legislation would have won him acceptance in any state's progressive legion: he supported public education, prohibition, and railroad and corporate regulation; he advocated a forestry board, an antilobby law, a child labor law, and an elective judiciary; he led the fight to allow larger cities to adopt commmission government. One of his favorite pastimes was baiting corporations in general and the G. and S. I. Rail-

11. Balsamo, "Bilbo and Mississippi Politics," 13–24.

12. Poplarville *Free Press*, May 16, 1907; Kirwan, *Revolt of the Rednecks*, 136–41.

road in particular. When his colleagues rebuffed a serious effort to have the company investigated, Bilbo descended to derision, introducing a ten-thousand-dollar appropriation to enable the line to extend its track to the capitol steps, the better for private cars to distribute their "hot birds, cold drinks, and long black cigars."[13]

The sarcasm prompted a journalistic rebuke that began a forty-five-year verbal feud between the fledgling politician and Jackson *Daily News* editor Fred Sullens. If Bilbo were aspiring to succeed Mark Twain, Sullens suggested, perhaps he should be left alone, for genuine humor was rare enough that "all budding genius should be cultivated," even if it meant cluttering up the senate journal with "embryonic efforts." Besides, he confessed, "we have sufficient curiosity to 'try anything once.'"[14]

That 1908 session has been seen as the turning point for progressive reform in Mississippi, and Bilbo was in the forefront of the forces for progress. When the legislature adjourned, he returned to Poplarville to practice law. Since the lawmakers met biennially, he had a year and a half to mend political fences before the next regular session. He also found time in 1909 to attend law courses at the University of Michigan, but he earned no credit.[15]

The legislature reconvened in 1910 amidst one of the hottest political duels the state had ever seen. By the time the session adjourned, Bilbo had forever crashed beyond the role of an obscure piney-woods legislator. United States Senator Anselm J. McLaurin died suddenly in December, 1909, and the legislature faced the chore of selecting his successor. Vardaman's supporters brought great pressure to bear in behalf of the White Chief, who had lost a bitterly contested primary race for the other Senate seat in 1907. Although several applicants placed their names before the Democratic joint legislative caucus in January, 1910, Vardaman's claim to McLaurin's seat appeared compelling.[16]

Everyone conceded that Vardaman would run away with a popular vote. But there would be no statewide primary until 1911, and a legislative election to fill the unexpired term was a different matter. Even in the legislature, however, the White Chief could mount a formidable campaign, especially since the lawmakers labored under the scrutiny of the publicity-aroused farmers. Vardaman's followers were stunned,

13. Hamilton, *Progressive Mississippi*, 62, 78–79.

14. Jackson *Daily News*, February 16, 1908.

15. Charles G. Hamilton, "The Turning Point: The Legislative Session of 1908," *Journal of Mississippi History*, XXV (1963), 99; Balsamo, "Bilbo and Mississippi Politics," 35–37.

16. Kirwan, *Revolt of the Rednecks*, 178–84.

therefore, when the opening session of the caucus of Democratic legislators voted to keep its proceedings secret. Since Mississippi was a single-party state, the official and open vote of the legislature would be no more than a formal ratification of a decision already reached by the closeted caucus. The anti-Vardaman group realized that their only hope was to keep several candidates with strong local followings in the field until their backers could be wooed away from Vardaman as a second choice. From the pack emerged LeRoy Percy as the strongest challenger. Father of William Alexander Percy, he was the flower of Delta manhood, and he entered the race, said his son, not to gain office but to defeat Vardaman, who though "a likeable man, as a poolroom wit is likeable," was "surely not one to sit in the councils of the nation." He was simply "an exhibitionist playing with fire." [17]

For six weeks the balloting dragged on, with each day's legislative business prefaced by a closed-door meeting of the caucus. The daily ritual proceeded amidst swirling rumors of smoky hotel-room conclaves where political brokers bought and bartered votes like market securities, where hungry upstart lawmakers sought to parlay their coveted votes into judgeships, money, or just a share of the free-flowing whiskey that lubricated the electoral machine. Finally, on Washington's birthday the legislators selected Percy, 87–82, sparking a barrage of accusations and demands for an investigation of the "secret caucus." In late March a Hinds County grand jury indicted L. C. Dulaney, a prominent Percy backer, for attempted bribery. The prosecution's star witness and purported victim was none other than the freshman senator from Pearl River, who testified that Dulaney had paid him $645 to switch his vote from Vardaman to Percy. Bilbo's enemies in the senate offered a resolution to expel him. The debate, which became an open investigation of the bribery charges, fell somewhere between circus and melodrama, with Bilbo insisting that he had set out to expose the horse-trading tactics of the Percy people by catching them in the act.

He spun a lurid tale of a police-arranged payoff at a black Jackson bordello, aborted at the last minute by Dulaney. Several leading Vardaman men corroborated the story, but Dulaney gave a detailed refutation. The Percy senators closed with a parade of character witnesses who questioned Bilbo's integrity, after which the two-week hearing ended with the expulsion vote falling one short of the necessary two-thirds. The anti-Vardaman group then entered a resolution declaring Bilbo's story "a trumped-up falsehood utterly unworthy of belief," and

17. *Ibid.*, 191–93; Percy, *Lanterns on the Levee*, 143–44.

demanded his resignation. He was, said the document, "unfit to sit with honest upright men in a respectable legislative body." Despite a boycott by Bilbo's supporters, the diminished Senate passed the measure 28–1.[18]

The entire carnival was reenacted at Dulaney's trial in Yazoo County, at the end of which a jury acquitted him in early December. The accuracy of Bilbo's story is impossible to determine with certainty, but of the political consequences there is no doubt. In the senate censure he had found his empty sleeve, and he determined to dangle it before the voters in 1911. At the close of the legislative session he launched a speaking tour to render his side of the bribery affair and in town after town droned through the facts of the case to polite but uninspired audiences. It was an awkward and slow start, convincing perhaps, but not rousing. Then at a late May rally near McComb he struck a nerve. In a vicious indictment of the secret caucus, Bilbo worked the crowd of mostly poor dirt farmers into a frenzy of indignation. Each bitter thrust at the Percy faction evoked thunderous acclaim, and for more than two hours he assailed wealth and privilege and argued the cause of the rednecks. Bilbo had discovered "the people" and thereby his political self.[19]

Throughout the rest of the year he peddled his version of the caucus from courthouse steps or, if denied that, as he often was by hostile county officials, from any makeshift platform where the brogan and overall crowd would gather. And how they thronged!—a thousand in Tishomingo, three thousand at North Carrollton, five thousand at Lauderdale Springs. When the organizers of a Newton rally refused to let Bilbo speak, his admirers threw together a jerrybuilt rostrum within earshot and then bellowed with glee as spectators stampeded to him, magnetized by his oratory.[20]

And there rained on Mississippi such oratory as had never been heard, even from the lips of the White Chief. Bilbo served up a mixture of coarse wit in barnyard vernacular "salted," as V. O. Key described it, "with bastard King Jamesian orotundities." Percy loyalists, meanwhile, were neither idle nor silent. Eager to vindicate the caucus vic-

18. Green, *The Man Bilbo*, 31–34; Nannie Pitts McLemore, "The Progressive Era," in McLemore (ed.), *History of Mississippi*, II, 49–52. See also *Investigation of the Charges of Bribery*.

19. Balsamo, "Bilbo and Mississippi Politics," 54–56, 60–61; Thurston E. Doler, "Theodore G. Bilbo's Rhetoric of Racial Relations" (Ph.D. dissertation, University of Oregon, 1968), 40–43.

20. Balsamo, "Bilbo and Mississippi Politics," 62–67.

tory, they were already touting Percy for the 1911 primary, in which Vardaman was sure to challenge for the full term. It was just as essential to stop Bilbo, who obviously had his eye on the lieutenant governor's office. Bilbo was, Percy warned, "a characterless man, a self-confessed liar, a self-accused bribe-taker . . . and a moral leper." R. H. Henry's Jackson *Daily Clarion-Ledger* called him a "repudiated man with no reputation to protect," and Sullens labeled him a "pimp" and a "frequenter of lewd houses." The Man matched them epithet for epithet. Henry, he sneered, was an "old gouty-legged, dunghill cock . . . who has lied about me until he has gotten swayback," and Sullens was "a degenerate by birth, a carpetbagger by inheritance, a liar by instinct, a slanderer and assassin of character by practice, and a coward by nature." The summer air sizzled with political lightning; it was a vintage Mississippi campaign.[21]

When Dulaney was acquitted in December, Bilbo announced his candidacy and raised the rhetorical stakes, if that was possible. When he labeled Percy supporter Washington Gibbs "a renegade confederate soldier," the old rebel tracked him down and caned him on a Yazoo City street. Sullens headlined: WAR HORSE OF YAZOO BROKE GOOD WALKING STICK OVER HEAD OF POPLARVILLE PERVERT. Bilbo transcended all bounds of propriety in a speech at Blue Mountain College, where he called J. J. Henry "a cross between a hyena and a mongrel . . . begotten in a nigger graveyard at midnight, suckled by a sow, and educated by a fool."[22]

Henry's friends warned that any retaliation would only aid Bilbo and Vardaman, but the insult was too severe. On July 6, Henry boarded a train at Starkville, tracked Bilbo to the smoking car, and summarily pistol-whipped him on the spot. At nearby Sturgis, Bilbo got off the train and a doctor treated him briefly before a special train rushed him to Jackson. Meanwhile, Henry surrendered himself to the authorities. But Bilbo preferred to wreak his justice at the polls rather than the bar, and he squeezed as much political mileage as possible out of the incident. From the hospital, where he remained for several weeks, came frequent press releases detailing Bilbo's "courageous recovery." In a splendid stroke of political timing he took the stump at a "second coming" to Sturgis just before the primary. Swathed in bandages that hardly veiled the precious wounds, Bilbo was the political martyr par excellence, and it paid off handsomely.[23]

21. Key, *Southern Politics*, 242; Balsamo, "Bilbo and Mississippi Politics," 68–69.
22. Balsamo, "Bilbo and Mississippi Politics," 71–74.
23. Wilmuth Saunders Rutledge, "The John J. Henry–Theodore Bilbo Encounter, 1911," *Journal of Mississippi History*, XXXIV (1972), 360–71; A. H. Longino to J. J.

Bilbo's stock in the Vardaman camp had risen steadily throughout the campaign. The two men were united by a common cause, censure of the secret caucus, and a common clientele, the mass of poor farmers. Adversaries hurled the term *redneck* at them in derision, but the followers of Vardaman and Bilbo received it with pride, often sporting red neckties as a sort of perverse badge of honor. Bilbo, as was his wont, carried matters to extravagance, wearing red pajamas, red socks, and red galluses. When Sullens ill-advisedly wondered in print why Bilbo wore red suspenders and a red tie, The Man responded artlessly that he wore suspenders to keep up his pants—and the tie to keep up his courage.[24]

On primary day Vardaman and Bilbo swamped their opponents, to the shock and dismay of the conservative press. Friends, however, celebrated with a ditty:

Vardaman on the main line,
Alexander on the switch,
Bilbo in the sleeping car,
And Percy in the ditch.

Vardaman led his nearest opponent by almost 50,000 votes out of 130,000 cast, and Percy limped home last with barely 15 percent of the vote. Bilbo did almost as well as his mentor, carrying 68 of 80 counties and finishing within 3,000 votes of the White Chief's own total. The victory was more than Bilbo's successful introduction to statewide politics; it was in large measure his real political birth. Conceived in the secret caucus and shaped by the 1911 campaign, he emerged with all the parts in place—the flamboyant oratory, the slashing, aggressive style, the knack for martyrdom, and above all a hypnotic mastery of the redneck imagination. After 1911 it was only a matter of growth and development.[25]

The election was also important for the state, because it paved the way for the completion of the reform program, sweeping aside many of the conservative legislators who had blocked progressivism heretofore. And thanks to Bilbo's dynamism, though it was somewhat erratic, the 1911 campaign energized a progressive constituency among the poor farmers, a constituency that would become the backbone of Bilbo's po-

---

Henry, April 15, 1911, T. C. Lowery to Henry, April 10, 1911, both in Marion Henry Papers, Mitchell Library, Mississippi State University, Starkville.

24. Green, *The Man Bilbo*, 37–38.

25. Interview with Thomas P. Brady, Mississippi Oral History Program (hereinafter cited as MOHP), Vol. II, 23, McCain Library, University of Southern Mississippi, Hattiesburg; Balsamo, "Bilbo and Mississippi Politics," 75–77.

litical future and the backbone of whatever future liberalism would have in Mississippi.[26]

In a strange epilogue to the primary, some of the Delta diehards found the idea of Bilbo's success so abhorrent that they tried to deny him the office by quietly backing James T. Lester, the Socialist candidate, in the general election. Lester garnered three times as many votes as his party's gubernatorial candidate and carried Sunflower and Washington counties and lost Adams by only two votes and Issaquena by three. Despite those efforts, when the legislature convened in 1912, Bilbo took the oath as lieutenant governor in the senate chamber before a bevy of jubilant supporters who sang "Amazing Grace," led by the White Chief himself.[27]

With the reform faction in solid control of most of state government, calm seemed to prevail in 1912. It was merely the eye of the storm. In 1913 a bitter rivalry erupted between the lieutenant governor and the new chief executive, Earl Brewer. Brewer had run unopposed in 1911 and had been able to remain independent of both major factions and on relatively good terms with both. But he had his eye on a Senate seat, and Bilbo's growing command of the small-farmer vote was a significant obstacle to his attaining it. Moreover, Bilbo, too, had ambitions, probably for the governorship in 1915. The first skirmish came in 1913 over a scandal in the state prison system. Brewer declared his intention to investigate the situation thoroughly, while the prison board, dominated by Vardaman favorites, tried to circumvent the governor with a probe of its own. In a special legislative session in June, the house backed the governor, and Bilbo marshaled the senate behind the board. Round one was a draw. A jury convicted two board members of minor offenses, but Bilbo was able to minimize the political damage.[28]

Round two began later that year when a Vicksburg grand jury indicted Bilbo and Senator George Hobbs for bribery in connection with a bill to create a new Delta county. Brewer appeared for the prosecution and testified that he had helped devise a scheme to catch the conspirators in the act. The defense argued that the whole thing was a political ploy by Brewer to discredit Bilbo, and the jury acquitted both men. The following legislative session dissolved into a battleground between the rival politicians and ended in March, 1914, without the passage of a single piece of significant legislation.[29]

26. Hamilton, *Progressive Mississippi*, 105–106; Grantham, *The Democratic South*, 49–50.

27. Hamilton, *Progressive Mississippi*, 103–107.

28. Balsamo, "Bilbo and Mississippi Politics," 80–82.

29. *Ibid.*, 82–92. For Hobbs's version of the affair, see George A. Hobbs, *Bilbo, Brewer, and Bribery in Mississippi Politics* (Nashville, 1917).

In the summer Bilbo, for the second time, announced for statewide office in the wake of a bribery scandal; this time he sought the state's highest post. The 1915 primary campaign proved much more tranquil than the previous one, though conservatives again assailed Bilbo's character in harsh terms. His four opponents seemed united against him, appearing together at rally after rally, often accompanied and supported by Brewer. Bilbo himself ran a more positive campaign, advancing an elaborate and typically progressive platform that called for a state highway commission, a tax commission, a juvenile reformatory, a school for the mentally retarded, a corporate watchdog commission, a Blue Sky law, an equitable tax structure, an increase in school funds, and adoption of the initiative and referendum. In August the voters awarded The Man a stunning first-primary victory. The prospect of Bilbo in the governor's chair prompted Fred Sullens to suggest replacing the eagle on the capitol dome with a "puking buzzard" and its counterpart on the state seal with a "carrion crow."[30]

But the crow that rankled Sullens for the next four years was that which he had to eat, and Bilbo's performance as chief executive fed him a steady diet of it. "We must give the devil his due," the editor grumbled at the end of the term, "and frankly admit that Theodore's administration has been one of substantial achievements." Indeed, Bilbo's governorship, according to one historian, "marked the climax of the progressive era in Mississippi." The governor early established good relationships with most lawmakers and then implored, prodded, cajoled, and pressured them into passing a legislative program that remains unsurpassed by any four-year period in modern Mississippi history. His most outstanding feats were the creation of a state tax commission and equalization of tax assessments throughout the state, which gave Mississippi its most efficient revenue system since antebellum days. In 1918 the state budget was in the black for the first time in recent memory. Under Bilbo's whip hand the legislature gave Mississippi a board of bank examiners, a highway commission, a pardoning board, a tuberculosis hosital, a charity hospital, a training school for delinquents, a compulsory school-attendance law, a Blue Sky law, a tougher antilobby law, equalization of school fund distribution, adult night classes, and the largest appropriation ever for education. In addition, Bilbo proposed other items that were rejected by a conservative house of representatives. Even his severest critics acknowledged that it was a remarkable record.[31]

30. Balsamo, "Bilbo and Mississippi Politics," 93–104; Green, *The Man Bilbo*, 50–53.

31. William D. McCain, "The Triumph of Democracy, 1916–1932," in McLemore

However, by 1918 the Vardaman-Bilbo dominion was beginning to crumble. The senator, who had aligned himself with midwestern progressives like George Norris and Robert La Follette, remained popular only so long as domestic reform dominated the Congress. Vardaman's unswerving support of Woodrow Wilson's New Freedom progressivism had won him widespread acclaim back home, but when international issues brutally intruded on the public consciousness, some of the associations that were popular in peacetime became distasteful in war. The White Chief joined the "little group of willful men," who opposed what they saw as Wilson's "unneutral" neutrality in the face of world war. Vardaman's stubborn idealism doomed him politically.[32]

Amidst the war hysteria and rampant jingoism, Mississippians scorned Vardaman for his intransigent opposition to the president. Gulfport Congressman Byron Patton Harrison sensed a unique opportunity to advance and announced that he would challenge Vardaman in 1918 on a platform of patriotism and loyalty to Wilson. Bilbo, with his eye on the 1922 Senate primary for John Sharp Williams' seat, decided to seek Harrison's vacated House spot. Four candidates opposed the governor, the most formidable being Judge Paul B. Johnson of Hattiesburg. Vardaman and Bilbo both lost badly. Vardaman's unpopular antiwar position undoubtedly undid him, but the governor's problems were manifold. For one thing, the wartime fervor, heightened for Mississippians by the Senate race, overshadowed the kind of economic and social issues that were Bilbo's bill of fare. His association with the White Chief, who was now commonly condemned as a slacker, did not help, while his efforts to distance himself from his former leader only antagonized the Vardaman loyalists. Many voters simply resented a sitting governor's seeking another office with more than a year and a half remaining in his term.[33]

But the most damaging issue was a bill that the governor had signed into law almost unnoticed in 1916. To eradicate Texas tick fever from the state and to remove a federal quarantine on all Mississippi beef, the legislature had approved a measure requiring farmers to dip their cattle every two weeks. Having to drive stock to public vats and immerse them in an arsenic solution seemed a dangerous nuisance to Mississippi farmers, and determined, sometimes violent, resistance emerged, especially in south Mississippi. Although Bilbo had not spon-

(ed.), *History of Mississippi*, II, 60–73; Balsamo, "Bilbo and Mississippi Politics," 105–24.

32. Holmes, *The White Chief*, 292–93, 298–319.

33. *Ibid.*, 342–46; Balsamo, "Bilbo and Mississippi Politics," 127–35.

sored the bill, he had signed it. Now Johnson was determined to hang it around the governor's neck and was proclaiming the news, with the aid of a cowbell, from stumps throughout the Sixth District. By the time the legislature adjourned and Bilbo was able to leave the capital to campaign, the force of his speeches was all but muted by the lingering echo of the judge's cowbell. Even some of the faithful found the eradication effort a strain on their loyalty, begetting one of those enduring aphorisms of Mississippi politics: "I'm fer Bilbo but I'm agin dippin'." When the last August returns trickled in, The Man's enemies for the first of many times pronounced him politically dead. Had there been a certificate, it must surely have listed the cause of death as Texas tick fever. Bilbo would later frame his demise in a more exalted metaphor: "I was," he declared, "crucified on a cross of ticks."[34]

When his term expired in 1920, Bilbo returned to Poplarville for the first time in a decade to farm and to practice law. Through inheritance and purchase he had acquired several hundred acres of land, including a handsome pecan orchard. Bilbo enjoyed farming immensely, but it would always be a second love. Politics was never far from his thoughts. He considered entering the 1922 senatorial primary for John Sharp Williams' seat, even if it meant challenging the old apostle Vardaman. Although his relationship to the White Chief remained cool, Bilbo finally bowed out, leaving the race to Vardaman, Belle Kearney of Madison County, and Hubert Stephens of New Albany. Bilbo did little work for Vardaman early in the campaign, and the worn and ill old war horse appeared doomed. Unwilling to see the reform faction demolished, however, Bilbo finally took the stump for his old ally, and to the amazement and chagrin of the experts, helped push Vardaman into a first primary lead. The alarmed conservatives rolled out all of their guns in support of Stephens, who triumphed in the runoff. But Vardaman's surprising strength underscored the stubborn vitality of the old progressive faction, and with the White Chief now retiring to a daughter's care in Birmingham, the mantle of undisputed leadership passed to Bilbo.[35]

The newly invested potentate decided to seek a second gubernatorial term in 1923 and for the third time launched his campaign in a whirlwind of controversy. Lee Russell, who had become governor in 1920 as

34. Interview with John Oliver Emmerich, MOHP, Vol. XVI, 6–13; Balsamo, "Bilbo and Mississippi Politics," 131–35; Poplarville *Free Press*, October 25, 1917; Gloster *Record*, January 20, 1922.

35. Balsamo, "Bilbo and Mississippi Politics," 135–39; Bilbo to W. D. Robinson, January 2, 1921, in W. D. Robinson Papers, No. 1214, Southern Historical Collection, Wilson Library, University of North Carolina, Chapel Hill.

something of a Bilbo protégé, had since antagonized his erstwhile ally and mired himself in a sensational scandal involving a former secretary. In February of 1922 Frances Birkhead sued Russell for $100,000, charging that he had seduced her and forced her to undergo an abortion that left her permanently injured. The trial unfolded in Russell's hometown of Oxford in December. When the prosecution was unable to produce its star witness, the jury took hardly half an hour to acquit the governor. That star witness was Bilbo, who allegedly knew all about the affair and was willing to tell it to a jury to embarrass Russell. However, on the eve of the trial, the former governor mysteriously ignored a summons and vanished into the piney woods. Fred Sullens claimed that the deputy who finally found Bilbo had combed all of Pearl River County and was about to give up when he was stopped by the wail of a heifer calf. Tracking the sound to a nearby barn, he found the illustrious fugitive huddled in a stall with a very dismayed young cow. The whole affair was a pitiable case, the editor mused. Some people were sorry for the governor, some for Miss Birkhead, and some for Bilbo. "But personally," he declared, "all of our sympathy goes to the heifer calf."[36]

In any case, Bilbo insisted that since he had acted as Russell's counsel, lawyer-client confidentiality protected any information that he possessed. Judge Edwin Holmes was unimpressed and sentenced him to thirty days in jail and fined him a hundred dollars. The sentence was later reduced to ten days, and upon his release Bilbo declared his candidacy for governor from the Lafayette County jailhouse steps. Running against him were Judge Percy Bell of Greenville, Mike Conner, Lester Franklin, and Henry Whitfield. Bilbo surprised almost everyone by making the runoff, though he eventually succumbed to Whitfield by sixteen thousand votes. For the second time in five years Bilbo was pronounced politically dead but refused a proper burial. In fact he was encouraged by his showing and believed that he had taken great strides in reviving the old Vardaman faction. Enough of the loyalists had come out of hiding to give him thirty-two counties in the second primary.[37]

Immediately Bilbo began building for 1927. With borrowed money,

36. Miss Birkhead claimed that Bilbo and another friend of Russell's promised that she would be made the governor's private secretary if she would stay out of sight during the legislative session of 1920. They eventually convinced her to leave the state and promised that she would "be taken care of." Frances Birkhead to Brunini and Hirsch, January 24, 1922, in Papers of the Committee on the Judiciary, 74th Cong., Records of the United States Senate, Record Group 46, National Archives; John Oliver Emmerich, *Two Faces of Janus: The Saga of Deep South Change* (Jackson, Miss., 1973), 63–64.

37. Balsamo, "Bilbo and Mississippi Politics," 139–49.

he established a weekly political paper, the Mississippi *Free Lance*, and flooded the state with free copies, followed hard by paid solicitors peddling subscriptions at two dollars a year. By 1926 circulation topped seventeen thousand. Whatever backsliding the reform faction had done in 1923 was partially offset by the performance of the business-oriented Whitfield administration. Bolstered by a conservative legislature, the new governor put the ax to much of the progressive program of his recent predecessors. The rednecks seethed at what they considered the coddling of corporate interests, and Bilbo fanned the flames with the *Free Lance*.[38]

By the end of 1926 he had a statewide organization preparing for the next year's primary, and the field looked uncommonly manageable. Only Conner offered formidable opposition. But Whitfield's sudden death in March elevated Dennis Murphree to the top post and to legitimate candidacy for a full term. Defending the Whitfield record, Murphree vowed "to defeat Bilbo and remove the scourge of Bilboism" from the state forever. The Man lashed back, labeling Murphree a corporate tool and offering a progressive platform highlighted by a call for a state textbook printing plant and an extensive highway program. Armed with a brick in each hand, Bilbo mounted the stump to assure the people that the Good Lord had blessed Mississippi with clay for bricks and the devil had provided convicts for labor. "Why my countrymen," he thundered, "we can lay the bricks on one side and run off'em for a hundred years. We can turn'em over and run on the other side for a hundred more years, and then we can stand'em up on end and run them right into Kingdom Come." It was the kind of logic that must have appalled William Alexander Percy, whose ideal of political eloquence was "Father" uplifting the uninformed with a dispassionate and enlightening discourse on the intricacies of the tariff or the Panama tolls question. But the rednecks preferred seasoned King James to vapid, albeit erudite, political prose, and they squealed with delight at their man's antics: "Hurrah for Bilbo! Amen! Hallelujah!" It was, if not respectable, much more fun than respectability.[39]

And for Bilbo it was much more effective. He came within 1 percent of a first-primary victory. Conner, who ran third, endorsed Murphree, but Bilbo anticipated an easy win in the runoff. Then a last-minute ploy

38. *Ibid.*, 149–53; for Bilbo and the *Free Lance*, see Lynda Lawrence Blackwelder, "Theodore Gilmore Bilbo: The *Mississippi Free Lance* Years, 1923–1927" (Master's thesis, University of Southern Mississippi, 1975).

39. Saucier, "The Public Career of Bilbo," 56–60; Roman J. Zorn, "Theodore G. Bilbo: Shibboleths for Statesmanship," in J. D. Salter (ed.), *Public Men: In and Out of Office* (Chapel Hill, 1946), 286; Percy, *Lanterns on the Levee*, 149.

by Masonic Grand Master George Myers made the second primary much closer than expected. Myers sent a letter to Masons throughout the state charging that Bilbo intended to back Al Smith for the Democratic presidential nomination in 1928. Bilbo vehemently denied that he would support any candidate who opposed prohibition, but the accusation was damaging. He barely slipped into a second term by fewer than ten thousand votes.[40]

Bilbo's second administration proved to be the most frustrating period of his political career. Facing a hostile and conservative house of representatives under the domination of the Big Four leaders of black-county Bourbonism, he failed to accomplish any of his major legislative goals. The proposal for a half-million-dollar, state-owned textbook printing plant was vigorously opposed by commercial publishers as well as local printers, who feared that the facility would eventually absorb all of the state's printing business. After intense lobbying by these groups, the house rejected the printing plant scheme in 1928 despite a herculean effort by the governor and firm endorsements from the Mississippi Education Association and the state Federation of Labor. Encouraged by this initial victory, the house then thwarted every other major proposal by the governor, including a sales tax to reduce the state deficit. After Bilbo stubbornly vetoed every alternative revenue measure, the session ended with the budget in disarray. The governor vowed to call a special session in the fall, hoping to arouse enough public support in the interim to bring the lawmakers to heel.[41]

National politics intervened. When the Democrats nominated Smith —wet, Catholic, and urban—to oppose Herbert Hoover for the presidency, the Ku Klux Klan and prohibition groups worked feverishly to crack the Solid South. It was a time of decision for party leaders whose dry, Protestant constituents balked at the prospect of supporting Smith. Some, like Hugo Black in Alabama, equivocated under Klan pressures. In Mississippi, Pat Harrison and Bilbo remained loyal and found themselves paradoxically invoking religious tolerance in defense of racial intolerance. Harrison, with a possible cabinet post at stake, led the way in trying to persuade the voters that a Republican victory posed a danger to white supremacy that thoroughly overshadowed Smith's Catholicism. Besides, Bilbo added, Smith did not have "enough religion to hurt" anybody anyway. For Bilbo it was the very first time he had employed race as a major political weapon, but when he used it, he used it to great effect. In a Memphis address he accused Hoover

40. Balsamo, "Bilbo and Mississippi Politics," 149–61.
41. *Ibid.*, 162–76.

of dancing with Mississippi's black Republican national committeewoman, Mary Booze, at a Washington social gathering. Republicans faced the dilemma of denying the charge and antagonizing northern blacks or admitting it and angering white southerners. Hoover's advisors chose the former, but it did no good, at least in Mississippi, where Smith swamped the Republican by a six-to-one margin. During the campaign Bilbo spoke in several other southern states as well as forty counties in Mississippi. His appeal to the small farmers perhaps made the difference in Klan-ridden Alabama, where he was the featured speaker at the final Smith rally in Birmingham's municipal auditorium and where Smith edged Hoover by a mere seven thousand votes.[42]

The governor returned to Jackson and the special legislative session in October to lead the fight for his highway program, which included a sixty-million-dollar bond issue and a new appointive highway commission. The Big Four were determined to deny Bilbo such a patronage pool, and they had the votes. The house also again rejected the printing plant and sales tax, leaving Bilbo no choice but to accept the conservatives' revenue package.[43]

Undaunted, the governor called the lawmakers back for another special session in June of 1929. This time the case for his highway plan was bolstered by an imminent cutoff of federal funds. The existing commission failed to meet federal standards, and an independent auditor issued a report criticizing the commission's inefficiency and shoddy bookkeeping. But the conservative house stood firm and after a long and bitter fight adjourned without enacting a highway program. In the next year's regular session, Bilbo reluctantly accepted a compromise, a three-man elected commission with sufficient power to satisfy the Federal Bureau of Roads. He also accepted a repugnant revenue measure but took great pains to deny any responsibility for it. Bilbo's second administration left a bitter and barren legislative record that stood in stark contrast to the achievements of his first term. But Mississippi was not the only state government to end the twenties in ignoble fashion. Most southern states, led by Arkansas and North Carolina, suffered from swollen per-capita debts, much of them caused by efforts

42. Ben G. Edmondson, "Pat Harrison and Mississippi in the Presidential Elections of 1924 and 1928," *Journal of Mississippi History*, XXXIII (1971), 349–50, Richard C. Ethridge, "Mississippi and the 1928 Presidential Campaign" (Master's thesis, Mississippi State University, 1961), 82–85; Martha H. Swain, *Pat Harrison: The New Deal Years* (Jackson, Miss., 1978), 21–24; Virginia Van der Veer Hamilton, "The Senate Career of Hugo L. Black" (Ph.D. dissertation, University of Alabama, 1968), 76–81.

43. Balsamo, "Bilbo and Mississippi Politics," 182–86.

to make up for past deficiencies in government services. The real culprit was the sheer poverty of the region.[44]

The most controversial action of Bilbo's second administration occurred away from the legislative battlefield. For almost a decade, the University of Mississippi had been plagued by a variety of problems, chief among them being paltry legislative appropriations and a long-standing tradition of political interference in the school's administration. One of Governor Whitfield's first official acts had been to replace the university's chancellor, Joseph N. Powers, a Bilbo appointee, with Alfred Hume, whose brother-in-law had managed the 1923 Whitfield campaign. In 1929 a Southern School Association report found a multitude of deficiencies including a "somewhat weak" faculty, many of whose degrees came from the University of Mississippi itself. Whitfield recognized that a major overhaul of Mississippi higher education was in order. To secure an authoritative analysis of the problems, he turned to the mecca of American progressive education, the University of Wisconsin, which provided a commission under Professor Michael V. O'Shea to conduct the study. Whitfield died, however, before he was able to implement any of the recommendations in the report.[45]

When Bilbo took office in 1928, he sent to the legislature several proposals based on the O'Shea report. Two of them created quite a political stir. One was a reorganization of higher education under an eight-member college board, one member appointed per year for eight-year terms. The plan was designed, said Bilbo, "to remove our educational institutions as far as it is possible from political turmoil, strife, and partisanship . . . so that no governor . . . could appoint the majority of said board and thus disrupt the proper functioning of our educational institutions."[46]

The second proposal was to consolidate the state's existing major colleges into a single "greater university" in Jackson. Not only was the concept drawn directly from the O'Shea report, but it was supported by numerous legislators, two former Ole Miss chancellors, and a majority of the university's student body. The major obstacle was Chancellor Hume, who with considerable political prowess marshaled the university community, the city of Oxford, and Bilbo's political opponents against the measure. In February, 1928, opponents chartered a special train that brought the entire legislature to Oxford, where they

44. *Ibid.*, 188–206; James T. Patterson, *The New Deal and the States: Federalism in Transition* (Princeton, 1969), 6–10.

45. Hardy Poindexter Graham, "Bilbo and the University of Mississippi, 1928–1932" (Master's thesis, University of Mississippi, 1965), 1–5, 75.

46. *Ibid.*, 21–26.

were royally entertained and lobbied. At the closing banquet Hume delivered an emotional address in which he declared: "Gentlemen, you may move the University of Mississippi. You may move it to Jackson or anywhere else. You may uproot it from the hallowed ground on which it has stood for eighty years. You may take it from these surroundings that have been dear to the thousands who have gone from its doors. But Gentlemen, don't call it Ole Miss. . . . I would suggest that you bury Ole Miss in the hills of Lafayette County, and give it a decent burial." To Hume, said the Jackson *Daily Clarion Ledger*, should go credit for reversing the sentiments of a hostile legislature, which promptly returned to Jackson and rejected the governor's proposal. Even Bilbo's old antagonist Sullens chastised the lawmakers for their shortsightedness and affirmed that "Oxford is, always has been, and always will be, a stupid country town."[47]

Encumbered by a hostile legislature and stagnant college administrations, Bilbo then resorted to a drastic weapon, his appointive power. Here, as elsewhere, he was wont to make a little political hay to reap along with the ideological harvest. The situation offered a prime opportunity to reward friends and punish enemies while cleaning up what the governor thought was a mess in higher education. In May, 1930, Bilbo made three appointments to the board that governed the University of Mississippi, Mississippi Agricultural and Mechanical College, and Mississippi State College for Women. The additions gave him a majority of supporters on the board, which promptly fired the heads of the three schools. Bilbo was also able to replace the president of the State Teacher's College. There followed what critics charged was a wholesale slaughter of faculty and administrators that cost the state colleges their accreditation by the Southern Association of Colleges and Secondary Schools. The howl that rose from the governor's enemies was enough to attract severe censure from the national press.[48]

While some of the changes were patently political, there is ample evidence that the overall design was a sincere effort to improve higher education. It boiled down largely to a conflict of educational philosophies between Bilbo and Hume. Bilbo saw state schools as extensions

47. *Ibid.*, 7-11.

48. Balsamo, "Bilbo and Mississippi Politics," 210–18; Aubrey Keith Lucas, "The Mississippi Legislature and Mississippi Public Higher Education, 1890–1960" (Ph.D. dissertation, Florida State University, 1966), 91–94; John K. Bettersworth, *People's College: A History of Mississippi State* (Tuscaloosa, 1953), 291–98; Allen Cabaniss, *The University of Mississippi: Its First Hundred Years* (Hattiesburg, 1971), 141–49; John B. Hudson, "The Spoils System Enters College: Governor Bilbo and Higher Education in Mississippi," *New Republic*, September 17, 1930, pp. 123–25.

of democracy, training institutions for the equipping of the common man for useful citizenship. Hume embraced a more traditional view, a kind of educational trickle-down, wherein by turning out cultured examples of the ruling class, the university improved the lot of society as a whole. A leader of the legislative opposition later confessed that the governor's proposal was "the most heroic thing I have ever known any politician in Mississippi to do. . . . I was wrong and he was right." The most extensive study of the whole controversy concludes that Bilbo's actions, rather than "wrecking the University . . . as was once thought," really jolted "the institution out of its former languid complacency and . . . contributed, either directly or indirectly, to the school's future progress and development."[49]

Nonetheless, the short-term effects of the desperate course proved disastrous for the colleges. Although the extent of the dismissals, which included several Bilbo supporters, was greatly exaggerated, and though most of the replacements bore impeccable academic credentials, the almost universal enmity of the Mississippi press turned the whole affair into just another Bilbo scandal.[50]

On top of all this came the devastation of the depression: falling cotton prices, foreclosures, bankruptcies, and a mounting deficit. The day Bilbo left office in January, 1932, was without doubt the low point of his political life. Surely, hoped his enemies, he would finally shuffle off to the political graveyard and discreetly expire. In fact on the eve of the 1931 elections someone circulated the following obituary: "Funeral Notice: The friends, acquaintances, and former political supporters of Theodough Graftmore Bilbo (alias Theodore G. Bilbo) are invited to attend his political funeral, which will be held at the governor's mansion on Tuesday, August 4 at 7 P.M. or as soon thereafter as the election returns can be counted. Final obsequies and interment at the Juniper Grove Baptist Church, adjoining the pecan orchard, near Poplarville. No flowers requested, no crying. Rest in Peace."[51]

But like the earlier rumors of Bilbo's political demise, this one, too, proved greatly exaggerated. Barely two years later The Man would again rise from the political grave to win a statewide election, this time to the United States Senate. He would enter that body as a proven progressive, though in some quarters acknowledgment of his early progressivism has come grudgingly. One reason has been the South's repu-

49. Graham, "Bilbo and the University of Mississippi," 30–33, 123–24.

50. Balsamo, "Bilbo and Mississippi Politics," 212–21.

51. Anonymous handwritten note (n.d.) in Theodore G. Bilbo Papers, McCain Library, University of Southern Mississippi, Hattiesburg.

tation for monolithic conservatism, which for so long fostered the notion that progressive democracy never existed, much less flourished, in the region. Not until Arthur Link pointed the way in the 1940s did scholars direct much serious attention to the region's reform tradition. By that historian's standards, Bilbo's progressive credentials are impeccable. All of the issues by which Link validated southern claims to progressivism were part and parcel of Bilbo's political ideology: railroad and trust regulations, direct primaries, initiative and referendum, commission government, corrupt practices and child labor legislation, penal reform. Even after middle-class elements began to reshape the reform movement in Mississippi, Bilbo's progressivism remained what it had always been. He never became a business progressive.[52]

Two things, however, did distinguish Bilbo from other southern progressive leaders. One accents something familiar about the social and economic texture of Mississippi; the other reveals something startling about Bilbo's politics.

The startling fact is the conspicuous absence of race as a prominent campaign tactic in Bilbo's rise as a progressive. It is especially startling in light of the intense racial rhetoric that marred his final few years and earned him national notoriety as a paradigm of racial bigotry. But the fact remains, and it stands in stark contrast to the tactics of not only Vardaman and other redneck leaders but to those of "respectable" southerners as well. Even a relative moderate like Hoke Smith of Georgia, once accused of being soft on white supremacy, "seized the issue," as T. Harry Williams says, "and ran off with it." For Carter Glass, Josephus Daniels, and others, economics always took a back seat to race—but not for Bilbo. Only in the 1928 presidential campaign did he discuss race to any significant degree, and even then he was merely following the lead set by such "respectable" politicians as Pat Harrison and John Sharp Williams.[53]

Certainly Bilbo embraced white supremacy as devoutly as any southerner, probably more so than most. It is intriguing, however, that he considered segregation an accepted fact of southern life and therefore saw no need to drag race into the political arena. Moreover, while Bilbo left no doubts about his opposition to racial equality, he sometimes rendered reasoned and temperate public pronouncements on race relations. In 1926 he wrote in the *Free Lance*: "Let us treat the

52. Arthur S. Link, "The Progressive Movement in the South, 1870–1914," *North Carolina Historical Review*, XXIII (1946), 172–95.

53. Williams, *Romance and Realism in Southern Politics*, 60; Ethridge, "Mississippi and the 1928 Presidential Campaign," 82–83.

negro fairly; give him justice; teach him that the white man is his real friend." Or even while condemning proponents of equal educational and political opportunity for blacks, he argued that "if . . . [they] wish to secure better service on the common carriers . . . for our colored population and better living conditions for them by methods in harmony with the segregation laws . . . we are ready to stand with . . . them and strive . . . to that end." But even those comments were rare and came in response to specific, isolated situations. Generally Bilbo was simply silent on the issue of race.[54]

The second distinguishing aspect of The Man's progressivism concerns his general style and issued from that crude commonness that Percy so eloquently proscribed. Bilbo's buffoonery was at once both intrinsic and calculated. He could, as Wigfall Green depicts, accompany the menfolk "behind the barn to relieve his kidneys just as he had shared his spleen with them on the stump." While particular instances of such antics might be designed to flaunt his identification with the common farmers, the impulse was as genuine in him as it was in them—not, as Green suggests, a reflex of false democracy.[55]

One of the reasons progressivism faded in the South, says T. Harry Williams, was the very lack of such leaders who could "provide psychological outlets that a rural and poor people craved and needed: a sense of identification with their spokesmen." For Williams that kind of outlet was all the more necessary because reformers so often failed to deliver the goods. He pointed to Bilbo and Cole Blease of South Carolina as examples of men who "stroked the ego of democracy" because they had no substantial program to offer. Or as C. Vann Woodward put it: "By some obscure rule of succession, Bleases tend to follow Tillmans and Bilbos to succeed Vardamans. The new type leader could hardly be said to have had a program or a party. Instead, he had prejudices and a following." But Bilbo did have a program, one which "no other leader of the plebeian masses" could match, said Tindall. And he did deliver the goods, at least as often as any other southern progressive including "ultra respectables" in neighboring states. Dewey Grantham attributes the "excess and irrelevancies" of such men as Bilbo more to the enormity of the task of dethroning conservatism than to any endemic southern propensity for demagoguery. Nowhere was that task more formidable than in Mississippi.[56]

Yet historians continue to puzzle over southern progressives in gen-

54. Doler, "Bilbo's Rhetoric of Racial Relations," 69–70, 84–85.

55. Green, *The Man Bilbo*, 39.

56. Williams, *Romance and Realism in Southern Politics*, 62–63; Woodward, *Ori-*

eral and "demagogues" like Bilbo in particular. The distinctly liberal convictions of many modern scholars cause them to shrink from the apparently anomalous union of reform politics, which claims their praise, and racial demagoguery, which demands their censure. Some, like Williams, resolve the dilemma by minimizing the demagogues' progressive achievements. But the records of Vardaman and Bilbo make that a dubious proposition when applied to Mississippi. Other historians, like Sheldon Hackney, have quibbled over whether Dixie's reform surge was more neo-Populist than progressive, whether its driving force was radical agrarian or urban middle class. But again such distinctions are hardly meaningful for pre–New Deal Mississippi, which was so overwhelmingly agrarian and most of whose farmers were so abjectly poor. Still others have even viewed progressivism as a conservative effort to stabilize the status quo. J. Morgan Kousser goes so far as to declare the movement a "reactionary revolution." This view, too, is obviously difficult to apply to the Vardaman-Bilbo era in Mississippi.[57]

Those who have faced up to the patent progressivism of Vardaman and Bilbo have, like Vardaman's biographer Holmes, often judged their racism as no worse but only more outspoken than that of conservatives, who are then doubly damned for being both racist and illiberal. Unable to deny Vardaman's progressivism, Holmes denies him status as "an advanced liberal" for failing to realize that it was impossible to uplift the poor whites while holding down the blacks. As Robert Dean Pope points out, however, certain historical examples seem to suggest that lower-class economic improvement among the favored race in a segregated society is possible after all. In any case Holmes offers no evidence that it is not possible. In fact Bilbo viewed the New Deal in just such terms, as a program to improve the lot of dispossessed southern whites within the context of the racial status quo, and Franklin Roosevelt gave him little reason to question that perception. Also, as Pope adds, Holmes fails to address the issue of whether the virulence of Vardaman's racism made any difference, ignoring "the important distinctions between Vardaman and men who did not regu-

---

gins of the New South, 392–93; Tindall, *Emergence of the New South*, 24–25; Grantham, *The Democratic South*, 49–51.

57. Sheldon Hackney, *Populism to Progressivism in Alabama* (Princeton, 1969), ix–xv; Kousser, *Shaping of Southern Politics*, 261–65. For progressivism as a conservative force, see Raymond H. Pulley, *Old Virginia Restored: An Interpretation of the Progressive Impulse, 1870–1930* (Charlottesville, 1968), and Jack Temple Kirby, *Darkness at Dawning: Race and Reform in the Progressive South* (Philadelphia, 1972).

larly incite crowds to a pitch of racial fury." While Pope probably had in mind more gentlemanly figures like John Sharp Williams and LeRoy Percy, no one fits the description better than Bilbo. The Man incited crowds to fury all right, but rarely about race.[58]

In light of this historical debate Bilbo's role in the evolution of Mississippi politics becomes all the more intriguing. He shared with Vardaman a common political program that included political democracy, corporate regulation, taxation of wealth, and government welfare for dispossessed whites. But the two men's differences are perhaps more revealing than their similarities. Vardaman was a Delta man whose early political philosophy was shaped by black-county Bourbonism. Even as that philosophy became transformed by the ideals and realities of redneck politics, the White Chief retained significant vestiges of his black-county heritage. He had not been born a Bourbon but had married into aristocracy and wealth, the widow whom he wedded in 1884 bringing to their union an established social pedigree and a three-thousand-acre plantation. Throughout his career, long after he had abandoned Bourbon politics, Vardaman continued to affect aristocratic manners and dress and to covet acceptance by upper-class society.[59]

But perhaps the most enduring aspect of his Delta background was the profound importance that he continued to place upon white supremacy. It has been customary to account for Vardaman's race-baiting as mere pandering to the prejudice of lower-class whites, and there was certainly no dearth of such prejudice among his constituency. But the extent to which the racial diatribes explain Vardaman's appeal to the rednecks remains problematic. In fact the only gubernatorial race that he ever won was in 1903, when he was supported by such distinguished Bourbons as LeRoy Percy and John Sharp Williams. In that race Vardaman carried only eleven of thirty-one white counties but twenty-eight of thirty-nine black counties, including all but three in the Delta. Even in the 1907 Senate race against Williams, Vardaman lost seventeen of thirty-seven white counties. Not until 1911 did his candidacy provoke a distinct division between black and white counties, and in that election, race was for the first time a negligible factor in Vardaman's campaign. Based on a statistical analysis of those three

58. Holmes, *The White Chief*, 270, 388; Robert Dean Pope, "Of the Man at the Center: Biographies of Southern Politicians from the Age of Segregation," in J. Morgan Kousser and James M. McPherson (eds.), *Region, Race and Reconstruction: Essays in Honor of C. Vann Woodward* (New York, 1982), 102–104.

59. Holmes, *The White Chief*, 12–21; Kirwan, *Revolt of the Rednecks*, 225–27.

elections, Kousser suggests that both Vardaman's support and his opposition were attributable primarily to issues other than race.[60]

How, then, does one explain his political race-baiting? Holmes insists that it flowed from a sincere commitment to white supremacy. If that is true, Vardaman's racial rhetoric was derived not so much from his encounter with poor-white prejudice as from the social conventions of his native Delta. It was, after all, the Delta sages who had made the reestablishment of white supremacy their political life's work. And it was William Alexander Percy who declared segregation to be "the cornerstone . . . of interracial peace," the questioning of which would mean "the shattering of race relations into hideous and bloody ruin." Percy's class deplored Vardaman's brand of racism not because it differed so much from their own in substance, but because the White Chief shamelessly paraded it naked before the voting public. But the real objection lay deeper still. It is true that the rednecks to whom Vardaman appealed were devoid of the kind of racial paternalism in which many aristocrats prided themselves. As Percy noted, the poor whites may even have nursed a secret fear of their own inferiority "to the Negro," which compelled them "to do something to him to prove to themselves their superiority. At their door must be laid the disgraceful riots and lynchings gloated over and exaggerated by Negrophiles the world over." But it was not Vardaman who taught the rednecks to express those fears in political terms. Delta politicians had spent decades warning the peckerwoods of the dangers of black rule. What rankled the Bourbons now was that the primary law had given poor whites a decisive political voice and Vardaman was invoking race to promote, not deference to Delta leadership, but rebellion against it.[61]

There is little doubt that the commons gloried in their hero's raw and extravagant depiction of the black menace. But then they tended to relish rhetorical excess on any subject. The crucial question is whether it was the substance of the racist harangues or their style that was more determinative of voting behavior. Vardaman's concept of the black man's place in society differed little from that of his conservative opponents, as those opponents often took great pains to make clear. Few Bourbons were really as "enlightened" and paternal in their racial views as Percy anyway. What distinguished Vardaman from his Re-

60. Holmes, *The White Chief*, 111–12, 251; Kousser, *Shaping of Southern Politics*, 233–35. Election figures are from Francis Glenn Abney, *Mississippi Election Statistics, 1900–1967* (Oxford, Miss., 1968), 33–38, 166. Population figures are from Economic Research Department, Mississippi Power and Light Company (M.P.&L.), *Mississippi Statistical Summary of Population, 1800–1980* (Jackson, Miss., 1983).

61. Percy, *Lanterns on the Levee*, 307–308, 20.

deemer forebears was not the logic of his racism but the mode of its expression.

Racism alone, then, hardly explains either the rednecks' devotion to Vardaman's cause or his enemies' opposition to it. His pronouncements on economic justice were every bit as titillating to poor-white sensibilities, and here the content was as significant as the style. Vardaman's huge victory in 1911 demonstrated that he could win without peddling the race issue and that class politics could be every bit as potent as racial politics. Most of Bilbo's career was predicated on that notion.

Bilbo's background and style were profoundly different from those of the White Chief. He was born and reared in a white county of the piney woods, and his family's status, while by no means destitute, was substantially more humble than Vardaman's. His political orientation was molded from the beginning by a white-county environment. He never saw politics through the lens of Reconstruction, redemption, and race relations, as the young Vardaman had under the tutelage of old Redeemers like George and Money. Life in a black county with all its emotions, anxieties, and patterns of experience was completely foreign to Bilbo.

Also, Bilbo was a product of south Mississippi, where there were not only more white counties but more sawmills, more railroads, and probably more anticorporation sentiment than anywhere else in the state. In addition, south Mississippians chafed under a legislative apportionment that they believed discriminated in favor of not just the Delta but all of north Mississippi. Vardaman ran poorly in south Mississippi, even in many white counties, until the secret caucus thrust Bilbo into the limelight and linked him to the White Chief's cause. (See table.)

In 1911, when Vardaman was a candidate for the Senate, Bilbo ran for lieutenant governor in his first bid for state office. The older man had already run four statewide campaigns and had served a four-year term as governor. Only two years earlier Bilbo had been virtually unknown outside his own district. Yet Vardaman carried a higher percentage of the vote than Bilbo in only ten of twenty-one white counties in north Mississippi and in only nine of twenty-five white counties in south Mississippi. Vardaman's total vote was hardly 3,000 more than Bilbo's out of a total of over 129,000 votes cast. In the black counties Vardaman outpolled Bilbo in thirty-two of thirty-three. The issue in 1911 was the secret caucus, and that issue had been created not by Vardaman but by Bilbo. Never again would Vardaman run a race in

Vardaman's Percentage of the Total Democratic Primary Vote in the White Counties in South Mississippi.

County	1903—Governor (second primary)	1907—Senate	1911—Senate
Amite	51	61	67
Clark	30	38	58
Covington	61	53	65
Franklin	54	38	52
Greene	16	35	61
Hancock	50	32	56
Harrison	54	36	48
Jackson	45	34	37
Jasper	30	41	53
Jones	47	51	60
Lauderdale	52	46	60
Lawrence	46	43	63
Lincoln	56	62	69
Marion	54	50	69
Newton	62	48	64
Pearl River	44	60	76
Perry	55	40	69
Pike	49	65	68
Scott	41	42	67
Simpson	43	53	60
Smith	44	65	68
Wayne	34	45	63

Source: Glenn Abney, *Mississippi Election Statistics, 1900–1967* (Oxford, Miss., 1968), 35–38, 96–97.

which he was more closely identified with Bilbo, and never before or after 1911 did he run a stronger or more class-oriented campaign.[62]

Charles G. Hamilton suggests that many lower-class whites were never at home with Vardaman's upper-class ways. "They appreciated having a leader like that," Hamilton said, "but they didn't—well, there is an old saying around here that you wouldn't let Bilbo associate with your hound dog, but he's one of the best men you could ever have in public office." A cursory examination of Bilbo's campaigns seems to reveal a voting pattern more class-oriented than even in Vardaman's case. The 1911 campaign for lieutenant governor was the first of seven state-

62. Holmes, *The White Chief*, 239–40. Figures are from Abney, *Mississippi Election Statistics* and M.P.&L., *Mississippi Statistical Summary of Population.*

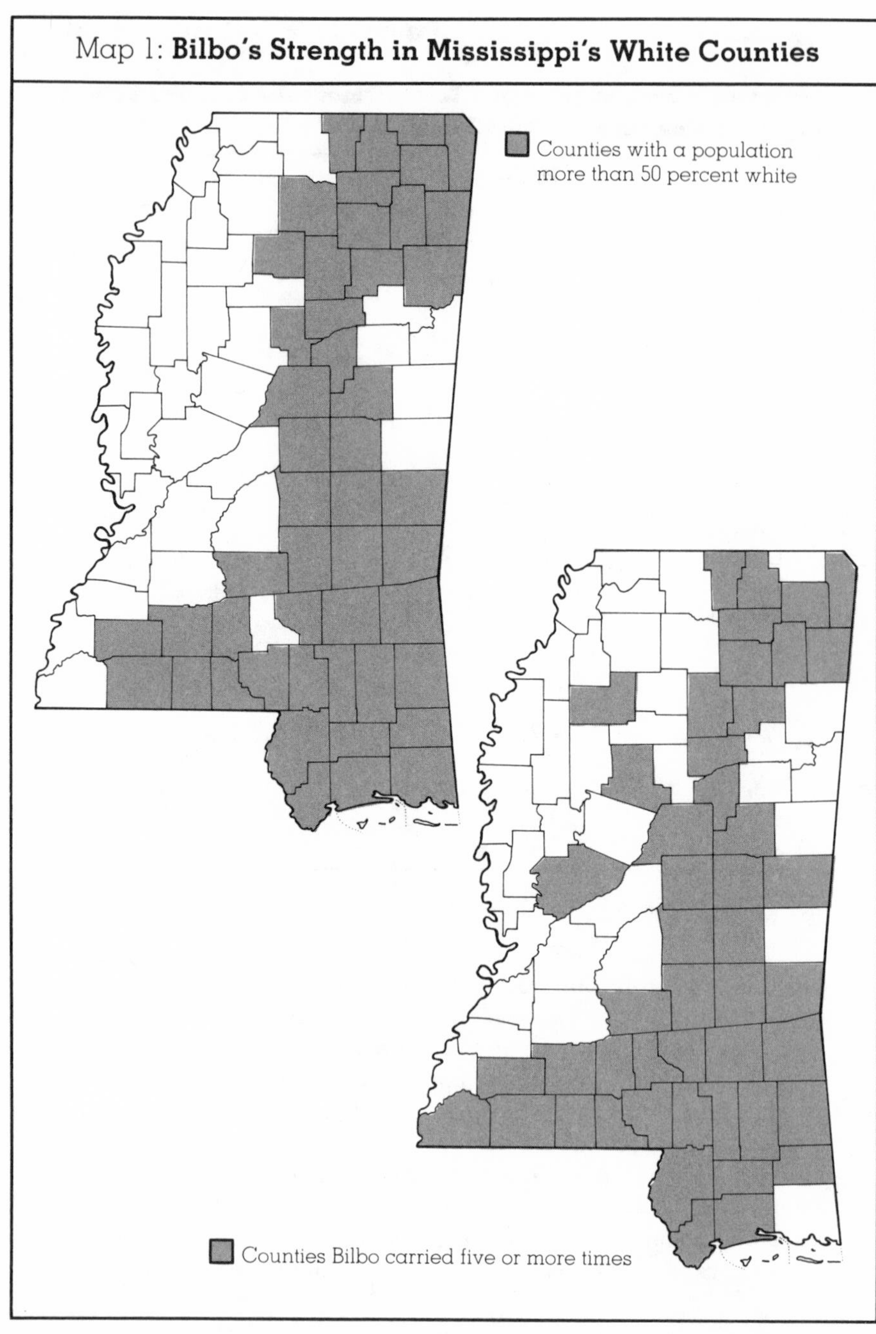

Sources: For all three maps, election figures are from Frances Glenn Abney, *Mississippi Election Statistics, 1900–1967* (Oxford, Miss., 1968); population figures are from Economic Research Department, Mississippi Power and Light Company, *Mississippi Statistical Summary of Population, 1800–1980* (Jackson, Miss., 1980); data on per-capita income are from Mississippi State Planning Commission, *Progress Report on State Planning in Mississippi* (Jackson, Miss., 1937), 130.

Map 2: **Bilbo's Weakness in Mississippi's Black Counties**

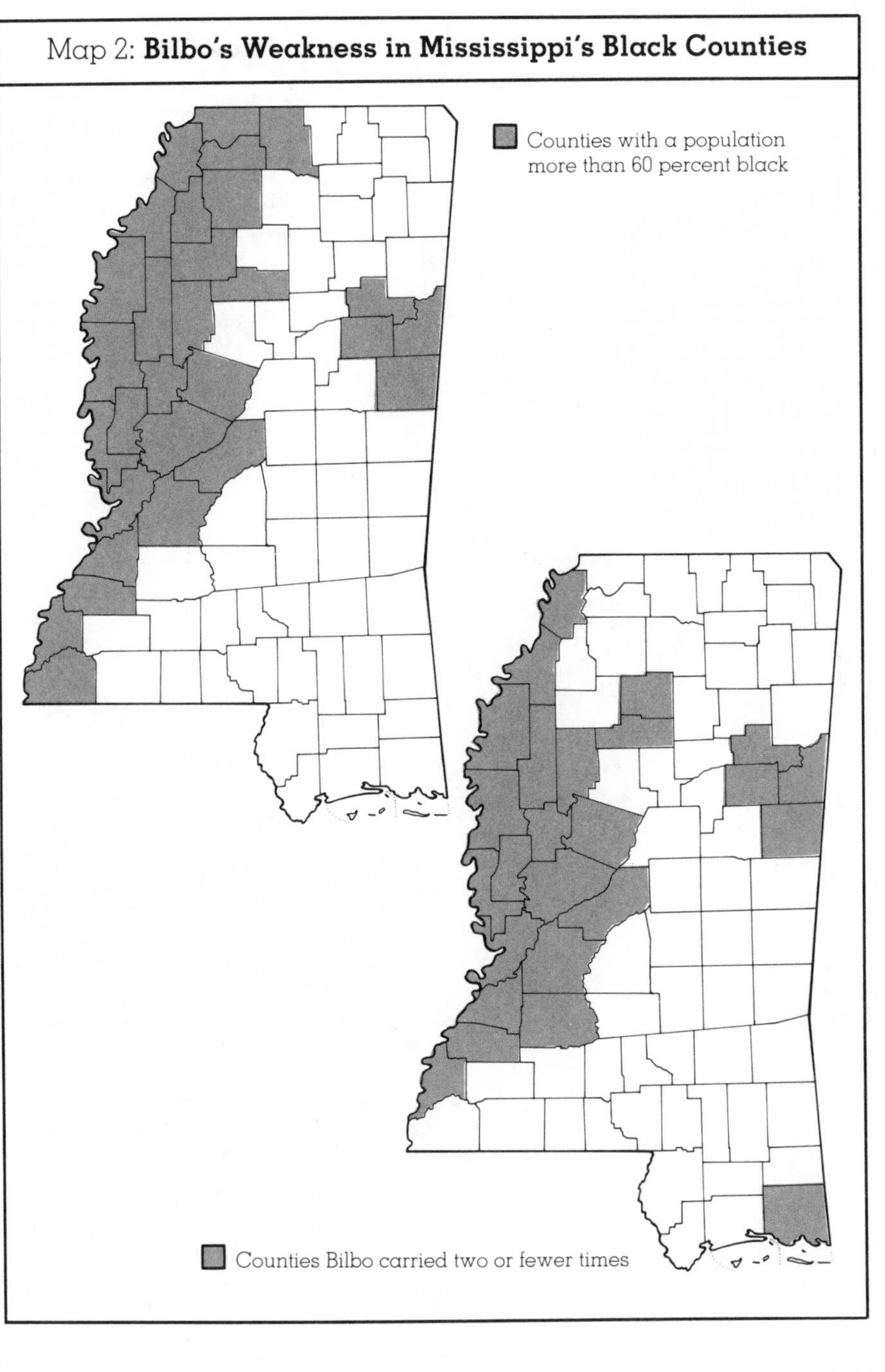

Map 3: **Bilbo's Strength in Mississippi's Low-Income White Counties in 1934**

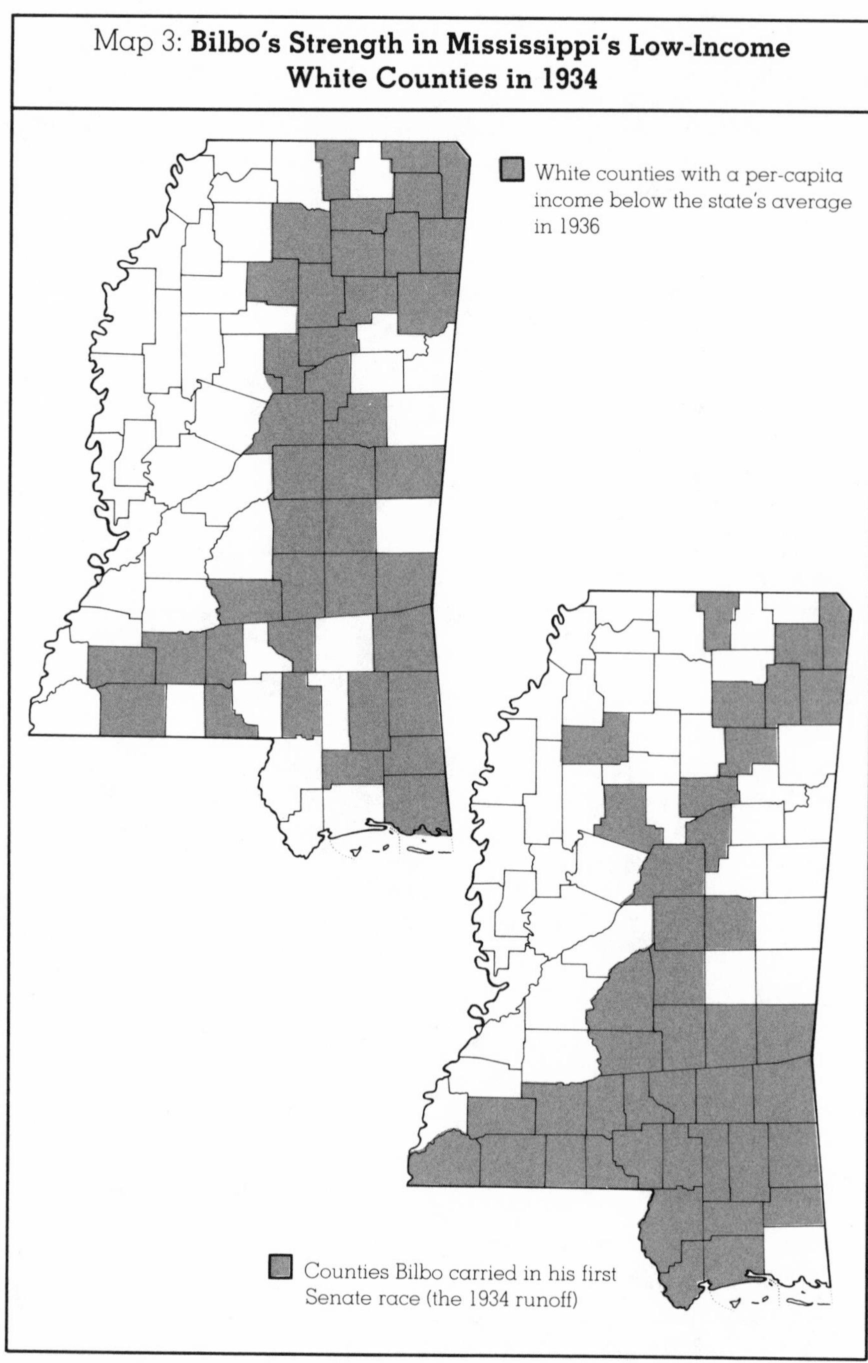

Note: This 1934 race perhaps best typifies Bilbo's support, because it was a runoff against a single, formidable incumbent with an established conservative reputation. The only aberration is a minor friends-and-neighbors effect around Stephens' home county of Union in northeast Mississippi, where Bilbo lost several counties that he usually carried.

wide races he ran. Of the twenty-one counties that Bilbo carried all seven times, eighteen were white and sixteen were in the southern half of the state. Of those he carried in at least four of the seven races, 79 percent were white. There were only thirteen counties that Bilbo carried no more than twice; twelve of them were black, and nine had the highest average farm land value in the state. Of the forty-eight white counties, he carried all but three in a majority of his races; of thirty-four black counties, he lost twenty-two of them in more than half of his races (see Maps 1 and 2). Of the twenty-eight counties with the lowest average farm land value, twenty-four of them supported him in at least a majority of his races. Indeed, it was Bilbo, even more than Vardaman, who recast Mississippi politics along class lines (see Map 3).[63]

The tragedy for Bilbo was that success with the rednecks came at the expense of credibility with "respectable" progressives. This was especially true of his reputation among those outside the South, whose perception of him was almost totally molded by a universally hostile Mississippi press. His immoderate and earthy rhetoric "created the image that was Bilbo," and while it endeared him to the peckerwoods, it quarantined him from more "respectable" liberal brethren. That isolation would be especially debilitating when he entered the intellectually stuffy world of New Deal bureaucrats and the clubby atmosphere of the United States Senate. The Man would never be able to live down his own perverse success; what would take him to Washington would disarm him once there.[64]

What made it doubly devastating was that Mississippi's economic problems were of such magnitude that they were unlikely to be solved without federal help. As Walter Davenport explained, the poor farmers had wrested state government from the hands of the "Ole Massa School," and their leaders distributed "what the ruling classes of the past left." But "unhappily, Ole Massa didn't leave much."[65]

63. Charles G. Hamilton, personal interview with the author, March 3, 1983; Abney, *Mississippi Election Statistics*, 104–105, 116–17, 120–21, 55–56, 59–60, 67–68; M.P.&L., *Mississippi Statistical Summary of Population*. Land values are based on *Sixteenth Census, 1940: Agriculture*, Vol. I, part 4, pp. 386–93. Figures are for 1930.

64. Doler, "Bilbo's Rhetoric of Racial Relations," 201.

65. Key, *Southern Politics*, 230–43; Walter Davenport, "Brethren and Sisters," *Collier's*, March 16, 1935, p. 19.

Chapter Three

New Deal Senator

Neither defeat nor marital trouble nor poverty was new to Bilbo in 1932, but the force of their convergence that year left him nearer desperation than he had ever been. He held an odd relationship to wealth, dreaming of ostentatious living and pursuing it vigorously when he could, but seemingly happy with the sardines-and-crackers existence that was more often his lot. He once advised his son that happiness and contentment were tied more to inward attitudes than external circumstances. "I can readily understand," he said, "how the poorest member of our race . . . can be happy even in abject poverty—even when denied all the luxuries and good things in life."[1]

In Bilbo's case that was more than platitudinous twaddle. Like the Apostle Paul he seemed to have learned both to be full and to be hungry, to abound and to suffer need. For Bilbo, if not for the Apostle, that insight by no means precluded a healthy indulgence in the good things of life. For years he planned and prepared for the construction of his "Dream House" on the old family place at Juniper Grove, stockpiling timber from his own land, bricks from an old mill that he had purchased, and magnificent walnut columns from the old state capitol, purchased at auction, it was rumored, for a dollar apiece.

With mortgages that jeopardized future solvency, Bilbo bought a good deal of additional land. By 1932 he owned three thousand acres and an almost completed Dream House, but he also faced thirty thousand dollars worth of obligations, which left him, as he termed it, "poor as Job's turkey." In August he lost the Dream House to a federal court auction to satisfy a five-hundred-dollar debt. Fortunately it was purchased by a cousin, H. K. Rouse, from whom Bilbo got it back in 1935, thanks to a loan from the Federal Land Bank.[2]

As Willard Bond said, "Money just didn't mean anything" to Bilbo. It was a personal luxury of conscience—more a deficiency, some ar-

1. Bilbo to Theo Bilbo, Jr., November 15, 1935, in Bilbo Papers.

2. Green, *The Man Bilbo*, 62–63; Robert J. Bailey, "Theodore G. Bilbo: Prelude to a Senate Career, 1932–1934" (Master's thesis, University of Southern Mississippi, 1971), 4–9.

gued—that wreaked financial havoc on creditors and friends alike. He was forever dipping into other people's available cash for day-to-day expenses. The wife of a political ally remarked that though Bilbo was a lively and entertaining guest, his occasional visits to their Gulf Coast home were always a mixed blessing. Whatever ready cash graced her husband's pockets upon The Man's arrival was likely to be spent or to depart with the illustrious but beggared visitor. Even the dignity of the United States Senate could not quell his pecuniary shamelessness. The most distinguished of visitors often found themselves invited out to dinner and left holding the check. Bilbo unblushingly wrote one that the "splendid meal you gave us while you were here has just about exhausted itself and we are hungry again. Ain't it awful to be poor?"[3]

He was a bill collector's nightmare. To save the farm, he pledged his first year's Senate salary without flinching, and he parried other creditors' pleas and threats with equally exasperating ease. "Keep the gates of mercy open," he answered one. "I will arrive a little later." To another, who agreed to settle an account for only 30 percent of the total debt, Bilbo mailed a slight overpayment, confessing to the attorney who negotiated the agreement that he often wrote checks for some small percentage over the proper amount when he feared the draft might not be honored. The creditor's brief elation over the "seeming generosity" helped to soften the "fearful shock" that would surely follow. Besides, he told his astonished counsel, what better way to conceal "from the prying eyes and eternal vigilance of other creditors" a nest egg that might someday "return . . . in an hour of need"?[4]

Sometimes The Man could dismay friends and creditors at a single stroke. A New Orleans bank once lent him six thousand dollars only on McComb Mayor X. A. Kramer's assurance that it would be repaid promptly. When Bilbo fell three months behind on the interest payments, Kramer implored: "For God's sake, Bill, handle these things in a manner that would be a credit to you. As a matter of fact my own credit is involved." The impenitent senator explained that he was doing his best to repay, noting that his friend might be more sympathetic had he ever known poverty firsthand. "But here's hoping," the senator added, "you will draw on your imagination." Bilbo seemed quite content being, as he put it, even with the world: he owed as many people as he did not owe. Nor did his insolvency make him niggardly. How-

3. Willard F. Bond to Wigfall Green, September 1, 1958, in Green Papers; Mr. and Mrs. Bidwell Adam, personal interview with the author, May 30, 1979; Bilbo to Doug Kenna, January 7, 1935, in Bilbo Papers.

4. Bilto to International Harvester Company (New Orleans), n.d., Bilbo to Frank W. Foote, July 6, 1935, Bilbo to Garland Lyell, July 13, 1935, all in Bilbo Papers.

ever deep the debt or relentless the collectors, Bilbo could never seem to refuse his children, who not infrequently plied him for small subsidies. The will that could resist the eternal vigilance of the most hard-hearted creditor easily gave way to the importunities of a son and daughter struggling to make it on their own.[5]

After 1932 Bilbo's marital difficulties added to the financial strain. Politics absorbed not only most of his time and energy but his devotion and affection as well. He had little left over for his wife and children. Moreover, the gossip about his infidelity seemed to embarrass him even less than did his financial woes. Sometimes he even betrayed a perverse pleasure in the swirling rumors, which he thought projected an image of uncommon virility. When Bilbo left the governor's office, he and Mrs. Bilbo separated. He wished the parting to be formal and permanent. She refused, so he was saddled with monthly support payments: twenty-five dollars per month until he secured a federal job in June, 1933, fifty dollars thereafter until he went to the Senate, and a hundred dollars after that. Also, he paid the note, insurance, and taxes on the Robinson Street house in which Mrs. Bilbo lived in Jackson.[6]

In general Bilbo's treatment of his wife was hardly a credit to his character. Her own behavior, while sometimes erratic, certainly did not merit the callousness and scorn that he heaped upon her. "I have long ceased to have any love for you," he wrote from Washington, "and any talk of reconciliation is an absolute waste of time." For him the marriage obligation, like an old political alliance that had served its immediate purpose, could now be discarded in the face of shifting circumstances. Bilbo lived as if marriage, and all else for that matter, were simply a function of politics, and he seemed to cultivate an insensitivity to the personal anguish that his attitude and behavior inflicted upon his wife. "I care nothing whatever about you," he wrote, "and would not live with you under any circumstances whatsoever."[7]

One exchange particularly captures the tragedy of their relationship, their complete failure to understand each other and her helplessness in the face of his cruelty. One January she upbraided him for refusing to send some pecans for Christmas from the orchard in Juniper Grove. "I

5. X. A. Kramer to Bilbo, January 13, 1939, Bilbo to Kramer, January 19, 1939, both in Bilbo Papers; interview with Alma M. Reyer, MOHP, Vol. LXXXIX, 36; Bilbo, Jr., to Bilbo, October 11, 1935, Bilbo to Jessie Lamar Smith, February 15, 1935, both in Bilbo Papers.

6. Green, *The Man Bilbo*, 86–87; Bailey, "Bilbo: Prelude to a Senate Career," 28–29; Bilbo to R. W. Wall, January 9, 1935, Bilbo to Linda Bilbo, January 18, 1935, both in Bilbo Papers.

7. Bilbo to Linda Bilbo, January 18, 1935, in Bilbo Papers.

wonder if you did not get choked on pecans," she wrote bitterly, "especially those grown on those trees which I worked so hard setting out on over a hundred acres—cutting the dynamite, putting on the fuse, setting off the fuse—taking a plank along to get trees straight and measuring the ground to get the trees in line. You must admit I got them straight when you drive by and look down those rows and see what a success I made in getting the lines straight from every direction. What a living monument to me—your conscience must hurt you if you have one." Bilbo's response was pitiless: "If you think it is a monument to your industry and frugality, then you are welcome to it. . . . Ten or twelve dollars would have paid for ordinary labor to have done all that you did." What to her was a symbol, however trivial, of a life of sacrifice and faithful devotion, to him was simply cheap labor.[8]

She eventually resorted to the only real weapon in her possession, the ability to embarrass him publicly, and she was often shamelessly abetted by his political enemies. Soon after Bilbo took his Senate seat, she invaded Washington, checking into the Wardman Park Hotel, where he lived. For three days he refused to go home, certain that she was "on the warpath" and determined "to create a scene or to generate unfavorable publicity." He appealed to their son to help reconcile her to a peaceful and quiet divorce and to keep her out of his hair in the meantime. In 1938 she finally accepted a twenty-thousand-dollar settlement that dissolved their thirty-five-year union, though she struck one final blow at his dignity by announcing her candidacy in opposition to his reelection two years later.[9]

Bilbo's dealings with his son were not burdened by the kind of hostility that ruined his marriage, but they lacked the enduring devotion and personal intimacy of a healthy relationship. He seemed unwilling or unable to give himself to anyone, to be intimate with anyone. It was as if the political personality were the only real Bilbo. His soul was a political ideology, and his true family was the electorate. On them he showered whatever filial affection he possessed. His letters to Theo, Jr., usually resembled either the empty rhetoric of a public official or the back-room banter of a political crony. Rarely was there the kind of deep warmth one might expect from a devoted and loving father. Occasionally a bolt of frustration and resentment flashed through the son's correspondence. Responding to a rebuke for not writing, Theo, Jr., reminded his father how few times he had visited the son at mili-

8. Linda Bilbo to Bilbo, January 26, 1936, Bilbo to Linda Bilbo, January 30, 1936, both in Bilbo Papers.

9. Green, *The Man Bilbo*, 95–96; Bilbo to Bilbo, Jr., January 7, 1935, Bilbo to Jessie Lamar Smith, March 30, 1935, both in Bilbo Papers.

tary school or at West Point or anywhere else. "You know as well as I do," he lamented, "that I have never had a real home as other kids have, all I've had to tie to was my love for you and Mother. . . . Ask yourself this question. 'How well do I know Theo?' You couldn't know much about me because you have been with me so little." But such outbursts were rare, and the relationship remained amiable if not intimate, the loyal son stoically yielding to the political exigencies that had rendered him virtually an orphan.[10]

Unable or unwilling to remedy his family and financial deficiencies, Bilbo by all means possessed the wherewithal and the will to attack his political problems, and he did so in short order. The 1930 census had cost Mississippi one of its congressional seats, and the legislature simply combined two of the existing districts for the 1932 election. Many believed the new district's population, which exceeded the proper figure by more than a hundred thousand, rendered the reapportionment law unconstitutional, and they challenged it in the courts. Had the challenge succeeded, the seat would have become an at-large place to be filled by a statewide election, a prospect that chilled the state Democratic executive committee. That body was now controlled by Bilbo's enemies, who knew that no other congressional candidate was likely to best him in a statewide race. In August, when a federal court enjoined the party from holding district elections, the committee ignored the injunction and ordered the election anyway. Desperate to keep Bilbo out of office, the respectable element rolled out the weapon that had been most effective against Bilbo's kind since the days of their fathers, the race issue. Congressman Will Whittington warned, "If Congress controls elections for Congress, white supremacy will be destroyed." To the profound relief of The Man's enemies, the Supreme Court in October upheld the redistricting law and lifted the injunction. Bilbo then respectfully withdrew and promised to support the Democratic nominees. For those who had so recently and joyfully buried Bilbo, it was a close and ominous encounter with his political resurrection.[11]

The incident was particularly sobering for Mississippi's two senators, especially Hubert Stephens, who faced reelection in 1934. The thought of Bilbo grazing freely in the political pasture for two years while they were tied to legislative duties a thousand miles away left

10. Bilbo to Bilbo, Jr., November 15, 1935; Bilbo, Jr. to Bilbo, June 11, 1936, both in Bilbo Papers.

11. Bailey, "Bilbo: Prelude to a Senate Career," 11–27; "Statement in Bilbo Debate," n.d., Box 43, Speeches, in Will Whittington Papers, Williams Library, University of Mississippi, Oxford.

Stephens and Pat Harrison cold. Aware of Bilbo's financial woes, Harrison, with importunate urging from Bilbo, scrambled to find him a job in the new Democratic administration. The trick was to place him in a position just attractive enough to satisfy but obscure enough to smother him politically. Bilbo first asked to be collector of internal revenue for Mississippi or national director of agricultural extension work, both befitting the dignity, he thought, of a two-time governor. Harrison vetoed one, and Secretary of Agriculture Henry Wallace, the other.[12]

In desperation Harrison called upon the new agricultural adjustment administrator, his old friend George Peek. Bilbo was, Pat assured Peek, a capable and loyal Democrat, and the AAA chief agreed to find Bilbo an adequate position. As the relieved Harrison started for the door, he decided that he had better hedge his bets. Bilbo was a capable administrator all right, he reminded Peek, but he probably ought not be doing any public speaking. His style might prove embarrassing. Again the senator started to leave and again he hesitated. After a further affirmation that Bilbo would do a creditable job, he warned that it might not be wise to let him handle a lot of money. This time Harrison got all the way out the door before conscience again halted him. Sticking his head back into the office, he offered a final testimony to Bilbo's competence before suggesting that a careful screening of his female staff might remove any undue temptation from The Man's path. "OK, Pat," Peek chortled, "I see just what you mean. Your man Bilbo is going to make a great public servant if I just gag him, bind him, and geld him. He's hired on that basis."[13]

After Harrison called Wallace to emphasize "what a *great* favor it would be," the secretary and Peek both agreed to "pigeonhole" Bilbo for Pat's sake. They conferred on him a six-thousand-dollar-a-year job "assembling current information records . . . from newspapers, magazines, and other published sources." In short, Bilbo kept a scrapbook for the AAA, "gloomily cutting out newspaper clippings with the help of a secretary who looked," said Joseph and Stewart Alsop, "as though she had entered government service in the administration of Millard Fillmore." Bilbo titled himself "Advisory Counselor," but his enemies dubbed him the "Pastemaster General." It was, said one historian of the AAA, the classic example of a political appointment. The job could have been better handled by "a first rate clerk." Rexford Tugwell

12. "The Reminiscences of Marvin Jones," 1953, Columbia Oral History Collection (hereinafter cited as COHC), 693–94; Bailey, "Bilbo: Prelude to a Senate Career," 30; "The Reminiscences of Henry Agard Wallace," 1951, COHC, 273–74.

13. Joseph Alsop and Stewart Alsop, *The Reporter's Trade* (New York, 1946), 20–21.

thought the deal was humiliating and immoral, though he hinted that it might have been the price Roosevelt paid for Harrison's support for much of the early New Deal.[14]

Gradually Bilbo began to chafe under the ridicule of the press, and as the 1934 Senate primary drew closer, gratitude turned to resentment. He felt, with some justification, that Harrison had deliberately belittled him. "I starved and waited and waited and starved," he later told a friend, "and finally was given an embarrassing, humiliating assignment which became a joke." In February of 1934 he resigned and three months later announced for Stephens' Senate seat.[15]

The campaign was an unusually docile affair by Bilbo standards. The kickoff rally was an all-day picnic at Poplarville where Bilbo presented his twenty-seven-plank platform, which included cash payment of the veterans' bonus, government control of federal reserve banks, old-age pensions, unemployment insurance, wages-and-hours legislation, and general support for the New Deal. He had always been supported by the poor people, he said, and since the depression had made everybody poor, everybody would vote for Bilbo. Stephens, from New Albany, had served two rather quiescent Senate terms in the tradition of LeRoy Percy and John Sharp Williams. A colorless campaigner at best, Stephens was in 1934 plagued by ill health and a crippled foot and had not intended to stand for reelection until he discovered that Bilbo might inherit the seat. His campaign offered a simple theme: support for the president's program, an assertion that amazed his Senate colleagues, who considered him distinctly anti–New Deal. The only other serious candidate was former state attorney general Ross Collins, who was eliminated in the first primary and endorsed Stephens in the runoff. Harrison's opposition to Bilbo was well known, but he took no active part in the race. However, he was probably responsible for a presidential summons that in the heat of the campaign called Stephens to Washington for an important consultation with Roosevelt. Fred Sullens declared it a tacit endorsement of the incumbent, though the White House denied it. It was futile anyway, as Bilbo edged Stephens by some 7,500 votes.[16]

In January of 1935 Bilbo moved into a radically new and somewhat

14. "Reminiscences of Wallace," 273–74; Alsop and Alsop, *The Reporter's Trade*, 20–21; Van L. Perkins, *Crisis in Agriculture: The Agricultural Adjustment Administration and the New Deal, 1933* (Berkeley, 1969), 99; Rexford G. Tugwell, *In Search of Roosevelt* (Cambridge, 1972), 275–76.

15. Bilbo to Henry Hart, May 28, 1936, in Bilbo Papers; "The Reminiscences of Chester Charles Davis," 1953, COHC, 296–300.

16. Bailey, "Bilbo: Prelude to a Senate Career," 51–83; Swain, *Pat Harrison*, 76–79; interview with Purser Hewitt, MOHP, Vol. X, part 2, p. 26.

alien setting—the national government. It had been a quarter of a century since he had been a lawmaker, and for the first time he had to deal with colleagues and adversaries, administrators and politicians who were isolated from the power and interest of the redneck masses. For the first time in his long career, he was himself somewhat removed from the sources of his political sustenance. In Washington he was out of his element, and he would never really adapt to the new environment.

Despite rumors to the contrary, the new senator appeared "dressed up" to take the oath of office. To those who said that he had run for the Senate just to get a parking place—parking had been a problem for him at the AAA—he crowed that he now had "a million dollar garage." More important, he declared that he came to Washington 100 percent for Roosevelt. He hardly had time to read the pending bills at first, because he was deluged by mail. The magic of The Man's identity with his constituents made him possibly the most accessible—and most annoyed—of southern politicians. The humblest of dirt farmers and sawmill hands felt perfectly comfortable and justified in sitting down to write Bilbo as he might write a well-placed uncle or cousin, with the full expectation that his senator could and would promptly and personally dispatch whatever bit of business was demanded, however trifling or grand. Bilbo was one of them, and they treated him accordingly.[17]

The day he arrived at his new office he found a pile of two thousand letters already awaiting replies. Most of them were pleas for jobs. "Folks won't give us a chance to find out what it's all about," he complained, "but we asked for this when we were asking for votes . . . so all we can do is grin and bear it." Out of his own pocket—or someone else's, more likely—he hired two extra stenographers who worked nights and Sundays, and still the pile of letters mounted, increasing by seventy-five or eighty per day. Many were scrawled in pencil on the backs of ledger sheets, envelopes, and even paper bags. Eventually he somehow got them all answered.[18]

Harrison's enormous influence had helped Bilbo secure a choice office and his pick of committee assignments, including Agriculture and Commerce. In the chamber, however, he sat with other newcomers near the back, though often he moved forward to some unoccupied desk for a better view of the proceedings. He was slow to concede the singular irrelevance of normal floor debate, a discovery that must have pained him sorely. He once petitioned the Rules Committee to install a

17. Jackson *Daily News*, January 3, 1935, p. 14.

18. Bilbo to Cecil Travis, January 12, 1935, Bilbo to W. C. Norris, May 6, 1935, Virginia Simmerman to Bilbo, October 15, 1935, all in Bilbo Papers.

public address system in the chamber. It was embarrassing, he complained, to be chased from some senior senator's seat in the midst of a speech. More likely he was frustrated that the poor acoustics might limit his own oratorical access to the galleries, though he pledged, in obeisance to Senate custom, to remain silent his first year. To the amazement of almost everyone, he did so.[19]

If he was silent on the floor in 1935, he was his "loquacious, audacious" self elsewhere, and by no means was he inactive or indifferent. His first session was a momentous one for the New Deal as well as for certain southern senators. The Second Hundred Days of 1935 swung the New Deal in a new direction, and several moderately conservative southerners who had hitherto followed the president faithfully now began to entertain serious doubts. Chief among them were Majority Leader Joseph Robinson of Arkansas, Finance Committee Chairman Harrison, Vice-President John Nance Garner of Texas, and Senator James F. Byrnes of South Carolina. Eventually all but Robinson would abandon Roosevelt to join a loose alliance of Republicans and conservative Democrats that smothered the New Deal in the late thirties. Their prominence in the conservative coalition helped fix in the public—and academic—mind the image of a monolithically conservative South.

It was as if "economic determinism abruptly stops at the Mason-Dixon line," said William Carleton. Writing in 1947, long after "facile economic determinists" had "glibly" reduced politics to economics everywhere on earth but Dixie, Carleton suggested that the persistent legend obscured a southern liberal tradition that has often outweighed the region's conservatism. To illustrate he pointed ironically to Bilbo, who by that time had become the hated symbol of southern obstruction of black civil rights. Yet his first-term voting record, insisted Carleton, was the envy of the most liberal of northern New Dealers. That record seems all the more remarkable when it is considered in light of the unfolding of the New Deal as a whole, with particular emphasis upon those congressional groups who abandoned Roosevelt after his first term: the southerners, the old progressives, and rural Democrats. Bilbo had more in common with those groups than with any in Congress, but after 1935 he would follow a completely different road from the one they chose.[20]

19. Bilbo to Bilbo, Jr., January 7, 1935, in Bilbo Papers; Jackson *Daily Clarion Ledger*, March 8, 1935, p. 1; *Congressional Record*, 74th Cong., 2nd Sess., 10, 365.

20. William G. Carleton, "Why Call the South Conservative?" *Harper's*, July, 1947, pp. 61–67.

Historians have argued over the New Deal perhaps as much as any issue in recent American history. Amidst the unresolved questions stand two certainties. First, in 1933 and 1935 an unparalleled torrent of reform legislation burst forth from Congress. But second, after 1935 the flood slowed to a trickle, so that by 1939 what had been a legislative gusher became a dry well.

In 1932 Franklin Roosevelt forged a political coalition that crushed Hoover and the Republicans. It was, according to Arthur Schlesinger, a marriage of the "politics of organization" with the "politics of ideology." The former sprang from "the princes and potentates of the party," the urban bosses and the old southern Wilsonians who directed the Democratic machine. Apart from a mildly conservative respect for business values, tempered, especially among the southerners, by the legacy of New Freedom progressivism, its adherents carried little ideological baggage. With an ardent reverence for the spoils system, they valued party loyalty above conservative sensibilities and could be trusted to dispatch the president's program faithfully and effectively.[21]

The other wing of the Democracy consisted of a hodge-podge of reformers, labor enthusiasts, maverick politicians, and liberal intellectuals. Unfettered by such niceties of political office as patronage and reelection campaigns, these men seized politics as the bondsman of ideas, as a means of putting government to work remaking society. Their attitude toward party professionals was generally contemptuous. "Politicians," said Rexford Tugwell, "never have a program for anything beyond elections. That event to them is a kind of apocalypse beyond which the future is a blank." The ideologues had little more reverence for the legislative process, wherein the professionals held absolute sway. What to the politician was a hallowed ritual, was to these visionaries "a messy business, to be got over as quickly as possible, like an attack of the mumps."[22]

Roosevelt hoped to make the Democrats a majority party by luring to this union "the forgotten man at the bottom of the economic pyramid." Offering himself as the spokesman and protector of those who felt excluded by a business tradition enshrined by a decade of Republicanism, he drew to the party and to himself the gratitude and allegiance—and expectations—of millions of farmers, laborers, minori-

21. Arthur M. Schlesinger, Jr., *The Politics of Upheaval* (Boston, 1960), 409–410. Vol. III of Schlesinger, *The Age of Roosevelt*, 3 vols. to date.

22. Rexford G. Tugwell, *The Brains Trust* (New York, 1968), 224; Joseph Alsop and Turner Catledge, *The 168 Days* (Garden City, N.Y., 1938), 82–83.

ties, and intellectuals. From this amalgam emerged the foundational coalition that supported the early New Deal.[23]

But the union was shaky, and its internal friction aggravated the traditional jealousy between the White House and Congress. Seeking imagination and daring to combat psychological as well as economic depression, Roosevelt inevitably turned to the idealists to staff the New Deal agencies and bureaus, to Tugwell and Hopkins and Ickes. But administrators must have laws to administer, and in the realm of lawmaking, two factors drew the president to the professionals, especially those in the Senate. No Democratic president could hope for legislative success without the support of the senatorial oligarchs, but their sympathies were far more conservative than those popular at the other end of Pennsylvania Avenue. These were "progressives" not "liberals," and their progressivism was the New Freedom variety: regulated competition, equal opportunity, and states' rights. They feared big government, big labor, and big deficits. But they also feared depression, and in 1933 party loyalty made them willing to follow Roosevelt where they might not have ventured on their own.[24]

The other thing that made these Democratic regulars indispensable to the White House was the recalcitrance of the old Senate progressives. Whether Democrats like Burton K. Wheeler of Montana, insurgent Republicans like William E. Borah of Idaho, or mavericks like Robert La Follette, Jr., of Wisconsin, these old crusaders were as ideologically in tune with the Democratic idealists as any other group in Congress. But Roosevelt had no confidence in their willingness to work together or with him. "Your progressives," he told Tugwell, are wonderful men, but they "have the general characteristic of complete unreliability." They were "individualists" who could not even agree on what progressivism was, let alone on how to turn it into law. Their high-minded ideological purity would never sanction the kind of flexibility necessary for the rough-and-tumble horse trading of practical politics. "They were the best standers-on-principle we had," Roosevelt told Tugwell. "But the principle always turned out to be whatever happened to interest them as individuals—or maybe as politicians." As Tugwell himself later concluded, "They cannot lead, they will not follow, and they refuse to cooperate."[25]

23. James MacGregor Burns, *Roosevelt: The Lion and the Fox* (New York, 1956), 133; Schlesinger, *Politics of Upheaval*, 410–15.

24. Schlesinger, *Politics of Upheaval*, 410–15; James T. Patterson, *Congressional Conservatism and the New Deal: The Growth of the Conservative Coalition in Congress, 1933–1939* (Lexington, Ky., 1967), 64–67, 130–33.

25. Schlesinger, *Politics of Upheaval*, 413–15; Edward Francis Hanlon, "Urban-

In his first two years in office, Roosevelt secured from a willing Congress an impressive list of recovery measures, and he did so largely because of the cooperation of the Senate grandees: Garner, Harrison, Byrnes, and Robinson. In those famous first hundred days of lawmaking, there was something for almost everyone in the coalition. The Agricultural Adjustment Act (AAA) was a boon to farmers. The National Industrial Recovery Act (NIRA), with its cartel-like code authorities, made significant concessions to business—too many to suit the old progressives, though in the long run apparently not enough to satisfy businessmen. For workers there was Section 7(a) of the same law, which guaranteed the right to collective bargaining and endorsed, in principle, minimum-wage and maximum-hour regulation. For the destitute, especially in the cities, there was a Federal Emergency Relief Act (FERA). No one approved of everything Congress did in those hectic days, but Roosevelt was willing to act boldly, and after four years of economic crisis, few were willing to stand in his way.

For many Americans things got better, but for most they remained far from good. The political result was a severe strain on the seam that held the Democratic party together. The very success of the coalition threatened to undo it. The elections of 1934 reflected the success; the congressional session of 1935 exposed the danger.

As those whom the New Deal had helped went to the polls, they swelled Democratic strength to 69 in the Senate and 322 in the House. Many of those votes came from previously non-Democratic groups, especially in the cities of the North: labor, immigrants, and the urban poor. Roosevelt had delivered them from political bondage, and now they expected him to lead them to the promised land of economic security. Add to that the rantings of the false prophets—Huey Long, Francis Townsend, and Father Charles Coughlin—and the pressure pushing Roosevelt toward further action became irresistible. He was not sure, however, that the professionals, especially the southern senators, would go along.

During the first few months of 1935, Roosevelt seemed paralyzed by indecision. Liberals worried that he had made his peace with the conservatives at the expense of their own dream of finishing the work begun two years earlier. Five months dragged by with the enactment of but a single piece of significant legislation, a massive work-relief bill. Then in May two events jolted the president to the realization that he

---

Rural Cooperation and Conflict in the Congress: The Breakdown of the New Deal Coalition, 1933–1938" (Ph.D. dissertation, Georgetown University, 1967), 119; Tugwell, *The Brains Trust*, 489–93.

must risk his coalition to save it. In early May the U.S. Chamber of Commerce condemned the New Deal, and while a hurt and angry Roosevelt wondered whether anything he could do would please businessmen and keep them in the coalition, the Supreme Court struck down the NRA. The centerpiece of the recovery program was gone and with it labor's gains in Section 7(a) and a considerable amount of government's control of business. Roosevelt refused to stand idle while the court threatened to undo the whole New Deal. In a flurry of renewed legislative vigor, he marshaled congressional forces for a Second Hundred Days. The lawmakers, eager for an early adjournment to escape the ravages of Washington's summer, recoiled under a series of orders that certain bills must pass: a social security act, a new banking law, Senator Wagner's labor relations act, a public-utilities holding company act, and a "soak-the-rich" tax bill. Under the whip hand of an aroused president, the weary Congress labored from June to late August in the capital's sweltering heat to construct the foundation of the American welfare state.[26]

Congress eventually gave Roosevelt everything he asked for in some form or other. Liberals, even the old progressives, were delighted at what appeared to be the opening salvo of an assault on big business. Others, moderate conservatives, became uneasy. Among them were Harrison and Robinson, who were especially fearful of the effects of the labor bill on southern industry, the relief bill on the federal budget, and the tax bill on business. They went along, as they had in 1933, but with increasing reluctance and anxiety. By the end of the session, they had become "silent opponents" of much of what the New Deal was doing.[27]

Those who thought Bilbo came to Capitol Hill harboring fears similar to those of so many of his southern brethren were soon disabused of that notion. He backed the president on almost every detail, and when he did wander off the New Deal reservation, it was usually in what was considered a leftward direction. Like Hugo Black, he often joined the old progressives in an effort to push further along the new course Roosevelt had set for the New Deal than even the president was willing to go in 1935. On only one major issue, the veterans' bonus, did he completely defy White House leadership, and that was hardly a conservative move. Those who were surprised should not have been. A glance at Bilbo's 1934 platform shows that he had called for many

26. William E. Leuchtenberg, *Franklin D. Roosevelt and the New Deal, 1932–1940* (New York, 1963), 145–50; Dexter Perkins, *The New Age of Franklin Roosevelt, 1932–1945* (Chicago, 1957), 26–40.

27. Patterson, *Congressional Conservatism and the New Deal*, 64–76.

of the very things that the Second Hundred Days accomplished: redistribution of income ("soak-the-rich" tax), federal control of reserve banks (banking act), old-age pensions and unemployment insurance (social security act), a public-works program (work-relief bill), and wages and hours regulation. Often those issues that most disturbed his fellow southerners were the ones he supported most vigorously.[28]

If the southern leaders were looking for signs of budget consciousness, Roosevelt dampened their hopes early. In his January message to Congress, the president asked for a $4.8 billion work-relief program. The New Deal had already spent over $2 billion on relief, yet nine million workers were still without jobs, and the number of Americans receiving some kind of public assistance was a staggering twenty million. The president believed that the dole was morally degenerating and should give way to a public-works effort that would put 3.5 million people to work at a "security wage," higher than the dole but enough below industrial wages to encourage private employment. State and local authorities would have to assume all responsibility for unemployables. It was the greatest single appropriation by any government anywhere and, financed by borrowing rather than taxes, the largest addition to the national debt—all to be spent at Roosevelt's discretion.[29]

This Emergency Relief Appropriation Act sailed through the House but met predictable opposition from Senate conservatives, many of whom preferred the cheaper dole and most of whom shrank from handing the president almost $5 billion to spend virtually as he pleased. The resistance delayed the bill for two months, cluttering the calendar with waiting legislation and betraying the administration's vulnerability to Senate opposition. Not all of the trouble came from the right. Roosevelt's lieutenants had hardly disposed of Virginia conservative Harry Byrd's amendment to cut the appropriation to $2 billion when La Follette tried to raise it to $9 billion. Although the effort was easily defeated, Bilbo joined western progressives like Bronson Cutting and Edward Costigan to support La Follette. It was the first of many times The Man would find himself in harness with the old progressive war horses, pulling the president faster than he felt he could safely go.[30]

With the bill mired in Senate debate, William Green of the American

28. Virginia Hamilton, "Senate Career of Hugo Black," 83; Bailey, "Bilbo: Prelude to a Senate Career," 55–61.

29. Leuchtenburg, *Roosevelt and the New Deal*, 123–25; E. Pendleton Herring, "First Session of the 74th Congress," *American Political Science Review*, XXIX (1935), 491–93; Paul K. Conkin, *The New Deal* (New York, 1967), 53–58.

30. Schlesinger, *Politics of Upheaval*, 268–69; Hanlon, "Urban-Rural Cooperation and Conflict," 223.

Federation of Labor (AF of L) attacked the security wage provision. Afraid the lower relief pay would drag down general wage rates, the labor chief suggested that the relief pay scale should equal the "prevailing wage" paid by private employers in any project area. Senator Pat McCarran of Nevada offered such a prevailing-wage amendment, and under an intense AF of L lobbying effort, the Senate approved it by a single vote in late February. The president had to have the bill returned to committee to allow time to muster votes against the amendment. Finally, in late March, facing a threatened veto, a reluctant Senate reversed itself and restored the security wage. But the senators did not sell themselves cheaply. They wrung from the administration consent to an amendment that required Senate approval for any appointment to a relief position paying five thousand dollars or more. The patronage-starved lawmakers had sneaked aboard Harry Hopkins' ship, and he would spend much of his time thereafter shooing them away from the rudder.[31]

Bilbo held fast against the McCarran amendment throughout the fight, despite AF of L pressure that included a personal telephone call from Green. When the Mississippi Labor Federation urged him to back the prevailing wage, he reminded them that he had always been a friend of labor, and that meant "organized labor as well." Roosevelt had promised not to let relief wages undermine industrial wages, he assured them, and he was willing to trust this president who had "done more for labor . . . than all other administrations combined." Besides, he grumbled, he did not intend to "let William Green, a Republican, sitting back in a swivel chair enjoying a salary of twice as much as I receive, tell me when to hop." In the showdown over the McCarran amendment he voted no, as he had a month earlier. He then joined sixty-seven other senators in approving the relief bill, which, says Paul Conkin, launched "the largest welfare program of the New Deal."[32]

Bilbo's support for relief spending by no means ended in 1935, even though the issue caused a major sectional dispute within the New Deal camp. Southerners, said James T. Patterson in his study of congressional conservatives and the New Deal, became "profoundly stirred" over the ever larger appropriations that followed the initial grant.

31. Robert E. Sherwood, *Roosevelt and Hopkins: An Intimate History* (New York, 1948), 66–68; Arthur W. MacMahan, John D. Millett, and Gladys Ogden, *The Administration of Federal Work Relief* (Chicago, 1941), 269–74.

32. Bilbo to P. H. Adams, June 28, 1935, Bilbo to J. H. Kuriger, March 12, 1935, Bilbo to M. L. Richie and W. G. Byers, February 26, 1935, all in Bilbo Papers; Conkin, *The New Deal*, 58.

Southern congressmen feared that far too much relief money found its way to northern cities. There, many of the beneficiaries were urban blacks, newly arrived from the plantations and towns of the South where relief checks were much skimpier than elsewhere. The labor drain was enough to cause concern, but what really disturbed men like Harrison and Robinson was the growing voice of northern blacks within Democratic politics. The senators held their peace in 1935, but spending would later become for them, as it was for their friend Jimmy Byrnes, "one of the prominent issues."[33]

If relief was one pillar of the New Deal welfare system, social security was the other, "the supreme symbol of the welfare state," as Conkin has suggested. Unlike much of the legislation of the Second Hundred Days, the social security measure had been an administration bill all along. It was based upon the recommendations of a committee on economic security that Roosevelt had established in 1934. The proposal the president presented to Congress on January 17, 1935, outlined a national system of compulsory retirement insurance. At age sixty-five, workers (and such substantial groups as farmers and domestics were not covered) would receive benefits from a fund supported by payroll taxes on employers and employees. The amount each participant paid into the fund determined the level of benefits he received. The law also provided for a joint federal-state system of unemployment insurance and matching federal funds for state expenditures on the disabled and dependent mothers and children.[34]

Bilbo played no visible role in the bill's passage, but there is no doubt that he supported it vigorously. Early in the year, an Arkansas woman wrote him to protest "the pitiful dole . . . that Roosevelt wants to give" the elderly under the White House proposal. She warned that old people had discovered that only political power prevailed and were organizing to fight: "When a man is in the street hungry and naked, he will listen to anyone who will promise food and clothes. . . . Long, Townsend, and Coughlin did not happen by accident." Bilbo rushed to defend the president. "Just remember," he reminded her, "that the one man, who has contributed more to the relief of the American people than any other man living or dead, is Franklin Delano Roosevelt." Without his "bold and intrepid leadership," there would be no old-age pension of any kind. "At a crucial moment in the life of this Republic, the President . . . struck with his imperial scepter the rock of the Na-

33. Patterson, *Congressional Conservatism and the New Deal*, 144–45; James F. Byrnes, *All in One Lifetime* (New York, 1958), 85.

34. Conkin, *The New Deal*, 60–62.

tion's resources and started spontaneously flowing the rivers of relief to a long suffering people."[35]

Yet Bilbo would not follow even Moses without murmur. Some liberals criticized the insurance features of the retirement systems, pointing out that no other welfare system dodged government responsibility for old-age security or financed benefits from worker paychecks. Bilbo's concern was rather for those already too old to work. Since they had not paid into the system, they could not draw from it. While the bill did require the federal government to supplement existing state pension programs on a dollar-for-dollar matching basis, wide variations in state payments made the provisions patently inequitable. When Borah offered an amendment to guarantee everyone over sixty-five at least thirty dollars a month regardless of the amount the state contributed, Bilbo again found himself voting with old progressives like Wheeler and California's Hiram Johnson to extend welfare measures beyond presidential preferences. The Senate rejected the amendment, but Bilbo continued to fight for what he considered a more equitable pension system.[36]

The progressive bloc did score major victories that session on business regulation and taxes. Wheeler introduced an administration bill that would have automatically liquidated any public-utility holding company that could not demonstrate the economic need for its existence. The House removed this "death sentence" provision, but the bill remained a formidable antimonopoly measure and provoked a massive lobbying effort by utility companies. Considering Bilbo's populist heritage, it is no surprise that he joined the progressives on this one. He stood his ground for the measure despite a barrage of letters and telegrams from investors in Mississippi power companies demanding that he oppose the bill. "These holding companies," he responded to a constituent complaint, "are mere leeches, veritable parasites feeding upon and sucking the very lifeblood of that class of industries you seek to protect." The passage of the act was the high-water mark for New Deal trustbusters like Tom Corcoran and Ben Cohen, who wrote the bill, and their ideological mentors Justice Louis Brandeis and Harvard law professor Felix Frankfurter.[37]

This Brandeis-Frankfurter bias against giant corporations was also

35. Mrs. S. H. Whitfield to Bilbo, April 4, 1935, Bilbo to Whitfield, April 18, 1935, both in Bilbo Papers.

36. Leuchtenburg, *Roosevelt and the New Deal*, 132; *Congressional Record*, 74th Cong., lst Sess., 9631–34.

37. Leuchtenburg, *Roosevelt and the New Deal*, 154–57; Bilbo to Dr. D. G. Rafferty, February 27, 1935, in Bilbo Papers.

visible in the Revenue Act of 1935. This tax measure constituted the administration's response both to the heightened antagonism of business and to Huey Long's share-the-wealth agitation. It afforded the most striking example of Bilbo's divergence from most of his southern colleagues, including Harrison. On June 19, Roosevelt, who had given no indication that he would ask for any kind of tax bill, suddenly sent Congress a message calling for an array of inheritance, gift, and income levies whose obvious intent was to redistribute wealth. As the last words echoed through the stilled chamber, the senators sat in stunned silence until a gloating Long strutted to the aisle to pronounce an irreverent "Amen."[38]

Roosevelt had known the message would be a bombshell, especially for Harrison, who would be "so surprised," the president exulted to Raymond Moley, "he'll have kittens on the spot." It was a landmark in national tax policy, and it galvanized the progressives into action. When the president's ambivalence about when he expected action on the proposal allowed the apprehensive party leadership to dally, it was La Follette who seized the initiative. He and twenty-one other senators signed a round robin vowing to keep Congress in session until the tax bill was enacted. There among the autographs of Norris, Costigan, Borah, and the other progressives was the name Theodore G. Bilbo. It was not the first time he had joined this company on the tax issue. Earlier he had supported La Follette's vain effort to retain disclosure provisions of the Revenue Act of 1934 making tax returns in higher brackets accessible to the public.[39]

A tax bill, soak-the-rich or otherwise, had to negotiate the Senate Finance Committee, where Chairman Harrison was not the only member whose fiscal conservatism balked at social taxation. Harrison wanted to hold the issue over until 1936, but Roosevelt could not afford to squander the momentum his message had generated. The president insisted that the revenue act must pass in 1935. On its way through the Senate gauntlet, however, the bill absorbed some crippling blows from conservatives. Harrison, who handled the measure for the administration, allowed the mutilation either in a sincere effort to make the bill passable or from a sinister design to tame its social-reform features. In any event, the animal that emerged was hardly the soak-the-rich dragon that the president had loosed on June 19. Nevertheless, it was acclaimed as a new departure in government revenue policy, and the principle of social taxation took its place among the

38. Leuchtenburg, *Roosevelt and the New Deal*, 152.

39. Raymond Moley, *After Seven Years* (New York, 1939), 310; Jackson *Daily News*, June 22, 1935, p. 1; *Congressional Record*, 74th Cong., lst Sess., 4526.

other gods of relief and social security in the New Deal pantheon. Bilbo's enthusiastic endorsement of the tax scheme in its early fire-breathing form stood in vivid contrast to the anxious acquiescence of Harrison, who, according to Martha Swain, was "embarrassed over an obligation to support a proposal with which he did not agree in order to bolster a president with whom he could not afford to break the year before they both faced reelection." In fact when Harrison finally found opportunity to abandon the New Deal train, tax policy would be one of the first places he would backtrack.[40]

The other major accomplishment of the Second Hundred Days was the National Labor Relations Act. When Senator Robert Wagner of New York introduced it early in the year, he received a rather tepid response from the White House. But he fought on without administration support, and he fought effectively. Only after Wagner had steered the measure through the Senate and the court had destroyed Section 7(a)'s protection of labor did Roosevelt declare the bill "must" legislation. Perhaps the Wagner Act was not "the most radical legislation passed during the New Deal," as James M. Burns has suggested, but it was a drastic step toward redressing the imbalance between the power of labor and the power of business. It guaranteed workers the right to bargain collectively and established a National Labor Relations Board to hear worker complaints and to conduct elections wherein a company's employees could choose whatever union they wanted to represent them. It also legalized strikes and boycotts and forbade such "unfair labor practices" as blacklisting and yellow-dog contracts.[41]

Bilbo supported Wagner throughout, helping defeat an amendment to legalize company unions and voting for the final version of the bill. He even joined his progressive friends in a futile effort to append Hugo Black's provision for a thirty-hour work week to the bill. Harrison, by contrast, was a "silent opponent" of the measure, though he voted for it, as Swain explains, because "he was simply as politically tuned to 1936 as were FDR and a majority of Congress." Bilbo's enthusiastic support of the Wagner Act was a significant portent of his coming departure from the mainstream of southern congressional sentiment. He would remain an unflagging supporter of Roosevelt's labor policy, an issue that more than any other would offend southern New Dealers and drive a wedge into the Democratic coalition.[42]

On only one piece of major legislation, the bonus, did Bilbo com-

40. Schlesinger, *Politics of Upheaval*, 331–34; Swain, *Pat Harrison*, 105–22.

41. Burns, *Roosevelt: The Lion and the Fox*, 215–20.

42. *Congressional Record*, 74th Cong., lst Sess., 5235, 7675, 7681; Swain, *Pat Harrison*, 97.

pletely defy the administration, and then he was simply fulfilling an explicit campaign pledge. In 1934 he had promised to remain "unalterably committed to the immediate cash payment" of the bonus that Congress had earlier agreed to pay veterans for their service in the World War but that would not fall due until 1945. Bilbo supported Texas Congressman Wright Patman's inflationary bill calling for the issuance of two billion dollars in greenbacks to finance immediate payment. Both houses passed it, but the Senate failed to override a presidential veto. Bilbo defended his support of the bonus with a quote from Roosevelt's own secretary of the interior, Harold Ickes: "It is more important in these times to preserve the morale of the people than it is to balance a set of books."[43]

It was fitting that Bilbo would defend his single significant departure from the administration in the words of an old Bull Moose progressive who sat in this later Roosevelt's own cabinet. Like the old progressives, Bilbo was delighted with the Second Hundred Days, and when he did clash with the administration, he was usually in their company. His initiation into the Senate had coincided with the most productive single congressional session of the thirties, and he emerged as a staunch New Dealer. He had backed Roosevelt with enthusiasm on relief, social security, antitrust legislation, taxes, even labor legislation. While many of his fellow southerners were growing anxious about where Roosevelt might be leading them, Bilbo was a willing follower. Soon, however, after the 1936 election, even the old progressives would balk at the president's new departures. When the New Deal ran off and left them, Bilbo went with it.

But that would come later, and in 1935 Bilbo had more on his mind than federal legislation. Mississippi politics was never far from his thoughts, and 1935 was statewide election year. Those who hoped the exigencies of congressional responsibility or at least sheer geography would remove his power, if not his interest, from state politics were sorely deluded. When someone suggested that he voluntarily remain merely an interested observer, Bilbo recoiled in mock horror: "impossible, unthinkable, outrageous, preposterous—what brand were you drinking when you dictated this" advice. From the day he took office until the August primary, the demands of lawmaking had to compete with the Mississippi governor's race for his attention.[44]

43. Bilbo to Irvine I. Weitzenhaffer, May 2, 1935, in Bilbo Papers.

44. Bilbo to L. O. Crosby, July 1, 1939, in Bilbo Papers.

Chapter Four

Hooey or Huey, It Means the Same Thing

Five men made the governor's race in 1935, and together they illustrated how the crosscurrents of friends-and-neighbors politics could swirl one-party factionalism into ideological turmoil. Paul Johnson, candidate of the "runt pigs," ran on a progressive platform that advocated free textbooks, higher teacher pay, cheap car tags, and a statewide eight-month school term. Yet he was backed by Mike Conner, perhaps the most conservative of Mississippi's business progressives. The real darling of the runt pigs was Bilbo, but he chose to support Hugh White, another business-minded conservative, who had lost the 1931 primary runoff to Conner. The only other real contender in 1935 was Lieutenant Governor Dennis Murphree, who had filled the governor's office briefly upon Whitfield's sudden death in 1927. Ironically, White was one of those who had helped persuade Murphree to seek a full term as governor in 1927 and had contributed heavily to his campaign. White's opposition now in 1935 was thoroughly overshadowed by Murphree's bitter hostility toward Conner, which fell with full force on the governor's candidate, Johnson.[1]

The feud had begun over Conner's attempt to secure the appointive highway commission that Bilbo had tried but failed to get during his second term. When the elected commissioners, led by Brown Williams, successfully lobbied the house to kill the proposal in 1932, Conner worked to defeat the reelection bids of all three, without success. The controversy reached a climax in 1934 when Conner asked the legislature for a constitutional convention, which the highway commission opposed. Afraid a convention might grant Conner the appointive commission that the legislature had denied him, the commissioners turned to Murphree, now presiding over the senate, to help them kill the con-

1. Skates, "World War II and Its Effects," 129; Jackson *Daily News*, February 6, 1935, p. 6.

vention proposal. The senate vote was a dead tie, and Murphree's deciding "nay" endeared him to the commissioners. They now gratefully backed his gubernatorial bid, and a bitter Conner believed that Murphree had torpedoed his whole administration to secure the support of Brown Williams and the commission.[2]

The two other men in the race were Dr. E. A. Copeland of Jackson and Lester Franklin, neither of whom was given much chance of winning. Franklin, while not a serious contender, did pose a problem for White because he entered a credible claim for the backing of the Bilbo faction. In fact Bilbo's law partner, Judge W. S. Shipman, chaired the January meeting at which Franklin announced his candidacy to a gathering that included several of the Bilbo faithful. At the campaign kickoff in Tupelo, Franklin presented a "new deal" platform that he unflinchingly termed "socialistic." It aimed to redistribute wealth by having the legislature peacefully but "literally and bodaciously take it away from the rich and give it to the poor." It is obvious why Bilbo found it difficult to lead some of his people from Franklin to White. In light of Franklin's slim chances of victory, it is equally obvious why Bilbo made the effort. Bilbo even tried to lure his old friend out of the race with promises of a comfortable appointment in Washington, but Franklin apparently spurned the bait.[3]

The senator had hardly located his notorious capitol parking space before he fired off to White a veritable treatise on Bilbonic politics: "You must be the people's candidate. . . . It takes votes to win an election. Get a Ford car, drive it yourself and 'take to the woods.' Stay out of the cities and towns and present your cause to the people of the rural section. . . . Get with the folks, stay with the folks, sympathize with the folks, and discuss with the folks in a positive and uncompromising way the issues and problems that *affect them*. . . . Nothing succeeds like success, and in politics you must create the impression that you are a winner." For a man whose inclinations ran naturally to Ford cars and sardines and crackers, posing as a man of the people was no problem; indeed, posturing was hardly involved. But selling a wealthy businessman like White to "the folks" would be a challenge, and Bilbo knew it. Soon after he wrote White, the senator set about

2. Memphis *Commercial Appeal*, February 17, 1935, Sec. 5, p. 5; Lynn Cook Hartwig, "The Mississippi Highway Program, 1932–1945" (Honor's thesis, University of Southern Mississippi, 1969), 8–13; McCain, "The Life and Labor of Dennis Murphree," 186.

3. Jackson *Daily News*, January 18, 1935, p. 1; Jackson *Daily Clarion Ledger*, May 12, 1935, p. 1; Bilbo to John Burkett, February 14, 1935, Bilbo to Dr. J. H. McClosky, July 16, 1935, both in Bilbo Papers.

convincing his own supporters that the lumber titan was really "just a 'redneck' like the rest of us who made a few dollars through the fortunes of the World War." When H. L. Simmons complained of White's style of living, Bilbo assured him that he had seen White's house and that it hardly rivaled the servants' quarters on The Man's own farm in Pearl River County. Beneath the bluster, however, Bilbo betrayed doubts. He hoped White would listen to "his real friends who know something about the masses instead of . . . a few high-hatting corporation spellbinders."[4]

Several of Bilbo's county managers found White hard to digest. One begged to be "excused" from supporting him, pleading, "I've tried my damnedest to take him on, but I can't for the life of me get reconciled to his kind. [He] goes around addressing these little Jacee [*sic*] commerce clubs and cornbread and black eyed pea aristocratic organizations which I detest." White's supporters had always been anti-Bilbo, and worst of all was Fred Sullens: "I simply find it laboring to be with Fred Sullens, in any situation."[5]

With so much major legislation pending, Bilbo found it difficult to get away from the capital, but from Washington he did what he could to steer the campaign. Confident that the Johnson vote would never go to Murphree, Bilbo hoped for a White-Murphree runoff and planned to undermine Johnson quietly, using federal patronage. Johnson's success depended upon the support of Conner, who controlled not only state appointments but also the Federal Emergency Relief Administration (FERA) machinery in Mississippi. If Bilbo could discreetly transfer relief patronage away from Conner, he could erode Johnson's strength, eliminate him in the first primary, and woo the Johnson vote for White in the runoff.[6]

Bilbo himself did not have the necessary leverage with Hopkins and Roosevelt, but Pat Harrison did, and the junior senator reminded his colleague of Conner's designs on Harrison's seat, which was up for renewal in 1936. Since Huey Long, who had already helped Conner into the governor's office in 1931, was now threatening to help the governor unseat Harrison, Pat could hardly afford to be indifferent. As early as November of 1934, FERA Regional Director Malcolm Miller informed Hopkins of rumors that Conner would challenge Harrison in 1936. But Miller and Mississippi FERA Director Charles Braun dis-

4. Bilbo to Hugh White, January 7, 1935, Bilbo to H. L. Simmons, January 12, 1935, both in Bilbo Papers.

5. S. R. King to Bilbo, March 8, 1935, in Bilbo Papers.

6. M. J. Miller to Harry Hopkins, November 24, 1934, FERA Field Reports, Mississippi, in Harry Hopkins Papers, Franklin D. Roosevelt Library, Hyde Park.

counted such talk and seemed confident of Conner's competence and sincerity. They had either seriously misread Conner or grossly misled Hopkins, because in August the governor wrote to a friend in Washington that Harrison's anxiety about Conner's plans for 1936 "may be well-founded." Conner would, indeed, seek the Senate post in 1936 and in a strange turn of events would be supported by Bilbo himself. But in 1935 the two senators pulled in harness to transfer relief patronage from the governor to themselves.[7]

Bilbo had already begun to receive complaints that his people were being shortchanged on patronage. Many Bilbo supporters blamed Harrison and spoke openly of working against him the following year. One warned that the FERA, which "has more effect on Mississippi than any other [agency]," was in the firm grip of Conner, who was using it for a free ride to the Senate. Late in January, Bilbo asked Hopkins to investigate the flood of complaints about politics in Mississippi's relief program. A week later Bilbo informed Harrison of a "general uprising" among Bilbo supporters and hinted that it would be difficult "to go to them next year and line them up for you" if jobs were not forthcoming. On February 21, Bilbo asked Roosevelt to grant the two senators joint authority over all federal projects and patronage in Mississippi. "It is vitally important," he urged, "that a complete change be made in the FERA organization in Mississippi. As operated now it is a political machine controlled in every detail by the present Governor of Mississippi, who was not your friend at Chicago, and is most certainly not our friend." That assessment of Conner would bear Bilbo bitter fruit a year hence, but it served its purpose in 1935.[8]

The Reverend Wayne Alliston, head of the Baptist Hospital in Jackson, was appointed Mississippi director of the new Works Progress Administration (WPA), which would handle all work relief under the Emergency Relief Appropriations Act of April 8. Braun would continue to dispense FERA relief until that agency's funds were exhausted, after which Alliston would control all work relief for Mississippi. Bilbo boasted to a south Mississippi associate, "I have been able to smash Conner's political machine into smitherenes." In a similar message to White campaign manager Hiram Patterson, he gloated, "It is goodbye Paul." Bilbo was certain that he had effectively relegated Johnson to the status of an also-ran before the campaign had even

7. M. S. Conner to M. R. Diggs, August 20, 1935, Official File (hereinafter cited as OF) 300, in Franklin D. Roosevelt Papers, Franklin D. Roosevelt Library, Hyde Park.

8. B. A. Bush to Bilbo, February 27, 1935, Bilbo to Hopkins, January 29, 1935, Bilbo to Harrison, February 5, 1935, Bilbo to Roosevelt, February 21, 1935, all in Bilbo Papers.

officially begun, and the White organization trained their guns on Murphree.[9]

Murphree, meanwhile, was trying to woo the Bilbo people without antagonizing his own following by drawing too close to The Man himself. In mid-May, just as Bilbo was shutting off the Conner-Johnson patronage flow, John Fraime, Cecil Inman, and other Murphree supporters somehow coaxed Bilbo's son-in-law, Lamar Smith, into open support of the lieutenant governor. At Murphree's campaign kickoff in Calhoun City, Smith took the stump on Murphree's behalf. "Never in my life," wailed a stunned Bilbo, "was I so completely knocked out, surprised, disappointed, and disgusted. . . . John Fraime and his gang must have promised him the earth and the fulness thereof, or they must have paid him more than William Jennings Bryan ever received for any speech in his life."[10]

But the incident gave Bilbo a chance to take a more active role against Murphree on White's behalf, and he wrote to friends to clarify his position. In 1928 when he had assumed the governor's office, Bilbo said, he had found Cecil Inman of the state tax commission and Attorney General Rush Knox elbow-deep in corruption. He had refused to reappoint Inman, and the legislature had impeached Knox. He could never, Bilbo insisted, watch "this same crowd" return to power. Besides, he explained, Murphree "is just a dam, [*sic*] cheap, weak, peanut politician . . . and I am strong as horse-radish for Hugh White." With Patterson's approval, Bilbo sent a form letter to five thousand supporters throughout the state explaining his role in the governor's race. Disclaiming any desire to dictate how anyone should vote, he said he nonetheless felt his friends had a right to know his inclinations. He intended to vote for White, who was a neighbor and a friend and would make a good governor. Murphree, on the other hand, had never been his friend, Bilbo said, and he could not support the lieutenant governor under any circumstances. Never one to let political ideals obscure financial reality, he also suggested to Patterson that the White headquarters advance him two hundred dollars for postage.[11]

Bilbo hoped the letter would not unduly antagonize the Murphree

9. Jackson *Daily News*, May 12, 1935, p. 1; Bilbo to F. C. Hathorn, April 15, 1935, Bilbo to H. J. Patterson, April 11, 1935, Bilbo to A. S. Coody, April 13, 1935, all in Bilbo Papers. For the New Deal relief agencies in Mississippi see Larry F. Whatley, "The New Deal Public Works Programs in Mississippi" (Master's thesis, Mississippi State University, 1965) and Whatley, "The Works Progress Administration in Mississippi," *Journal of Mississippi History*, XX (1968), 35–50.

10. Bilbo to Hathorn, May 17, 1935, in Bilbo Papers.

11. Bilbo to Dr. R. B. Clark, June 24, 1935, Bilbo to Friends, June 24, 1935, Bilbo to Hiram Patterson, June 24, 1935, all in Bilbo Papers.

people, but he need not have worried. During the heat of the campaign, Conner confided to a friend in Washington that he had aligned his whole organization behind Johnson because his "chief concern and business was to secure the elimination of Murphree from the run-off." Conner's bitterness toward Murphree, translated into Johnson's caustic campaign style, surpassed by far any of Bilbo's transgressions and provoked a counterattack by the lieutenant governor that diverted most of Murphree's hostility away from White.[12]

Neither Johnson nor Murphree ignored White completely. In a speech at Bassfield, Johnson scoffed that White was such a political novice that "he wouldn't know the difference between the constitution and a Sears, Roebuck catalogue." Murphree ridiculed Bilbo's support of White and charged that it was a payoff for White's financial contribution to the senator's 1934 campaign. It was amusing, he suggested, to think of White and Bilbo in the same boat. They had not always been so friendly. Murphree said that he himself had "refused to run for governor in 1927 against Bilbo until White came to see him, begged him to run and told Murphree that he was the only man who had a chance to defeat Bilbo; that the election of Bilbo might destroy the era of progress and development on which the state had started; that it was Murphree's patriotic duty to lead the forlorn hope and try to beat Bilbo. . . . Murphree ran, and White spent thousands of dollars trying to beat Bilbo for governor in 1927."[13]

The continuing effects of depression were creating pressures neither Bilbo nor the White campaign strategists had anticipated. In Mississippi in 1935 there were still stories of men begging house to house and doing chores for food, poor blacks picking through garbage cans for food for their families. Above all there was a great outcry for jobs, and the demands that politicians take care of their own were relentless. As word spread of the relief shakeup, expectations among Bilbo's followers increased proportionately. Alliston was squeezed between his orders for impartial and efficient administration and growing impatience for the spoils of victory.[14]

When opponents accused White's organization of buying support with promises of WPA jobs, Alliston forcefully denied that politics would play any role in his agency. Bilbo's followers became alarmed. They were incensed when Alliston began to staff the organization with

12. Conner to Diggs, August 20, 1935, OF 300, in Roosevelt Papers.

13. Hansford Simmons to Bilbo, May 29, 1935, in Bilbo Papers; Jackson *Daily News*, June 22, 1935, p. 8.

14. E. A. Fitzgerald to Bilbo, January 19, 1935, Cecil Travis to Bilbo, February 12, 1935, both in Bilbo Papers.

officials from the old FERA apparatus. County leaders warned that if the rank-and-file supporters perceived that Bilbo was unable to deliver jobs, their loyalty would be sorely tested by Johnson's promises. Some blamed the confusion on Harrison, who, they argued, could drive Conner and Johnson from the federal trough if he wanted. Cecil Travis warned that Murphree and Johnson were taking advantage of Bilbo's apparent impotence and that it was hurting White significantly. "Somebody somewhere along the line," Travis concluded, "certainly has been plowing with our heifer." Bilbo was concerned enough to share the information with Harrison.[15]

In early July, Alliston explained that he was trying to accommodate Bilbo's friends but that all the unrestrained crowing about a clean sweep was publicizing the issue and making the task difficult. "They all want everything done at once," he moaned, "and that makes the pot boil and the steam drifts immediately into Washington and then they block my plans." After all, Hopkins was the boss, he argued, and "I am bound to do what he asks done, or get out." Alliston had earlier told Bilbo, "I am absolutely not having anything to do with it . . . because I want my record to be *WHITE*." He had been accused of naïveté, he said, but assured the senator that he was just playing political "possum": "I am not letting people know that I *do* know what it is all about; but, brother, I will be there when the knowing is over! I am for you 10,000 per cent."[16]

Bilbo seemed pacified and tried to calm his troops. He warned that an overnight wholesale turnover would debilitate any agency and asked supporters to trust that Alliston would place the right men in the important posts. In his best King Jamesian imagery, Bilbo chided the doubters: "I am sometimes [led] to exclaim, 'Oh ye of little faith!' Remember we will eventually gather all our friends under our wings, as a hen doeth her brood. Let no one grow disheartened or grow impatient for though the mills of our Administrators or Directors may grind slowly, they eventually will grind exceedingly fine."[17]

But the situation began to change dramatically as Johnson gained on a faltering Murphree. Yet White's advisors still believed it would be White and Murphree in the runoff and pleaded for the senator to come to Mississippi and speak for the candidate, especially in the north-

15. Jackson *Daily Clarion Ledger*, July 10, 1935, pp. 1–2; Travis to John L. Smith, July 2, 1935, E. G. Nelson to Bilbo, July 9, 1935, Travis to Smith, June 29, 1935, all in Bilbo Papers.

16. Wayne Alliston to Bilbo, July 9, 1935, Alliston to Bilbo, June 28, 1935, both in Bilbo Papers.

17. Bilbo to S. E. Childers, July 13, 1935, in Bilbo Papers.

eastern hill counties, where Bilbo was so popular. He had already paid an unannounced visit to Mississippi in early June, during which supporters turned his Royal Hotel suite into a revolving door as over 1,100 of them paraded through to meet with him during the two-day stay in Jackson. His two weeks in the state had revitalized a sagging campaign, and Patterson now begged him to return.[18]

It seemed that not only White and the rednecks, but the institution of Mississippi politics yearned for The Man's return to the wars whose centerpiece and lifeblood he had been for almost three decades. The Jackson *Daily News* reported that in the final week of the primary the electorate remained unmoved by the major gubernatorial candidates, and the entire press agreed that it was the most quiescent state election in years. It was beginning to look as though the huge election night extravaganza planned by the *Daily News* might play to an empty house. Across from the newspaper office, on the Taylor Furniture Company Building, hung a huge screen on which would be flashed returns reported by two hundred correspondents around the state. Some wondered if anyone would care enough to attend.[19]

If Mississippi politics ached for Bilbo, it was a longing by no means unrequited. On July 17, as the campaign swept into its final three weeks, Bilbo advised his friend John Burkett that he would soon be in Mississippi but wanted no one to know. He was writing, he insisted, "to get you on fire and to put all the high-life in 'kingdom come' on Hiram Patterson and the White organization. Spare no time; spare no expense; spare no effort. You can sleep after the 6th of August."[20]

But the White strategists had badly miscalculated. On election night, as bleary-eyed spectators milled through discarded Dixie cups, broken Fudgesicle sticks, and crushed Old Gold butts along the roped-off block and a half of Capitol Street, the giant screen showed that Johnson was clinging stubbornly close to White. Long after the last straggler had folded his camp chair and sleepily shuffled off to a welcome bed, after the last of the ham sandwiches and Orange Crush and Patina cigars had been packed away, Johnson overhauled White. His total continued to climb the next day like the temperature, which by Thursday topped 104 degrees just as the last trickling returns thrust him into the lead. The sweltering temperatures persisted into the second primary, which began under a blistering heat wave that prompted an en-

18. Patterson to Bilbo, July 9, 1935, Bilbo to Jimmie Pierce, June 25, 1935, both in Bilbo Papers.

19. Jackson *Daily News*, August 1, 1935, p. 1, July 26, 1935, p. 1, August 5, 1935, p. 1, August 6, 1935, p. 1.

20. Bilbo to Burkett, July 17, 1935, in Bilbo Papers.

terprising Jackson merchant to fry eggs on a Capitol Street manhole cover to entertain shoppers wilting under the midday heat. Bilbo loved it hot, and he was about to generate some political heat of his own. Dog days in Mississippi and election time—Bilbo was in his element.[21]

The specter of Huey Long manipulating Mississippi politics handed Bilbo just the kind of issue he could exploit so masterfully. Despite candidate Bilbo's 1934 threat to "raise more hell than Huey Long" in the Senate, most observers knew that he cared little for his Louisiana neighbor's style and even less for his interest in Mississippi politics. The two men did have a lot in common. Both were spokesmen for the masses—demagogues, some said—and both were reformers. But they also had significant differences. Bilbo was far more traditional than Long and much more modest in his ambitions, both personal and ideological. Bilbo had no visions of a brave new world. Rather he sought simply to drive the money changers from the temple of democracy. He endorsed no mass sociopolitical movement but believed that the Democratic party, wrested from the clutches of the corporate octopus and restored to true representatives of the common man, was the proper vehicle to restore government to the people.[22]

The two men's response to Franklin Roosevelt clearly illustrated their differences. Long had no confidence that the New Deal would solve the problems of the depression, and he came eventually to detest the president personally. Bilbo, however, admired Roosevelt profoundly, and it was more than expedient admiration. He genuinely believed that Roosevelt was the people's friend and one of the greatest of America's presidents. Like Long, he sometimes grew impatient with the president's pace, but he believed in the New Deal and voted accordingly.[23]

Roosevelt early recognized Bilbo as a political friend, and the administration hoped that his presence in the Senate would provide a lightning rod to divert some of the Kingfish's fire away from the president. Bilbo's ability and apparent willingness to neutralize Long's expanding influence might also explain much of Harrison's civility, even helpfulness, toward his longtime Mississippi foe. Many in the press entertained a morbid lust for a spectacular clash between the two gladiators of bombast. A Memphis reporter suggested that should the event transpire, Vice-President Garner could reduce the national debt substantially by charging admission to gallery spectators. As Bilbo de-

21. Jackson *Daily News*, August 8, 1935, p. 1; Jackson *Daily Clarion Ledger*, August 10, 1935, p. 1.

22. T. Harry Williams, *Huey Long* (New York, 1969), 562; Allan A. Michie and Frank Ryhlick, *Dixie Demagogues* (New York, 1939), 107.

23. Williams, *Huey Long*, 5–6.

Governor Bilbo during his first term (1916–1920)
Courtesy Mississippi Department of Archives and History

James K. Vardaman
Courtesy Mississippi Department of Archives and History

The "Pastemaster General" and his secretary

UPI/Bettmann Newsphoto

Pat Harrison and Senator-elect Bilbo leaving the White House after a conference with FDR in late 1934

Wide World Photos

Leading Political Figures of Mississippi in the 1930s

Photographs courtesy Mississippi Department of Archives and History

Martin Sennett "Mike" Conner

Hugh L. White

Paul B. Johnson

Dennis Murphree

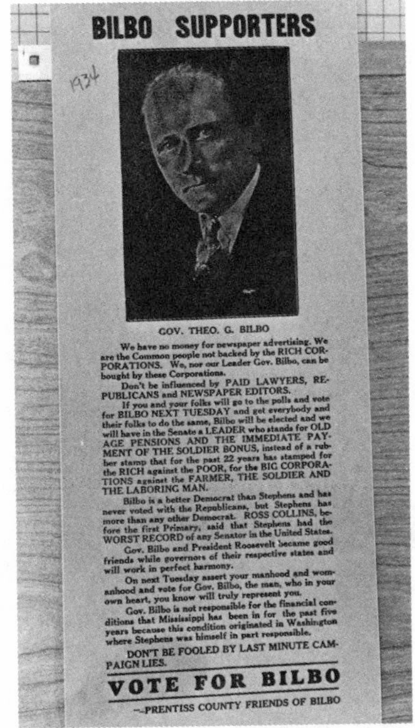

BILBO SUPPORTERS

1934

GOV. THEO. G. BILBO

We have no money for newspaper advertising. We
are the Common people not backed by the RICH COR-
PORATIONS. We, nor our Leader Gov. Bilbo, can be
bought by these Corporations.

Don't be influenced by PAID LAWYERS, RE-
PUBLICANS and NEWSPAPER EDITORS.

If you and your folks will go to the polls and vote
for BILBO NEXT TUESDAY and get everybody and
their folks to do the same, Bilbo will be elected and we
will have in the Senate a LEADER who stands for OLD
AGE PENSIONS AND THE IMMEDIATE PAY-
MENT OF THE SOLDIER BONUS, instead of a rub-
ber stamp that for the past 22 years has stamped for
the RICH against the POOR, for the BIG CORPORA-
TIONS against the FARMER, THE SOLDIER AND
THE LABORING MAN.

Bilbo is a better Democrat than Stephens and has
never voted with the Republicans, but Stephens has
more than any other Democrat. ROSS COLLINS, before the first Primary, said that Stephens had the
WORST RECORD of any Senator in the United States.

Gov. Bilbo and President Roosevelt became good
friends while governors of their respective states and
will work in perfect harmony.

On next Tuesday assert your manhood and womanhood and vote for Gov. Bilbo, the man, who in your
own heart, you know will truly represent you.

Gov. Bilbo is not responsible for the financial conditions that Mississippi has been in for the past five
years because this condition originated in Washington
where Stephens was himself in part responsible.

DON'T BE FOOLED BY LAST MINUTE CAM-
PAIGN LIES.

VOTE FOR BILBO

—PRENTISS COUNTY FRIENDS OF BILBO

A Bilbo campaign flyer from the 1934 Senate race

Courtesy McCain Library, University of Southern Mississippi

Senator Bilbo
Courtesy McCain Library, University of Southern Mississippi

Capital reporters relished the prospect of a clash between the Kingfish and The Man, who had vowed to "raise more hell than Huey Long." They were disappointed when Bilbo declared himself "too busy . . . to be monkeying with 'the wild man from Borneo.'"
Scripps-Howard News Service

Bilbo campaign truck, 1934
Courtesy McCain Library, University of Southern Mississippi

Fred Sullens presents Bilbo with a new pair of red galluses at a Hugh White victory rally in 1935.
Courtesy McCain Library, University of Southern Mississippi

Mississippi's "original third-termer" for Roosevelt: Bilbo at the 1940 Democratic national convention
Courtesy McCain Library, University of Southern Mississippi

Bilbo campaigning for the national Democratic ticket in 1940
Courtesy McCain Library, University of Southern Mississippi

The Mississippi delegation to the 1941 presidential inauguration. The men in the front row are (*left to right*) Senator Pat Harrison, Bilbo, Governor Paul Johnson, and Lieutenant Governor Dennis Murphree.

Courtesy McCain Library, University of Southern Mississippi

Bilbo's Dream House in Pearl River County

Courtesy McCain Library, University of Southern Mississippi

Mrs. Linda Bilbo at the Pearl River County courthouse, where she testified during divorce proceedings instituted by Senator Bilbo. He had always returned to her following previous separations, she told reporters, but "he hasn't come back this time. . . . I'm still waiting."

Wide World Photos

Bilbo and admirers. As a friend of his put it, "Girl friends was his great weakness."

Courtesy McCain Library, University of Southern Mississippi

At the Dream House

Courtesy McCain Library, University of Southern Mississippi

Bilbo speaking in 1940

Giles–Black Star

Bilbo addresses a crowd at a political rally. William Alexander Percy said of his supporters: "They were undiluted Anglo-Saxons. They were the sovereign voter."

Courtesy McCain Library, University of Southern Mississippi

"The people loved him," Percy said, "because they understood him thoroughly . . . he was one of them."

UPI/Bettmann Newsphotos

parted for the capital in December, 1934, he concluded his farewell news conference in Jackson with assurances that Mississippi was safe from a Long invasion. "Say, how do you spell 'hooey?'" he teased. "H-O-O-E-Y," someone responded. "Oh well," he beamed, "'hooey' or 'Huey,' it means the same thing."[24]

But Mississippi's new junior senator had also pledged to respect congressional decorum, and this latter promise superseded any inclination or expectations regarding his conduct toward his Louisiana colleague, even to the extent of a complete first year's silence on the Senate floor. Bilbo was willing to live and let live. Besides, he quipped, "I am too busy trying to keep faith with the people of Mississippi to be monkeying with 'the wild man from Borneo.'" Nonetheless, he needled Long at every opportunity. When the E-Z Chemical Company offered a sample box of voice pastelles, Bilbo declined but suggested that Long could probably use a whole case. A New York speaker's bureau invited him to debate Long some Sunday afternoon in a New York City theater. Bilbo presented a detailed justification for his polite refusal: (1) He didn't care to go skunk hunting on Sunday—"it's the Lord's Day"; (2) no matter how skillfully a skunk is skinned, he leaves his stink; (3) he had promised a year's silence; (4) he had no desire "to amuse, free of charge, the morbid and curious public mind by haranguing with [a] bleating Jackass." Some said the two men's paths did cross in 1935 at a Washington night spot. In the Senate the following day Bilbo appeared sporting a black eye and Long a bandaged left hand. Details of the alleged altercation were sketchy. Bilbo claimed that he had had a slight auto accident. When asked if his wounded hand had been at all connected with Bilbo's eye, Long simply said that he had contracted an unusual case of athlete's foot.[25]

The real showdown between the two came in the second primary of the governor's race. Lester Franklin had openly bid for the support of Long's Mississippi followers in the first primary, though the Kingfish himself was conspicuously silent about the race. Then on the eve of the vote, word apparently came down that Johnson was the anointed. Colonel S. P. McCall, a Louisiana conservation officer stationed at Biloxi, reported that he had received a call from Long himself, direct-

24. "Bilbo: Mississippi's Mighty Atom Explodes in Huey's Face," *Newsweek*, August 24, 1935, p. 10; W. D. Robinson to Colonel Louis McHenry Howe, February 13, 1935, Howe to Robinson, February 18, 1935, both in Robinson Papers; Memphis *Commercial Appeal*, May 19, 1935, Sec. 5, p. 6; Jackson *Daily Clarion Ledger*, December 9, 1934, p. 1.

25. Bilbo to T. W. Smith, January 16, 1935, Bilbo to H. H. Norton, January 21, 1935, Bilbo to Thomas Brady, March 7, 1935, all in Bilbo Papers; Williams, *Huey Long*, 715.

ing him to get to work for Johnson. Meanwhile, Louisiana Share Our Wealth club members poured across the state line urging their Mississippi brethren to turn out for Johnson.[26]

Long knew that his open support would be the kiss of death, giving Johnson's opposition the issue of outside interference to play upon, so after getting his man into the runoff, he backed up a step. A few days after the primary he issued a letter to heads of Share Our Wealth clubs in Mississippi instructing them to keep their hands off the governor's race regardless of what either candidate might say "*for* or *against* us." Johnson had solicited no help, and he had offered none, Long insisted. "We are sure to be repudiated no matter who wins." In light of Long's intervention in Conner's behalf in 1931, the current Conner-Johnson alliance, and Long's threats and Conner's designs against Harrison in 1936, the disclaimer proved a thin veil. In fact Long told an Associated Press reporter in Washington, "I don't want poor people penalized with a rapacious millionaire type like Hugh White serving as governor and I thought I had a right to say so."[27]

From the opening gun, Long's intervention put Johnson on the defensive. Franklin, who felt cheated of Long's support, and Murphree, whose integrity Johnson had viciously assailed in the first primary, both endorsed White. Only Hubert Stephens, whom Bilbo had humiliated the previous year, and Conner remained in Johnson's camp. The judge kicked off his second-primary campaign by declaring that the basic issue was "whether Hugh White with his millions can buy or corrupt the electorate of Mississippi, or shall the people rule with their own government. . . . Murphree has done sold out to White again." Murphree and Franklin, Johnson said, had offered him support in exchange for payment of their campaign debts, but he had refused. Moreover, all the talk about Long was Bilbo's doing. Endorsement by the Louisiana senator would be appreciated, Johnson said, but it had not been solicited. In fact, he said, he had never even met Long or spoken to him or written him.[28]

To the White forces Long was not just an issue; he was "the sole issue." White's chief editorial backer, Fred Sullens, ran a five-part series

26. New Orleans *Times Picayune*, August 6, 1935, p. 1.

27. Huey Long to Miles Reid (copy), August 13, 1935, in Bilbo Papers; New Orleans *Times Picayune*, August 14, 1935, p. 1; Huey Long, *Every Man a King: The Autobiography of Huey Long* (New Orleans, 1933), 275–76; Moley, *After Seven Years*, 305; Jackson *Daily News*, August 11, 1935, p. 1.

28. Jackson *Daily News*, August 9, 1935, p. 1; Dennis Murphree to Friends, August 10, 1935, in Record Group 27, Vol. 839, Dennis Murphree Papers, Mississippi Department of Archives and History, Jackson; Jackson *Daily Clarion Ledger*, August 10, 1935, p. 1.

on the dangers of Longism, written by a young Louisiana editor named Hodding Carter. Carter, former head of the Associated Press's Mississippi Bureau, ran a small newspaper in Hammond, the *Daily Courier*, with which he had waged a relentless editorial war against the Long machine. Sullens now gave him a chance to carry the fight to Mississippi, and Carter warned from the pages of the Jackson *Daily News* that scores of Share Our Wealth officials were making daily forays into Mississippi, organizing clubs and beating the drums for Johnson.[29]

White virtually ignored all other issues in the race. Often introduced to speak by Murphree leaders in the various counties, he hammered away at the dictator theme. Long ruled Louisiana with an iron hand, and a Johnson victory would surrender Mississippi to his dominion. The Kingfish coveted control of Mississippi as a springboard to national power, White warned, and he wanted control of the Mississippi delegation to the 1936 Democratic convention. Every vote for White would help protect Mississippi from "sinister" outside influence. As for Long's puppet Johnson, said White, if he forgot how to say "rich man," his entire political vocabulary would be extinct.[30]

While White wooed the voters, Bilbo wooed the president. He reminded Roosevelt of Conner's opposition at the 1932 convention and his general coolness toward the New Deal. He begged Roosevelt to replace the heads of several federal agencies in Mississippi. The National Reemployment Service, FERA, and the Rural Rehabilitation Administration were all integral parts of the Conner-Johnson-Long machine, he warned, and they negated any advantage WPA patronage might have given White. If Roosevelt would sweep away those "political manipulators for Long . . . I will deliver the goods whenever and wherever Mississippi's name is called," Bilbo promised. "We are in a death struggle with Huey Long, his men, and his money, and we need your help." As he was leaving Washington to campaign for White, Bilbo solicited the powerful influence of his Mississippi colleague. He implored Harrison, who was to attend an important White House conference on August 18, to impress upon the president the absolute necessity of these changes. "Don't ask," he urged, "demand it." Obviously Bilbo was out to feather his own nest as much as to help White, which explains why much of what he requested was ignored.[31]

Bilbo had not originally intended to take the stump for White, but Johnson's sweeping success in the first primary and the threat of Long's

29. Jackson *Daily News*, August 9, 1935, p. 1, August 13, 1935, p. 1.

30. Jackson *Daily News*, August 15, 1935, p. 10, August 16, 1935, p. 10.

31. Bilbo to Marvin MacIntyre, August 18, 1935, Bilbo to Roosevelt, August 18, 1935, Bilbo to Harrison, August 18, 1935, all in Bilbo Papers.

intervention in the second gave him both a reason and an excuse to do what he yearned to do anyway. A frolic in the hot springs of Mississippi election waters would be therapeutic to his political soul. He decided to intervene and landed running, to the delight of his redneck partisans, who spread the word of his coming as effectively as the more sophisticated media of many of his contemporaries.

His first appearance was scheduled for August 19 in Brookhaven, and "before he was up and dressed" requests began pouring in from all over the state for him to speak. Although his address had not been announced until that very morning, by evening the little Whitworth College auditorium groaned under the weight of a crowd that filled the seats, the aisles, the windows, and spilled out over the campus outside. They came despite the threat of rain, from Wesson and Beauregard, from Bogue Chitto and Jayess, from Bude and Roxie. They came in brogans and overalls and in ill-fitting Sunday suits. They came in automobiles, in wagons, and on foot, and they came singly, by families, and even by communities. They came to be wooed, entertained, or enlightened, or simply to escape the drudgery of the farm. But they all came, and they came by the hundreds, to bask in the splendor of The Man's oratory.[32]

And he did not disappoint them: "I'll start by calling Huey Long public enemy number one—and from there I'll get worse." Long had no concern for Johnson, Bilbo said. He merely wanted to control as many southern statehouses as possible so he could destroy the Democratic party and obstruct President Roosevelt. Reading from Long's own *Every Man a King*, Bilbo described the Kingfish's involvement in Conner's race for governor in 1931. "I'm here fighting for Franklin Roosevelt," Bilbo told the audience, who considered themselves and their kind, of all people, to be among the country's forgotten men and women. "I'm here fighting for Mississippi. I'm here fighting for you." These were people for whom luxury was a new pair of shoes and capital was what they carried in their pockets, and Bilbo reminded them that when the Senate debated the soak-the-rich tax bill, Huey Long "caught a train to New York to mix gin fizzes." At every mention of Roosevelt's name, the audience roared its acclaim. Hecklers, the bane of genteel politicians, were grist for Bilbo's mill. When a spectator suggested that White's platform was nothing like the one on which he had run in 1931, the former Sunday school organizer and sometime lay Baptist preacher reminded the wavering that "the Apostle Paul was

32. Jackson *Daily News*, August 19, 1935, p. 1; New Orleans *Times Picayune*, August 20, 1935, p. 3; Jackson *Daily News*, August 20, 1935, pp. 1, 10.

murdering Christians" until he saw the light on the road to Damascus. The heckling dissolved amidst a thunderous guffaw.[33]

The following day's account of the speech in Sullens' *Daily News* included a column of EXPLODING BOMBSHELLS FROM THEO'S BIG GUN! Sullens recounted Bilbo's blessing to "go ahead and take Huey Long's money if you need it, but vote for White," and his warning that "if you belong to Huey Long, you belong to him body, soul, boots, and breeches." But the Brookhaven crowd did not belong to Huey Long or Paul Johnson or even to Hugh White. They belonged to Bilbo, and apparently they were his, body, soul, boots, and breeches—and votes![34]

The scene was repeated every day for more than a week, as Bilbo crisscrossed the state, speaking five and six times a day: at Magee and Tylertown, at Ackerman and Eupora, at Iuka and Ripley and Pontotoc. Some said the crowd he addressed in Meridian was the largest in that city's history. When a section of bleachers collapsed, officials begged people to go home and listen on the radio. No sooner had several thousand left than others appeared, pushing and shoving their way to get within earshot of the platform.[35]

The campaign had its ugly moments. At Forest, Johnson waved a telegram that he said was from Mrs. Bilbo and succumbed to the crowd's importunate shouts to read it. Mrs. Bilbo, who had been estranged from the senator since he left the governor's office, insisted that her husband's support of White could not possibly be sincere. She had traveled with Bilbo for a quarter century, she said, and could recite his speeches by heart. He had always denounced corporate men like White, the rich and powerful. They opposed everything he stood for. On the other hand she praised Johnson as "an honest, upright, Christian man, unusually smart and well qualified to serve Mississippi as governor." The next day Johnson accused Bilbo of abandoning his wife. "No wonder Bilbo knows so much about relief," he scoffed, "his own precious wife had to go on it last year."[36]

Meanwhile the White camp raised the race issue. The candidate claimed to have been heckled at Tupelo by "a big buck negro" who would have said more if two White associates had not threatened "to cut his throat from ear to ear." Johnson complained about White's

33. Jackson *Daily News*, August 20, 1935, pp. 1, 10; New Orleans *Times Picayune*, August 20, 1935, p. 3, August 21, 1935, p. 2, August 22, 1935, p. 2.

34. Jackson *Daily News*, August 20, 1935, p. 1.

35. *Ibid.*, August 21, 1935, pp. 1, 8.

36. Jackson *Daily Clarion Ledger*, August 21, 1935, pp. 1, 3; "Bilbo v. Bilbo," *Time*, September 2, 1935, p. 14; Memphis *Commercial Appeal*, August 22, 1935, p. 13.

"nigger circular," which associated Johnson with Share Our Wealth organizing of black voters. With some hyperbole he called it "the most scurrilous campaign literature used in Mississippi since the Civil War" and blamed it on Bilbo. But there is no evidence that it was Bilbo's idea. In fact White's friend Sullens had been raising the same issue long before Bilbo left Washington for Mississippi. The editor charged that Long had praised black Congressman Oscar DePriest and warned that "any man who organizes negroes for a political or quasi-political purpose here in the South is a public enemy." The two incidents had negligible effect on the election, but they marred an already bitter campaign. Bilbo, interestingly in light of his reputation, was the victim of one and only incidentally involved in the other.[37]

As the campaign approached the August 27 showdown, it became more and more apparent that Bilbo was the show. He drew more of Johnson's fire than did White, and in an anomaly that must have taken the breath from veterans of Mississippi's political wars, Fred Sullens day after day extolled the virtues of the man he had spent a career scorning. Conservatives and progressives alike must have doubted their sanity as they read: "Bilbo is performing a great national service . . . and . . . must be credited with having made a heroic and unselfish effort." And: "If victory perches on the banner of simon-pure Democracy in Mississippi Tuesday night, give to Theodore G. Bilbo a goodly share of the credit. He has waged a valiant battle." Any doubts that The Man was the central figure in the campaign disappeared when the election eve statewide radio broadcast carried his speech from Laurel rather than the candidate's from Jackson. Meanwhile, Johnson concluded his campaign at Gulfport with the declaration "Bilbo is a humbug and a fraud."[38]

The tragic death of Will Rogers stole the public's attention from the campaign during the weekend before the runoff. He and Wiley Post were buried on Friday. On Tuesday, Bilbo buried Paul Johnson and Huey Long.[39]

As if to underscore the violence of Mississippi politics in general and this race in particular, an election-day knife-and-gun battle at Lorena left one dead and several wounded a mere twenty yards from a Smith County polling booth. Things were relatively calmer at the *Daily News*

37. Jackson *Daily News*, August 20, 1935, p. 5; Jackson *Daily Clarion Ledger*, August 22, 1935, p. 1; Jackson *Daily News*, August 18, 1935, p. 6.

38. Jackson *Daily News*, August 22, 1935, p. 1, August 26, 1935, p. 6; Jackson *Daily Clarion Ledger*, August 27, 1935, p. 1.

39. Jackson *Daily News*, August 16, 1935, p. 1.

election party in downtown Jackson, where more than ten thousand turned out to await the returns. The crowd swelled out into President Street, snaked around the corner into Capitol Street and beyond the Jitney Jungle grocery store, out of range of the big screen but not the loudspeakers. One Johnson supporter clanged a cowbell and scattered minor scuffles erupted, but by and large the spectators were civil.[40]

After all precincts had reported, White had a 12,000-vote victory (182,771 to 170,705), carrying fifty counties to Johnson's thirty-two. The following day a crowd of two hundred at Osyka, near White's birthplace of McComb and on the Louisiana line, celebrated by hanging Long in effigy. Affixed to the dummy victim was a sign that read, HUEY P. LONG DID NOT PASS. Bilbo wired Roosevelt that "the first treatment to that madman Huey Long in his efforts to break the solid Democratic South was administered yesterday. I am keeping the task assigned to me always in mind. Several more doses will be administered in due and ancient form." The president replied: "Thank you for your telegram. I am watching your smoke." Young Hodding Carter, who would later deem Bilbo the most unworthy senator ever "to represent a supposedly intelligent and free people," added his congratulations to Bilbo along with an invitation to "run for governor of Louisiana any time you feel like it."[41]

The White organization staged a victory party at Poindexter Park in Jackson on Friday night. Lieutenant Governor–elect J. B. Snider and Judge Garland Lyell shared presiding duties, and the music of Lee Hardcastle and his Castles of the Air softened the celebrants before subjecting them to the speakers. Everyone sang "Let Me Call You Sweetheart" to Mrs. White, who smiled demurely as someone bestowed the accompanying orchid and lilies of the valley. Then came the laborious train of soporific oratory—congratulations and thanksgiving, glorying in the past campaign and anticipating the coming administration—but mostly vacuous and innocuous homily. Finally, the governor-elect spoke, including in his remarks a "special acknowledgement . . . of the incomparable service . . . and masterly addresses

40. Jackson *Daily Clarion Ledger*, August 28, 1935, p. 1; Jackson *Daily News*, August 28, 1935, p. 9.

41. *Mississippi Blue Book: Biennial Report of the Secretary of State to the Legislature of Mississippi, 1935–1937*, p. 155; New Orleans *Times Picayune*, August 29, 1935, p. 1; Bilbo to Roosevelt, August 28, 1935, Roosevelt to Bilbo, August 30, 1935, both in President's Personal File (hereinafter cited as PPF) 2184, Roosevelt Papers; Hodding Carter, *Where Main Street Meets the River* (New York, 1952), 182–83; Carter to Bilbo, August 29, 1935, in Bilbo Papers.

. . . of Senator Bilbo." The evening's highlight came when Bilbo took the stage in shirt sleeves while his old antagonist Sullens "affixed . . . to the Senatorial trousers, fore and aft" a bright new pair of red galluses to repair the ones damaged during a verbal assault on a heckler in Laurel on election eve. Although not exactly necessary—the senator was a cautious man; he wore suspenders and a belt—the gift provided a fitting trophy for Bilbo's triumph, for it was his victory as much, if not more, than it was White's.[42]

In what turned out to be a prophetic observation, Bilbo declared, "If Paul Johnson would take a bath every day and night, fumigate himself and get rid of the Huey Long stink we might consider him four years hence." In 1939 Bilbo would help Johnson win the governor's office that he had just denied him in 1935.[43]

Bilbo revealed to the gathering at Poindexter Park that he would, probably at the behest of the administration and Harrison, make a national speaking tour against Long during 1936. In less than a month it became unnecessary because Long was felled by an assassin in Baton Rouge. The tragedy left Bilbo by no means repentant of his scorn for the fallen fellow senator or the remnants of his political machine. Bilbo protested to the attorney general's office when it was rumored that the Justice Department might compromise with the Long crowd concerning an investigation of tax evasion by members of Long's organization. The government should probe deeper, The Man argued, and put the whole lot in federal prison. When Share Our Wealth's Gerald L. K. Smith hinted in a national radio broadcast that Bilbo had been involved in Long's death, Bilbo called him "a contemptible, dirty, vicious, pusillanimous, with malice aforethought, damnable, self-made liar" and suggested that he crawl back into the pulpit and keep his nose out of politics. Bilbo had been in New Orleans the Friday before the assassination, but he had gone to seek a loan from the Federal Land Bank. He had seen no one, he said, but "a hard-hearted banker whose eyes were so cold that I nearly froze to death in his office." Besides, he added callously, why would anyone pay to have Long killed when thousands of Louisianians would gladly do it for nothing.[44]

On the surface Bilbo's role in the 1935 race seemed to make little ideological sense. He shunned the most progressive gubernatorial can-

42. Jackson *Daily News*, August 31, 1935, p. 14; Jackson *Daily Clarion Ledger*, August 31, 1935, p. 1.

43. Jackson *Daily News*, August 27, 1935, p. 7.

44. New Orleans *Times Picayune*, August 31, 1935, p. 1; Jackson *Daily News*, September 16, 1935, pp. 1, 12; New York *Times*, September 10, 1935, p. 37.

didate in favor of a millionaire businessman who, in his only previous statewide race, had won more counties in the Delta than any other section of the state. In supporting White over Johnson, Bilbo appeared to deny his liberal heritage and to betray his poor-white constituency. But several other factors clarify the picture somewhat. First is the nature of executive office in Mississippi, wherein the governorship is much more political than it is powerful. No one knew better than Bilbo that electoral success was not easily translated into administrative success. Although the chief executive's control of state patronage gave him substantial influence in statewide elections, the real locus of power in state government was in the legislature. The governor's inability to succeed himself and the effects of one-party factionalism diffused what little power the executive did have. Local elections, including legislative races, remained fairly independent of statewide politics.

Second, the factionalism necessarily produced shifting alliances, which made ideological alignment even more difficult. The system fostered a gubernatorial politics that was more negative than positive, especially for those, like Bilbo in 1935, who were not candidates but whose political future would be affected profoundly by the outcome of the election. It was simply more important to defeat enemies than to elect ideological friends. Bilbo could not have supported Johnson in 1935 without strengthening Conner, whose conservatism was every bit as unpalatable as White's. The Conner-Johnson partnership raised serious questions about how progressive a Johnson administration might have been. More important, it forced Bilbo to choose between Conner and White, and a quick glance at the political influence that the former already held in his hands made the choice rather obvious.

In the third place, there was a good bit of personal animosity between Bilbo and both Johnson and Conner, and as The Man would reveal the following year, he could carry a personal grudge to extravagance. Johnson had defeated Bilbo for Congress in 1918, and the two men cordially disliked each other thereafter. Although Bilbo had helped Conner become Speaker of the house in 1916, they had fallen out since and had said some harsh things about each other in the campaign for governor in 1923. White, on the other hand, got along fairly well with Bilbo and had even supported him for the Senate in 1934.

The decisive factor, however, was probably the shadow of the Kingfish, and more was involved than simply the sanctity of Mississippi politics. Certainly Bilbo did not want Long involved in Mississippi elections, but despite all the uproar during the campaign, Bilbo was probably confident that he could take care of Long before the voters of Mississippi. What was really at stake was control of the state Democratic delegation to the 1936 national convention. A victorious Conner-Johnson faction, backed by Huey Long, raised the specter of a Mississippi Democratic party hostile to Roosevelt and Harrison as well as to Bilbo. The New Deal was certainly an issue in the 1935 race, with Bilbo, Harrison, and White on one side and Conner, Johnson, and Long on the other. There is little doubt that Roosevelt saw the election in those terms. Bilbo was not completely comfortable supporting White, who would repay The Man's efforts by opposing him for reelection in 1940. Bilbo simply had no alternative. He might have remained on the sidelines in 1935 had Johnson not made such a strong bid in the first primary.

Bilbo believed in Roosevelt and the New Deal and, like the administration, he saw Long's bid for control of southern Democratic delegations as a real threat in 1936. Moreover, Bilbo simply did not care for Long-style bossism. In an interview with a Memphis reporter, he perhaps summarized his feelings about the 1935 race.

> "Senator, you're the Kingfish now, eh?"
> "I'm just old Bilbo."
> "Bilbo the Boss?"
> "Naw, just old Bilbo. Bilbo the Man. Old Man Bilbo. No boss about it."
> "Well, you had a little something to do with the election of your friend Hugh White, didn't you?"
> "The people of Mississippi did it. I just helped."[45]

But Bilbo was the Kingfish now, at least in Mississippi, and in December he crowned his successful first year in the Senate with the opening of the Dream House in Pearl River County. It was a rustically lavish affair in typical Bilbo fashion. Rather than risk an oversight in a guest list, he simply threw open the doors and publicly invited to the open house "all who have ever heard the name of 'Bilbo.'" In Mississippi, that could only have exempted the deaf.[46]

On the weekend before Christmas hundreds descended upon little Juniper Grove to celebrate The Man's splendor and to revel in his generosity: a hundred pounds of cheese, ten cases of crackers, six hundred tins of sardines, five gallons of dill pickles, fifty gallons of ice cream, ten layer cakes, five boxes of oranges, five boxes of apples, five crates of grapes, five pounds of sugar, eight hundred nickel cigars, enough coffee

45. "Mississippi's Two Edged Sword," *Literary Digest*, September 4, 1935, p. 4; Memphis *Commercial Appeal*, September 22, 1935, Sec. 4, p. 5.

46. Bilbo press release, November 11, 1935, in Bilbo Papers.

"for everyone," and fifty gallons of claret that possessed "plenty of jurisdiction." As Bilbo later told a friend, whatever architectural deficiencies the house may have had, "one trip through the basement and everything was lovely thereafter." Indeed, as 1935 drew to a close, everything did seem lovely. But the euphoria would not survive the following year.[47]

47. New York *Times*, December 22, 1935, p. 9; Bilbo to A. H. Alvis, January 14, 1936, in Bilbo Papers.

Chapter Five

From Hell to Breakfast

Bilbo's political friendship with Harrison had been precarious from the start. It was an aberration ideologically and personally, and it collapsed abruptly in 1936 over a disputed federal judicial appointment. Ironically, the controversy had erupted the previous year while Bilbo was out of Washington campaigning tooth and nail for Harrison's old friend Hugh White. The death of Judge Nathan P. Bryan in early August created a vacancy on the Fifth United States Circuit Court of Appeals. Since no Mississippian had ever served on the court, there was general acknowledgment that the state should get the seat. The question was which Mississippi jurist would get the nod. One held a presumptive claim. Several years earlier Federal District Judge Edwin R. Holmes had almost been elevated to a similar vacancy. Only a petty political squabble over his replacement on the district court had prevented his promotion. Holmes, who had married a daughter of John Sharp Williams, commanded support from a substantial segment of the Mississippi bar, including the senior senator, who held an unrivaled reverence for the judge's father-in-law.[1]

The 1935 nomination and confirmation might have proceeded perfunctorily but for the venerable tradition of senatorial prerogative and a politically injudicious ruling that Holmes had rendered twelve years earlier. During the Lee Russell–Frances Birkhead scandal in 1923, Holmes had sentenced Bilbo to thirty days in jail and fined him a hundred dollars for failing to answer a subpoena to testify for the plaintiff. The judge ordered Bilbo released after ten days and remitted the fine, but the conviction for contempt of court remained on record.[2]

Now, twelve years later, Bilbo sat in that august body whose objections to judicial appointments were rarely overridden by a chief executive. It was highly unlikely that Roosevelt and Attorney General Homer Cummings would have sent Holmes's name to the Senate over Bilbo's opposition, notwithstanding Harrison's enormous influence

1. Saucier, "The Public Career of Bilbo," 138–40.

2. See Chapter Two.

with the administration and on Capitol Hill. But the junior senator was conveniently leaving town for Mississippi to take the stump for White in the governor's race. Before he left on August 15, Bilbo called Harrison aside to the Capitol porch just off the Senate chamber to ask the status of the judgeship. Exactly what transpired in that conversation was ever after a matter of dispute between the two and bred a personal animus that profoundly affected Bilbo's Senate career and drastically altered the shape of Mississippi politics.[3]

Harrison claimed he told Bilbo that he intended to submit Holmes's name but assured him that Cummings would have to investigate the application and endorsements and would not make the appointment before adjournment. Pat insisted that Bilbo never offered the least opposition to the nomination. Bilbo's recollection was that he had declared he would never agree to the confirmation of someone who had jailed him "without rhyme or reason." Whatever the case, Bilbo departed for Mississippi to do battle against Huey Long and the enemies of the administration. Then suddenly, late on August 23, the day before adjournment, Cummings called Harrison to say that he had decided to appoint Holmes and was sending his name to Roosevelt. Harrison later testified that he told Cummings he had assured Bilbo that the nomination would not come up that session and that he did not know his colleague's feelings on the matter. It was the attorney general, Pat insisted, who decided that to wait would be unfair to Holmes, who would have to resign his district judgeship before he was confirmed for the circuit court. So while Bilbo rained political fire and brimstone on Huey Long and Paul Johnson a thousand miles away, the Holmes nomination quietly slipped into place on the Senate calendar. Knowing that the nomination was already safely on its way to the Senate, Harrison wired Bilbo of the day's events and encouraged him to wire his position to the attorney general immediately. "It would not do," he said, "for nomination to come to Senate and fail of confirmation."[4]

The Man was not impressed with the mock urgency. By the time Harrison's wire caught up with him at Corinth, it was too late to reply that day. He had already heard of the appointment in Oxford, where he had spoken earlier that afternoon. On the way to his next engagement, he drafted a message to Cummings and Roosevelt expressing his opposition to Holmes and his resentment that "a committee of the

3. U.S. Congress, Senate, Committee on the Judiciary, *Hearings Before a Subcommittee of the Committee on the Judiciary, U.S. Senate, on the Nomination of Judge Edwin R. Holmes for Judge of the United States Circuit Court of Appeals for the Fifth District* (hereinafter cited as *Holmes Hearings*), 74th Cong., 2nd Sess., 1936, pp. 59–63.

4. *Ibid.*; *Congressional Record*, 74th Cong., 2nd Sess., 3992.

Mississippi Bar Association has come to Washington to force this appointment when they know I am here at home fighting Huey Long in the interest of Pat Harrison, President Roosevelt, and the Democratic Party. Senator Harrison assured me this matter would be held over until my return." The next morning he wired a blunt response to Harrison: "I most positively object to the confirmation of Ed Holmes, and I don't mean maybe."[5]

Why would Roosevelt have made the appointment in the face of such stern opposition? He did so because Harrison had shrewdly veiled that opposition from him. On August 20, three days before the last-minute call from Cummings, Harrison had urged the president to nominate Holmes, noting that the entire Mississippi delegation joined in the endorsement. Upon receiving Bilbo's protest, Roosevelt responded that the nomination had gone to the Senate the previous afternoon "several hours before your telegram was received." It was made on the "assurance that it had unanimous support and I certainly understood this included you," he said. "I am deeply sorry for the misunderstanding." When Harrison received Bilbo's wire of the twenty-fourth, he gallantly requested that the nomination be returned to the Judiciary Committee and go over to the next session. Although a bitter skirmish loomed over Senate confirmation, Harrison had already won the war by securing the presidential appointment. The Senate, as Pat later assured the president, he could handle well enough.[6]

Harrison's pretense that he had no hint of Bilbo's objection to Holmes appears rather lame, for Pat had already had a taste of Bilbo's stubbornness regarding appointments. Early in 1935 the newly arrived junior senator had opposed the confirmation of Mississippian Eugene Sykes as chairman of the Federal Communications Commission. Sykes, who began his career as a Bilbo appointee to the Mississippi Supreme Court, had become anti-Bilbo by the time he joined the FCC board in 1927. Bilbo charged that in 1934 Sykes had used the agency to support Hubert Stephens' reelection bid. Bilbo lost the fight against Sykes, but the tenacity with which he waged it ought to have been a firm clue that he would not fail to use his new office to settle old political scores when afforded an opportunity.[7]

5. *Holmes Hearings*, 64–65.

6. *Ibid.*, 60; Roosevelt to Cummings, August 23, 1935, MacIntyre to Roosevelt, January 6, 1936, both in OF 208, Roosevelt Papers; Roosevelt to Bilbo, August 24, 1935, in Bilbo Papers.

7. Edwin E. Meek, "Eugene Octave Sykes, Member and Chairman of Federal Communications Commission and Federal Radio Commission, 1927–1939," *Journal of Mississippi History*, XXXVI (1974), 380.

Bilbo had certainly left his friends no room for doubt concerning his view of the Holmes candidacy. Early in July, as the political vultures were already circling over Judge Bryan's yet unrelinquished seat, Bilbo's old law partner Stewart Broom staked his claim to the district judgeship should Holmes move up. Bilbo acknowledged that he had heard the rumor about Holmes but thought there was nothing to it. Besides, he chided, "since when did you get the idea that I would vote to be of assistance to him on the bench. It would take a lot of persuasion for me to change my mind about this shriveled nincompoop." Later, when the Washington County Bar Association endorsed Holmes as "a fair, impartial and brilliant jurist . . . who has endeared himself to all who have had the pleasure of coming in contact with him either on or off the bench," Bilbo took cordial exception. "I had the misfortune," he scoffed, "of coming in contact with him on the bench . . . and he very promptly sent me to jail . . . so you can readily see . . . that Judge Holmes played hell in endearing himself to me."[8]

Before and during the hearing on the appointment, Bilbo begged Roosevelt to withdraw the nomination and even sent him a copy of the plea he would make against Holmes before the Judiciary Committee. The president asked his secretary, Marvin MacIntyre, to "take care of this rather delicate matter." MacIntyre encountered a "perturbed" Harrison who insisted that withdrawal of Holmes's name would "finish" him (Harrison) in Mississippi. He reassured the secretary that he could take care of the matter before the Senate, that the administration ought to leave the nomination to him. Bilbo knew that his chances against Harrison in the Senate were nil, but he was determined to fight "as long as there is a pea in the dish." If he could not defeat Holmes, he would "give his sponsor hell." As matters progressed, this latter option became an obsession. "He may beat me in Washington, but we will see what we can do about it from Yellow Rabbit to Vinegar Bend," Bilbo wrote John Burkett. "I'm in the market for a colleague who will show some respect for me," he told the press. "I'll fight him [Pat] from hell to breakfast." One reason Bilbo pursued his vain opposition to Holmes so stubbornly was to get the whole matter on public record for the electorate to see.[9]

Bilbo indeed faced an uphill fight in the Senate. His real objection to

8. Bilbo to Broom, July 6, 1935, Edward J. Bogen to Bilbo, September 11, 1935, Bilbo to Bogen, September 16, 1935, all in Bilbo Papers.

9. Bilbo to Roosevelt, March 2, 1936, MacIntyre to Roosevelt, January 6, 1936, both in OF 208, Roosevelt Papers; Bilbo to W. A. Shipman, February 19, 1936, Bilbo to John Burkett, January 13, 1936, both in Bilbo Papers; "Bilbo: 'Ex-Pastemaster General' Turns on Man Who Got Him Job," *Newsweek*, February 1, 1936, pp. 16–17.

Holmes, the 1923 jailing at Oxford, seemed rather picayune by itself, so Bilbo immediately set himself to uncover some more conventional malfeasance. When the Judiciary subcommittee met to hear the case in late January, Bilbo was replete with charges but bereft of witnesses. By February 3 the subcommittee was almost ready to report to the full Judiciary Committee, but just as Chairman Edward Burke of Nebraska was ready to gavel what should have been the final meeting to order, Bilbo handed him a written request to reopen the hearing. Reluctantly the subcommittee agreed to give Bilbo a chance to go to Mississippi in search of witnesses. After another delay in late February, Burke called time on Bilbo, and the subcommittee met for its final sessions on March 5 and 6.[10]

Bilbo produced three charges against Holmes: he had unlawfully jailed Bilbo in 1923 for political reasons; he had approved some questionable transactions by the receiver of a Gulfport bank; and he had often rendered sentences more severe than statutes allowed. The Birkhead case had become legendary in Mississippi politics. Holmes had sent him to jail, Bilbo told the subcommittee, simply because he was the champion of a political faction that the judge despised. He had not wanted to testify in 1923, Bilbo explained, because any information he possessed had been obtained as Russell's lawyer and was therefore confidential. He would have answered the summons anyway, but the case was scandalous and highly publicized and he wanted nothing to do with it. He thought he was legally protected by a long-standing statute that exempted a witness, even under subpoena, if he lived outside the district of the case and more than a hundred miles from the trial site. He had tried to explain as much to Holmes, Bilbo said, in what amounted to a de facto plea of nolo contendere. But the judge neither acknowledged his remarks nor asked whether Bilbo desired to plead at all, but "summarily announced that he held me in contempt."[11]

Holmes betrayed his vindictive intent, Bilbo continued, by sentencing him to jail *and* fining him, whereas the law called for one or the other but not both. He was released only when Holmes realized the error and when conservative friends persuaded Holmes that being jailed by a Bourbon judge was merely winning Bilbo votes. It was pointed out that the law under which Bilbo thought he was protected had been amended only two months before the subpoena had been issued. Bilbo argued that neither Holmes nor any of the trial lawyers

10. *Congressional Record*, 74th Cong., 2nd Sess., 4024–27; Bilbo to Edward Burke, Key Pittman, and Tom Connally, January 14, 1936, Bilbo to Burke, Pittman, and Warren Austin, February 21, 1936, both in Bilbo Papers.

11. *Holmes Hearings*, 9-11.

had known of the change. The amendment still required an application to the court to show cause why someone outside the district should be subpoenaed. There was no such application on record in the Birkhead case regarding Bilbo; his subpoena was in the same form as all others in the case. "From the day I was cited for contempt unto this good hour," Bilbo declared, "I have not yet been able to find any lawyer who has ever known or heard of anyone having been cited for contempt under such circumstances except me by Judge Holmes." [12]

The second charge involved two Gulfport banks that had entered receivership during the depression and whose liquidation had been supervised by Judge Holmes's district court. Bilbo argued that Holmes had allowed and approved the "dissipation of the assets of those banks," that he "specifically authorized" disposal of certain bank assets "for grossly inadequate prices," that many debtors to the banks who were thereby bailed out of financial difficulty were "abundantly able to pay," and that several of them were "personal and political friends" of the judge. The transactions constituted a severe loss to the depositors and creditors of the banks, who were not allowed the benefit of notification, much less a proper hearing. Such flagrant "political favoritism" made Judge Holmes unfit to sit on the circuit court, Bilbo insisted.[13]

At this point Bilbo, not very subtly, dragged into the hearing the financial status of Holmes's benefactor and Bilbo's newly made enemy, Pat Harrison. A Bilbo witness testified that one of the "personal and political friends" who had received special treatment from Holmes was none other than the distinguished senior senator from Mississippi, who had dipped into the judge's "favoritism" to the tune of almost thirty thousand dollars. Harrison, who was in attendance, seethed as the testimony proceeded and rose at the first opportunity to vindicate himself. Livid, but controlled, he apologized for taking up the committee's time, lamenting that he was forced to do so only because his name had entered the proceedings. Like many others, he had plunged into the land boom of the twenties and had made what he thought was enough money to live comfortably the rest of his life. Then came the crash, and he was forced to repossess property that he had sold at high prices. After paying taxes on it for over a decade, Pat admitted, he was indeed insolvent. He had also incurred several personal notes and endorsed others on the banks in question. "I have done everything possible to try to reduce those obligations, and have reduced them, and in time I will pay them," he declared. Moreover, Pat added, the settlement

12. *Ibid.*, 12–18.
13. *Ibid.*, 20–21; *Congressional Record*, 74th Cong., 2nd Sess., 4001–4011.

with those banks had been approved by a depositors' committee. Glowering at his junior colleague, he charged that the issue had been introduced not to thwart Holmes but to hurt Harrison. And *that* "I can take care of before the people of Mississippi," he warned, banging his fist on the table.[14]

Bilbo lamely responded that "there were many people of prominence and of wealth whose claims were compromised" and that he was sorry Harrison's name had been injected into the hearing. Such was hardly the case. Bilbo had first learned of the Gulfport bank situation from his friend John Lumpkin in May of 1935, when he and Pat were still friendly. Lumpkin told Bilbo that the liquidating agent had made an application for a loan that was denied. Some of the depositors believed Harrison had derailed the loan because the failed bank held a large note against him. Lumpkin doubted that. Nonetheless, the bank had made several questionable loans, he said, and "the accusation is strong against our friend, to my sorrow." He suggested that if Bilbo could help the depositors get a $600,000 loan, most of them (several thousand) would support White in the governor's race. At the time, Lumpkin, Bilbo, and Harrison were all yoked together in the White campaign. But Bilbo was too agile a politician and too shrewd a gambler not to hedge his bets. He filed the information, however deeply, for future reference. A friend of Harrison's later remarked: "Bilbo had a lot of elephant in him. He never forgot."[15]

When Pat challenged him on the Holmes issue, Bilbo dredged up the letter and went to work. He sent lawyer friends scurrying over Harrison County in search of evidence to substantiate the story. He even sent his secretary to the comptroller of the currency to secure a list of the assets and liabilities of the Gulfport banks. On February 17, in the midst of the Holmes hearings, Comptroller J. F. T. O'Conner wrote Bilbo that the records were confidential and accessible only to bank officials or a Senate committee. Apparently Harrison had learned of Bilbo's plans, because O'Conner added incidentally that the senior senator had recently requested information regarding Bilbo's own settlement of a debt to the receiver of the First National Bank of Jackson. Pat was denied the records on the same basis as Bilbo.[16]

14. *Holmes Hearings*, 23–31, 61–62; "Taxmaster," *Time*, June 1, 1936, pp. 10–12.

15. *Holmes Hearings*, 65; John Lumpkin to Bilbo, May 5, 1935, in Bilbo Papers; Wilburn Buckley oral history interview, 21, in John C. Stennis Collection, Mitchell Library, Mississippi State University, Starkville.

16. Bilbo to Bidwell Adam, January 4, 1936, J. F. T. O'Connor to Bilbo, February 17, 1936, both in Bilbo Papers.

Bilbo, spoiling for a fight and already frustrated by his adversary's subtle but powerful influence in the Senate, fired off a detailed account of "definite and reliable information" about his own "dealings with, and obligations to, all of the failed State and National Banks in Mississippi." He invited—more nearly dared—his colleague to reciprocate. A few days after the hearings ended, Harrison returned Bilbo's letter, remarking piously: "It is useless to me. I think you ought to know me well enough to know that I believe a man's private dealings are one thing, and his official acts are another." Pat failed to note why he took the trouble to solicit "useless" information from the comptroller in the first place.[17]

Bilbo's final charge against Holmes was that he had illegally sentenced "hundreds" of Mississippians without statutory authority. Several of them, Bilbo declared, had even been released because they had been sent to the Atlanta federal prison with excessive sentences. In fact, so many had been returned for "correction of erroneous sentences," he said, that Holmes had almost stopped sending prisoners to Atlanta.[18]

But The Man's rhetorical magic, so captivating to the multitudes of the piney woods and red clay hills, left the subcommittee unmoved. The nomination proceeded with a favorable recommendation to the full committee, which sent it on to the Senate floor, where it was scheduled for consideration on March 19. Here now was Bilbo's last appeal, and he had to make the most of it. Whatever misery the year of self-imposed senatorial reticence had inflicted on him was about to be expiated in a torrent of bombast that would tax congressional ears already jaded by three years of Huey Long's oratory.[19]

On March 18 Bilbo sent each senator a copy of the subcommittee hearings and a letter summarizing the plea that he would make on the floor. When he rose to speak the next day, he began with a lavish tribute to senatorial custom and a review of his own strenuous effort to observe its every jot and tittle, even the long-standing convention of "remaining deathly silent for a period of a whole year." He knew, however, that "whispering subtleties or softly pedaled rumors" among the chamber's inner circle, those "guardians and defenders of the common law of Senatorial propriety," could like "a single drop of poison . . . spread and expand into an effervescent vapor, permeating every nook

17. Bilbo to Harrison, February 24, 1936, Harrison to Bilbo, March 10, 1936, both in Bilbo Papers.

18. Burkett to Bilbo, March 4, 1936, in Bilbo Papers.

19. *Congressional Record*, 74th Cong., 2nd Sess., 3987.

and cranny of the Senate chambers until the minds of its constituted occupants became impregnated with this lethal gas."[20]

Bilbo was warming to the task. He begged that each member would take great care not to judge the Holmes issue "purely on the basis of the personal equation as applied to myself and my distinguished colleague, Senator Harrison." The objection to Holmes was, he insisted, more than a personal affair. "This nominee's perfidy, favoritism, partiality, ignorance or prostitution of the duties of his office" are so flagrant, he said, that it would be unfair to ask lawyers who must deal with him on the bench to come forward and testify against him. Despite a lot of noise from a few lawyers who coveted his district judgeship, Holmes's supporters "dared not" offer a resolution of endorsement at the recent annual meeting of the Mississippi Bar Association, Bilbo proclaimed.

> His record of judicial incompetency and abuse of the powers vested in him is unparalleled in the courts of this country . . . and finds no equal except in the records made by Lord Chancellor Jeffreys in England and Lord Braxfield, his counterpart, "blood-thirsty wearers of the ermine" whose fiendish delight was in the imposition of extreme sentences and whose cruelty and political profligacy knew no bounds. If these facts are permitted to be shown . . . they will present a record of such judicial stupidity, of such crass ignorance of the law or of such a willful and premeditated abuse of his powers as will astound and amaze the members of this great deliberative body.[21]

He had been refused the opportunity to produce sufficient witnesses to prove his case, Bilbo said. While Holmes had paraded twenty-three witnesses before the subcommittee, he had been allowed but four. He merely wanted a fair chance to present his argument by having the nomination recommitted to the committee for further hearings. Holmes had mistakenly sentenced Bilbo in 1923 because he had not read the particular law involved, Bilbo concluded. "If the Senators will let me take him back to committee for a couple of weeks I will teach him some more law." But it was all to no avail. The motion to recommit failed, 59–4.[22]

The Holmes controversy proved a pivotal issue in Bilbo's first term. It eroded his influence with the administration and among his colleagues and virtually reversed his relationships with Harrison and

20. *Ibid.*, 3987–88; Bilbo to Henry F. Ashurst, March 18, 1936, in Judiciary Committee Papers.

21. Bilbo to Ashurst, March 18, 1936, in Judiciary Committee Papers.

22. *Congressional Record*, 74th Cong., 2nd Sess., 3988–91, 4032; Bilbo to Ashurst, March 18, 1936, in Judiciary Committee Papers.

Conner. In the Senate, Harrison's early friendship had worked wonders for Bilbo. He had arrived in Washington with a reputation that was not likely to endear him to most senators, and his initial sally into floor debate did nothing to enhance that reputation. He had antagonized and assailed one of the most popular and influential men in the Senate, the very man who had enabled him to gain what little credibility he enjoyed in that body.

With the administration, too, Harrison had been a great help to Bilbo. Whatever patronage he had secured in 1935 came largely as a result of Harrison's efforts, but from now on, the flow of federal jobs would almost dry up. Whereas Harrison had been somewhat indifferent to the makeup of the WPA, now he became quite active with most of the activity aimed at squeezing Bilbo's supporters out of the agency. Even Bilbo's unflagging support of the New Deal could not offset his colleague's influence with the Roosevelt bureaucracy. Not until 1937, when Harrison openly began to oppose the president on major issues, did the administration begin to smile on Bilbo, and then only slightly. So long as Harrison remained in the Senate, Bilbo got the short end of the patronage stick.

Heretofore the two senators had been allies if not intimates. Now they became inveterate enemies, personally and politically. The enmity was so intense as to drive Bilbo into the arms of the faction he had spent all of 1935 trying to destroy, the Conner machine. By the time Holmes was confirmed, Bilbo had made up his mind to do everything possible to see Harrison defeated in the 1936 primary, even if he had to support Mike Conner. That meant a complete restructuring of Mississippi's factional alignment. Harrison had proved himself Bilbo's superior in senatorial politics, but Bilbo now set out to prove himself undisputed master of Mississippi politics.

Chapter Six

In the Market for a Colleague

It has been suggested that Bilbo contrived the Holmes controversy as a mere pretext to oppose Harrison in 1936. That hardly seems the case. Nothing Bilbo had done since coming to Washington indicated any political antagonism toward his colleague. In fact he seemed committed to Harrison's reelection and had done a great deal to bring it about, performing yeoman duty in the cause of Hugh White, knowing that success meant the transfer of state patronage to Harrison's old friend at the direct expense of the only man who seemed likely to challenge Pat in 1936, Governor Mike Conner. He had worked tirelessly to deprive Conner of federal patronage. Although Bilbo had a vested interest in WPA jobs himself, it hardly made sense to disarm completely the only major challenger to a man whom he hoped to see defeated.[1]

As late as December of 1935, Bilbo was begging Roosevelt and Public Works Administrator Harold Ickes to delay the release of PWA highway funds for Mississippi until January when White, rather than Conner, would control them. The Man had made clear to his own followers that he intended to back Pat "with all there is in me" and had even sent Harrison a complete list of Bilbo precinct leaders. It seems highly unlikely that Bilbo entertained any serious thoughts of opposing Pat until the Holmes affair erupted.[2]

That is not to say that Bilbo had become a genuine admirer of Harrison's. The two men had never been close. Although they had cooperated back in 1918 when Harrison unseated Vardaman, by the mid-1930s they had come to represent two distinct and antagonistic

1. Saucier, "The Public Career of Bilbo," 141.

2. Hartwig, "Mississippi Highway Program," 16–21; Harold Ickes to Bilbo, November 15, 1935, Secretary of Interior File, October, 1935–1936, Container 253, in Harold Ickes Papers, Library of Congress; E. D. Kenna, personal interview with the author, June 3, 1979; Bilbo to Ickes, November 12, 1935, Bilbo to Dr. Willis Walley, May 6, 1935, Bilbo to Harrison, February 24, 1936, all in Bilbo Papers.

constituencies: Bilbo, the rednecks of the hills and piney woods; Harrison, the middle classes of the towns and cities and the Bourbon remnants of the Delta. More important, Bilbo sulked in the giant shadow that Harrison cast over him in Washington, personally and politically. He coveted Harrison's control of patronage. He still chafed at the indignity of the "pastemaster generalship," convinced that Harrison could easily have secured him a more respectable position in 1933. He envied Harrison's prestige, his access to administration policy makers, his popularity with the press, his eminence in Washington social circles, his influence on the floor, and his power in the cloakroom. In a moment of revealing candor, Bilbo wrote a friend:

> He has not given me any more consideration since I have been in the Senate, except where he was forced to, than you would give the negro servant in your home. He owns a nice home in Washington. He has been here for 26 years. He has had every opportunity to ingratiate himself with the social life of Washington, but he has been so afraid that I might gain some recognition that during all this time, both while I was working in the Department of Agriculture, and since I have been his colleague in the United State Senate, he has never invited me to share a meal with him in public and I have never even been invited to enter his home.[3]

Bilbo was not without incentive to get rid of Harrison. Pat had opposed him in 1934 and was not unlikely to do so again in 1940. He would surely be much less dangerous to Bilbo out of office than in. But all these irritants were present in 1935, when Bilbo was sincerely lining up his forces for Harrison's reelection. The decisive factor was the Holmes nomination. Bilbo's earlier response to Sykes had demonstrated his willingness to inject personal pique and vengeance into the appointment process, but it had also shown his willingness to forgive and forget causes lost honestly. But he felt betrayed by the way Harrison, with the Holmes affair, had deceptively and haughtily sidestepped Bilbo's own senatorial prerogative. Admittedly impotent in Washington, he would strike at Harrison from his own (Bilbo's) strength, the registered voters from Yellow Rabbit to Vinegar Bend. Just before taking his case to the Senate floor, he wrote a friend: "From the hour that Pat succeeds in cramming Holmes down my throat until I am called 'up yonder' or 'down yonder,' I have proposed in my mind and heart to give him pure, unadulterated hell. . . . If he can give me more hell than I can give him, I am sport enough to take it on the chin."[4]

3. Bilbo to Henry Hart, May 28, 1936, in Bilbo Papers.

4. Interview with Bidwell Adam, MOHP, Vol. XXXIV, 18–19, 79–81; interview

It seems strange that through the summer of 1935 Harrison allowed Conner appointees to remain in the WPA. Perhaps he hoped appeasement would keep the governor out of the race. More likely, he had the good sense to realize that the tools he was providing to build political fences for Bilbo might instead be used to dig his own political grave. Even more likely, Harrison had decided by September that he was no longer so dependent on Bilbo's influence with the redneck vote. Pat's own good friend White was safely elected governor and soon to inherit Conner's state patronage, and the old enemy Long was safely buried in Winn Parish, unable to marshal the Share Our Wealth forces as he had done for Conner in 1931. Indeed, soon after the 1935 primary and Long's assassination, complaints about Harrison's WPA activities began to pour into Bilbo's office. "I think something's wrong with Pat," a friend from Ripley wrote. "When he was here I sensed an attitude rather of disdain, as if he could give you only what he wanted." The friend suggested it was time to look for someone else to back in 1936.[5]

In light of the long-standing bitterness between Conner and Bilbo, it seemed logical that the senator would look for another horse to back. For a time it appeared that Toxey Hall of Columbia might get into the Senate race. Hall had been a district attorney in south Mississippi for almost a quarter of a century and, except for Bilbo, had been White's most effective platform speaker in the 1935 campaign. Despite a great deal of pressure, however, Hall refused to be coaxed into the race. Bilbo never seemed enthusiastic about Hall or any other possible third candidate, probably because no one else could mount a realistic challenge to Harrison. Moreover, after Johnson's defeat in 1935, the Harrison-White faction replaced the Conner machine as the major threat to dominate state politics. Since Mississippi's factionalism placed a premium on balancing the opposing political powers, by February Bilbo was making overtures to Conner through A. D. Russell, a Magee newspaper publisher. Russell conveyed Bilbo's invitation to confer in Washington as soon as the Holmes matter was dispatched, and returned with news that Conner was eager for an arrangement with the Bilbo forces. The eventual face-to-face meeting occurred in mid-April in Jackson rather than Washington. Bilbo, who usually headquartered at the Royal Hotel when he was in Mississippi, left his suite at 4 P.M., and during the next six hours, the two former governors temporarily buried a decade of political enmity.[6]

---

with Heber Ladner, MOHP, Vol. XXX, 36–37; Bilbo to Forrest Jackson, March 16, 1936, in Bilbo Papers.

5. Orbrey Street to Bilbo, December 5, 1935, in Bilbo Papers.

6. Memphis *Commercial Appeal*, January 19, 1936, Sec. 4, p. 5; Bilbo to George

The new alliance left Bilbo's followers in a quandary. In less than a year their man had circled back on himself twice. He had begged, badgered, and bullied them into harness for their old enemy White, largely out of fear of a Conner-backed Paul Johnson governorship. Now he was driving them right back over the field they had just planted. Much like those countless mules that the 1933 cotton plow-up had sent tromping down the forbidden rows, Bilbo's people were bewildered at being ordered to do what they had been taught was unthinkable, to support Mike Conner. Harrison was no friend, one wrote, but Conner was "a mighty bitter pill to swallow." Another summarized their dilemma well: "First. We have no love for Pat Harrison. Second. We don't want to vote for Mike Conner. Third. We don't want to take a walk." A third even appealed to Harrison to reconcile with Bilbo. Bilbo "is the most powerful man in Mississippi," he warned. "He is a real vote getter, for he knows every 'pig trail' in the state and half the people by their first name."[7]

But there would be no reconciliation. Bilbo was intent on attacking Harrison, and Conner was the only weapon available. He was determined to strike a straight blow with what many of his supporters considered an awfully crooked stick. He had gone so far in his earlier support of Harrison as to provide him with a list of Bilbo's own precinct campaign managers—six thousand names!—from the 1934 race. Send it back, Bilbo now demanded, "and don't keep a copy."[8]

A master at the factional game, Bilbo set about neutralizing the key personalities whose endorsements might carry large blocs into the opposing camp. Harrison was already hard at work. Pat had secured Dennis Murphree an appointment to the National Emergency Council and Lester Franklin a place on the legal staff of the Federal Trade Commission. He named as his campaign manager Norfleet Sledge, a close friend of Lieutenant Governor J. B. "Billy" Snider, who controlled several northern Mississippi newspapers. The only big guns left were White and Johnson, and Bilbo went to work on both. He wrote White in late January, voicing his grievances against Harrison. He hinted that Harrison's role in his old friend's 1935 campaign had been equivocal at best and begged White not to endorse Harrison until Bilbo could explain to him "the whole picture." White agreed to hear Bilbo out before making any statement, but The Man must have known he was

Mitchell, April 19, 1936, A. D. Russell to Bilbo, February 17, 1936, Bilbo to Dr. Harvey Garrison, April 19, 1936, all in Bilbo Papers.

7. Mitchell to Bilbo, April 3, 1936, T. I. Halbert to Bilbo, April 9, 1936, R. R. Baird to Harrison (copy), February 27, 1936, all in Bilbo Papers.

8. Bilbo to Harrison, February 24, 1936, in Bilbo Papers.

unlikely to drive a wedge between Harrison and the governor. Indeed, White eventually endorsed Harrison and often accompanied him on the speaker's platform as he stumped the state.[9]

Overtures to Johnson proved more successful. Bilbo knew that he would have little leverage with a man to whom he had just denied the governorship, but Conner himself had fought hard for Johnson in 1935. More important, Johnson was irate at Harrison's failure to stop Bilbo from using the WPA against him in the earlier campaign. From Bilbo he expected as much, he wrote to a friend, but he had been "Pat's friend for 25 years" and had counted on his old friend's assurance of support. Yet he "would not open his mouth" in protest of the tactics Bilbo employed. In fact, during 1935 "Harrison and Bilbo were as close as the Siamese twins." While Harrison was in Mississippi, Johnson had begged for a conference in Gulfport, but the senator had refused even to see him.[10]

At Bilbo's urging, Conner sent Kenneth Toler, a reporter for the Memphis *Commercial Appeal*, to Hattiesburg to get an exclusive interview with Johnson, including the expected endorsement. Johnson apparently committed himself to Conner but chose to delay any public announcement. It did not come until July, when Johnson appeared at a rally in Ellisville to declare himself "red hot for Conner." Bilbo hoped that Johnson's support would pay at least two extra dividends: first, an endorsement by the Jackson *Daily Clarion Ledger*, which had backed Johnson in 1935, and second, attacks by Harrison that would alienate Johnson's friends. Neither came. T. M. and R. M. Hederman and their newspaper endorsed Harrison, and Pat was astute enough to order his people to "lay off" Johnson.[11]

As with White in 1935, Bilbo foreswore any designs on running Conner's campaign. He would be "fresh and wide open" with suggestions but urged Conner to reject whatever advice did not suit him. It would be Conner's campaign, Bilbo insisted. "I am just going to be a good soldier." It is difficult to determine how sincere The Man was about Conner's rejecting, but there is ample evidence that he meant what he said about his own suggesting. No one knew the quirks of the electoral mind or the contours of factional politics better than Bilbo.

9. Memphis *Commercial Appeal*, February 23, 1936, Sec. 4, p. 4; Hattiesburg *American*, July 22, 1939, p. 3; Mitchell to Bilbo, March 11, 1936, Bilbo to White, January 28, 1936, Bilbo to White, April 19, 1936, all in Bilbo Papers.

10. Paul Johnson to W. W. Whitaker, May 15, 1936, in Kenneth Toler Papers, Mitchell Library, Mississippi State University, Starkville.

11. Bilbo to Conner, April 14, 1936, in Bilbo Papers; Jackson *Daily Clarion Ledger*, July 17, 1936, p. 1; Swain, *Pat Harrison*, 135.

He knew that the motives of Mississippi voters were varied and often petty and that it was easier and more fruitful in the long run to avoid making enemies than to try to make friends. He suggested that Conner set up a second-floor headquarters on Capitol Street in Jackson—"in the center of the 'drag'"—and staff it with innocuous underlings who would raise no one's factional hackles. He sent Conner a list of precinct leaders and recommended a young Pearl River County protégé, Heber Ladner, whom Conner made statewide manager. Most of all, as he had done with the previous campaign, Bilbo preached the doctrine of organization. It was a presidential election year, and control of the county Democratic conventions was essential. Those delegates would name the county executive committees, which would then choose election managers. Controlling them was often "half the battle," Bilbo declared in something of an understatement. The first step in the delegate process was the key, and he urged Conner to organize his friends quietly but effectively and to flood the precinct meetings with them. The outcome of the conventions would decide the election, he warned, so "do not let any of your friends sleep until this part of the fight is finished."[12]

Newsweek called it "the most raucous, name-calling, hair pulling campaign in recent Mississippi history." That, of course, hinged on how one defined *recent*. Actually the campaign was rather tame until Bilbo took the stump in July, much to the dismay of Harrison's backers. It had been twelve years since Pat had faced opposition, and his staff had apparently become inured to the urbanity of the capital and the decorum of the legislative ritual. It was irksome to have to descend into the political pit and combat "Bilbo with his showmanship and political lies which the ruralities swallow like a bass swallows a fly." Friends grudgingly advised Harrison to cast aside dignity and grieved, as one aide put it, that their man would have "to start skinning a skunk" to survive in Mississippi, where "the voters are interested in little things and they overlook the chance of Commonwealth betterment to give way to petty prejudices." But Bilbo was a master of "little things" and veritably reveled in prejudice, grand or petty. As he once reminded a Yankee reporter, in Mississippi issues were scarce and voter interest in them downright rare. On the other hand, Bilbo himself was a living testimony to the popular appeal of personality. A candidate need not bother himself with what an opponent was for or against, Bilbo ex-

12. Bilbo to Conner, April 14, 1936, Bilbo to Conner, April 22, 1936, both in Bilbo Papers.

plained. "You just show he's a low down blankety blank." And The Man could blankety-blank with the best of them.[13]

As he had done the previous year, Bilbo took the stump in a race in which he was not running, upstaged the legitimate candidates, made himself the star attraction, and turned a dull show into a blockbuster. When Harrison dredged up some of Bilbo's earlier criticism of Conner, Bilbo responded that Mike had been his baby all along. Thereafter, Pat referred to Conner as "Mother Bilbo's Tootsie Wootsie." Bilbo went after the veteran vote by attacking Harrison's early opposition to the bonus legislation. In 1935 Wright Patman of Texas had introduced a bill requiring immediate payment of the full bonus that World War veterans were due to receive in 1945. When Roosevelt declared the inflationary measure unacceptable, Harrison introduced a compromise prepared by several Senate Democrats who faced reelection in 1936. The Senate rejected it and passed the original bill, which Roosevelt promptly vetoed. Harrison was one of the forty senators who voted to sustain that veto. Pat had contributed nothing to the passage of the bonus, said Bilbo, and anyone who thought he had was a "plain, ordinary, copper-lined, copper-lidded, copper-headed, consummate damn fool." The bonus would have passed, he scoffed, if Harrison had been in the jungle frolicking with monkeys and coconuts instead of in Washington. But it had in fact been Harrison who in 1936 introduced the watered-down Patman bill, which was again passed and vetoed. This time, however, Harrison voted to override the president. "Political expediency," said Martha Swain, "led him to line the pockets of the Mississippi veterans before he asked for their vote." His discretion paid off handsomely in endorsements by the principal veterans groups in 1936.[14]

On the Gulf Coast, Bilbo revived the charges of Harrison's role in the financial demise of the Gulfport banks. The Man's friend Bidwell Adam began referring to Harrison as "Promissory Pat." During a speech at Bay St. Louis, Bilbo accused Harrison of trying to buy reelection with patronage. "I want to talk to you Harrison men," he said, and warned that it would be unwise for them to put all their eggs in

13. "Primary: Pat Overwhelms Mike as Mud Flies over Mississippi," *Newsweek*, September 5, 1936, pp. 9–10; Paul J. Miller to Edwin Halsey, July 25, 1936, in Edwin Halsey Papers, Senate Historical Office, Washington, D.C.; Swain, *Pat Harrison*, 136–37; Jerome Beatty, "Mississippi Pearl," *American Magazine*, February, 1935, p. 95.

14. Swain, *Pat Harrison*, 99–103; Herring, "First Session of 74th Congress," 994–95; O. R. Aultman, "Second Session of the 74th Congress," *American Political Science Review*, XXX (1936), 1102; Jackson *Daily Clarion Ledger*, August 19, 1936, p. 7.

Pat's basket. "Where is 'Red' Favre?" he shouted, referring to the chancery clerk of Hancock County. "I'd like for him to hear this." Apparently Favre had heard enough already from Bilbo's sound truck, which was blaring outside the windows of his first-floor courthouse office. The rotund Harrison stalwart rose from his desk and rumbled up the steps to the second-floor speaker's stand in the nearest approximation to an infantry assault a man of his bulk could mount. "Here I am," he shouted, as he swung at the startled speaker. Bilbo nimbly ducked only to slam his forehead into the microphone. Undaunted, he recovered and counterpunched. Before either warrior could strike a solid blow, several men dragged away the struggling Favre, who shouted, "You can't talk to our Harrison men that way!" The flash in Bilbo's blue eyes gave way to a twinkle as he chided, "I'm sorry our friend can't take a little kidding." With his collar open and his tie askew, he plunged ahead with the speech. But Favre had the last word—or at least deprived Bilbo of it. Before retreating to his office, he pulled the plug on Bilbo's sound truck, to the disappointment of the crowd lounging outside on the courthouse lawn.[15]

Throughout the summer Bilbo continued to complain about Harrison's use of WPA patronage. Harrison had pressured Hopkins to "investigate" charges of political activity in the Mississippi WPA in early 1936. The result was a shakeup that sifted a great many Bilbo people out of the agency and shifted power from the district directors to the state office, which was now under the control of Harrison's WPA watchdog, Assistant Director Roland Wall. Throughout May and June, Wall tried to bypass the regional WPA office to secure increases in personnel and projects, usually without success. In early July there was a meeting of district and state officers in Jackson to discuss the problem. Whatever agreement Harrison had reached with Hopkins in Washington must have become lost in the bowels of bureaucracy, because the regional office was represented at the meeting by Charles Braun, a former Conner appointee to the Mississippi ERA. He rejected the proposed increases out of hand. A flustered Harrison dashed off a complaint to Hopkins with the ominous warning that unless something were done, he would find it "impossible . . . to defend WPA." That bit of political intimidation was good for an immediate two-million-dollar allocation from discretionary funds under Hopkins' control.[16]

15. Jackson *Daily Clarion Ledger*, August 19, 1936, p. 7; New York *Times*, August 18, 1936, p. 7; Biloxi *Daily Herald*, August 18, 1936, pp. 1, 5; Bay St. Louis *Sea Coast Echo*, August 21, 1936, p. 1.

16. Catherine Blanton to Harrison, July 6, 1936, Harrison to Blanton, July 6, 1936,

On the eve of the primary, Wall secured a 450-man increase in the Tupelo district, which was considered the crucial battleground between Conner and Harrison. F. M. McLaury, the field-agent-in-charge for the WPA Division of Investigation, frankly reported that the personnel increase was purely a political move to neutralize the Bilbo-Conner strength in that area. It was approved anyway. Meanwhile, Ellen Woodward, the national director of the WPA Women's Work Division, was monitoring the progress of her old friend Harrison's campaign, discussing campaign strategy with the state director and initiating investigations of Bilbo's friends in the agency.[17]

As the campaign hit its stride, things began to look bleak for Conner. Harrison added endorsements by prominent labor and farm organizations to those already secured from the Veterans of Foreign Wars and Disabled American Veterans. President William Green of the AF of L worked actively for the incumbent, winning the support of most Mississippi railway unions and a unanimous endorsement by the executive board of the Mississippi Federation of Labor. Edward O'Neal of the American Farm Bureau Federation and Mississippi Commissioner of Agriculture J. C. Holton marshaled their forces in Harrison's behalf. Harrison's staff even found a crowd-rouser who could hold his own with Bilbo, The Man's former law partner Stewart C. "Sweep Clean" Broom. Broom, who styled himself a "professor" of Bilbo politics and still a true believer, wooed The Man's followers with claims that he was saving Bilbo from himself. Conner had never been a friend and was not now, said Broom. When Mike finished leeching Bilbo in the present campaign, he would turn around and oppose him in 1940 "as sure as there's a hound dog in Georgia." Washington life had addled The Man's mind. He had swapped the head-clearing sardines and crackers for caviar and hotel dining. "Cav-eh-ah," Broom bellowed, "it ain't a thing in the world but Russian catfish eggs, and it upset him and disordered him," spawning "tantrums," an affliction common to "actors, actresses, politicians, and babies," and similar to "running fits" in dogs. The only remedy, Broom declared, was "a first

---

Harrison to Hopkins, July 8, 1936, all in Pat Harrison Papers, Williams Library, University of Mississippi, Oxford.

17. F. M. McLaury to Roger J. Bounds, August 19, 1936, in Work Projects Administration Papers, Division of Investigation, Miscellaneous State File, Mississippi, Record Group 69, Records of the Work Projects Administration, National Archives; M. J. Miller to Alan Johnstone, May 17, 1936, Miller to Roland Wall, May 17, 1936, both in WPA Papers, Central Files, General Subject Series, Section 131.3, WPA Records; transcript of telephone conversation between Ellen Woodward and Wayne Alliston, August 13, 1936, in Ellen Woodward Papers, Mississippi Department of Archives and History, Jackson.

class political spanking." He then evoked guffaws and squeals of delight as he wheeled a doll buggy around the platform to the strains of "Yessir, That's My Baby."[18]

Broom's motives were less pristine than they appeared. When the Holmes nomination had been first rumored, Broom had petitioned his former law partner for Holmes's district judgeship with political logic matched only by Bilbo's own. He had not supported Bilbo just to share the spoils of victory but because he thought it was right and in the nation's best interest, Broom explained. He would "be controlled by the same high motives in the future, but . . . it will be a derned sight easier to believe you are the greatest statesman in Mississippi if I get this appointment." By January, 1936, when it was obvious that Bilbo could not accommodate him, Broom wrote that he would settle for the clerkship of the district court but warned that "somebody is going to get gored . . . if this isn't attended to." At the same time, he was advising Bilbo to join with Conner in the Senate race because Harrison could never win. Between January and June both his high motives and his political analysis got severely modified. But all this was unknown to the voters and in no way diminished the impact of Broom's platform antics.[19]

Harrison was not without his own crowd-pleasing theatrics. In several speeches he read "with great emotion" excerpts from Bilbo's 1933 letter thanking Harrison for finding him the AAA position. Bilbo had chosen a strange way of expressing gratitude, Harrison said. Then solemnly placing his hand over his heart, he declared: "I hate no man. Hate destroys the heart that harbors it. But I must confess to you that I hold a man in utter contempt who has treated me this way."[20]

More worrisome to Bilbo than all the dramatics were reports of Conner's lack of organization. Harrison controlled even the party convention in Bilbo's home county of Pearl River. The situation was similar in Lamar, Hancock, and Lauderdale counties. Bilbo's son-in-law, Lamar Smith, reported that "active" Conner men were hard to find, while wherever he went even the Conner supporters could identify Harrison's managers. Three-fourths of Bilbo's own leaders in south Mississippi were actively campaigning for Harrison, and there was no evidence that things were better elsewhere. Harrison clubs were abun-

18. J. Wayne Flynt, "A Vignette of Southern Labor Politics—The 1936 Mississippi Senatorial Primary," *Mississippi Quarterly*, XXVI (1972–73), 89–97; Swain, *Pat Harrison*, 138–40; "Broom or Bilbo," *Time*, August 24, 1936, pp. 22–23.

19. Stewart C. Broom to Bilbo, July 2, 1935, Broom to Bilbo, January 6, 1936, Broom to Bilbo, January 25, 1936, all in Bilbo Papers.

20. Buckley interview, 17–20.

dant, whereas similar groups for Conner were nonexistent. When the state convention met in mid-June, it was owned by Pat Harrison.[21]

Then the incumbent inadvertently handed Bilbo and Conner a ready-made issue. Soon after Norfleet Sledge became campaign manager, Harrison got him placed on the federal payroll as advisor for the majority on the Senate Finance Committee. With a good deal of help from correspondent Hilton Butler and publisher James Hammond of the Memphis *Commercial Appeal*, Bilbo milked that mistake for all it was worth. Hammond suggested getting photocopies of warrants issued to Sledge, and Bilbo sent Butler to Washington with a request to Henry Morgenthau for the copies. Bilbo from the stump and Butler from the editorial page etched in voters' minds the image of Sledge drawing an annual salary of three thousand dollars for supplying Democrats on the Finance Committee with "expert advice," doubtlessly delivered long-distance from Mississippi where he was busily managing the chairman's campaign. The picture was not lost on the depression-ridden poor of Mississippi. The *Appeal* endorsed neither candidate but engaged in a running dispute with Harrison over journalistic ethics that drew attention to the issue and did the senior senator's cause no good.[22]

Harrison explained that using congressional staff as election workers was standard procedure and offered supporting statements from Majority Leader Robinson and Senate Financial Clerk Charles F. Pace. And if there was to be quibbling about federally salaried campaign staff, he added, Sledge's pittance paled in comparison to the ten thousand dollars drawn annually by Conner's number one operative, Bilbo. Despite the obvious validity of Harrison's defense, the move was a substantial blunder that set back a campaign that was almost home free.[23]

The fundamental issue in the race, however, was who would more effectively support the New Deal, and with Roosevelt's reelection campaign helping to nudge other issues into the background, Harrison held a decided advantage. His true relationship to the New Deal had been somewhat ambivalent. Much of the legislation of the preceding four years had grated on his conservative sensibilities, but he had been a loyal supporter of the administration and had played a major role in securing what did pass, especially social security and the revenue acts.

21. Lamar Smith to Bilbo, May 20, 1936, Smith to Bilbo, June 6, 1936, Heber Ladner to Bilbo, June 14, 1936, all in Bilbo Papers.

22. Memphis *Commercial Appeal*, August 15, 1936, p. 4, August 20, 1936, p. 6; Hilton Butler to Bilbo, August 8, 1936, Bilbo to Butler, August 9, 1936, Bilbo to Henry Morgenthau, Jr., August 9, 1936, all in Bilbo Papers.

23. Swain, *Pat Harrison*, 138–39.

His realistic compromises saved countless bills from certain death, according to some commentators; others charged him with sabotaging the New Deal through legislative dilution. The only opinion that mattered in 1936 was the president's, and he said little about Harrison in the early months of the year. Bilbo knew that Roosevelt's intervention on Harrison's behalf would be Conner's death knell, so he did all he could to prevent it. Apparently he secured something of an assurance of public neutrality before he left the capital. At least, that is what he implied in his speeches in Mississippi. "The President has positively assured me," Bilbo declared on the eve of the state Democratic convention, "that he will not take any part in the Mississippi Senatorial race this summer."[24]

Roosevelt's silence frustrated Harrison's staff, but finally in June the president spoke out. While in Arkansas he told a group of Mississippi editors that Harrison was "one of the most valuable assets of the nation and the Democratic Party." The following month, when Mississippi Congressman Aubert Dunn told an audience that Roosevelt wanted Harrison reelected, Bilbo reminded Roosevelt of his neutrality pledge. He also reminded James Farley of the president's promise and warned him not to let his personal affection for Harrison lead him to interfere in a primary of a state that was 100 percent for Roosevelt. Both candidates were good Democrats and should be allowed to fight it out without outside interference. When Dunn asked the White House for a statement to verify his own assertion of the administration's preference for Harrison, he was politely refused. But Roosevelt had decided that he needed Harrison, and if he could not help him openly, he would do so indirectly.[25]

Two weeks before the primary Roosevelt ordered Secretary of the Treasury Henry Morgenthau to request a meeting between the president, Harrison, and House Ways and Means Committee Chairman Robert Doughton to discuss important tax revision. Roosevelt then issued a highly publicized "urgent" call for Harrison to come to Washington for an important White House conference. Bilbo noted that the same tactic had been used in Hubert Stephens' cause in 1934, but that hardly dimmed the halo of importance cast by the exploding flashbulbs at Jackson Airport, where Harrison boarded a Chicago and Southern airliner for Washington. The cameras captured the loyal New Dealer abandoning his own reelection campaign to rush to the presi-

24. *Ibid.*, 103–104; Bilbo to Charles Snow, June 9, 1936, in Bilbo Papers.

25. Swain, *Pat Harrison*, 141–42; Bilbo to James Farley (copy), July 27, 1936, James Farley to Emil Hurja, August 17, 1936, both in Container 186 (Papers of Emil Hurja, Campaign Reports, 1936), James Farley Papers, Library of Congress.

dent's rescue. Nothing Bilbo did could erase the image of indispensability that dotted Mississippi newspapers the next day.[26]

To enhance the picture, Harrison sought to project himself as being no less vital to the Democratic party's politics than to the administration's finances. He asked Mississippi National Committeeman Louis Jiggitts to wire Farley concerning Harrison's role in the national campaign and then personally drafted a response to the telegram and sent it to Farley by way of Senate secretary Edwin Halsey. It modestly read: "No man in the Senate stands higher than Pat Harrison. As a Democrat he is loved throughout the Nation. We have received, and will receive as many requests for him to speak in the different parts of the country as any other leading Democrat. His influence grows, and we are anxious for his contest in Mississippi to be finished in order that he can go as soon as possible throughout the country making speeches for the reelection of our ticket. No Democratic leader is held in higher esteem and affection by President Roosevelt."[27]

Bilbo tried hard to portray Conner as a better New Dealer than Harrison. He harped on Harrison's basic conservatism, his connection with the likes of Bernard Baruch, and his equivocation on TVA. Bilbo urged his candidate to toot the New Deal horn while The Man sang Conner's praises to Roosevelt. "You will not regret the election of Governor Conner," he assured the president. "He is young, aggressive, and progressive, [and] . . . he will make a good Administration Senator." But nothing Bilbo said about Conner in 1936 could unsay what he had said in earlier years. Bilbo's own reference to Conner's association with Huey Long and opposition to the New Deal haunted him from Harrison ads in newspapers all over Mississippi.[28]

Most observers thought it would be an extremely close vote, but Harrison need not have worried. He swept eighty of eighty-two counties and outpolled Conner by more than sixty thousand votes. It was a landslide. Most analyses attributed the victory to Harrison's ability to identify himself with the New Deal and to reap credit for the avalanche of federal money that had cascaded over Mississippi since 1933. Other factors played their part. Pat controlled federal patronage and had access to campaign funds Conner could not hope to match. On the

26. Henry Morgenthau Diary, Book 29, pp. 147–48, 162, 186, Franklin D. Roosevelt Library, Hyde Park; John Morton Blum, *From the Morgenthau Diaries: Years of Crisis, 1928–1938* (Boston, 1959), 319–20.

27. Harrison to Halsey, August 6, 1936, Louis Jiggitts to Farley (copy), n.d., Joseph Guffey to Farley (copy), n.d., all in Halsey Papers.

28. Swain, *Pat Harrison*, 135, 281; Harrison to Halsey, July 15, 1936, in Halsey Papers; Bilbo to Roosevelt, July 27, 1936, in Bilbo Papers.

eve of the primary, George Mitchell informed Bilbo and Ladner, who spent the night at his Tupelo home planning a full slate of speeches for the following day, that they might just as well quit campaigning. "It's all over, you can forget it," he said, "the moneychangers have arrived." It is impossible to determine how much Harrison spent, but more than one commentator noted that Bernard Baruch "contributed heavily" to the campaign chest to keep one of the politicians from his "Old Masters" collection in power.[29]

Conner's deficiencies were probably as important as Harrison's attributes. Bilbo, while unable to deliver many of his own followers, no doubt caused numerous defections among Conner's traditional backers. It had been an unholy alliance from the start. Also, there was the sales tax that Conner had rammed through the state legislature during his governorship and that still rankled consumers and merchants alike. There was the animosity of the powerful highway commission with whom Conner had feuded for so long. Perhaps most important, and almost unmentioned, was the low voter turnout, fewer than 200,000 compared with more than 350,000 in 1935. It was not so much that Bilbo could not deliver his votes to another candidate, even an unpopular one. He had done that the previous year. But he could only deliver them if they turned out to vote, and without local elections it was difficult to lure his largely rural constituency from their labors to the polls. It was Harrison's people, the literate middle classes of the towns and cities, who usually dominated federal elections in Mississippi. Moreover, a new stringent Corrupt Practices Act disfranchised innumerable voters who had heretofore been qualified. The largest decreases, which approached 50 percent in some counties, resulted from changes in poll-tax procedures. No longer could sheriffs allow tardy taxpayers to pay on election day and backdate the receipts to the February 1 deadline. The receipt book now had to be turned over to the circuit court by March 15, and voters were required to bring to the polls a valid receipt or duplicate to receive a ballot. Again, those most affected tended to be Bilbo people.[30]

29. Heber Ladner, personal interview with the author, August 26, 1983; Swain, *Pat Harrison*, 143–44; Harold Ickes, *The Inside Struggle, 1936–1939* (New York, 1954), 164. Vol. II of *The Secret Diary of Harold Ickes*, 3 vols.; Jordan A. Schwarz, *The Speculator: Bernard M. Baruch in Washington, 1917–1965* (Chapel Hill, 1981), 184–87, 257.

30. Swain, *Pat Harrison*, 143; New York *Times*, August 25, 1936, p. 10. In the counties that Bilbo carried in the 1934 runoff against Stephens, the total vote decreased by 3,171. In the counties that Stephens carried, there was a net increase of 3,398 votes. *Mississippi Blue Book, 1935–1937*, pp. 173, 142.

The outcome of the primary had grave consequences for Bilbo. Some believed the disaster would make it much more difficult for him to win votes for himself in the future and impossible for him to win them for someone else. Such hopes were doomed to frustration. In 1939 Bilbo would help win the governor's office for the very man to whom he had denied it four years earlier, Paul Johnson. In 1940 he would gain easy reelection himself over the very man whom he had made governor in 1935, Hugh White.

The real damage to Bilbo came in Washington. Harrison's anger and contempt for Bilbo became boundless, and he used his enormous prestige to thwart The Man at every turn and make him an object of scorn among fellow senators. More costly at the moment was Harrison's influence with the administration. He was determined to squeeze Bilbo out of the patronage picture, and so long as the administration needed Pat's power and prowess in the congressional wars, he was likely to have his way. Not until Harrison soured on the New Deal and openly defied Roosevelt on major issues would Bilbo have much hope of breaking Pat's monopoly of federal jobs. The largest prize was the WPA, and even before the primary ended, Harrison was at work purging the agency of Bilboism.

Chapter Seven

Politics and Human Misery

Ironically the WPA was at first a political bonanza for Bilbo. After all, when the agency was established in 1935, he and Harrison were allied against Conner, and Pat's only interest in relief patronage was to prevent its use against his own interests. Federal patronage traditionally had not been very important in Mississippi politics anyway, though widespread unemployment and the New Deal's proliferating alphabet agencies were changing that dramatically. But before the split with Bilbo in 1936, Pat could afford to be generous with federal jobs, and he gave his colleague relatively free rein over WPA.

By the time Bilbo took office, the fires of expectation were raging among his supporters, and he was already feeling the heat. Many anticipated a wholesale slaughter of Stephens appointees with easy pickings after the carnage, and each day without news of a massacre deepened their dismay. Despite his defeat Stephens had been able to place his secretary and campaign manager, George Neville, in a six-thousand-dollar-a-year post and numerous other friends in lesser positions. Stephens even secured an appointment for himself on the board of the Reconstruction Finance Corporation (RFC) early in 1935.[1]

During the 1934 campaign Bilbo had assured the voters that if they would relieve the incumbent of his senatorial burdens, he would be delighted to help the administration find Stephens a less trying federal position elsewhere. Now Bilbo was on the spot. His challenge would surely have torpedoed the RFC appointment, but true to his word he endorsed his old enemy. Many of the faithful were irate. Fulfilling campaign promises is one thing, wrote George Mitchell, "but I do not think it is necessary for you to act a fool." Bilbo defended his decision as judicious humanitarianism. It would get Stephens out of Mississippi and perhaps facilitate loans to Mississippi borrowers. Besides, Bilbo

1. Memphis *Commercial Appeal*, February 24, 1935, Sec. 5, p. 4.

argued, "He's old, sick, crippled, and probably broke—he ought to be after all he spent to beat me last summer. . . . I see no harm in being gracious."[2]

But disaffection in the ranks was troublesome. After three years without the benefits of public office—three depression years—Bilbo loyalists were eager for jobs, and many of them believed that Harrison was deliberately denying them the spoils of victory. A group of them petitioned Bilbo to submit his colleague an ultimatum: loosen the patronage reins or face opposition from the Bilbo people in 1936. There is no question that Bilbo himself fully intended to align his forces for Pat in 1936, but the troops were certainly restive. He argued that Harrison was one of the strongest men in the capital and could do more for the state in a brief congressional session than others had done in a lifetime. "I am going to support Pat with all there is in me," he told a Warren County follower, "even after I know that he did everything he could for Stephens last summer. . . . Mississippi needs Pat in Washington and he has just now got to the place where he can render a great service."[3]

Bilbo did, however, use the dissatisfaction to pry some jobs from Harrison's grip. There is a "general uprising" in the Bilbo camp, he told his colleague, and lining them up in 1936—"which I am very anxious to do"—could be difficult if they were to spend 1935 outside the fence watching Stephens' friends feeding at the public trough. "To be perfectly frank," he concluded, "my friends ought to have at least half of the federal jobs now available in Mississippi. As it is they have practically nothing."[4]

Pat refused to allow the axing of any appointments that he and Stephens had already made, but he agreed to give Bilbo's recommendations for new jobs priority until there was "an equitable distribution" of patronage. The pending Emergency Relief Appropriations Act (ERAA) promised equity with a vengeance, and soon. In late 1934 the administration had reassessed its relief program and decided to concentrate federal efforts in a central works agency, initially funded at $1.5 billion and aimed at reducing the relief rolls by hiring employables for works projects.[5]

2. Bascom N. Timmons, *Jessie H. Jones: The Man and the Statesman* (New York, 1956), 267–68; George Mitchell to Bilbo, January 26, 1935, Bilbo to Clyde Willoughby, March 16, 1935, both in Bilbo Papers.

3. Memphis *Commercial Appeal*, February 24, 1935, Sec. 5, p. 4; Bilbo to G. C. Bryan, March 7, 1935, Bilbo to Dr. Willis Walley, May 6, 1935, both in Bilbo Papers.

4. Bilbo to Harrison, February 8, 1935, in Bilbo Papers.

5. Statement issued by Senator Pat Harrison, June 30, 1935, in Harrison Papers, University of Mississippi.

What began as a quest to grab the FERA reins from Conner became an effort to control a huge new relief organization in Mississippi. As early as January, 1935, Bilbo urged Hopkins to investigate complaints of political mischief in Mississippi. Above all, he warned, the FERA needed a thorough cleaning out, because as matters stood it was controlled from top to bottom by Conner, who was not friendly to Roosevelt or Harrison. Harrison was by no means oblivious to the governor's plans. As early as July, 1933, Pat's friend Phil Stone of Oxford had complained to Louis Howe and Jim Farley that administration appointments "over the protest of Senator Harrison" were helping Conner "build up a political machine to run against" Pat in 1936. Conner's failure to secure the highway patronage solidified his resolve to maintain control of federal relief jobs, but Congress shattered those hopes when it required Senate confirmation for any position paying five thousand dollars or more. Apparently Mississippians were not the only Democrats in Congress who were tired of voting huge expenditures only to see rival factions back home reap much of the political benefit. From now on senators would control federal relief patronage, and since Pat had offered his new colleague equity, the ERAA promised to be a Bilbo windfall. By April, Mississippi courthouse gossip buzzed about the impending "Bilbo shakeup" in the relief organization. As talk of the junior senator's growing influence continued, "the crop of Bilbo folks . . . increased wonderfully."[6]

Conner had endured the mounting gossip with a bewildered silence, but in mid-April he fired off a lengthy public letter to Hopkins. Its petulant defense of the record of the Mississippi ERA hardly veiled Conner's seething but impotent resentment at having the patronage rug so unceremoniously jerked from under him. ERA had been "conducted entirely free of political consideration," he insisted, and "no reputable citizen who has made the slightest effort to inform himself will make a contrary assertation." The disreputable and uninformed were apparently legion. If there was to be a change, Conner complained peevishly, it would be "a matter of common courtesy" to inform the chief executive. He received no official response from Hopkins, but the answer came on the night of May 11 when Wayne Alliston, Bilbo's handpicked man, was announced as the new WPA administrator for Mississippi.[7]

6. Bilbo to Hopkins, January 29, 1935, Bilbo to Roosevelt, February 21, 1935, both in Bilbo Papers; Phil Stone to Howe, July 21, 1933, OF 400, in Roosevelt Papers; James T. Patterson, *The New Deal and the States*, 57–60; H. L. Simmons to Bilbo, April 21, 1935, in Bilbo Papers.

7. Conner to Hopkins, April 15, 1935, in Federal Emergency Relief Administration

The new state relief czar returned from Washington accompanied by John Burkett, Bilbo's 1934 campaign manager. Burkett, who was to be a top assistant in the new agency, was soon besieged by job seekers. He had already sent Bilbo a list from which to choose those to be consulted about various appointments. The senator was aware that many of his supporters were cool toward White and instructed Burkett to review each county situation with key campaign people before any commitments were made and to make sure WPA would not be used for any of the other gubernatorial candidates.[8]

In late May, Burkett sent Bilbo twelve names as possible directors for the six WPA districts. Bilbo marked out two names and returned the list with comments that clearly reflected his concern for the political impact of the appointments. He seemed as interested in their effect in 1936 as in the ongoing governor's race. With state patronage at stake in the 1935 election, some observers viewed White's election as the key to Harrison's race the following year. Moreover, behind Johnson and Conner stood Huey Long, whose Share Our Wealth chapters were becoming as ubiquitous among the rednecks as the kudzu that was beginning to overrun their red clay hills. It looked as though Pat might have his hands full in 1936.[9]

One name on Burkett's list, Roland Wall of Brookhaven, was clearly there primarily for the senior senator's benefit. Wall had never been an ardent Bilboite, and his major asset in Bilbo's mind was his influence with Mississippi veterans, whom Harrison had sorely antagonized with his opposition to bonus legislation. A few weeks later Drew Wall, a Bilbo supporter from southwest Mississippi, cautioned his chief that the appointment of Roland Wall would be a mistake. "We understand," he wrote, "that this Mr. Wall was not for you [in 1934]. He is the only Wall we know who was not for you. He is not related to us." Within a year Bilbo would desperately wish he had heeded that warning.[10]

About the same time, another portentous assessment, this one concerning Alliston, appeared in the Jackson press. Fred Sullens wondered in his *Daily News* column "how Wayne Alliston, one of the most genial and lovable of men, is going to fire 'em and still keep that broad smile on his face." Others wondered, too, especially longtime Bilbo supporters whose employment future in large measure hinged on the

---

Papers, Central Files, State Series, Mississippi, Section 400, WPA Records; Jackson *Daily News*, May 12, 1935, p. 1.

8. Burkett to Bilbo, April 20, 1935, Bilbo to Burkett, May 17, 1935, both in Bilbo Papers.

9. Bilbo to Burkett, May 25, 1935, in Bilbo Papers; Moley, *After Seven Years*, 305.

10. Drew Wall to Bilbo, June 20, 1935, in Bilbo Papers.

new director's decisiveness. They were not encouraged when Alliston firmly proclaimed that there would be no politics in the WPA. They were incensed when he announced that his agency would absorb much of the "Connerized" ERA personnel. Nonetheless, while Alliston was vehemently denying that the senators had handpicked his staff, he was assuring Bilbo that all was well. "You can always depend upon me," he vowed. "I am doing everything that I can possibly do to make this set-up just exactly the apple of your eye." However sincere (and in contradiction of his public pronouncements) those promises were, they would not hold up.[11]

At the moment, though, Bilbo appeared to hold the reins. Early in June after a two-week visit to Mississippi, the junior senator returned to Washington accompanied by Alliston. When the director returned to Jackson a week later, he announced the new district heads, all drawn from the Burkett list. Conner fought back as best he could. At a national governors' conference held in June in Biloxi, he led a minor assault on fellow Yale alumnus and former Mississippi relief administrator Aubrey Williams, who addressed the state executives as Hopkins' representative. Conner abruptly interrupted Williams to ask if the WPA was to be a "patronage proposition." Williams, taken quite by surprise, uttered some innocuous platitude about cooperating with state authorities and tried to continue. But Conner doggedly pursued the issue until Williams relented: "No, it is not a political set-up." At that point John Ehringhaus of North Carolina blurted, "Well, it's being made that," and the dogs were loose on Hopkins' dazed aide.[12]

Conner's complaint was apparently well placed. By late June ERA staff, none of whom was allied with either senator, were shifting into the new agency in strategic positions. Whatever their impact on the functioning of relief operations, the news of their appointments spawned a psychological cyclone in the Bilbo camp. As social workers invaded WPA headquarters on the eighteenth floor of the Tower Building in Jackson, the senator's troops saw it as a victorious Conner offensive, and Bilbo found a real storm of protest brewing in his ranks. From all over the state came complaints: that local ERA people were boasting that they would control the new organization and business would continue as usual; that it appeared Bilbo could not get people jobs but that Conner and Johnson could; that all the talk was hurting the White

11. Jackson *Daily News*, May 19, 1935, p. 1, June 22, 1935, p. 1, June 27, 1935, p. 1; Alliston to Bilbo, May 21, 1935, in Bilbo Papers.

12. Jackson *Daily Clarion Ledger*, June 15, 1935, p. 10, June 23, 1935, p. 1, June 14, 1935, p. 1.

campaign; that Pat ought to be able to help and people were blaming him for the mess. Jackson attorney Cecil Travis bluntly summarized the situation. The Bilbo faithful needed jobs desperately, he urged, and while they were willing to support White or anybody else Bilbo chose, his failure to deliver so far was making them vulnerable to the promises of other candidates, especially Johnson. All the talk of a politically neutral WPA and the influx of ERA people were confirming appearances. Surely, Travis concluded, "it is about time for Bilbo to start raising hell in Washington."[13]

It was a familiar crop. Bilbo had raised his share of it during three decades of Mississippi politics. He put his hand to the plow immediately, but Washington was new ground for him and the soil proved resistant. He urged Hopkins not to let "political snipers and schemers" mislead him with wolf cries about Alliston erecting a political machine. The senators would take the responsibility, he promised, if Hopkins would give the state director a free hand in choosing his people.[14]

If Bilbo's Washington hell-raising produced a puny yield, his workers back home were bringing in a bumper crop. Alliston complained in early July that the impatience of Bilbo's followers was making misery. After all, he reminded Bilbo, "Hopkins is running this affair and I am bound to do what he asks done, or get out." Burkett informed Bilbo that the force behind Hopkins' actions was pressure from Conner. The national office, he complained, simply transferred ERA people to WPA without bothering to inform the state administrator. Noting that in at least fourteen states ERA and WPA were headed by the same person, he urged Bilbo to get Alliston named ERA Director in place of Conner's man, Charles Braun. When Bilbo got nowhere with Hopkins, he took it up with the White House. Roosevelt's secretary, Marvin MacIntyre, informed Hopkins that Bilbo had been by to request that "Allison" [*sic*] be made "Mississippi Administrator." The president had agreed to the change if Hopkins did not object, but Hopkins responded obtusely that Alliston *was* WPA administrator. "I don't understand what the Senator has in mind." The incident clearly demonstrated how difficult it was for the White House to keep up with even fairly important activities in its far-flung domain. It also exemplified the kind of bureaucratic legerdemain that Bilbo could never fathom and that plagued his every effort to turn WPA to his own ad-

13. Jackson *Daily News*, June 27, 1935, p. 1; E. G. Nelson to Travis, June 24, 1935, Nelson to Travis, June 29, 1935, Travis to Bilbo, June 26, 1935, Travis to John L. Smith, July 2, 1935, Travis to Smith, June 29, 1935, all in Bilbo Papers.

14. Bilbo to Hopkins, June 28, 1935, in Bilbo Papers.

vantage. For him, maneuvering Washington officialdom was like pushing a chain.[15]

To his enemies, however, Bilbo seemed anything but impotent in patronage matters. As the Johnson campaign sputtered and faltered from the shock of the WPA announcement, the judge accused the White forces of promising jobs in return for votes. It was common talk, Johnson charged, that Bilbo would whip Johnson with the WPA. Many former Johnson backers, even some who had originally petitioned him to run, now scurried for cover as Bilbo boasted of White House support and threatened that only those who backed White could get jobs. The slick little operator had seduced both Harrison and the president, Johnson fumed, and was constructing a potent political machine upon their gullibility. The judge appealed to Pat and to Roosevelt but to no avail; the White House did not even respond until the day after the election. Johnson insisted that he was not accusing the president of manipulating the WPA. Roosevelt, he said, had simply failed to stop Bilbo.[16]

But if White's victory was at all attributable to the WPA, it was from the psychological rather than the real effect of WPA jobs. F. M. McLaury of the agency's Investigation Division minimized the charges made by White's opponents. More significant, Bilbo loyalists continued to complain that many, if not most, jobs were going to anti-Bilbo people. Bilbo put what pressure he could on Alliston, wondering how so many "anti's" were getting in the set-up. He suggested that they not be approved no matter who recommended them. "Hadn't you better quit being so damned agreeable?" he asked Burkett. It was all right to hire "anti's" if no good Bilbo people were available: "Of course, we aren't playing politics but I want my friends taken care of."[17]

After August, 1935, Bilbo's patronage problems got worse rather than better, as Harrison's attitude changed toward Bilbo and the WPA. Heretofore Pat had apparently been somewhat indifferent to the agency's operation so long as it did not become a political machine to

15. Alliston to Bilbo, July 9, 1935, Burkett to Bilbo, July 10, 1935, both in Bilbo Papers; Marvin MacIntyre to Hopkins, August 16, 1935, Hopkins to MacIntyre, both in WPA Papers, Central Files, State Series, Mississippi (hereinafter cited as WPA Papers, Mississippi), Section 630.

16. Statement by Paul B. Johnson, March 24, 1936, in WPA Papers, Division of Investigation, Case Files, Mississippi, Johnstone Investigation (hereinafter cited as Johnstone Investigation), Exhibit 459.

17. McLaury to Dallas Dort, August 24, 1935, in WPA Papers, Division of Investigation, New Orleans Office, General Correspondence; Travis to Bilbo, November 26, 1935, Bilbo to Alliston, October 21, 1935, Bilbo to Burkett, July 17, 1935, all in Bilbo Papers.

be used against him. He seems to have made a sincere effort to let Bilbo use WPA to begin to acquire a fair portion of the federal patronage pie. But Harrison's fears about a Conner-controlled agency were more than balanced by a gnawing anxiety about a Bilboized WPA. Pat probably preferred that WPA regional and national officials run the agency without interference, to the dismay of job-hungry loyalists of both Conner and Bilbo. Harrison seemed content to let the two men neutralize each other, confident that his own influence with the administration could forestall any drastic changes.

By 1936 the entire situation had changed. White's victory, which Bilbo had worked so hard to achieve, and Long's death reduced Harrison's dependence on Bilbo's influence with the redneck vote. This perhaps explains Pat's willingness to push the Holmes nomination even at the risk of antagonizing his junior colleague. But with Bilbo openly backing Conner's bid for Harrison's seat, Pat realized that he would have to take the Mississippi WPA in hand to protect his interests.

As early as October, 1935, Harrison's friend Ellen Woodward had warned that Bilbo's influence over the WPA might be dangerous and suggested that Harrison investigate the situation before it got out of control. In November, Harrison sent WPA Personnel Director B. A. Bush a list of friends to be consulted concerning future appointments, and Bush forwarded the names to the district directors. The effort turned up the man who would prove to be Harrison's Trojan horse in Bilbo's patronage army, Roland Wall.[18]

Wall, director of the Brookhaven district, quickly complied with Bush's request and encouraged Harrison to "write and make any recommendations for the giving of jobs or making appointments of any of your friends in this territory. . . . You can rest assured that I will . . . do everything I can to make such appointments or give jobs to . . . anyone that . . . will be helpful or advantageous to you." Wall had already placed several veterans, he said, and had "taken the occasion to drop the word" that the request had come from Harrison. Perhaps there might be "some special work" among veterans or "others that may have been antagonistic to you in the past," he suggested. "If such should be the case, I want you to feel free to call on me because I want to help or serve you in any way that I can."[19]

The transparency of the invitation was not lost on Harrison. By the

18. Woodward to Harrison, October 8, 1935, in Woodward Papers; J. C. Davis to Harrison (copy), November 30, 1935, in WPA Papers, Johnstone Investigation; Bush to Bilbo, January 18, 1936, in Bilbo Papers.

19. Wall to Harrison (copy), November 29, 1935, in WPA Papers, Johnstone Investigation.

middle of January, John Burkett reported to Bilbo that Wall was being elevated to some sort of troubleshooting position under Alliston and that he was displacing Bilbo's friends as rapidly as he dared without attracting undue attention. Wall's promotion was obviously designed to increase his range beyond the single district in order to make contacts for Harrison's interest in the senatorial primary. In addition, Eugene Fly, Mississippi collector of internal revenue and Harrison's primary patronage lieutenant, was spending a lot of time on the eighteenth floor of the Tower Building in the WPA office. "Every time I stick my head out," said Burkett, "he is coming or going. . . . Some deep politics are being discussed and planned here now." Bilbo quickly warned Alliston not to allow Wall too much rein: "He is only a recent friend of mine, and I am having a world of complaint from his district."[20]

By February, Bilbo was "in the market" for a new colleague, and Harrison's assault on the WPA was in full gear. Pat asked WPA Assistant Director Aubrey Williams for a complete list of WPA administrative and supervisory personnel. "He wants our entire organization," Williams told Regional Director Malcolm Miller, but "doesn't want his name associated with the request." Williams told Miller to cooperate, and the ax soon began to fall on Bilbo's friends in the agency.[21]

Early in March, Harrison convinced Hopkins to send an investigator to Mississippi, and Alan Johnstone, who had just completed a well-publicized investigation of the West Virginia WPA, was ordered to Mississippi to "observe the operations" and "take any steps . . . necessary to insure . . . efficient operation." Before leaving Washington, Johnstone called on Bilbo, who said he had nothing to hide, that he had been for his friends since the WPA began and was still for them but had done no more than make recommendations. Johnstone asked if he and Harrison were friends. Bilbo replied that they had been until the Holmes fight, which had nothing to do with the WPA. Conner had probably gotten the majority of WPA patronage, Bilbo said, because Pat had allowed so many ERA holdovers in the new agency. After Johnstone left, Bilbo warned Alliston of the investigation, noting that

20. Burkett to Bilbo, January 8, 1936, Burkett to Bilbo, January 15, 1936, Burkett to Bilbo, January 26, 1936, Bilbo to Alliston, January 13, 1936, all in Bilbo Papers.

21. Transcript of telephone conversation between Aubrey Williams and Malcolm Miller, February 18, 1936, in WPA Papers, Mississippi, Section 610; Julius Marx to Bilbo, February 24, 1936, in Bilbo Papers; Memphis *Commercial Appeal*, March 1, 1936, Sec. 4, p. 5.

Johnstone would want to inspect the director's correspondence and files. "Throw the door wide open to him," Bilbo advised.[22]

After a week-long investigation, Johnstone and his staff recommended major changes. They suggested that all administrative and supervisory appointments be resubmitted to the state director, who should then review their records. Those that were satisfactory would be maintained, but all others should be released. The result was what the Memphis *Commercial Appeal* called a "complete shake-up." Johnstone's report concluded that political influence in hiring both staff and relief workers had been negligible but recommended a significant reduction in projects, workers, and administrative staff. That reduction became the press that was used to squeeze Bilbo's influence out of the agency. In late April, Alliston told Bilbo that things had "certainly been disturbed" since the investigation. Scores of people had been laid off—supervisors, paymasters, engineers; and numerous projects had been eliminated. "It is certainly causing a howl."[23]

Johnstone had one ancillary duty to perform. Just before he left for Mississippi, the press began to carry stories that WPA money was being used to build textile factories for private businesses. John Edelman, research director of the American Federation of Hosiery Workers, charged that Harrison was "bringing pressure to bear upon government agencies to subsidize sweatshops in Mississippi." In several Mississippi cities, the WPA built "vocational schools" that were in reality factory buildings to be leased to industrial concerns at nominal rent. The projects were inspired by Governor White's BAWI program, in which state and local governments sought to entice northern industry to Mississippi using tax breaks and publicly funded facilities. When the WPA eventually stopped work on the "vocational schools," White continued construction of several of them with state funds.[24]

The hosiery workers union charged that when local workers re-

22. Hopkins to Johnstone, March 10, 1936, in WPA Papers, Johnstone Investigation; Bilbo to Alliston, March 13, 1936, in Bilbo Papers.

23. Statement of Alan Johnstone, March 27, 1936, in WPA Papers, Mississippi, Section 610; Memphis *Commercial Appeal*, April 5, 1936, Sec. 4, p. 5; J. Marshall Carr to Bilbo, April 3, 1936, Alliston to Bilbo, April 29, 1936, both in Bilbo Papers.

24. Press release by Robert W. Horton, March 13, 1936, Reference File, Work Relief, 1935–1936, in Raymond Clapper Papers, Library of Congress; Raymond Clapper, "Politics in the WPA," *Review of Reviews*, April, 1936, p. 70; Alliston to Hopkins, March 9, 1936, in WPA Papers, Johnstone Investigation, Exhibit 339. Mississippi labor leaders charged that the BAWI approach bred anti-union sentiment, especially in north Mississippi. The program attracted low-wage "carpetbag" companies, many of which were fleeing organized labor in other places. One union official charged that BAWI made

fused to work for the low wages paid by one of the WPA-built plants in Columbus, the employer imported prison labor under contract from Oklahoma. Officials also reported that a union investigator was driven out of Columbus by local police. Another of the plants was built at Brookhaven, where Wall as WPA director signed the project proposal and as mayor of Brookhaven signed a ten-year lease to the Brookhaven Garment Company for a mere dollar. The Brookhaven Garment Company was a subsidiary of the Stahl-Urban Company, which had ceased similar production in Terre Haute, Indiana, after a rash of labor disputes.[25]

The New York *Herald Tribune* reported that "there was fire in the WPA chief's eyes" when Hopkins told a press conference that the agreement to lease the "vocational schools" to private companies had been reached without his approval. He vowed that the buildings would not "find their way" into private hands "for any use whatever. Wait till I get to the bottom of this, and I'll write your story for you," he promised reporters, "and it'll be just as hot as you want it." Hopkins' failure to follow that threat with decisive action would cause his successor considerable grief.[26]

On March 16 Assistant Administrator Howard Hunter told Johnstone that Hopkins was "particularly anxious" to get a firsthand report on the situation, especially any records showing the basis on which the projects were approved and whether there was any need to pursue an investigation of possible conspiracy. Johnstone reported that all work on the schools had ceased and the WPA was trying to recover whatever funds had been invested in them. The decisiveness of that affirmation would likewise haunt Hopkins' successor.[27]

It is almost certain that the whole Johnstone investigation was an effort to appease Pat Harrison. The major result of the shake-up was that beginning in the spring of 1936 Roland Wall ran the WPA in Mississippi. In a letter to Johnstone, Wall remarked that he "could appreciate the fact that [the] Washington office probably would not want to

---

Mississippi the country's "industrial junkyard." Donald C. Mosley, "The Labor Union Movement," in McLemore (ed.), *History of Mississippi*, II, 265–66.

25. Press release by Horton, in Clapper Papers; J. C. Capt to Administrator (WPA), March 15, 1939, OF 444c, in Roosevelt Papers; James McCann to Clara M. Beyer (copy), August 8, 1938, in WPA Papers, Mississippi, Section 610.

26. McCann to Beyer (copy), September 1, 1938, in WPA Papers, Mississippi, Section 610.

27. Howard Hunter to Johnstone, March 16, 1936, in WPA Papers, Johnstone Investigation, Exhibit 375; statement by Johnstone, March 27, 1936, in WPA Papers, Mississippi, Section 610.

. . . put in writing some of the things we discussed about our Mississippi situation and future program." Miller reported to Hopkins that he had had several conferences with the "very close friend and associate of Senator Harrison," Eugene Fly, who was delighted at the recent "turn of affairs." Alliston soon became little more than a pliant figurehead. "He will do anything I tell him to," Miller assured Hopkins, and Alliston himself explained to Bilbo, "Mr. Wall is here by instructions of Mr. Hopkins and Mr. Malcolm J. Miller." Bush wrote Bilbo, "We are up against every pressure in the world that the senior Senator can bring forth."[28]

Bilbo wasted no time in attacking Wall, charging that Wall's candidacy for reelection as mayor of Brookhaven violated WPA regulations. Miller had expressly instructed Alliston in February that "where anyone employed by us in an administrative capacity becomes a candidate for public office in Mississippi . . . their resignation would be immediately required." Bilbo demanded Wall's resignation, but Miller advised Hopkins that "it would practically wreck the Mississippi WPA" if Wall were removed, and recommended that he be retained as deputy administrator. Hopkins agreed but warned that the WPA could "call it a day in Mississippi" if Wall played politics with the agency.[29]

Hopkins had placed himself in a compromising situation that Bilbo quickly exploited. Arguing that it was unfair to allow Wall to remain in the WPA when others who chose to run for office had been asked to resign, Bilbo listed several who had been forced out. He even offered an amendment to the pending Deficiency Appropriation Act making Hopkins' directive a statutory requirement. At that point even Alan Johnstone advised Hopkins to demand that Wall resign as mayor and relinquish his nomination for the new term or get out of the WPA. Hopkins did not agree. Bilbo also told Hopkins that Wall had known that the Brookhaven "vocational school" was really a factory for "Eastern capitalists" when he approved the project for WPA money. At the same time Bilbo dispatched his friend Heber Ladner to find

28. Wall to Johnstone, May 15, 1936, in WPA Papers, Mississippi, Section 610; Miller to Hopkins, February 13, 1936, in WPA Papers, Central Files, General Subject Series, Section 132.3; transcript of telephone conversation between Miller and Hopkins, April 29, 1936, WPA, Mississippi, in Hopkins Papers; Alliston to Phil A. Armitage, May 21, 1936, Bush to Bilbo, May 23, 1936, both in Bilbo Papers.

29. Miller to Alliston, February 11, 1936, in WPA Papers, Central Files, General Subject Series, Section 132.3; Bilbo to Hopkins, May 9, 1936, in Bilbo Papers; Miller to Hopkins, May 5, 1936, in WPA Papers, Mississippi, Section 630; transcript of telephone conversation between Miller and Hopkins, April 29, 1936, WPA, Mississippi, in Hopkins Papers.

someone to oppose Wall as an independent candidate for mayor in the general election. But he cautioned, "If you can't do it, forget it," and Ladner apparently forgot it.[30]

Again in July, with the senatorial primary in full swing, Bilbo urged Hopkins to remove Wall. Not only was he in direct violation of Hopkins' own regulation and federal statute, but he was using the WPA—"discharging people, hiring people, releasing projects, and other such activities"—in behalf of Harrison in the primary. Bilbo warned that he did not want to hurt the Roosevelt administration by attacking WPA publicly, but he would explain matters to Mississippi's voters if necessary.[31]

Bilbo's charges were not entirely groundless. In May, Wall had written Johnstone regarding those undocumented discussions "about our Mississippi situation." He asked Johnstone to "advise" Miller of Hopkins' agreement to allow the Mississippi office to release, on its own, "such projects as in our opinion, should be released," and to certify for relief jobs "additional men of the class and character that should be certified." Johnstone then informed Miller that he and Hopkins had agreed with Wall that regional office requirements regarding new projects could be "relaxed" in Mississippi's case and that requisite funds should be made available.[32]

Throughout the primary campaign there were rumors of a massive WPA purge. Harrison often referred in campaign speeches to his little red book and his little black book. In the first were the names of those who supported him; in the other, those who did not. Those two registers, he threatened, would be crucial references for future WPA applicants. "We are going down the line to do some purging," he told a Jackson crowd. Immediately after trouncing Conner in the primary, he left for Washington with Fly and Wall and the little black book in tow. Anxiety ran rampant among federal jobholders in Mississippi, and the fears were well founded. Harrison's campaign manager, Norfleet Sledge, noted that the situation just after the primary was "more trying than even . . . the campaign with hundreds of people even into the late hours of the night having conferences regarding employment and other matters." Reports were pouring into Harrison headquarters in response to queries concerning the loyalty of WPA workers during the

30. Bilbo to Hopkins, May 9, 1936, in Bilbo Papers; *Congressional Record*, 74th Cong., 2nd Sess., 7566; Johnstone to Hopkins, May 25, 1935, in WPA Papers, Mississippi, Section 630; Bilbo to Heber Ladner, May 26, 1936, in Bilbo Papers.

31. Bilbo to Hopkins, July 13, 1936, in Bilbo Papers.

32. Wall to Johnstone, May 15, 1936, Johnstone to Miller, May 18, 1936, both in WPA Papers, Mississippi, Section 610.

campaign. It was not long before Bilbo people began to disappear from WPA payrolls. "I curse the day that WPA was born!" Bilbo declared.[33]

Bilbo realized that Alliston would not or could not resist the pressure from above, and so long as he remained director, Wall would rule the WPA in Harrison's interest. If he could force Alliston out, the new director would have to be confirmed by the Senate, and Bilbo was confident that Roosevelt would not let Harrison run roughshod over him on another controversial appointment. Bilbo turned on Alliston with a fury. "You can't hide behind Harry Hopkins or Pat Harrison or anyone else," he said. "I do not blame Roland Wall nor any of the Pat Harrison parties and manipulators because I know that you are clothed with all the authority on earth to prevent those outrages." He was, said Bilbo, no more than "a little peanut cringing politician, ready to bow and scrape at the feet of anyone who, you think, is in a position to disturb your ease, comfort and emoluments."[34]

Bilbo insisted that Alliston tell Hopkins how Harrison and Wall had used the WPA in the Senate primary and that he demand the right to rehire those being fired. When Alliston took no action Bilbo assailed him bitterly in the weekly article that he contributed to the Poplarville *Free Press*. By November he was demanding that Alliston resign. "I believed you," he said, even while Harrison was having the WPA investigated, but "I now understand your type. . . . Of course none of us is perfect. We have all sinned and come short of the glory of God, but your short-comings are so tragic and pitiable until words fail me in their portrayal."[35]

Convinced that Hopkins was willingly cooperating with Harrison, Bilbo took his case directly to the president, whom he found surprisingly responsive. Roosevelt urged Hopkins to send "an outside investigator to check up on WPA in Mississippi," and Hopkins dispatched J. C. Capt to conduct an inquiry. Capt impressed Bilbo as a "strong Roosevelt man," who would give him a fair hearing. By early 1938 Capt was in Mississippi interviewing people who, Bilbo told him, could "substantiate beyond every reasonable doubt" that Wall had

33. Memphis *Commercial Appeal*, September 6, 1936, Sec. 4, p. 5; Swain, *Pat Harrison*, 144–45; Norfleet Sledge to Mrs. Sledge, September 11, 1936, Homer F. Benson to Catherine Blanton, September 2, 1936, Frank Hughes to Harrison, September 1, 1936, all in Harrison Papers, University of Mississippi; Bilbo to Armitage, September 23, 1936, in Bilbo Papers.

34. Bilbo to Alliston, October 7, 1936, Bilbo to Alliston, November 5, 1936, Bilbo to Alliston, November 11, 1936, all in Bilbo Papers.

35. Bilbo to Alliston, September 28, 1936, Bilbo to W. T. Reese, November 20, 1936, Bilbo to Alliston, November 11, 1936, all in Bilbo Papers.

played politics for Harrison and had driven Bilbo's friends from the agency. The "slaughter" had been so complete, Bilbo complained, that he could not even suggest a foreman or local worker from his own Pearl River County.[36]

Most of the witnesses were Bilbo people, and each detailed the litany of "abuses" that Wall had perpetrated. More convincing were people like former WPA Commodity Division Director Walter Davis of Kosciusko, who insisted that he had never supported Bilbo in his life. He told Capt that shortly after the primary he had been summoned to Harrison's room at the Edwards Hotel in Jackson, where Harrison accused him of supporting Conner. When he denied it, said Davis, the senator produced a complete list of the workers in the commodity division and asked how each one had voted. "He went far enough," Davis continued, "to ask me how some of the women voted who were engaged in packing dried milk and who were working on a security wage." Davis insisted that he did not know how any of them had voted and was surprised Harrison would ask. Pat seemed "mad and ill-tempered," so Davis said little else. A month later he was fired.[37]

In late March, Wall was in Washington in connection with the investigation. He returned to Mississippi "in a very bad frame of mind," according to Bilbo's friend B. A. Bush. Wall had threatened to "clean house" of Bilbo people, and Bush wrote Capt to ask if those who testified would now be fired. Aubrey Williams promised that no one would suffer for telling the truth but that every charge would have to be substantiated.[38]

Meanwhile Bilbo was pleading his case to James Roosevelt, who was serving as White House liaison on Capitol Hill. "Your father has promised me to remove Roland Wall," Bilbo said, and urged the younger Roosevelt to persuade FDR that Harrison's constituency was a hotbed of growing anti–New Deal sentiment and that Wall's control of WPA was solidifying their grip on the Mississippi Democratic party. A few days later Roosevelt reported that his father had instructed him to do what he could about Wall immediately. Events seemed to be working in Bilbo's favor. Since the president had torpedoed Harrison's bid for the majority leadership the previous summer, Pat had been edging away

36. Roosevelt to Hopkins, June 11, 1937, General Correspondence, FDR, in Hopkins Papers; Bilbo to Hugh Wall, February 16, 1938, Bilbo to J. C. Capt, February 23, 1938, both in Bilbo Papers.

37. Walter Davis to Hopkins (copy), March 7, 1938, in Bilbo Papers.

38. Bush to Capt, April 1, 1938, in WPA Papers, Mississippi, Section 610; Robert M. Newton to Bilbo, April 2, 1938, in Bilbo Papers; Williams to Bush, April 6, 1938, in WPA Papers, Mississippi, Section 610.

from the administration and by mid-1938 was in open revolt, especially on New Deal tax and labor policies. He was also, some said, pushing the Mississippi congressional delegation toward rebellion.[39]

Bilbo painted for the president's son the grim picture of a conservative faction of Mississippi Democracy, catapulted to power by New Deal patronage yet leading to the 1940 national convention a delegation hostile to the very spirit of the New Deal. Pointing to his own steady reliability in the Senate, Bilbo promised to prevent such an outrage if only Roosevelt would help "quietly, without any noise or fuss," reorganize federal patronage in Mississippi. "We are chasing the bag of gold at the end of the rainbow," he concluded, ever to hope that Harrison would again be reconciled to the president and his program. The younger Roosevelt invited Bilbo to visit him to discuss the matter further.[40]

In early June, Bilbo suggested that Wall be replaced by T. G. Gladney, WPA Engineer for Mississippi. At almost the same time Aubrey Williams sent Roosevelt a nomination form and recommended Wall. James Roosevelt, who had asked to be informed when a recommendation came through for Mississippi, stressed to his father, "This is the man Senator Bilbo is so opposed to." The president ordered his secretary to hold the nomination.[41]

Meanwhile, Malcolm Miller had been urging Williams to go ahead and appoint Wall as soon as possible. He did so with the understanding that Harrison and Hugh White had already suggested Wall to Roosevelt, who had agreed. Miller was mistaken, however, because Roosevelt, in a handwritten note to Hopkins, insisted that "Roland Wall . . . should not go in" and suggested Gladney as a good man who should be acceptable to both senators. On June 25 Hopkins told Harrison that he thought it best to maintain the existing situation, so for the time being Wall remained acting administrator. Wall was not pleased.[42]

All the while Bilbo was working feverishly to rid himself of Wall for

39. Bilbo to James Roosevelt, February 14, 1938, James Roosevelt to Bilbo, February 18, 1938, both in Bilbo Papers; Swain, *Pat Harrison*, 163–65.

40. Bilbo to James Roosevelt, March 23, 1938, in James Roosevelt Papers, Franklin D. Roosevelt Library, Hyde Park; James Roosevelt to Bilbo, March 30, 1938, in Bilbo Papers.

41. Bilbo to James Roosevelt, June 8, 1938, OF 400, in Roosevelt Papers; Williams to Roosevelt, June 13, 1938, James Roosevelt to FDR, June 14, 1938, OF 444c, in Roosevelt Papers.

42. Miller to Williams, June 28, 1938, in WPA Papers, Mississippi, Section 610; Roosevelt to Hopkins, n.d., Correspondence from the President, in Hopkins Papers; Hopkins to Harrison, June 25, 1938, in WPA Papers, Mississippi, Section 630.

good. He begged for a conference with the president but could not get one until September. Meanwhile the Washington bureaucracy slipped through his fingers like water. In late August he fretted to Roosevelt that the Washington WPA office had done nothing about the presidential request concerning Mississippi; everyone with authority to act seemed to be out of town. He begged the president to order Assistant Administrator Corrington Gill to appoint Gladney, or even Capt, immediately. "No one can object if Mr. Hopkins sends a man out of his own office," he argued.[43]

As rumors proliferated, Bilbo's enemies grew restless. Congressman Dan McGehee wrote his colleague Will Whittington and suggested that the entire Mississippi delegation ought to wire Hopkins in support of Wall. "I know what it means to each of us who have opposition," he said. If Bilbo got his way, "the WPA would be a complete organization that would give us hell." Whittington, McGehee, and John Rankin all wired Hopkins that the Mississippi delegation was perfectly pleased with Wall. A few days later Harrison sent word to Marvin MacIntyre that Wall's removal would "raise hell with the situation." He demanded a conference before any action was taken, "so I can have a complete understanding about this. If my head is to be chopped off, I would like to know about it first."[44]

Bilbo, too, was still trying to see the president. He had been in the capital two months, he explained to Roosevelt, but knowing how busy the president was, he had not insisted on a conference. He pleaded for just a few minutes "to discuss . . . matters of vital importance to you and the Administration." To the president's secretary he was more petulant. "Don't you think that four years of one hundred percent loyalty . . . would entitle me to at least an opportunity to talk with the President?" He would remain in the city until he was granted a conference, he said.[45]

MacIntyre finally arranged for Bilbo to see Roosevelt at Hyde Park on September 9, and the senator came away from "a very satisfactory interview" convinced that he had won his case. But his friend B. A. Bush cautioned that Jim Farley was pressuring Hopkins for his old

43. Bilbo to MacIntyre, June 22, 1938, Bilbo to Roosevelt, August 20, 1938, Bilbo to MacIntyre, August 29, 1938, all in Bilbo Papers.

44. Dan McGehee to Will Whittington, July 2, 1938, Whittington to Hopkins, both in Whittington Papers; John Rankin to Hopkins, August 22, 1938, McGehee to Hopkins, August 29, 1938, both in WPA Papers, Mississippi, Section 610; Harrison to MacIntyre, September, 1938, in Pat Harrison Papers (microfilm), Mitchell Library, Mississippi State University, Starkville.

45. Bilbo to Roosevelt, September 6, 1938, Bilbo to MacIntyre, September 6, 1938, both in PPF 2184, Roosevelt Papers.

friend Harrison. Bush warned that while men like Farley, Hopkins, and MacIntyre would certainly not cross Roosevelt, they could scatter a lot of bureaucratic debris in his path.[46]

It was a prescient warning. Within a week Wall had fired Gladney, allegedly for boasting that he would soon be state administrator and would clean house. Again Bilbo begged Roosevelt for someone from the Washington office to run the Mississippi agency independently of the state's congressmen and senators. Aubrey Williams put Roosevelt off at least until Hopkins' return, but the president, too, was apparently wearying of bureaucratic hide and seek. "We have got to remember this," Williams warned Miller, "that the President is not at all happy about that situation and we are all seemingly opposing him in what he wants to do and he is getting pretty sick of it." When he had tried to explain the Gladney firing, "the President didn't say much," said Williams. "He is very unhappy about it all." Roosevelt seemed perturbed that his own administrators were shielding the interests of one senator, who was saying some harsh things publicly about presidential policy, at the expense of another, who seemed thoroughly loyal. Bilbo finally gave up and went home, but he continued to bombard the White House with importunate correspondence.[47]

Matters took a dramatic turn in Bilbo's favor in December when Roosevelt nominated Hopkins as secretary of commerce and chose Colonel Francis G. Harrington to replace him as WPA administrator. One of Harrington's first moves was a regional reorganization that took Mississippi out of Miller's jurisdiction and placed it in Region Six, headed by George H. Field. Gone were the two WPA officials, Harry Hopkins and Malcolm Miller, who had shielded Harrison and Wall from Bilbo's hostility, even at the risk of angering the president. Another of Harrington's early decisions was to send Capt on another investigative junket to the Magnolia State before naming a new state director. In the meantime he ordered Wall to take a leave of absence.[48]

In March, Capt issued a report that contained six major charges

46. MacIntyre to Bilbo, September 6, 1938, Bilbo to Bush, September 10, 1938, Bush to Bilbo, September 7, 1938, all in Bilbo Papers.

47. Transcript of telephone conversation between Williams and Miller, September 13, 1938, in Aubrey Williams Papers, Franklin D. Roosevelt Library, Hyde Park; Bilbo to Roosevelt, September 17, 1938, Williams to Bilbo, September 23, 1938, both in Bilbo Papers; transcript of telephone conversation between Miller and Williams, September 26, 1938, in Williams Papers; Bilbo to Roosevelt, October 7, 1938, in Bilbo Papers.

48. Sherwood, *Roosevelt and Hopkins*, 105–107; Miller to Bilbo, February 18, 1939, in Bilbo Papers; F. C. Harrington to Wall, February 23, 1939, in WPA Papers, Mississippi, Section 610; Wall to Harrington, March 11, 1939, OF 444c, in Roosevelt Papers.

against Wall. The most damaging dealt with two of the "vocational schools" that were built in 1936, one in Brookhaven and one in Columbia. According to the report Wall had "joined with other officials . . . to improperly use WPA funds for the benefit of private persons." In the Brookhaven case, he had known from the beginning that the proposed building was to be a factory for the Stahl-Urban Company and had signed the lease as mayor—ten years for one dollar. He had discovered several weeks in advance that Hopkins intended to halt construction and admitted that he had then ordered three shifts put to work to finish the factory. At the Reliance Manufacturing Company of Columbia, he had allowed steel, cement, and lumber to be delivered to the work site two weeks after Hopkins had ordered work stopped and refused to allow district officials to remove the steel, which the City of Columbia eventually used to complete the structure.[49]

These allegations came not very long after Aubrey Williams had received complaints about Wall's role in those very incidents. In the late summer of 1938, a representative of the National Work Shirt Manufacturers Association complained to the Division of Labor Standards that after Hopkins so forcefully promised to punish such offenders, he had promoted one of the worst to acting director of the Mississippi WPA. The industry representative feared a similar southern prostitution of the recently enacted Fair Labor Standards Act. Under Hopkins the Washington WPA office had done nothing regarding Wall's role in the affair.[50]

When Harrington sent Wall a summary of the charges, the state director replied simply that he had not "joined with any sponsors of any projects to improperly use WPA funds." Harrington deemed that "very limited and general response" unsatisfactory in light of "facts which the evidence quite definitely established." He scolded Wall for "poor judgement and faulty administration"—a fairly generous assessment—but nonetheless intended to appoint him as administrator under certain stringent qualifications: (1) cessation of practices that resulted in the vocational school mess; (2) stricter observance of national and regional office directives; (3) "elimination" of inadequate personnel; (4) better intake and certification procedure. Hereafter Mississippi would be closely monitored by the regional office, he warned, and if conditions did not improve in three to four months, he would be

49. J. C. Capt to Administrator (WPA), March 15, 1939, OF 444c, in Roosevelt Papers.

50. Beyer to Williams (copy), August 25, 1938, in WPA Papers, Mississippi, 610; McCann to Beyer (copy), September 1, 1938, in WPA Papers, Mississippi, Section 630.

"compelled to obtain another Administrator." Finally, he insisted that Wall resign as mayor in compliance with federal law. There was "no option" concerning that matter, Harrington said, though the regulation had already been ignored in Wall's case for almost three years.[51]

Wall agreed to take the job on those conditions and responded to each directive individually. Regarding intake and certification he referred Harrington to Eve Gilmour, former regional office supervisor of the Mississippi employment division, who would confirm, he said, "that the Division of Employment here had tried to work with them to the best of their ability." That was a remarkable assertion considering some of Gilmour's earlier reports. In 1937 she had protested sternly that Mississippi officials were certifying relief applicants that the social workers considered ineligible. When Miller mentioned the matter to Wall, he became so exercised that the regional director had to "call him to order and terminate the conference." It was "the old question in Mississippi," Miller told Hopkins, of "Wall's influence with our Senior Senator," who wanted no interference at all by the regional office.[52]

Harrington informed the White House that he intended to appoint Wall on a conditional basis. "I did not feel," he said, "that I had any basis for dismissing Mr. Wall on account of bad administrative practices which had occurred three years ago, and felt that if I took this action *it would undoubtedly result in criticism of Mr. Hopkins*" (italics mine). He persuaded Bilbo to accept Wall's appointment on the temporary probationary arrangement. At the same time, Roosevelt ordered Harrington "to make a thorough investigation" of the Mississippi situation, preferably in person, to find out if Wall was playing politics and if so, to remove him. He suggested suspending Wall's appointment in the meantime.[53]

Wall tried to appease Bilbo. On April 1 he wrote the senator to suggest that though he knew Bilbo preferred someone else as state administrator, he harbored no "malice or ill will" and wanted Bilbo to feel free "to call on . . . the Works Progress Administration . . . for any assistance or service" he desired. Bilbo replied that he would treat the letter as any of the other "jokes" normally perpetrated on that day. But

51. Wall to Harrington (copy), March 18, 1939, Harrington to Wall (copy), March 21, 1939, both in OF 444c, Roosevelt Papers.

52. Wall to Harrington (copy), March 23, 1939, OF 444c, in Roosevelt Papers; Eve Gilmour to Miller, January 18, 1937, Miller to Hopkins, January 21, 1937, both in WPA Papers, Central Files, General Subject Series, Section 132.3.

53. Harrington to General Edwin Watson, March 27, 1939, Watson to Roosevelt, March 28, 1939, Watson to Harrington, March 28, 1939, all in OF 444c, Roosevelt Papers.

then "*every day*" had been April Fool's Day, he said, since Wall had come to head the WPA.[54]

In May, Harrington dispatched Deputy Administrator Howard Hunter to Mississippi to monitor Wall's compliance with the conditions of his appointment. Before leaving Washington, Hunter met with Bilbo, who gave him another list of people who would, he said, document "the prostitution of the WPA set-up in Mississippi." After Hunter completed the probe, Harrington decided to replace Wall temporarily, not because he had been guilty of any misconduct but simply as a precautionary response to the Mississippi political pot, which was again beginning to boil. It was a statewide election year, and the governorship was up for grabs between the conservatives and the "runt pigs." Bilbo, in a striking reversal from the previous campaign, backed Paul Johnson as the New Deal candidate and champion of the poor farmers.[55]

More was at stake in 1939 than Mississippi's top political office. The winning faction would take a giant stride toward control of the state delegation to the 1940 national Democratic convention, and Bilbo was doing everything possible to turn the race into a referendum on the New Deal. For more than three years Bilbo had been arguing that Harrison's supporters, who controlled the Democratic machinery in the state, were out to sabotage the New Deal at the first opportunity. When Harrison declared his support for his old adversary Mike Conner, an open critic of the New Deal, Bilbo's charges took on renewed plausibility. When Harrison's good friends Governor White and Ellen Woodward took the stump for Conner, the charges appeared indisputable. The Washington *Daily News* reported that most New Dealers hoped Bilbo, and not Harrison, would control Mississippi's 1940 delegation.[56]

Wall's position became especially tenuous, and Harrington decided to remove him from harm's way. In June he announced that Marvin Porter of South Carolina would replace Wall at least until the election was over. "Our Pat," crowed Bilbo, "is having a H—— of a time explaining away the fact" that his WPA boss had been removed. Bilbo boasted that he had simply marched down to the White House "and told the President the time had come for action," whereupon Roose-

54. Wall to Bilbo, April 1, 1939, Bilbo to Wall, April 4, 1939, both in Bilbo Papers.

55. Hunter to Bilbo, May 10, 1939, Bilbo to Hunter, May 17, 1939, Bilbo to Paul Johnson, May 17, 1939, all in Bilbo Papers.

56. Swain, *Pat Harrison*, 207–208; Thomas L. Stokes, "Harrison Gets a Jolt and New Dealers Grin," Washington *Daily News*, August 31, 1939, clipping in Reference File, Mississippi, 1938–1939, Clapper Papers.

velt "grabbed the telephone" and ordered Harrington "to get Wall . . . out of Mississippi at once. It was all done in a jiffy," Bilbo declared. Wall and Harrison claimed to be unconcerned about the development, but they were not able to convey that confidence to their friends in the Mississippi congressional delegation, who believed Wall's transfer was a prelude to his permanent removal. The congressmen were mortally terrified that if Bilbo gained control he would use the WPA and their own voting records to assail them, too, in 1940.[57]

In what some pundits deemed a smashing upset, Johnson rolled over Conner in the August runoff. New Dealers everywhere were delighted, and apparently so was the president himself. Bilbo reminded Roosevelt that he had promised all along Johnson could win if Wall was removed. "The result speaks for itself," he declared, and renewed his plea that Wall be removed permanently. It was vital, he insisted, if the New Dealers in Mississippi were to control the 1940 delegation. The next day the president wrote Harrington, "Why not keep Mr. Marvin Porter there as State Director?" Yet even from the Commerce Department, the long arm of Harry Hopkins still thwarted Bilbo's efforts to remove Wall. Harrington apparently persuaded Roosevelt to allow Wall to return in keeping with a promise he had made to Hopkins. In the fall Wall returned to Mississippi as WPA director.[58]

Not until after Harrison's death in 1941 was Bilbo able to get Wall ousted, though he was again replaced temporarily during Bilbo's reelection campaign in 1940. Beginning in 1939, however, the agency did become more responsive to Bilbo's appointments recommendations, perhaps because he began to bombard both the regional and national offices with them. Also, the new regional director, Lawrence Westbrook, seemed more congenial to Bilbo and more appreciative of his political loyalty. Westbrook had headed the rural rehabilitation program of the FERA and had been intimately involved with the struggle for the Bankhead-Jones Farm Tenancy Act. He had testified before the Senate Agriculture Committee, where he probably observed Bilbo's tireless efforts in behalf of tenant legislation. As former chairman of an agriculture committee in the Texas legislature and organizer of the Texas Cotton Cooperative Association, Westbrook had become

57. Bilbo to R. M. Newton, July 1, 1939, Bilbo to Paul Johnson, July 1, 1939, both in Bilbo Papers; Wall to Whittington, June 30, 1939, McGehee to Whittington, July 2, 1939, both in Whittington Papers; joint letter from Mississippi Congressmen to Roosevelt, February 10, 1939, in WPA Papers, Mississippi, Section 630.

58. Bilbo to Roosevelt, August 30, 1939, Roosevelt to Bilbo, August 31, 1939, both in Bilbo Papers; Roosevelt to Harrington, August 31, 1939, PPF 2184, in Roosevelt Papers; Bilbo to T. Brady, Jr., September 25, 1939, in Bilbo Papers.

acquainted with Bilbo's enthusiasm for New Deal farm policy, especially as it affected cotton interests. Whatever the case, Bilbo found Westbrook much more friendly toward him than Malcolm Miller or any other WPA official had ever been.[59]

The fight between Bilbo and Harrison for control of the Mississippi WPA offers an intriguing study of the impact of New Deal administrative policy on state politics. There is little dispute that in most states politics played an important, sometimes paramount, part in the functioning of the WPA.[60] As Robert Sherwood describes it, Hopkins himself—once Roosevelt taught him how to "square his conscience with the realities of the two-party system"—decided there was no way to be semipolitical so he became admittedly "all political." It seemed a grand opportunity to promote support for the New Deal. Many of the agency field men knew exactly how to do that: "give the good guys the jobs, the bad guys the gate." If Roosevelt's administrators had reserved patronage for their friends, according to James T. Patterson, they could have created "dependably liberal Democratic parties" that could have turned state governments into "bastions of progress." James M. Burns, too, argues that Roosevelt could have "liberalized" the Democratic party through "a patient, steady, well-planned battle of attrition against a host of state parties and their leaders in congressional and state offices."[61]

The South was especially ripe for such a revolution. Roosevelt was enormously popular, and there was no Republican opposition to cry foul. It was simply a matter of feeding patronage to the New Dealers and denying it to conservative Democrats. Yet just the opposite occurred in Mississippi. There is little doubt that Harrison monopolized

59. Whatley, "Public Works Program in Mississippi," 30; Bilbo to Harrington, April 10, 1939, Bilbo to Harrington, April 18, 1939, Bilbo to Harrington, May 19, 1939, all in Bilbo Papers; Sidney Baldwin, *Poverty and Politics: The Rise and Decline of the Farm Security Administration* (Chapel Hill, 1968), 62, 134; Paul Conkin, *Tomorrow a New World: The New Deal Community Programs* (Ithaca, N.Y., 1959), 132–33; Westbrook to Bilbo, June 11, 1940, Westbrook to Bilbo, November 27, 1939, both in Bilbo Papers.

60. For the WPA and state politics see Ronald Marcello, "The North Carolina Works Progress Administration and the Politics of Relief" (Ph.D. dissertation, Duke University, 1968); A. Cash Koeniger, "The New Deal and the States: Roosevelt Versus the Byrd Organization in Virginia," *Journal of American History*, LXVIII (1982), 876–96; Michael S. Holmes, *The New Deal in Georgia: An Administrative History* (Westport, Conn., 1975); Braeman, Bremner, and Brody (eds.), *The New Deal: The State and Local Levels* (Columbus, Ohio, 1975). Vol. II of Braeman, Bremner, and Brody (eds.), *The New Deal*, 2 vols.

61. Sherwood, *Roosevelt and Hopkins*, 68; Patterson, *The New Deal and the States*, 159, 168; James MacGregor Burns, *Deadlock of Democracy: Four Party Politics in America* (Englewood Cliffs, N.J., 1963), 168–69.

the state's federal patronage, and the WPA was by far the biggest prize. "The Administration has done everything for Harrison in Mississippi," Harold Ickes wrote in 1937, "even at the expense of Bilbo." As early as 1935 Aubrey Williams warned Malcolm Miller, "Regardless of all factors, you and I know that Harry [Hopkins] wouldn't agree to do anything that would get us out on a limb against him [Harrison]." With Wall running things in Jackson and Ellen Woodward funneling information from WPA headquarters to Harrison's office, very little the agency did in Mississippi escaped the senior senator's control.[62]

There is likewise no doubt that Harrison's constituency encompassed those "conservatives who controlled the . . . politics, economy, and social life" in Mississippi and who, according to Dewey Grantham, stood in the way of the kind of "far-reaching revolution" Roosevelt hoped to achieve in the South. So why did the administration, and Hopkins in particular, leave patronage, and consequent control of the state Democratic party, so totally in the grasp of such a faction?[63]

The reason for the coddling of Harrison in the early years was fairly obvious. For the sake of New Deal legislative success, Hopkins found it necessary to treat certain members of Congress with great care, and Harrison, as chairman of the Senate Finance Committee, was one of those who got "special attention." But the extent to which Hopkins was willing to accommodate Harrison's wishes substantially exceeded the demands of political expediency. After Roosevelt blocked Harrison's path to the Democratic leadership in 1937 and declared open war on southern conservatives with the purge attempt in 1938, it was apparent that Pat was going to go his own way regardless. He fought the administration vigorously on taxes and even relief spending and by 1939 was quietly throwing cold water on talk among state Democratic leaders of a third term for Roosevelt. Barely a week before the state convention in 1940, Harrison finally hopped aboard the third-term bandwagon when it was obvious that it was going to roll with or without him.[64]

Even then Hopkins continued to cater to Harrison's needs, at times

62. Ickes, *The Inside Struggle*, 170; transcript of telephone conservation between Williams and Miller, November 13, 1935, in WPA Papers, Mississippi, Section 610; transcript of telephone conversation between Woodward and Miss Cronin, October 23, 1936, transcript of telephone conversation between Miss Cronin and Ethel Payne, October 26, 1936, both in Woodward Papers.

63. Grantham, *The Democratic South*, 73–74.

64. Searle F. Charles, *Minister of Relief: Harry Hopkins and the Depression* (Syracuse, 1963), 162–63; Swain, *Pat Harrison*, 168–94, 234–36; Herbert Holmes to Harrison and Hugh White, February 27, 1939, Harrison to Holmes, March 11, 1939, both in Harrison Papers, University of Mississippi.

in apparent defiance of presidential directives. All this was done at the expense of Bilbo, whose loyalty to the New Deal was unflinching, even on as controversial an issue as wages and hours legislation. Perhaps part of the explanation lay in Hopkins' own presidential ambitions. By 1938 Roosevelt was grooming his relief czar as a possible successor, and Hopkins was not unwilling to use relief patronage as leverage in the quest. It would have been difficult for a man of Hopkins' background and temperament to gain the acquiescence of the southern conservative wing of the party, but if anyone's approval could have made him credible, it would have been Harrison's. Martha Swain notes that Hopkins was a singular and striking exception to Harrison's general disdain for the New Dealers. She attributes their friendship to the administrator's firsthand knowledge of the South. Yet it is hard to think that his three years of Red Cross work in the Southeast two decades earlier made Hopkins more attractive to Harrison than did three years of free-flowing patronage more recently.[65]

Whatever the causes, the Hopkins-Harrison alliance was real enough. Hopkins told a meeting of Democratic women in Memphis in 1937 that no one except perhaps Joseph Robinson had done more for Roosevelt and the New Deal than Harrison. In 1939 as secretary of commerce he even joined Harrison in criticism of Roosevelt's tax policy.[66]

The most amazing aspect of Hopkins' persistent partiality toward Harrison was that after 1937 Harrison joined the fight to cut relief spending while Bilbo fought valiantly for increases. The fight over the WPA "eighteen month" rule illustrated the paradox. In 1939 Congress added to the work-relief appropriation a requirement that everyone, except veterans, who had been on the WPA payroll for eighteen consecutive months be removed and made ineligible for recertification for thirty days. The following year John Danaher of Connecticut and Claude Pepper of Florida led an assault on the regulation, which had, said Danaher, left hundreds of thousands of people "in most destitute and most deplorable circumstances." Harrington himself had asked the Appropriations Committee to eliminate the rule, but the amendment failed by a large margin. Harrison was one of the forty-two who voted to retain the rule while Bilbo joined New Deal liberals

65. Samuel I. Rosenman, *Working with Roosevelt* (New York, 1952), 202; Marcello, "The North Carolina WPA," 259; Charles, *Minister of Relief*, 216–19; Swain, *Pat Harrison*, 251–52.

66. Memphis *Commercial Appeal*, May 9, 1937, Sec. 4, p. 6; Swain, *Pat Harrison*, 185; Charles, *Minister of Relief*, 217.

Pepper, Sherman Minton, Robert Wagner, and twenty-five others to vote against it.[67]

After 1937 Harrison continued to fight increases in relief spending and to bemoan what federal assistance was doing to the "rugged characters" of "tens of thousands" of Americans. During the same time, hundreds of letters were pouring into Bilbo's office from those whose "views of life and government" were undergoing the kind of transformation that Harrison lamented. Many were semiliterate or worse, and their scrawlings were usually in pencil on anything that could conceivably be used as writing paper. A sixty-three-year-old widow wrote that she and three daughters were without food and were asking "Bill Bo and Mr. Roosevelt for Some help." A Corinth widower with two children had been "layed off the WPA. . . . I am a poor man," he wrote, "haven't got anything at all, all I have to depend on is the WPA. . . . I sure will thank you a thousand times if you will help me get back to work."[68] A woman from Dennis wrote: "I am a widow woman 25, have two children, 2 and 4 to work for. Will you please help get me on the WPA. I signed up . . . at Tishomingo and havnt herd from it yet. I certainly do need some work to do, we are needing clothes very bad and can't get them and suffering for food I can't possibly make a crop and never last year. just hired out and hoed. and picked cotton and take in washing once a week. 50c. I owe a Dr. Bill $25 . . . but I can't pay it unless I can get Some work to do. I also owe a $10 Grocery Bill and cant get any more credit until I pay up. So please do all you can for me." From Pachuta another said: "i an writing to you for me a job if you pleasir, for i have not got any work to do but i sure Do kneed it mity bad for winter is coming and we have not got any clothes to wear and nothing to eat." A New Albany man was "*distressed* and *frantic* over being yet unemployed. . . . I want work," he begged. "I appeal to you—*Please*—and double please—ask somebody to place me at once." Broke as he always was, Bilbo sent him twenty-five dollars but begged him not to tell anyone: "So many want money—I can't help them all."[69]

If Mississippi had any of the "forgotten" men and women about whom Roosevelt talked, here they were. If there were Mississippians

67. Donald S. Howard, *The WPA and Federal Relief Policy* (New York, 1943), 519–22; *Congressional Record*, 76th Cong., 3rd Sess., 8310–15.

68. Swain, *Pat Harrison*, 190; Maud Burns to Bilbo, July 20, 1939, Green J. Knight to Bilbo, March 28, 1940, both in Bilbo Papers.

69. Lola V. Holley to Bilbo, February 1940, Evie Drury to Bilbo, October 31, 1938, Clarence Young to Bilbo, July 14, 1940, Bilbo to Young, July 31, 1940, all in Bilbo Papers.

"at the bottom of the economic pyramid," here they were. If Mississippi had citizens for whom the New Deal philosophy was especially tailored, here they were. But these were Bilbo's people—tenants, croppers, laborers, the "runt pigs" as Paul Johnson called them—and they believed in Bilbo. They looked to him, not as the average constituent looked to a politician, as a distant but ideologically sympathetic spokesman. They looked to him as a friend, as one of their own, as one who understood them, who felt their feelings, thought their thoughts, and spoke their words. "I come to you," one wrote, "because you are a friend of the poor and your aim is to do right by us, your people."[70]

It has been fashionable to attribute Bilbo's liberal leanings to elementary demagoguery, and perhaps it is true that "politics more than idealism" explained his consistent support for New Deal liberalism. But as Daniel Robison pointed out almost a half century ago, whether a man was considered a demagogue or a statesman often depended on "the respectability of his followers," at least in the eyes of those who considered themselves respectable. Since the primary beneficiaries of welfare liberalism in the South were the rednecks, their spokesmen tended, by definition, to be demagogues. Yet if Mississippi had a liberal constituency, the rednecks were it.[71]

When Otis L. Graham discussed those few old reformers who successfully made the transition to modern liberalism, he distinguished them from their "progressive" brethren of an earlier era by their delight that "the federal government was now committed to intercession against want." The progressive as liberal was one who "welcomed social action at the national level." Those with the most affinity for the welfare state, he argued, were the ones who had firsthand experience with the plight of the "urban lower classes," those whose constituents were the "people of the slums." But Graham could find no explanation in his scheme for "the unfeigned enthusiasm" of southerners, like Josephus Daniels, whose "ardent New Dealism" he found "astonishing." But why should the ardent New Dealism of a southerner, Daniels or Bilbo, be astonishing? "Only those progressives," said Graham, "who limited their hopes to a more humane treatment of the poor were able to find satisfaction in the achievement of Roosevelt's general welfare state." Certainly there were poor in the South, and certainly if

70. Joe C. Taylor to Bilbo, February 20, 1940, in Bilbo Papers.

71. Saucier, "The Public Career of Bilbo," 294; Daniel M. Robison, "From Tillman to Long: Some Striking Leaders of the Rural South," *Journal of Southern History*, III (1937), 298.

anyone demonstrated a conviction that the government ought to treat them humanely by tending to their welfare, Bilbo did.[72]

That is not to say that Bilbo was not first, last, and always a politician. No one with any sense of proportion would dispute that. He made every effort to turn his support for relief legislation to political advantage, going to great lengths to try to control the WPA in his state. But his doing so hardly distinguishes him from other New Dealers in the Congress or proves that he was any less committed in principle to the New Deal philosophy than they were. Yet his devotion to liberalism, no matter how consistent, was always suspect among the intellectual keepers of the liberal flame.

Unlike most eastern liberals, or even fellow southerners like Aubrey Williams or Claude Pepper, Bilbo acquired his ideals primarily from experience. He became committed to "humane treatment of the poor" as a result of long-standing and intimate empathy with the poor, not from the academic ambience of Yale or Harvard Law School. His liberalism was earthy and crude, as his people were earthy and crude. The slums of Mississippi were the hot, Delta flatlands or the barren, rugged clay of the northeastern hills. The people of those slums were the tenants, the sharecroppers, and the one-mule farmers who, like their fathers before them, clawed an earthy and crude existence amidst debt, disease, and despair. Bilbo knew he could hardly win their allegiance with a reasoned analysis of intricate economic or social policy. They would only follow someone whom they trusted, someone who understood them. Misplaced or not, that trust was firmly fixed on Bilbo. In the thirties they looked to Roosevelt and the federal government for relief in the most literal meaning of that term, and most of them looked to Roosevelt because Bilbo encouraged them to. As one explained to the president, "I and 8 in family has all away Ben for Mr. Billbo. We have helped him in ever way. I mean to help you on the Count of Mr. Bill Bo."[73]

Here was the New Deal constituency in Mississippi, but Hopkins almost squandered it. He stubbornly used the WPA to strengthen the leaders of the faction most hostile to the administration's philosophy. There is no apparent logical or ideological explanation for that political paradox. Perhaps the explanation lay not in logic or ideology at all, but in style. Dorothy Kinsella, in a study of three prominent liberal southern journalists, notes their frustration that liberalism failed to

72. Otis L. Graham, Jr., *An Encore for Reform: The Old Progressives and the New Deal* (New York, 1967), 103–12, 181.

73. Maud Burns to Bilbo, July 20, 1939, in Bilbo Papers.

win the allegiance of the masses. When confronted with a political choice between the respectable conservatives and the "demagogues," who commanded mass support, they chose the "traditional leadership," hoping to find there someone who would attack poverty and ignorance. "If the candidates were conservative, they were at least gentlemen who avoided flamboyant racist oratory and brought prestige to the South." But during the thirties Bilbo's oratory, while by all standards flamboyant, was but little tainted by the kind of racist drivel that would make him the "archangel of white supremacy" a decade later. He was simply too busy trying to get the federal government in gear against poverty and illiteracy—and keep his political fences mended—to be ranting about white supremacy, which he considered to be relatively secure anyway. For him economics was the issue during the New Deal, and race was not.[74]

Yet in the eyes of the lettered liberals of the East, it was not Bilbo but the journalists whom Kinsella describes who became the recognized "promoters of the New Deal." It was they who molded the northern image of the South and its politics, and perhaps that as much as anything helps explain the paradox of the political role of the WPA in Mississippi. Like their urbane counterparts in the South, Hopkins and Williams and their friends in the WPA found it more palatable to deal with a conservative gentleman than with a liberal "demagogue."[75]

74. Dorothy Kinsella, "Southern Apologists: A Liberal Image" (Ph.D. dissertation, St. Louis University, 1971), 54–55, 271–84.

75. *Ibid.*, 54.

Chapter Eight

Liberal New Dealer

The true test of Bilbo's transition from progressive to liberal came during Roosevelt's second term. He had backed the president faithfully during 1935's Second Hundred Days, but so had most southerners. He differed from his colleagues only in the eagerness with which he fell in behind Roosevelt, who now eased off the conventional Democratic path and edged toward forbidden social and economic terrain. As the landscape of the new course became more visible and the president's determination to continue along it became more fixed, an increasing number of Democrats, especially southerners, turned back toward the familiar road, though it meant becoming fellow travelers with Republicans. The Man, however, marched on with enthusiasm.

The events of 1936 confirmed Roosevelt in his new departure. With the election looming in November and with the "must" list of 1935 completed, the 74th Congress assembled in January in common agreement that it would be a brief session. Those hopes were dashed quickly by the Supreme Court, which in January struck down the AAA, forcing the lawmakers to construct a new farm program. Debate on the new Soil Conservation and Domestic Allotment Act and the holdover bonus controversy made for anything but a tranquil session, but in view of what had preceded and what would follow, 1936 resembled the eye of a storm. There was plenty of energy left for the fall campaign.[1]

It was a momentous election. Extending the trend of 1934, the Democrats swelled to unprecedented majorities in the Congress. There were so many in the Senate, in fact, that twelve freshmen had to hold their noses and sit on the Republican side of the aisle. In the presidential race Roosevelt swamped Republican Alf Landon by almost eleven million votes, carrying every state but Maine and Vermont. It was one of the most stunningly complete presidential victories ever and a resounding personal triumph for Roosevelt.

It was also a triumph for the New Deal—the New Deal of the Sec-

1. O. R. Altman, "Second Session of the 74th Congress," *American Political Science Review*, XXX (1936), 1086; Leuchtenburg, *Roosevelt and the New Deal*, 170–74.

ond Hundred Days. The coalition that swept the Democrats to victory in 1936 was not the same as that of 1932. This was a liberal coalition built on the urban masses of the North, on labor, and on the poor throughout the country. Such people revered Roosevelt because they believed that he had eased their economic pain and followed him because they dreamed that he could cure them altogether. As the president glanced over his shoulder at the throngs who had fallen in behind him, he must surely have seen the anxious hope in their faces and concluded that he could not stand still. He would have to continue the direction set in 1935. Yet when he turned forward again to face the Congress who would have to tread the path with him, he must have seen weary anxiety in the faces of men like Robinson, Byrnes, and Harrison, the leaders who had served him so faithfully and effectively but who nursed a growing dread of the unfamiliar ground they were now expected to traverse. Roosevelt would have to choose: the "new Democrats" cried out for advance, but old hands like Harrison wanted "to get under the shade and rest awhile."[2]

The president's second inaugural address did nothing to allay the fears of the Old Guard. "I see one-third of a nation ill-housed, ill-clad, ill-nourished," he declared, and "the Nation, seeing and understanding the injustice" of those conditions, demanded a remedy. Having pronounced that diagnosis, Dr. New Deal then prescribed the medicine: increased relief, a labor standards act, a public housing law, seven smaller regional TVAs, a new farm bill, executive reorganization, an NRA-type bituminous coal bill, and a farm tenancy act. It was an impressive work list, even for a Congress that gathered, as one reporter said, in "an atmosphere of profound awe" at the president's "unprecedented popularity." But the work list would remain unfilled. The congressional session of 1937 proved to be a watershed for the New Deal, the first time Roosevelt would go to the legislative well and draw up an empty bucket. He had decided on a bold stroke that, as it turned out, thoroughly blunted New Deal momentum and dissipated much of the political capital so carefully amassed over the previous four years and so magnificently consolidated in November.[3]

Roosevelt had determined on a surprise offensive against the last bastion of effective conservative opposition, the Supreme Court. Routed from their traditional stronghold on Capitol Hill, the defenders of the status quo had fallen back on the court as their last hope of stemming

2. Leuchtenburg, *Roosevelt and the New Deal*, 184–96; Swain, *Pat Harrison*, 164.

3. Burns, *Roosevelt: The Lion and the Fox*, 310–11, 291–93; O. R. Altman, "First Session of the 75th Congress," *American Political Science Review*, XXXI (1937), 1071.

the liberal tide. And it was no broken reed upon which they leaned. The justices had cast down both NRA and AAA, the twin pillars of the recovery program, and were threatening the newly laid foundations of welfare democracy. The court's invalidation in 1936 of a New York state minimum-wage law created what the president called "a no man's land" where neither state nor federal governments could operate. In 1937 the Wagner Act and social security seemed certain targets for the guns of judicial review.[4]

Taking the November triumph as a personal mandate to defend and extend the New Deal, Roosevelt decided to neutralize this lone but potent pocket of illiberal opposition; he decided to "pack" the Supreme Court. Keeping mostly his own counsel, he considered a variety of plans and finally settled on one devised by Attorney General Homer Cummings. Rather than present the solution as a straightforward effort to liberalize a court that was already severely divided ideologically —several of the crucial decisions had been by 5–4 vote—FDR called for a general reform of the judiciary, disingenuously justified by the age of the judges. There was a substantial backlog of cases, he argued, because the older judges could not keep up. The judiciary reorganization bill would allow the president to appoint a new justice for every sitting judge who failed to retire within six months after his seventieth birthday, up to a limit of six on the Supreme Court bench and forty-four in the lower courts.[5]

Before announcing the plan on February 5, Roosevelt had shared his intentions with but a handful of people; of the cabinet, only Cummings knew what was coming. The proposal gave an extraordinary jolt to congressional leaders who would have to steer it through the legislative shoals. For some, like Representative Hatton Summers of Texas, it was time to "cash in." For others, like Harrison, Byrnes, and Garner, it was at least a goad to reconsider the recent drift of the New Deal. What especially troubled the southerners was the persistent association in the public mind of the court plan with the recent sit-down strikes that the militant Congress of Industrial Organizations had used to bludgeon General Motors into a submissive contract. The workers had occupied factories and refused either to leave or to work. It was an assault on private property that deeply disturbed men like Harrison and their middle-class constituents. In an era when European dictators seemed to be rising on the backs of street rowdies and mob action, it seemed ominous indeed to see an American president straining to

4. Leuchtenburg, *Roosevelt and the New Deal*, 231–34.

5. *Ibid.*

quash the only institution that successfully resisted his wishes even as he refused to intervene to stop working-class "radicalism."[6]

The howl from conservatives was expected, but the telling blow came from liberals, in and out of Congress. Many who had heretofore marched behind Roosevelt refused to follow on this issue. Some feared for the court's dignity and independence; some worried over the president's patent vengefulness. Others simply resented the transparency of the pretext: "Too clever—too damned clever," remarked a formerly friendly newspaper. Further developments stripped the president's case of whatever credibility it might have had. In a series of spring decisions the court upheld a Washington state minimum-wage law, reversing its earlier position, and sustained the Wagner Act and the Social Security Act. When the Senate Judiciary Committee opened hearings on the reorganization bill, the opposition presented a letter from Chief Justice Charles Evans Hughes that trenchantly refuted the charge of inefficiency.[7]

Roosevelt himself had done what the Republicans and conservatives seemed incapable of doing on their own. He had provoked substantial liberal opposition to an administration position. Among the defectors were most of the old progressives. When Senator Burton K. Wheeler revealed his opposition, the conservatives recognized the value of having a Democrat with such unimpeachably progressive credentials leading the fight, and they willingly stepped aside to let him out front. Republicans reveled in the exquisite luxury of silently watching Roosevelt squirm under a challenge to his legislative authority orchestrated by Democrats, and it was the severest, most significant such challenge yet. So Wheeler led, moderate Democrats followed (Tom Connally of Texas, Joseph O'Mahoney of Wyoming, Bennett Clark of Missouri), Harrison and Byrnes kept quiet, and Garner went fishing in Texas. Democratic unity was disintegrating.[8]

What concerned other southerners delighted Bilbo; what alienated Roosevelt from other progressives endeared him to Bilbo. The inevitable liberal-conservative clash within the coalition was erupting, and Bilbo relished conflict. The New Deal was turning to his kind of politics. When Roosevelt attacked "organized money" and "economic royalists" and declared himself the candidate of the people, he was speaking Bilbo's language.

The Man had already launched his own assault on the court in the

6. *Ibid.*

7. Burns, *Roosevelt: The Lion and the Fox*, 297–305.

8. Leuchtenburg, *Roosevelt and the New Deal*, 234–35; Patterson, *Congressional Conservatism and the New Deal*, 111–18.

wake of the AAA decision a year earlier. Hurling Thomas Jefferson (on the dangers of judicial usurpation) with one hand and James Russell Lowell (on the adaptablility of the Constitution) with the other, he rained philosophical and literary fire on the New Deal's foes. It was not the 1780s, he sneered, and "the question today is, shall the power usurped on the part of the Supreme Court continue to be exercised over the solemn will of the people?" Bilbo assailed the autocracy of five of nine "old men in caps and gowns . . . [who] dared to question an act of Congress . . . no matter what the will of the people." He promised to submit a constitutional amendment to allow Congress to override a judicial veto by a two-thirds vote of each house. It was the same basic solution to the court problem that Tom Corcoran and Ben Cohen would unsuccessfully urge on Roosevelt the following January.[9]

"The fight for the forgotten man has just commenced," Bilbo wrote a constituent. "Of course, we all believe in orderly and constitutional government, but after all, nothing is higher in Government than the welfare of the masses." In the midst of the reorganization fight he introduced his amendment but emphasized that it was not intended as a substitute for the president's proposal, which Bilbo endorsed "one hundred percent." His own proposal would, however, provide a more enduring safeguard. He implored Hugh White to declare publicly his "whole hearted approval" of the court bill to bring pressure on Mississippi's wavering congressional delegation. The governor politely declined, lamely arguing that the president and the people knew where he stood. White's silence contrasted with resolutions of support for Roosevelt from Mississippi farm groups and the state bar association and a recent poll that showed Mississippi to be one of twelve states that favored the bill.[10]

Bilbo justified the president to constituents in his most orotund populist rhetoric. When one declared that Carter Glass's eloquent radio attack on the court proposal made him "ashamed and disgusted" with his own two senators, Bilbo responded that he was fairly disgusted with one of them himself. He declared surprise, horror, and grief that anyone could be so "gullible and credulous" as to be moved by "the unctuous, high-sounding and hypocritical explosions of old man Carter Glass, the aristocrat . . . and the known sympathizer and manipulator of the predatory interests. . . . He is old, feeble, irritable,

9. *Congressional Record*, 74th Cong., 2nd Sess., 9891–99; Alsop and Catledge, *The 168 Days*, 36–37.

10. Bilbo to F. L. Matthews, January 10, 1936, in Bilbo Papers; *Congressional Record*, 75th Cong., lst Sess., 2803–2804; Bilbo to White, March 28, 1937, White to Bilbo, April 2, 1937, both in Bilbo Papers; Swain, *Pat Harrison*, 148.

and senile . . . and when he dies," it would be splendid if "old Andy Mellon would pass out at the same time: [then] these two old corporate fossils could be buried in the same grave, on the right-hand side of the House of Morgan on Wall Street . . . where their sympathies and hearts have always been." The "money power," Bilbo declared, had been using the Republican party to pack the Supreme Court since Lincoln's day. They had stocked it and the lower courts with a galaxy of corporation lawyers, who "by their decisions . . . have glorified property rights by sacrificing human rights. The god of Mammon reigns supreme in their chambers. . . . My dear brother, this is a Democracy and Democracy shall and must rule this country," not "these old ossified, petrified, fossilized corporate minions of the predatory interests." It was a time for new blood, he concluded, "new, modern, Democratic men . . . whose lives and preachments . . . would . . . glorify human rights instead of property rights."[11]

In light of the court's reversal on the minimum-wage law, Bilbo added a postscript. The judges were so "old, senile, and childish," that they would not "stand their ground" under the pressure of the president's proposal. "They are weak," he declared, but warned, "Of course, you and I will be that way some day." It reminded him, he said, of a sign he had once seen in a Bogalusa, Louisiana, restaurant: "Don't talk about our coffee because you will be old and weak some day yourself."[12]

On May 18 Willis van Devanter, one of the court's four conservatives, announced his retirement, opening the way for Roosevelt to establish a slim liberal majority on the court with his appointment of a replacement. But FDR wanted more than a slim majority. With his reorganization bill in deep trouble, with other bills languishing on the Senate calendar, and with his party in disarray, he stubbornly refused to retreat. Then on July 14 came the crushing blow. Majority Leader Robinson, whose immense influence over his fellows constituted the bill's last hope, collapsed and died in his Washington apartment. More Democrats, loosed from their personal commitments to Robinson, scurried to the opposition, and eight days later the Senate voted to recommit the bill to the Judiciary Committee. Bilbo, with La Follette, Black, and seventeen other diehards, voted no. In August, Congress passed a face-saving judiciary reform bill that made procedural changes in the courts but was absolutely silent on the issue of additional judges.

11. Bilbo to Rev. W. A. Sullivan, March 30, 1937, in Bilbo Papers.
12. *Ibid.*

The lawmakers had for the first time stood on their hind legs and defied the president on a major issue.[13]

To aggravate the administration's misery, there was the problem of a new Senate majority leader. The issue had first surfaced when van Devanter had resigned and Robinson's Senate friends had virtually demanded that Roosevelt appoint the Arkansan to the vacancy. White House forces immediately began to lay the groundwork for the promotion of Assistant Majority Leader Alben Barkley of Kentucky to Robinson's post. The other contenders were Key Pittman of Nevada, Byrnes, and Harrison. The Mississippian had entered the contest, some said, simply out of pique over the administration's efforts on Barkley's behalf. On May 19 Harrison and Pittman withdrew, but Pat jumped back in when friends convinced him that his colleague from South Carolina would step aside in his favor. Harrison's candidacy became a rallying point for opponents of the court bill, and Robinson's death provoked a stampede to his side.[14]

Roosevelt faced an agonizing dilemma. Barkley was more liberal and more willing to execute White House orders, and his opponent had become a symbol of Senate rebellion against the administration. Moreover, Harrison's election to the leadership would leave the all-important Finance Committee in the hands of conservative William King of Utah. At the bottom of it all was Harrison's own conservatism, especially in fiscal matters. Roosevelt later worried aloud to Farley that Pat would sabotage his tax and spending policies. He "would repeal the Capital Gains Tax," the president warned. "He would do it now if he could."[15]

But to defile the hallowed ground of congressional custom and legislative independence with executive interference would be a desecration sure to inflame the wrath of Senate gods already restive under an overbearing White House. The president, however, had no choice. Behind a facade of public neutrality he hurled his troops into a feverish campaign to insure Barkley's success. To strengthen the Kentuckian's claim, Roosevelt addressed a letter to Barkley as assistant leader encouraging him to continue the fight for court reform. The obvious purpose of this "Dear Alben" letter and the intense behind-the-scenes executive pressure on certain senators infuriated even some of the president's most

13. Leuchtenburg, *Roosevelt and the New Deal*, 237–38; *Congressional Record*, 75th Cong., lst Sess., 7381.

14. Alsop and Catledge, *The 168 Days*, 239–40.

15. Swain, *Pat Harrison*, 154–55; James A. Farley, *Jim Farley's Story: The Roosevelt Years* (New York, 1948), 124–25, 181.

loyal supporters. Robinson's funeral train turned into a cross-country political auction with both sides seizing every opportunity discretion would allow to bid for the votes of the uncommitted or wavering. When the train pulled into Washington from Little Rock, the race was still too close to call.[16]

Harrison returned to the capital painfully aware that every vote would count, even Bilbo's. The two had not exchanged a single word since the 1936 primary, but when Byrnes solicited his vote for Harrison, Bilbo reputedly hinted that he might comply if the candidate himself would ask for it. After a moment's Faustian flirtation, Harrison decided there were limits to ambition. "Tell the son-of-a-bitch I wouldn't speak to him if it meant the Presidency of the United States," Pat bellowed.[17]

On July 21, at 10 A.M., seventy-five Democratic senators filed into Room 201 of the Senate Office Building. The acrimony nursed by six months of increasingly bitter controversy was almost as palpable as the Caucus Room's marble surface, and the mood was every bit as cold. The outcome was still very much uncertain as Carl Hatch of New Mexico and Kenneth McKellar of Tennessee collected the folded slips of paper from Key Pittman's hat. After a seemingly interminable count the vote stood dead even at thirty-seven as the teller fumbled with the final ballot. Barkley bit his pipe stem in two before the teller announced the name on the tiny piece of paper, Alben Barkley.[18]

There is some doubt about Bilbo's explanation of his vote; there is no doubt how he voted. "Barkley beat 'Our Pat' by one vote," he beamed, "and that was my vote." He had committed himself to Barkley, Bilbo explained, when it appeared that Robinson was going to the Supreme Court, before Harrison was ever a candidate. In fact he had urged Barkley to run and campaigned for him before Robinson's death. He could not compromise himself, he reasoned, by "flopping around" on the Senate floor.[19]

There were indications, however, that he did not decide how he would vote until the last minute. When McComb Mayor X. A. Kramer urged him to vote for Harrison, Bilbo grumbled, in a letter written be-

16. Alsop and Catledge, *The 168 Days*, 268–83; Tom Connally (as told to Alfred Steinberg), *My Name is Tom Connally* (New York, 1954), 192–93.

17. Swain, *Pat Harrison*, 159–60; George E. Allen, *Presidents Who Have Known Me* (New York, 1950), 70–71.

18. Memphis *Commercial Appeal*, July 22, 1937, p. 6; Alsop and Catledge, *The 168 Days*, 282–83.

19. Bilbo to Burkett, July 21, 1937, Bilbo to R. M. Newton, July 21, 1937, Bilbo to R. Q. Braswell, July 21, 1937, all in Bilbo Papers; Key Pittman to Pat Harrison, July 20,

fore the caucus, that Pat had snubbed him since the 1936 primary and had driven his friends from the WPA. "Notwithstanding all this," he said, "I am really thinking about voting for him and will decide between now and tomorrow at ten o'clock."[20]

Why, then, did Bilbo vote for Barkley? Harold Ickes attributed it to simple spite, observing that "it must be true that revenge is sweeter than most other feelings." Also, there is evidence that James Roosevelt had promised Bilbo administration support for his research-laboratory bill[21] and the prospect of increased patronage if he would vote for the president's choice for majority leader. But there were also reasons for The Man to swallow hard and support his fellow Mississippian. Most observers believed that he would have assured his own reelection in 1940 with a magnanimous vote for Harrison. Some of his closest lieutenants urged him "to silence Pat's supporters by voting for him." But this was not the first time that Bilbo had failed to do what his friends thought politically expedient when Harrison was involved. Besides, a vote for Barkley was consistent with Bilbo's record of support for the administration, and the court bill was, after all, then still at stake. Perhaps Bilbo's vote is best explained by that ubiquitous and inseparable union of politics and progressivism that characterized his entire public life. "The fight is on," he exulted to Mike Conner. "I am a leftist; Pat is a rightist, and . . . I am the boy that killed Cock Robin. What is the reaction of the people?"[22]

In an interesting epilogue to the court reform fight, Roosevelt named Hugo Black to the Supreme Court vacancy, only to have the press uncover the Alabama senator's former membership in the Ku Klux Klan. In a perversely fitting way, the president dragged controversy along the final few steps of the year-long wrangle over the judiciary. The appointment of a fellow southern liberal delighted Bilbo, who reminded opponents that the Senate had not quailed at the appointments of Mississippi's L. Q. C. Lamar or Louisiana's Edward Douglass White, despite their notorious participation in the post-Reconstruction Klan. Bilbo defended his vote for confirmation with an eloquent testimony to his own and Black's liberalism.

1937, in Political Correspondence, 1920–1940, "H," Key Pittman Papers, Library of Congress.

20. Bilbo to X. A. Kramer, July 20, 1937, in Bilbo Papers.

21. See Chapter Nine.

22. Ickes, *The Inside Struggle*, 170; Bidwell Adam to Bilbo, May 7, 1938; Bilbo to D. R. Smith, July 29, 1937, both in Bilbo Papers; Memphis *Commercial Appeal*, August 1, 1937, Sec. 4, p. 5; Bilbo to Newton, July 21, 1937, Bilbo to Conner, July 25, 1937, both in Bilbo Papers.

> I voted for the confirmation of Senator Hugo L. Black because during my association with him in the United States Senate I found him to be a friend of the forgotten and underprivileged man, a friend of labor, a friend of the great masses that have for so long a time been subjected to the exploitation of the over-privileged few. I reasoned that a man of his broad sympathies for the common people and his clear understanding of their problems, whether they were Jews, Catholics, Protestants, Hicksites, Orthodox Friends, or Klu Kluxers, with all of whom he had enjoyed close and intimate associations, who could draft and perfect legislation designed to lessen the oppressiveness of their burden and to improve their standards of living, most certainly could correctly interpret laws and rightly determine the question of their constitutionality.
>
> In voting for the confirmation of Senator Hugo L. Black, I was confident that I was acting "in the interest of the preservation of civil liberty and religious toleration" and in the interest of the economic freedom of the people of the United States.[23]

The court reform fiasco was a turning point for congressional opposition to the New Deal. It allowed those moderate Democrats who had grown uneasy about where Roosevelt had been leading them since 1935 an opportunity to abandon ship without being hanged by the electorate for desertion. Having once mutinied and survived, they would find it less threatening to challenge the captain thereafter. The court bill had been derailed by a coalition whose loose but definite structure, leadership, and methodology provided the experience and machinery for effective opposition in the future. At the same time, the fight substantially weakened the president's coalition. He could never again be sure of the southern oligarchs, other moderate and rural Democrats, or the western progressives. Worst of all, it shattered the myth of Roosevelt's invincibility.[24]

James Patterson rightly argues, however, that there would have been significant congressional resistance to Roosevelt's second-term program even had there never been a judiciary reform bill. The "new" New Deal, the urban liberalism of the Second Hundred Days, had splintered Roosevelt's original coalition along sectional and economic lines, and the issues that would dominate the second term—relief, labor, and housing—were just the kind to aggravate the split. The most devastating of the defections were those of the southerners because they so thoroughly dominated the congressional power structure. Without Robinson, Byrnes, Harrison, and Garner there would have been no Hundred Days, First or Second. But 1935 and 1936 had been troubling for them. They were uneasy with the antibusiness tone of

23. Bilbo to Robert Gray Taylor, October 5, 1937, in Bilbo Papers.
24. Patterson, *Congressional Conservatism and the New Deal*, 125–27.

both the Second Hundred Days and the presidential campaign. All but Garner were close to Bernard Baruch—his collection of "Old Masters," critics called them—and they increasingly looked to him for advice as the administration assailed the "Sixty Families" who controlled the economy and the "chiselling ten percent" of businessmen who were at the root of the nation's economic woes. As these old politicos grew more uncomfortable in the rarefied ideological air around the White House, they discovered a renewed attraction in the rural but fraternal atmosphere of Hobcaw, Baruch's lavish South Carolina estate. There they often hunted with him and his powerful business friends. Like Baruch they had approved the crisis action of the early New Deal but now believed that the emergency had passed and further drastic reform would erode business confidence and discourage recovery. In addition they cherished their power in the party and felt threatened by the growing influence of liberal urban elements. Behind it all lurked an unspoken but perhaps decisive fear. They were coming to see what bedrock southern conservatives like Carter Glass had seen earlier, that a liberalized Democracy under an all-powerful executive was a threat to white supremacy. For them the showdown had come, and at stake were the Democratic party and the New Deal. They must yield to Roosevelt's urban liberalism or somehow turn the administration back toward New Freedom progressivism.[25]

Roosevelt could perhaps have salvaged a senatorial majority had he been able to unite the remaining progressive elements, but he could not. Most of the old western progressives, horrified by the burgeoning power of government in general and the executive in particular, abandoned the president after 1936. They had never really trusted Roosevelt. To them labor and welfare legislation seemed merely a political sop to soak up urban votes and perpetuate FDR's presidency. Only Norris and La Follette were able to translate their progressivism into New Deal liberalism. Finally, many nonsouthern rural Democrats who had followed the administration on nonfarm issues during the first term refused after 1936 to extend their agrarian radicalism to urban interests. While the incipient conservative coalition, said Patterson, was not the unified and cohesive bloc some thought, "liberals . . . were hardly a coalition at all."[26]

If Bilbo harbored any reservations about the emerging welfare state,

25. *Ibid.*, 133–34, 95–99; Schwarz, *The Speculator: Bernard M. Baruch*, 184–87, 257.

26. Ronald Mulder, *The Insurgent Progressives in the United States Senate and the New Deal, 1933–1939* (New York, 1979), 292–307; Graham, *Encore for Reform*, 29, 39–40; Patterson, *Congressional Conservatism and the New Deal*, 325.

1937 opened wide the gate for his departure. Many of those who spoke for constituencies like his—southern, agrarian, progressive—had already scrambled through. But Bilbo did not share their aversion to Roosevelt's new direction. He remained not only a New Dealer but a vocal one, a veritable missionary proclaiming the gospel of welfare liberalism throughout rural Mississippi. On Capitol Hill, Bilbo's support for the president remained firm and outspoken.

The court fight had diverted attention from other legislation, but the sit-down controversy thrust the labor issue upon Congress even before the president's wages-and-hours bill reached the floor. On April 1, while the senators droned their way toward a weekend recess with debate on the Guffey coal bill, Byrnes launched a surprise counteroffensive against militant labor by introducing an amendment condemning sit-down strikes. Startled conservative Democrats and delighted Republicans leaped forward with heartfelt support and plunged the normally somnolent late-Thursday chamber into spirited debate. Robinson, who inwardly sympathized with the censure, nonetheless defended the president's interests and corralled enough votes over the weekend to block the amendment. Yet Byrnes had served warning that southern Democrats would not be bulldozed on the labor issue. Both Mississippi senators supported the president, but Bilbo's vote was enthusiastic while Harrison's was more like the majority leader's, reluctant.[27]

By the time the wages-and-hours debate erupted, reluctance had hardened into resistance. The battle came on the far side of the judiciary controversy, with Harrison smarting from Roosevelt's intervention in the leadership contest and sniffing the air of political independence. The opening salvo in his rebellion against the White House was a forceful statement of the South's case against federal labor standards. Southern industry, he argued, could not afford to pay its workers as much as New England and needed the kind of wage differential that had been built into the NRA and public works agencies.[28]

"Pat Harrison has gone off the deep end," Roosevelt responded. But the president faced a general uprising among southern senators over the issue. Extolling their region's natural advantages, climate, accessible raw materials, and cheap power, they insisted that the salubrious Southland could sustain men "comfortably and reasonably" on a much lower wage than could the North—though E. D. Smith's "fifty cents a day" strained even the dullest credulity. The primary attraction, as Turner Catledge of the New York *Times* reported, was "a plentiful

27. Patterson, *Congressional Conservatism and the New Deal*, 136–38.
28. *Ibid.*, 152.

supply of cheap, docile, dependable, and unorganized labor." The Deep South had begun to woo northern industry with the kind of concessions Harrison's friend Hugh White sponsored in his BAWI program: tax breaks and state or locally financed factories. It was BAWI that had inspired Mississippi WPA Director Roland Wall to divert WPA funds to construct the "vocational schools" that conveniently converted into ready-made factory buildings and were then leased to manufacturers at nominal rent.[29]

Federal wage-and-hour regulations threatened to negate the South's advantages, and southerners in Congress suspected a conspiracy to strike "a deadening blow to the New South." The Wagner Act had already ruffled southern feathers as in Tupelo, Mississippi, where, Congressman John Rankin charged, National Labor Relations Board agents had incited labor trouble that shut down the town's chief industry. The Tupelo incident perfectly mirrored the growing estrangement of middle-class southerners from the New Deal. Labor trouble had a loyal congressman and a model TVA city up in arms. Constituents vilified Hugo Black, who sponsored the fair labor standards bill in the Senate, while opponents like Harrison were deluged with praise.[30]

On the last day of July the administration had mustered enough votes to pass the bill only to see it die in the House in August. Revived in a special session later in the year, the bill expired again when the House sent it back to committee. Not a single Mississippi congressman voted to save it. Finally, after liberal New Dealer Claude Pepper won a reelection campaign in which labor standards was a major issue and after the bill had been revised to satisfy AF of L objections, the House passed it in May, 1938.[31]

The debate came to symbolize, said Willliam Leuchtenburg, the struggle "of Southern conservatives like . . . Smith against southerners of advanced views like Hugo Black." If so, the junior senator from Mississippi stood amongst the advanced. For him the wages-and-hours fight capped a career of support for organized labor stretching back to his lieutenant governorship, when he had refused to send troops to protect scabs during a strike against the Gulf and Ship Island Railroad. That decision had earned him "the lasting friendship and admiration" of Mississippi's railroad workers, said one union leader. As

29. Ickes, *The Inside Struggle*, 182; Leuchtenburg, *Roosevelt and the New Deal*, 261; New York *Times*, August 8, 1937, Sec. 4, p. 3; Swain, *Pat Harrison*, 163–64.

30. New York *Times*, August 8, 1937, Sec. 4, p. 3; T. R. B., "Washington Notes," *New Republic*, August 18, 1937, p. 45.

31. Leuchtenburg, *Roosevelt and the New Deal*, 261–62; Swain, *Pat Harrison*, 164–65.

Bilbo explained to a constituent, he was simply too loyal a Democrat "to repudiate the Platform or desert the President in his efforts to keep faith with the people."[32]

More likely his vote was an echo of his populist heritage. No corporate entity save the railroads roused the ire of piney-woods rednecks as did the sawmill companies whose predecessors had stripped much of south Mississippi bare around the turn of the century. Bilbo had cut his political teeth on the anticorporation issue, and he had gnawed the lumber industry down to the marrow. Thirty years later he was still fighting to protect sawmill workers. An employee of the Pearl River Valley Lumber Company, in an anonymous letter, begged him on behalf of all the workers to do whatever he could to see that the wages-and-hours bill passed. Every employee, said the mill worker, had earlier been forced to write a letter to Bilbo and Congressman Dan McGehee denouncing the bill. "The boss dictated every letter," he said. "They had us come into the office one by one, and we were told to write as they dictated 'or walk out.'"[33]

Bilbo hardly needed persuading. "I am one hundred percent for the wage and hour law," he told a lumberman who complained that it would drive sawmills out of business. "You know," Bilbo responded, "that a white man with a family could not maintain the American standard of living on the wages paid the common labor in the average sawmill. . . . Such laborers received just enough to eke out a miserable existence." To the suggestion that Congress should lower the minimum wage, Bilbo replied that if it were changed at all it ought to be raised: "In other words, the wage and hour law . . . has come to stay."[34]

Only eight southern Democrats voted for the bill in the Senate. Although Bilbo did vote to exempt agricultural workers, so did other southern liberals, including Pepper. And on every other major amendment, Bilbo voted with the liberals. There can be no question of his belief in fair labor standards. While his Mississippi colleague was justifying the ways of the South to the nation, Bilbo was evangelizing the folks back home on an issue that most southern spokesmen and most other rural Congressmen opposed vehemently.[35]

Bilbo also heartily endorsed Roosevelt's proposal for seven regional

32. Leuchtenburg, *Roosevelt and the New Deal*, 262; P. D. Williams to Bilbo, May 16, 1935, Bilbo to John F. Shows, August 5, 1937, both in Bilbo Papers.

33. Employees of Pearl River Valley Lumber Company to Bilbo, May 19, 1938, in Bilbo Papers.

34. Bilbo to C. Blankinship, December 9, 1938, in Bilbo Papers.

35. Patterson, *Congressional Conservatism and the New Deal*, 153–54; Bilbo to Roosevelt, October 11, 1937, PPF 2184, in Roosevelt Papers.

"little TVAs," though it never got off the ground in 1937. Had he been able, Bilbo would have laced Mississippi with TVA lines humming with public power for every hamlet in the state. He even tried, unsuccessfully, to coax TVA Director Arthur Morgan into investing in Mississippi bauxite to crack the "Mellon monopoly" on aluminum.[36]

But the aspect of TVA that intrigued Bilbo most was flood control. He wanted to extend Washington's responsibility from the Tennessee Valley to the entire nation. In his first year in the Senate he had secured half a million dollars for a flood-control navigation project on the Pearl River in south Mississippi. In 1936 he took his crusade for federal responsibility to the Senate floor. "If I can win this one fight," he boasted, "I will have done more for Mississippi than all the senators and representatives have done in fifty years."[37]

He proposed an amendment to a flood-control bill that explicitly acknowledged the federal government's "full burden and responsibility" for flood control and relieved state and local agencies of any of the cost of the projects covered in the bill. He wanted a "positive policy of total responsibility" by Washington. Armed with detailed research, including an Army Corps of Engineers survey recommending eight billion dollars worth of improvements on two thousand projects in all but four states, Bilbo swamped his colleagues with his own deluge of facts and figures. Flood control, he explained, was a national problem that encompassed drought and soil erosion as well as overflow and required a multifaceted solution integrating levee, dam, and canal work with reforestation and drought control. "What modern Pythagoras," he asked, "what Einstein of our own age," could possibly apportion the proper share of local costs and benefits of so extensive a program. His arguments convinced several senators, especially New Dealers like Joseph Guffey, Barkley, Black, and Harry Truman, but not nearly enough. Bilbo's last word on the issue was the verse "Who Owns the Mississippi River?" which he entered into the *Congressional Record.* "It occurred to me," he chided, "that if prose would not convince the Congress, perhaps poetry would do so." It did not.[38]

36. Bilbo to Arthur E. Morgan, March 28, 1935, Morgan to Bilbo, April 8, 1935, both in Bilbo Papers.

37. Jackson *Daily News*, May 10, 1935, p. 1, June 28, 1935, p. 1; Bilbo to Heber Ladner, January 28, 1936.

38. U.S. Congress, Senate, Committee on Commerce, *Hearings Before the Committee on Commerce on H.R. 6732, an Act Authorizing the Construction, Repair, and Preservation of Certain Public Works on Rivers and Harbors and for Other Purposes*, 74th Cong., lst Sess., 1935, pp. 519–27; *Congressional Record*, 74th Cong., 2nd Sess., 7681–97, 8003–8004.

Roosevelt emerged from 1937 with but a single legislative catch, a public housing law, and the conservative sharks mauled even that before he landed it. The original bill, which Robert Wagner of New York had first introduced in 1936, would have provided $700 million in loans to municipalities for slum clearance and low-cost housing. Wagner guided the measure through the Senate, but it foundered in the House from lack of presidential endorsement. Wagner tried again in 1937 but met the same revitalized rural-southern-conservative coalition that opposed the wages-and-hours-bill. Rural, especially southern, senators brashly acknowledged that their opposition stemmed from fears that the measure would primarily benefit urban centers. Harry Byrd of Virginia led the opposition and outflanked Wagner with an army of crippling amendments, the most damaging of which limited construction costs to four thousand dollars per four-room unit or a thousand dollars per room. Roosevelt, who had finally thrown his weight behind the bill, accepted the revision to appease the budget balancers. The liberals, bereft of presidential support, fell a vote short of blocking the amendment. Bilbo backed Wagner on every vote while Harrison helped Byrnes and Byrd orchestrate the opposition. The version that Congress finally approved shaved $200 million from the appropriation and hardly made a dent in the nation's housing needs. It did, however, mark a beginning for federal public housing policy.[39]

The 1938 session proved to be something of a second honeymoon for Roosevelt and the southern conservatives, who denied him, however, on one major issue, taxes. In 1936 Congress had bolstered the previous year's "soak-the-rich" levy with an undistributed-profits tax on business. Harrison, already retreating from his 1935 acquiescence to social taxation, developed a convenient illness that forced his absence from the Finance Committee and left the bill in the hands of Senator William King. The Utah conservative allowed the rates to be scaled back to merely symbolic proportions. La Follette, Bilbo, and the progressives favored the higher levies of the House version of the bill, as did the president. Even after a conference-committee compromise increased the Senate figure, Bilbo, Black, and Borah stubbornly refused to support the final version.[40]

By 1937 Harrison was openly hostile to New Deal taxation, advis-

39. Timothy L. McDonnell, *The Wagner Housing Act: A Case Study of the Legislative Process* (Chicago, 1957), 324–30; *Congressional Record*, 75th Cong., lst Sess., 8196.

40. Altman, "Second Session of 74th Congress," 1092–1101; *Congressional Record*, 74th Cong., 2nd Sess., 10475–76.

ing a national radio audience that even the meager corporate increases of 1936 had been a mistake. In 1938 he flaunted his newfound independence by railroading through the Senate a revenue bill that repealed the undistributed-profits tax and significantly slashed capital-gains levies. Counseled by Baruch and assisted by Byrnes and Garner, Pat led the upper house into utter repudiation of established New Deal tax policy, and he did so with a display of legislative skill and power that left the president's forces sitting in stunned and impotent silence. Bilbo, on the other hand, continued to back progressive taxation as energetically as he had in 1935. La Follette, who personalized every revenue debate with his annual amendment to increase income tax rates at the top end of the scale, could always count on the vote of one Mississippi senator.[41]

The other major Senate controversies of 1938 found the two Mississippians in agreement. A deep recession that began midway through 1937 melted much of the moderate conservative opposition to increased spending. Rural lawmakers indulged their urban colleagues with increased WPA expenditures in exchange for $212 million in farm-parity payments. Bilbo and Harrison supported both and also found themselves together behind the president's executive reorganization proposal. On this issue the archconservatives found alliance with western progressives like Wheeler, who led this fight as he had the court squabble, accusing Roosevelt of dictatorial ambitions. The reorganization bill was innocuous enough in itself; it had been recommended by a blue-ribbon commission of political scientists assembled in 1936 to suggest improvements in the executive branch. But the rise of totalitarian regimes in Europe tainted any move toward centralized authority, and the opposition, still tasting blood from the fight over judiciary reform, capitalized on public fears. The bill survived the Senate but died in the House, though Congress approved a much weaker bill in 1939.[42]

Following the 1938 session of Congress, Roosevelt attempted to "purge" conservatives from the party by actively campaigning for progressive Democrats in the 1938 primaries. The results were disastrous, especially in the South, where E. D. Smith, Walter George of Georgia, and Millard Tydings of Maryland all survived presidential opposition and returned to Washington more determined than ever to turn back

41. Swain, *Pat Harrison*, 171–79; Hanlon, "Urban-Rural Cooperation and Conflict," 21, *Congressional Record*, 74th Cong., lst Sess., 7691–92, 7699.

42. Patterson, *Congressional Conservatism and the New Deal*, 214–23, 238–41, 300–302; *Congressional Record*, 75th Cong., 3rd Sess., 4204.

the New Deal. With them came eight new Republican senators, six of whom replaced loyal Democrats, making the voice of Senate conservatism stronger than at any time since 1932.[43]

Historians have customarily divided the New Deal into two phases, the first encompassing the emergency recovery legislation of 1933–1934 and the second consisting of the establishment of welfare liberalism and ending with the passage of the Fair Labor Standards Act. David L. Porter, however, argues that after 1938 the New Deal entered a third stage, "characterized by a spirited battle between the New Deal Democrats" and the conservative coalition. The New Dealers fought for the expansion of presidential power, as exemplified by Roosevelt's renewed efforts to reorganize the executive branch, and against efforts to limit or scale back welfare programs, as typified by conservative attempts to reduce WPA expenditures. The strength of the Democratic component of the conservative coalition was centered among southern members of Congress, whom Roosevelt had already angered with the court reform proposal, the purge attempt of 1938, and his intervention against Harrison's bid for the Senate Democratic leadership. As Richard Polenberg suggests, the more responsive the New Deal became to northern urban interests, the more it alienated southern rural support. Beginning with the 1939 session of Congress, these southerners led the fight against growing executive power and increased relief appropriations. The legislative battles of 1939 and 1940 clearly defined the outer bounds of New Deal reform. The coalition failed to undo what had been accomplished since 1935, but the conservatives did draw a line beyond which they refused to allow Roosevelt to pass. It is perhaps unclear whether all who stopped short of the line could justly be labeled conservatives, but it would be difficult to describe those willing to go further as anything but New Deal liberals.[44]

It is noteworthy that in 1939, which saw the successful stalemate of the New Deal, Bilbo exerted his most energetic efforts to extend the two pillars of the welfare state, relief and social security, which he had helped to erect during his first Senate session. Since 1937 relief spending had been a whipping boy for opponents of the drift toward the welfare state. That year Roosevelt requested $1.5 billion to carry

43. Leuchtenburg, *Roosevelt and the New Deal*, 266–72; Floyd M. Riddick, "First Session of the 76th Congress," *American Political Science Review*, XXXIII (1939), 1023.

44. David L. Porter, *Congress and the Waning of the New Deal* (Port Washington, N.Y., 1980), ix–xiv; Richard Polenberg, "The Decline of the New Deal, 1937–1940," in Braeman, Bremner, and Brody (eds.), *The New Deal: The National Level*, 252.

WPA through fiscal 1938, and the House complied. But when the bill reached the Senate Appropriations subcommittee, Chairman Byrnes, after failing to slice half a billion dollars from it, secured an amendment forcing a local contribution of 40 percent for all projects and placing a 3 percent lid on administrative costs. The change would have reduced spending drastically since many local governments could not have met the requirement. On the floor Robinson offered a "compromise" reducing the local share to a still-crippling 25 percent and forcing local officials to take a virtual pauper's oath to receive exemption. Administration supporters throttled the Robinson amendment, and the president got his $1.5 billion, but formerly dependable southerners Robinson, Bankhead, and Harrison all voted for the compromise, registering a stern protest against escalating relief budgets. The issue was especially rankling to Harrison, who told the Mississippi Democratic Executive Committee in the summer of 1938 that the WPA was "sheltering" too much deadwood. Those sentiments were hardly encouraging to a president who hoped to liberalize the party in the South. Later that year Harrison took his criticism beyond the South, attacking burgeoning relief appropriations to Midwest audiences on a fall speaking tour.[45]

By 1939 the economy bloc had finally mustered enough force to pare presidential relief requests. Roosevelt asked for an $875 million deficiency appropriation to carry WPA through fiscal 1939, but the House slashed it by $150 million. Alva Adams' Senate Appropriations subcommittee accepted the House version, and the full committee boosted the figures only slightly. The ensuing floor fight spawned a furious bidding war in which Harrison and Garner teamed with Republican Leader Charles McNary in directing the effort to sustain the cut. The Senate resembled a trade fair, with the White House and its adversaries buttonholing senators in cloakrooms and corridors, offering rewards for support. On a tense roll call an amendment to restore the cut fell a single vote short, and the appropriation passed at the reduced level. Two weeks later Roosevelt again begged Congress to restore the $150 million to head off a real relief crisis. The House promptly cut it to $100 million. Barkley hastily convened a caucus and advised his fellow Democrats to go along with the House reduction, but the meeting dissolved into rancorous confusion, with Pepper threatening to lead a floor fight for the full $150 million. He made good that promise, and the president and his liberal diehards squared

45. *Congressional Record*, 75th Cong., lst Sess., 6032; Swain, *Pat Harrison*, 151–90.

off against Republicans, conservative Democrats, and even loyalists like Barkley and Truman.[46]

Bilbo, who had yet to waver on the spending issue, joined Pepper in the debate. He badgered Adams into admitting that WPA chief Harrington had indeed requested the money in subcommittee hearings and scoffed at the Colorado Democrat's complaint that local authorities often certified people for relief jobs who really did not qualify. There were over forty thousand on the relief rolls in Mississippi, Bilbo argued, and almost a hundred thousand more just as needy who had been certified for nearly three years, many in real danger of starvation. Instead of haggling about taking a few off the rolls, the Senate ought to be finding the funds to put those other ninety thousand to work. The proposed cut would pitch another four thousand a month "into the cold, without a job, on starvation, in need, in poverty." If a natural disaster left seven or eight hundred thousand Americans destitute, Bilbo reasoned, this Congress to a man would vote money for their succor. Yet these people were equally destitute, he pleaded, and "we hesitate to do our duty. . . . I hope there will be a sufficient number of Senators who have the humanity . . . to vote this $150 million." His eloquent appeal, with that of Pepper, and the votes of faithful New Dealers Sherman Minton, Joseph Guffey, La Follette, and Norris were to no avail. The Senate rejected the amendment, 49–28. The economy bloc was at last victorious. It was, said a triumphant Byrnes, "the beginning of the end of WPA."[47]

The following year Bilbo joined another effort to raise relief appropriations, but it too failed. He then turned to the Federal Surplus Commodities Corporation (FSCC) as a vehicle to offset the appropriation cuts and at the same time serve his other basic interest, agriculture. The FSCC, which had been established under another name by the NIRA and extended through 1942 by the AAA of 1938, operated as a food-stamp program. From local relief offices needy families secured stamps and used them to buy specified agricultural commodities from any local grocer. The grocer pasted the stamps on five-dollar cards and redeemed them from the Treasury.[48]

When Bilbo approached FSCC about extending the program to sev-

46. Porter, *Congress and the Waning of the New Deal*, 71–88; Patterson, *Congressional Conservatism and the New Deal*, 294–304.

47. *Congressional Record*, 76th Cong., 2nd Sess., 3878–80, 4103–4109; Byrnes, *All in One Lifetime*, 87.

48. Josephine Chapin Brown, *Public Relief: 1929–1937* (New York, 1940), 254–55, 355; Murray Benedict, *Farm Policies of the United States, 1790–1950* (New York, 1953), 355.

eral Mississippi cities and towns, Director Milo Perkins showed the senator similar requests from hundreds of other communities. Bilbo decided that the program needed a champion on Capitol Hill and launched a one-man crusade in the agency's behalf. He was not the only man in Washington who thought commodity distribution was an essential relief endeavor. Henry Wallace deemed it "one of the *very* good efforts of the New Deal" and in 1939, according to Russell Lord, considered its "directorship . . . the key spot in the whole Department."[49]

Bilbo was appalled that of twenty million Americans in 900 cities who qualified for stamps, only four million in 150 cities could get them. Yet Congress voted fifty million dollars in surplus goods for foreign refugee relief. In 1940, with the need greater than ever and with export markets squeezed by the European war, Congress chose to cut FSCC's budget by eighteen million dollars. That, he argued, was a senseless blow to an agency that offered such manifold benefits. Not only would it enlarge the domestic markets for farmers and serve as a kind of AAA for growers of nonbasic commodities, it would improve the life-style of the poor, urban and rural alike. It's dairy products, fruits, vegetables, and meats would fill the bellies, and its cotton mattresses would comfort the backs, of Delta sharecroppers as well as East Side immigrants and South Side blacks. La Follette took the floor to appeal for Bilbo's amendment as "only a small approach to one of the most important problems confronting the American people." Endorsed explicitly by the WPA and implicitly by the president, the appropriation earned Senate approval only to be cut in half by a conference committee.[50]

In 1939 Congress also decided to review social security. By then most friends of federal old-age assistance had come to consider the inequities in state pension programs for the elderly as a major problem. Paul Douglas, a University of Chicago professor and radical political activist, considered existing "pensions in most states . . . shockingly low" and warned that some states would try to keep them low despite federal aid. Douglas, Economic Security Committee Director Edwin Witte, and Social Security Board Chairman Arthur Altmeyer all recommended some type of federal assistance to poor states based on ability to pay rather than a standard matching ratio. The Social Security Board's 1938 list of recommendations to the president included a

49. *Congressional Record*, 76th Cong., 3rd Sess., 2147; Russell Lord, *The Wallaces of Iowa* (Boston, 1947), 469–72; "Reminiscences of Wallace," 569–71.

50. *Congressional Record*, 76th Cong., 3rd. Sess., 2148, 6360–62, 8230, 8240–47, 8925–30.

request for a variable grant structure based on ability to pay. Altmeyer deemed it "the most important recommendation for amending the public assistance titles" of the act. After three years of social security, state pensions varied as much as five to one, and only California matched the maximum federal grant. Niggardly appropriations had spawned long waiting lists in some states, and poverty, especially in mountain and southern states, strained budgets to the point of precluding adequate pensions.[51]

All this strengthened Dr. Francis Townsend and the supporters of his radical pension plan. Roosevelt had merely deflected their onslaught with the 1935 law, and its very inadequacy was pumping new life into the movement. In the congressional elections of 1938, the Townsendites joined with Republicans to fill the political atmosphere with pension promises, and the general commotion over old-age security assured the public of a congressional reassessment of the whole social security question in 1939.[52]

Bilbo decided to use the opportunity to renew the fight for a guaranteed minimum pension of thirty dollars regardless of state contributions. He even considered joining the Townsend tide if Congress failed to go along. Others had similar ideas. Senator Tom Connally proposed to amend the omnibus social security bill to increase the federal contribution to state pensions. The measure, which most southerners supported, provided two federal dollars for every state dollar up to a total of fifteen. Beyond that the ratio reverted to one for one, up to thirty-five dollars. When Connally's proposal passed, Senator Edwin Johnson of Colorado offered an amendment requiring all states to provide at least ten dollars a month or forfeit all federal funds. Although only seventeen states had adequate pensions to qualify under the restriction, enough Republicans joined Democrats from liberal pension states to pass the amendment.[53]

Neither change suited Bilbo. One he thought outrageous, the other inadequate. The existing matching arrangement "is so unrighteous," he charged, "that it is downright criminal." He introduced an amend-

51. Paul H. Douglas, *Social Security in the United States* (New York, 1936), 236–38; Edwin E. Witte, "Old-Age Security in the Social Security Act," *Journal of Political Economy*, XLV (1937), 42; Arthur J. Altmeyer, *The Formative Years of Social Security* (Madison, Wis., 1966), 96–98, 107; Abraham Holtzman, *The Townsend Movement: A Political Study* (New York, 1963), 103.

52. Patterson, *Congressional Conservatism and the New Deal*, 309; Holtzman, *The Townsend Movement*, 103–104.

53. Bilbo to Paul Johnson, March 30, 1938, in Bilbo Papers; *Congressional Record*, 76th Cong., lst Sess., 8899–8912; New York *Times*, July 14, 1939, pp. 1, 9.

ment of his own, which would have forbidden the states to reduce their current old-age pensions and would have supplemented each of them with a thirty-dollar federal contribution. The measure would have swelled the social security budget by $300 million to $400 million dollars more than the $80 million increase of the Connally amendment. Old-age security, Bilbo stressed, was a federal responsibility, and Congress owed it to the old people. Lawmakers could bewail the Townsend movement all they liked, he warned, but if they failed the elderly, they would get the Townsend nostrum whether they wanted it or not. "I have not much patience," he snapped, "with some who are economical, especially when it comes to appropriations for the welfare of the suffering citizens of this country." In the wake of a gush of defense expenditures, he professed amusement at talk of "balancing the Budget—whatever that means." After voting day after day, not millions or hundreds of millions, but billions for the army and navy and almost everything else imaginable, when "we get to the old men and women of this country who are suffering because of want, and poverty, and need, the distinguished Senator [Harry Byrd of Virginia] proposed to 'take it out' on the old folks. . . . If we have to economize anywhere, God forbid that we should economize at the expense of the old people who cannot help themselves."[54]

To those who argued that the states were better suited to take care of the elderly, Bilbo pointed out that per-capita income in thirty of the forty-eight states was below the national average. Mississippi, which was at the bottom of the heap, could hardly afford the paltry three dollars a month that it did pay in pensions yet was expected to pay fifteen dollars to get its full share of federal aid. The state could not afford it, he said, but its old people had just as much right to fifteen federal dollars as did the elderly of California and Massachusetts: "It is not our fault we are poor." Bilbo insisted that his proposal was not a raid on the Treasury but the settlement of a debt that the nation owed to its aged. "No one wants to spend the money of taxpayers ruthlessly and criminally," he concluded, but the people would surely support this justifiable use of public funds.[55]

Again his pleas fell on deaf ears. In a debate filled with acrimony, reported the New York *Times*, "the harshest treatment of the day" was visited upon Bilbo's amendment. He could not even muster the one-fifth required to force a roll-call vote, and his proposal was swept away in a thunderous no. For three weeks the social security bill lan-

54. *Congressional Record*, 76th Cong., lst Sess., 8921–25.
55. *Ibid.*

guished in conference committee, where the conferees wrangled over the Connally amendment. Altmeyer, who had assumed that the president endorsed the board's variable-grant proposal, appealed to Roosevelt to break the deadlock. He was stunned to find the president unalterably opposed to any but a fifty-fifty matching arrangement. The committee ultimately removed both Connally's and Johnson's amendments, and the final bill did little more than increase the total amount of federal aid and move the commencement date for old-age insurance benefits from 1942 to 1940. Bilbo, who had threatened to filibuster the conference report if it included Johnson's amendment, did not like the final version, but he acquiesced. Like most of his New Deal fellows, he knew the tide had turned.[56]

By 1940 the New Deal had run out of gas. The conservative coalition was not able to roll back the liberal gains, but it did block any further advance. Moreover, the domestic issues that had divided Democrats since 1937 became submerged in Roosevelt's efforts to meet the mounting foreign crisis with a unified party.[57]

Bilbo's legislative record during Roosevelt's second term distinguished him not only from southern conservatives and old progressives, most of whom abandoned the president in his march toward welfare liberalism, but also from many of his fellow New Dealers. James Patterson argues that the New Deal coalition foundered because so many of its constituents—agriculture, labor, and urban machines—remained apathetic to all but their own narrow interests. Lacking "breadth of vision" and "unity of purpose" they failed to forge an effective congressional coalition that could submerge provincial selfishness in favor of a broad social-welfare agenda. In addition, Roosevelt failed to liberalize state Democratic parties that continued to send to Congress men who harbored residual conservative fears about deficits, unions, and federal power in general, or whose "liberalism extended only to tapping the Treasury for purely local gains."[58]

If consistent support for the broad range of social and economic programs that the president pushed after 1936 constituted "breadth of vision" and "unity of purpose," Bilbo exhibited both. On every major issue he was squarely on the liberal side. On some—relief and social

56. New York *Times*, July 14, 1939, p. 29; Riddick, "First Session of 76th Congress," 1029–30; Altmeyer, *Formative Years of Social Security*, 111–13; Bilbo to Ed Terry, July 14, 1939, in Bilbo Papers.

57. Patterson, *Congressional Conservatism and the New Deal*, 337.

58. *Ibid.*, 334–37.

security—he fought especially hard. On others—public housing and wages and hours—he supported measures that won him few, if any, political points back home. He certainly deserved no medals for original intellectual contributions to welfare liberalism; nor was he a strategist in the congressional war for its implementation. But it would hardly be fair to deny him commendation for a faithful tour of duty as a loyal soldier in the New Deal army.[59]

59. The president's son, James Roosevelt, who served as White House liaison with Congress, remembered Bilbo as a "hard-working loyal Democrat," and Henry Wallace believed Bilbo's public image as a "bad fellow" was grossly overstated. James Roosevelt, telephone interview with the author, February 5, 1982; "Reminiscences of Henry Wallace," 275. Soon after Bilbo's election to the Senate, Hugh Russell Fraser wrote a scathing analysis of him in the *American Mercury*, in which he said that Bilbo had "labored with painstaking diligence and some genius to leave the mental, moral, and emotional aspects of the Mississippians more confused than he found them." In late 1939 Fraser wrote Bilbo to repent. "Your record in the Senate," he said, "has not only surprised me, but it is deserving of the highest commendation. I think if I were writing my article over again, I would have to devote considerable space to your generally progressive and liberal record. . . . Several of your votes . . . are outstanding. . . . Indeed, there were few roll calls which did not find you right. . . . The more you prove me wrong, the better I like it." Hugh Russell Fraser, "Bilbo: Mississippi's Mouthpiece," *American Mercury*, XXXVIII (1936), 424–32; Fraser to Bilbo, September 11, 1939, in Bilbo Papers.

Chapter Nine

Champion of the One-Horse Farmer

Discounting certain recurring scurrilous rumors, Bilbo had but two real passions. The most obvious was politics; the other was farming. By 1935 he owned considerable acreage in Pearl River County, though he was forever in danger of losing it to debts and taxes. Tenants worked most of it, and through the years he experimented with everything from pecans and pears to turkey hens. He even built a small sawmill. Amidst the crush of legislative business or the heat of political battle, Bilbo found time for weekly, sometimes almost daily, correspondence with his farm manager, Otho Stewart. These were not business letters; they were love letters, effused with fond affection and longing and weighted with the minutest instructions for the care of his beloved—the exact location and spacing of every pecan tree, the precise pitch for the roof of each turkey house, just the right motor (an old Buick engine) for the sawmill. "Give me a report on everything that is taking place on the farm," he implored Stewart. "You know how anxious I am about every detail." However inconstant Bilbo may have been in marriage, only one love ever really challenged his singular affection for politics, and that was farm life. To others she may have been homely and unmannered, but to him she was lovely beyond measure. Being in the capital at hog-killing time was especially excruciating. "How I wish I were there [Poplarville]," he exclaimed to Stewart one January. "I like hog brains better than anything in the world and sausage next best, but back-bones and dumplings are not so bad." Love truly can be blind.[1]

As a senator The Man was able to do more for Mississippi's farmers than he could ever have done at the state level. Harrison helped him get a place on the important Agriculture and Forestry Committee, where

1. Bilbo to Otho Stewart, January 4, 1936, Bilbo to Stewart, January 16, 1936, Bilbo to Stewart, January 27, 1936, all in Bilbo Papers.

he worked, said one commentator, "quietly and diligently" to become "a serious student of agricultural economics." He voted and acted as one would expect a rural cotton-belt senator to vote and act. He supported most administration farm proposals: AAA, soil conservation, Farmer's Home Act, rural electrification. When he did oppose presidential policy, he was usually in the company of the old progressives, as when he voted with Borah, Costigan, Cutting, Norris, and others to reduce the interest on federal farm loans from 4½ to 3½ percent.[2]

Bilbo had a keen eye for the special needs of his peculiar constituency—the poor farmers. In his first congressional session he persuaded the Senate to double its fifty-million-dollar seed-loan appropriation, though the House voted only forty million dollars and a conference committee compromised at sixty million. He secured fifteen thousand dollars for research on the causes and cure of swamp fever, which killed or debilitated the mules on which Mississippi farmers depended so heavily. The loss of a mule could devastate a small farmer, and in 1935, a single Mississippi county reported 1,400 cases affecting almost half the mules in the county.[3]

On issues affecting cotton Bilbo was especially vigilant. He urged Hopkins to use relief money to buy surplus cotton to make mattresses for poor families. When the Federal Surplus Commodities Corporation emerged to distribute surplus farm goods to relief families, he led the fight to increase its budget. The FSCC absorbed over two million bales of cotton between 1938 and 1940. As war approached, Bilbo urged that cotton be stockpiled as a strategic raw material. By 1934 the Commodity Credit Corporation had 11.5 million bales that farmers had pledged as collateral on loans since 1933. Bilbo suggested that the CCC transfer 7 million bales to the War Department, which estimated it would need that much for a four-year major war. He argued that if world markets knew that those 7 million bales were definitely immovable, the value of the remaining 4.5 million bales would rise immediately. Roosevelt refused, arguing that finished rather than raw cotton would be needed for war and that shifting the surplus from one government agency to another would not boost prices.[4]

2. Michie and Ryhlick, *Dixie Demagogues*, 104; *Congressional Record*, 74th Cong., lst Sess., 1809.

3. Herring, "First Session of 74th Congress," 995–96; Bilbo to W. D. Turnbough, February 5, 1935, Bilbo to W. E. Ayres, May 11, 1935, C. C. Smith to Bilbo, March 26, 1935, all in Bilbo Papers.

4. Copy of press release, December 11, 1935, in Bilbo Papers; Murray Benedict and Oscar C. Stine, *The Agricultural Commodity Programs: Two Decades of Experience* (New York, 1956), 20–21; *Congressional Record*, 76th Cong., lst Sess., 3602–3608;

On two cotton issues Bilbo found himself at odds with the administration. In 1938, the seething political caldron in Europe combined with government policy at home to drop American cotton exports to a sixty-year low. The following year Wallace and Roosevelt resorted to export subsidies to stimulate the flow of American cotton abroad. Bilbo was livid. He thought the program would benefit export merchants—middlemen—at the expense of both cotton farmers and domestic mills. He took to the radio to denounce the subsidies and threatened to filibuster any subsidy bill in Congress. Nonetheless, exports were subsidized, though only for about six months.[5]

The second issue was crop insurance. As part of the second AAA of 1938, Congress inaugurated an experimental insurance program on wheat, hoping to extend it to other commodities should it prove successful. It did not, and when Edward O'Neal and the American Farm Bureau Federation (AFBF) wrung a cotton-insurance program from Congress anyway, Roosevelt vetoed it. Bilbo had begged the president to approve the plan. "I believe strongly in crop insurance," Roosevelt responded, but wheat was costing too much already. The nation's agricultural base would have to improve considerably before other crops could be included. A year later, however, the pressure proved too great, and the southerners got their insurance plan, which promptly lost eleven million dollars in its first two years.[6]

Bilbo believed that his greatest achievement for cotton farmers—indeed his most valuable accomplishment as a senator—was his bill to create regional laboratories for research into industrial uses for agricultural products. He wholeheartedly embraced New Deal farm policy, but crop control was to him a temporary though necessary expedient. Only when new uses were discovered for farm products, he believed, could rural America prosper without financial transfusions from Washington. To that end he advocated, even in the 1934 campaign, a federal research laboratory dedicated to developing new uses for the South's main crop. "We must," he insisted, "get the people of the world to using more cotton."[7]

Bilbo to Roosevelt, April 5, 1939, Roosevelt to Bilbo, April 29, 1939, both in OF 258, Roosevelt Papers.

5. Donald C. Blaisdell, *Government and Agriculture: The Growth of Federal Farm Aid* (New York, 1940), 92–95; Broadus Mitchell, *Depression Decade: From New Era Through New Deal, 1929–1941* (New York, 1947), 207; Bilbo to W. L. Williams, April 3, 1939, in Bilbo Papers.

6. Roosevelt to Bilbo, May 15, 1940, OF 258, in Roosevelt Papers; Benedict, *Farm Policies of the U.S.*, 382–84.

7. Heber Ladner, personal interview with the author, August 26, 1983; Jackson *Daily Clarion Ledger*, December 9, 1934, pp. 1, 16.

He was not alone in his enthusiasm for the idea. Promoters of the concept called it chemurgy, and by the mid-1930s the movement had blossomed into something of a crusade. In May, 1935, Francis Patrick Garvan, president of the American Chemical Foundation, convened a chemurgic conference hosted by Henry and Edsel Ford in Dearborn, Michigan. Before the three hundred delegates—noted scientists, industrialists, and agriculturalists—dispersed, they organized the National Farm Chemurgic Council. There followed a flurry of local and regional conferences that swelled membership, so that by the third Dearborn convention in 1937, the year Bilbo introduced his bill, chemurgical legislation had a visible constituency.[8]

The bill, which Bilbo first introduced on April 12, 1937, would have appropriated a million dollars to build and maintain a regional chemical laboratory for research into new uses of southern agricultural products "for the purpose of providing new markets for southern farm crops." It also provided for $400,000 in each of the first four years of operation. Roosevelt quickly solicited from various agencies their views on the proposal. Harold Ickes, speaking for the National Resources Committee, was generally favorable. He had been pleased with the success of three existing laboratories, one for forest products in Wisconsin, one for corn-belt crops in Iowa, and one for soybeans in Illinois. His advisory and science committees supported federal aid for research in principle but stopped short of a specific recommendation of Bilbo's proposition. Harcourt Morgan of TVA was likewise generally favorable. The most enthusiastic response came from Secretary of Agriculture Henry Wallace, who was also impressed with the value of the three existing USDA laboratories. He told Roosevelt that Bilbo's measure was "fully justified" and had his "unqualified endorsement." Bilbo thus secured an important ally, one with the president's ear, and the White House confided to the senator that while the administration could not openly promote the bill, it would not oppose it.[9]

So Bilbo launched his laboratory bill without ceremony but also without controversy. Then it ran aground at the Bureau of the Budget. When Chairman E. D. Smith of the Senate Agriculture Committee solicited the Department of Agriculture's position on the measure, Wallace sent a favorable report to Acting Budget Director Daniel Bell.

8. Wheeler McMillan, *New Riches from the Soil: The Promise of Chemurgy* (New York, 1946), 32–36; William J. Hale, *Farmward March: Chemurgy Takes Command* (New York, 1939), 43–44; H. E. Erdman, "An Appraisal of the Movement to Increase Industrial Uses of Farm Products," *Scientific Agriculture*, XX (1939), 20.

9. *Congressional Record*, 75th Cong., lst Sess., 3367; Ickes to Roosevelt, May 17, 1937, Morgan to Roosevelt, April 22, 1937, Wallace to Roosevelt, April 21, 1937, Roosevelt to MacIntyre, April 22, 1937, all in OF 872, Roosevelt Papers.

Bell advised that because the secretary already had legislative authority to undertake the kind of research envisioned for the laboratory and because of the estimated cost of Bilbo's scheme, "this proposed legislation would not be in accord with the financial programs of the President." [10]

There was only one man who could help Bilbo now, Roosevelt, and Bilbo appealed to him as "one Southern cotton farmer to another." In the twenties Roosevelt had sought to rehabilitate his polio-stricken legs in the mineral waters of Warm Springs, Georgia, where he had seen firsthand the ravages of rural poverty in the South and had begun to ponder ways to eradicate it. He bought land, farmed, experimented, and tried to educate himself and his Georgia neighbors in ways to improve agriculture. He returned to political life with an abiding sense of the struggles of the South's poor farmers, and Bilbo's idea intrigued him as it quickened those sensibilities. Increased foreign production and the development of substitute fibers were making cotton farmers increasingly dependent on the domestic market, Bilbo argued, but to prosper, the South needed to grow and sell more than the eight million bales a year that were currently consumed at home. The only permanent solution was to find new ways for Americans to use cotton products.[11]

The Senate's legislative council had been aware, Bilbo continued, that the Bankhead-Jones Act of 1935 authorized the kind of research that his proposed laboratory would pursue but preferred the "broad and comprehensive" approach that his bill encompassed. Bell's ruling, however well-intentioned with regard to the president's concerns for economy, had derailed the proposal. "I must depend on you and you alone," he pleaded, to get it back on track. He reminded Roosevelt of his earlier assurance that there would be no opposition and urged him to have Bell withdraw the objection and allow Wallace to forward the favorable report to the Agriculture Committee. Bilbo even gave the president a copy of the blueprints and specifications for the proposed laboratory and a detailed accounting of the first five years' expenditures.[12]

Roosevelt apparently was impressed. "This proposed laboratory is really a good thing," he told Bell, and instructed him to find some way

10. Wallace to E. D. Smith, May 22, 1937, Daniel Bell to Roosevelt, July 1, 1937, both in OF 872, Roosevelt Papers.

11. Freidel, *FDR and the South*, 5–18; Bilbo to Roosevelt, June 10, 1937, OF 872, in Roosevelt Papers.

12. Bilbo to Roosevelt, June 10, 1937, Bilbo to MacIntyre, June 4, 1937, both in OF 872, Roosevelt Papers.

to approve its authorization with at least a small initial appropriation. Wallace recommended a joint state-federal project with one or more southern states furnishing the building and grounds for a laboratory devoted strictly to cotton research. The federal government would then pay $250,000 to equip it and $250,000 a year to operate it. Roosevelt advised Bilbo that if he would modify the bill along those lines, the White House would approve it.[13]

Bilbo now saw an opportunity to get the laboratory for Mississippi. He redrafted the bill, authorizing the secretary of agriculture to locate the facility in the first state to agree to provide the building and grounds, or, if more than one made offers, to choose "the state best suited to the purposes." He also sent Governor White a copy of the president's letter and urged him to be ready, when the bill passed Congress, to recommend that the Mississippi legislature immediately appropriate the land and money.[14]

The Agriculture Committee reported the rewritten bill unanimously, and the Senate approved it without a single dissenting vote in late July. Bilbo then went to work on members of the House, using every means of leverage he could grasp. He asked Senator John Bankhead of Alabama to encourage his brother, House Speaker William Bankhead, to expedite the bill's passage. He wrote letters and sent copies of the president's letter to southern congressmen, to Democratic members of the House Agriculture Committee, and to the Democratic leaders in the House. He especially prodded the Mississippi congressmen. William Colmer, at Bilbo's urging, tried to arrange to have the bill brought to the floor and passed by unanimous consent, but House Minority Leader Bertrand Snell balked. When Colmer reminded him that his Senate counterpart, Charles McNary of Oregon, had been cooperative, Snell snapped that McNary did not run minority affairs in the House. So the bill had to plod its way through committee, where it was vulnerable to major alteration.[15]

Bilbo's plan for quick passage began to unravel. Speaker Bankhead expressed fears that other controversial legislation would crowd the bill off the calendar and postpone House action until a later session, and Agriculture Committee Chairman Marvin Jones of Texas dropped

13. Roosevelt to Bell, June 11, 1937, Roosevelt to Bilbo, July 6, 1937, both in OF 872, Roosevelt Papers.

14. Bilbo to White, July 7, 1937, in Bilbo Papers.

15. Bilbo to John Bankhead, July 25, 1937, Bilbo to Congressmen, July 25, 1937, Bilbo to William Bankhead, July 28, 1937, all in Bilbo Papers; William Colmer to Bilbo, August 9, 1937, in Legislative Correspondence, Agriculture, 1937, William Colmer Papers, McCain Library, University of Southern Mississippi, Hattiesburg.

the first serious hint that the House might significantly modify the proposal. With an eye toward the need for nonsouthern support, Jones suggested that the bill might be broadened to cover other areas and other crops. He also pointed out that there already existed statutory authority for research. Mississippi Congressman Wall Doxey told Bilbo that Jones, in a committee discussion, emphasized that there was no real need for additional authority. Despite assurances of support for the principle of research, the congressman from Texas was dismantling Bilbo's laboratory. Doxey doubted that the bill would get anywhere with the committee but argued that at least Bilbo's bill would spur the secretary of agriculture to exercise existing authority to go ahead and build a laboratory.[16]

The committee finally agreed to summon a Department of Agriculture official to testify concerning the department's intention. After the hearing, the committee decided that the bill supplemented rather than duplicated existing provisions for research, primarily because of the requirement of state contributions, and reported the bill favorably. In the same report, the committee endorsed South Carolina Congressman Hampton Fulmer's effort to insert in the pending agriculture bill a $10 million appropriation for research. Nonetheless, Bankhead's warning came true when a weary Congress adjourned in August before the House acted either on Bilbo's bill or on a general farm bill to replace the invalidated AAA. By the time Roosevelt called the reluctant lawmakers back to the capital for a special session in November to pass a farm bill, the House had made Fulmer's proposal a substitute for Bilbo's bill. It provided $9 million for the secretary to construct an unspecified number of laboratories. Bilbo then offered an entirely new proposal as an amendment to the new farm bill. It provided for four regional laboratories on the same basis as the single laboratory of the earlier bill, with $250,000 to equip and another $250,000 to maintain each.[17]

Bilbo lobbied hard for bipartisan support for the measure, and the Senate debate reflected his success. Republican Arthur Vandenberg called the idea "the most constructive contribution to the possibility of farm relief that I have heard in the four weeks this rather amazing debate has been running. . . . I most emphatically approve his [Bilbo's] objective, and I congratulate him upon the contribution he has made."

16. Bankhead to Bilbo, July 30, 1937, Marvin Jones to Bilbo, July 31, 1937, Doxey to Bilbo, August 12, 1937, all in Bilbo Papers.

17. *House Reports*, 75th Cong., lst Sess., No. 1570, pp. 2–3; O. R. Altman, "Second and Third Sessions of the 75th Congress," *American Political Science Review*, XXXII (1938), 1099; *Congressional Record*, 75th Cong., 2nd Sess., 1726.

Of course, those sentiments reflected as much Vandenberg's conservative frustration with New Deal farm policy as his approbation of farm chemurgy. At the other end of the political spectrum, Claude Pepper added his "enthusiastic sponsorship" and urged the bill's adoption. The senators approved the amendment, again without a roll call.[18]

Congress again adjourned without passing the bill, but early in the regular session of 1938 it finally went to conference committee. Again Bilbo lobbied vigorously, pleading in personal letters to each Senate conferee to hold fast for his own version of the measure. What came out of that conference was surprisingly more than even Bilbo had expected. Whether by mistake or by design, the report, which both houses perfunctorily approved, authorized four million dollars for *each* of the first four years of operation beginning July 1, 1938, one-fourth for each laboratory. Later Congresses cut actual expenditures somewhat, but the federal government still spent ten million dollars on research laboratories during the first four years.[19]

Bilbo's next objective was to get the southern laboratory assigned to Mississippi. As the farm bill emerged from conference, Heber Ladner, then representing Pearl River County in the Mississippi legislature, offered to arrange an invitation for the senator to address a joint legislative session as soon as Roosevelt signed the farm bill. Although the final act did not require a state contribution, Bilbo felt that a liberal donation from the legislature would help convince Wallace to choose a Mississippi site. On March 1, Bilbo arrived in Jackson to urge the lawmakers to spend upward of half a million dollars and authorize municipalities to issue bonds to purchase land for his pet project.[20]

The Man's three years away in Washington had done nothing to diminish his popularity with the folks back home. If anything his absence had left a political heartache that had them yearning for a glimpse of their beloved, and they overran the new state capitol and thronged the House gallery for a precious few minutes of classic Bilbo oratory. He did not disappoint. The research laboratory "is my baby," he declared, "and they ought to let me bring it home where I can look after it." Texas was the only real competition, and the lawmakers could put Mississippi a leg up, he said, by appropriating the land and money for the facility. Leaving Jackson buzzing with research labora-

18. *Congressional Record*, 75th Cong., 2nd Sess., 1727–29.

19. McMillan, *New Riches from the Soil*, 299–303; *House Reports*, 75th Cong., 3rd Sess., No. 1767, pp. 7–8, 64–65.

20. Ladner to Bilbo, February 11, 1938, Bilbo to Ladner, February 12, 1938, both in Bilbo Papers.

tory boosterism, Bilbo carried his crusade to other Mississippi cities. By mid-March the legislature had done its part, despite warnings from Fred Sullens that state contributions would not influence Wallace in choosing the site.[21]

Bilbo returned to Washington to secure an amendment to the farm bill allowing the secretary of agriculture to proceed immediately with construction of the southern laboratory. All his efforts to get it for his home state failed, however, and Wallace chose New Orleans, primarily because it offered facilities unavailable in Mississippi. But The Man had come very close. In fact, had he been aware of the president's sentiments, he might have pushed harder and succeeded. Roosevelt told Wallace that he thought Bilbo's efforts had earned the laboratory for Mississippi, and Wallace later admitted that when he chose Louisiana, "Roosevelt didn't like it at all. He thought it would be marvelous to put it in Mississippi in the open country." [22]

Some critics have charged that chemurgy enthusiasts exaggerated the value and practicality of agricultural research and that the potential of the laboratories was grossly overstated. The laboratories did, however, make contributions. Most notable was the Peoria, Illinois, laboratory's development of a process that increased the production of penicillin dramatically, a critical discovery for a nation on the brink of war. All the laboratories made significant contributions to the war effort, and almost everyone hailed them as a giant step toward relieving the nation's agricultural woes. Wallace considered them essential, and Roosevelt himself believed that they held great promise. Everyone likewise acknowledged their paternity: they were indeed Bilbo's "babies," his quadruplets. When the southern laboratory was formally opened in 1939, several senators suggested to Wallace that the festivities would be incomplete without Bilbo, so he was invited to lay the cornerstone and, of course, to deliver an address.[23]

One other cotton issue absorbed a great deal of Bilbo's legislative energies. That was his crusade for a net-weight cotton bill. On this one, however, he failed miserably, because a significant segment of the

21. Jackson *Daily News*, March 1, 1938, pp. 1, 8, March 4, 1938, p. 1, March 16, 1938, p. 8; Bilbo to Wendell Black, April 1, 1938, in Bilbo Papers.

22. *Senate Reports*, 75th Cong., 3rd Sess., No. 1892; "Reminiscences of Henry Wallace," 275.

23. Erdman, "Appraisal of Movement to Increase Industrial Uses of Farm Products," 25–26; McMillan, *New Riches from the Soil*, 307–10; John Overton to Wallace (copy), June 6, 1939, Allen Ellender to Wallace (copy), June 10, 1939, Wallace to Claude Pepper (copy), June 13, 1939, all in Bilbo Papers.

cotton community refused to support him. Gin operators had for years covered cotton bales with heavy jute bagging, about twenty-one pounds counting metal ties. Since the bale was then valued according to its gross weight, the grower received cotton prices for the weight of bagging and ties worth much less than an equal amount of cotton. Farmers naturally came to believe that the system worked to their advantage and reveled in the thought of pinching Yankee mill buyers for $2.50 a bale in bagging and ties worth only half that much. What most did not realize was that buyers adjusted their quotations to compensate for noncotton weight.[24]

Worst of all, middlemen made a bigger killing than anyone from the practice, mostly at the growers' expense. Because several graders took samples from bales in transit and because handlers were allowed up to thirty pounds of covering, a bale's weight could increase by as much as nine pounds on its way to the mill. Middlemen simply patched the holes made by graders with the heaviest and cheapest jute, received cotton prices for it, and doubled their money. The added freight charges, higher fire-insurance costs, and damage from inferior covering ultimately came out of the grower's pocket in the form of price quotations that were adjusted for those factors. Some mills had voluntarily adjusted prices upward for bales covered in superior cotton bagging. The whole gross weight system was wasteful and costly (an extra fifteen to twenty million dollars a year), but the weight of custom and a powerful jute lobby had saddled the whole industry with it.[25]

For more than a decade Representative Hampton Fulmer of South Carolina had fought for a net-weight cotton bill, so when Bilbo got interested he naturally turned to Fulmer for support. In the spring of 1938, soon after Congress had enacted the second AAA, Fulmer outlined the case for net-weight cotton trading in a letter to Bilbo. The senator derived most of the argument for his own net-weight proposal directly from that letter. Fulmer had always linked the net-weight issue with standardization of bale covering, really hoping that a minimum requirement for the quality of all bale coverings would drive jute completely from the business to be replaced mainly by cotton covering. But

24. U.S. Congress, Senate, Committee on Agriculture and Forestry, *Hearings Before a Subcommittee of the Senate Committee on Agriculture and Forestry on S. 1228, a Bill to Provide for the Use of Net Weights in Interstate or Foreign Commerce Transactions in Cotton and for Other Purposes* (hereinafter cited as *Hearings on Net Weights*), 76th Cong., lst Sess., 5–14.

25. *Ibid.*; *Senate Reports*, 76th Cong., 3rd Sess., No. 1403, pp. 1–2; H. P. Fulmer to Bilbo, April 27, 1938, Wallace to Bilbo, April 19, 1939, both in Bilbo Papers.

the jute lobby, casting itself as the innocent victim of a cotton-mill plot to exclude jute from the market, had always marshaled enough votes to defeat Fulmer. Bilbo decided to separate the two issues.[26]

He first introduced his net-weight proposal in 1939 and chaired an agriculture subcommittee that held hearings on it in May. The National Grange, the Cotton Textile Institute, the Mississippi Farm Bureau Federation, and the Southern Commissioners of Agriculture all endorsed the bill. Several witnesses emphasized that cotton was the only agricultural product traded on a gross-weight basis. Almost every other nation in the international cotton trade used a net-weight system and therefore produced neat, trim, attractive bales. The American bale was the "tramp" of the trade, according to one cotton mill representative. Another said, "The American package is a stink in the industry, it is vile, it is terrible, and we ought to be ashamed of it." Others pointed out that though the bill would end the jute monopoly, it would simply force jute manufacturers to compete with producers of other bale coverings.[27]

One of the crucial voices in the debate would be the Department of Agriculture, which, like Fulmer, had linked the need for net-weight trading with standardization of bale covering. The department and the cotton mills feared that without minimum requirements ginners would go to a cheap covering and produce an even shabbier bale. Nonetheless, Wallace suggested that if Bilbo thought a standardization provision in the bill would doom net weights, he might try an administrative solution. He could amend the bill to authorize the secretary of agriculture "to prescribe regulations under which the net weight of cotton and the weights of bagging, ties, and patches might be determined for the purposes indicated." After Bilbo rewrote the bill along those lines, the department threw its weight behind it and sent a representative to the hearings to testify in its behalf. The department believed, the spokesman said, that passage of the bill would spark an instant jump in cotton-futures prices and a later increase in spot-market prices.[28]

But farmers were slow to believe, and several testified against the bill. Many would not be persuaded that net-weight trading would affect prices. Despite the groundswell of support for the measure among agricultural groups, the obstinance of the farmers was there to be tapped by its opponents. When North Carolina jute manufacturers

26. Fulmer to Bilbo, April 27, 1938, Fulmer to Stanley Andrews (copy), May 27, 1938, Hall Johnston to Marvin Jones (copy), May 23, 1939, Bilbo to Senators, May 9, 1938, all in Bilbo Papers.

27. *Hearings on Net Weights*, 5–8, 23, 51, 61.

28. *Ibid.*, 3, 9, 14; Wallace to Bilbo, April 19, 1939, in Bilbo Papers.

unloaded their worries on Senator Josiah Bailey, he warned that there was considerable support for a net-weight bill in Washington and suggested that opponents "circularize the farmers, who . . . are violently opposed." Unless farmer resistance could be unleashed, he warned, "there is every likelihood that the bill will finally pass." Even Bailey's own secretary acknowledged that farmers would eventually get a better price on a net-weight basis but feared that they would suffer during the period of transition until mills adjusted their prices. Those fears no doubt grew more vivid with each letter that descended on Bailey's office from the Carolina Bagging Company and other jute makers.[29]

The most powerful opposition came from Senator E. D. Smith of South Carolina, chairman of the Senate Agriculture Committee, "Cotton Ed" to his friends. Smith thwarted every attempt to get the bill up for floor consideration in 1939, but Bilbo decided to try again in 1940. This time the House passed the measure, and Bilbo threw the jute forces into a mild panic when he garnered enough votes in the Agriculture Committee to report the bill out over the chairman's objections. But again it died on the Senate floor, and Bilbo never got his net-weight law. Nonetheless, his effort reflected a progressive impulse that went all the way back to the cattle-dipping controversy of his first term as governor. As in earlier years, Bilbo was not afraid to drag his stubborn farmer followers kicking and screaming down the road of technological advance.[30]

On general farm legislation, Bilbo was sympathetic with New Deal policy. His own pronouncements on farm problems and solutions bore a striking resemblance to the underconsumption ideas of some of the Brain Trusters, especially Rexford Tugwell. Tugwell, the great prophet of economic cooperation and centralized planning, asserted that the various segments of the economy were so interdependent that when one suffered all suffered. If income in one sector was so low that those people could not purchase goods, everyone involved in producing salable goods was hurt. Prior to the depression, Tugwell said, "conspicuous among those who were thus starved of income . . . were the farmers of America." Ending the depression meant solving the problems of agriculture, and solving the agricultural problem meant correcting the imbalance between farmers and others in the economy. That, in turn, meant embracing what Tugwell termed "the single most important

29. *Hearings on Net Weights*, 40–49; Josiah Bailey to Bennett H. Perry, November 28, 1940, A. H. J. to E. Hervey Evans, April 9, 1940, both in Senatorial Series, Agriculture, 1939, Josiah Bailey Papers, Perkins Library, Duke University, Durham.

30. Bilbo to S. Odenheimer, July 25, 1939, in Bilbo Papers; A. H. J. to Evans, April 9, 1940, in Bailey Papers; *Congressional Record*, 76th Cong., 3rd Sess., 13750–51.

principle of national agricultural policy during the New Deal . . . parity." That, he insisted, required production control: "Until there was an effective demand, until cold and hungry people could buy . . . the products, reducing was the only practical procedure."[31]

Bilbo also embraced parity, with abandon. "The permanent establishment of the purchasing power of American agriculture will solve our problem," he declared. It was pointless to try to reclaim the export trade, as so many farm spokesmen in and out of Congress were advocating. In America were millions "who are hungry, who are improperly clothed, and who are improperly sheltered." "What this country needs," he concluded, in terms the good Baptist farmers back home understood, "is a little more home missionary work and less attention to foreign missionary work, governmentally speaking." If American farm wives had the money for a one-day shopping binge, he declared, they would spend five billion dollars on home necessities alone.[32]

Bilbo and Tugwell both believed that the export-subsidy schemes that dominated farm-bloc thinking throughout the twenties were more attractive to middlemen than to farmers. "The Agricultural bloc," said Tugwell, "belonged less to the farmers themselves than to the processors," who opposed production control because it would mean fewer goods to store, mill, pack, and ship. They preferred instead to attack low prices by means of dumping schemes or market agreements that would not threaten the volume of business by reducing production. Bilbo was one of the few cotton senators who was unalterably opposed to export subsidies.[33]

Like most farm legislators, he did not particularly relish crop control or see it as a permanent solution. Yet he supported the administration program, and with more than lip service. He played an important part in the struggle after 1936 to construct a permanent replacement for the invalidated AAA. Back in 1933, when Dr. New Deal and his army of agricultural economists had first invaded the capital, America's farmers were already all too familiar with depression. They had seen crop prices decline since the postwar bust of 1920–1921 while taxes and the cost of farm necessities steadily rose. The buying power of agricultural commodities was in 1933 only half of what it had been in 1914, and industrial net profits were half again as great as gross farm income. Attention

31. Rexford G. Tugwell, *The Democratic Roosevelt: A Biography of Franklin Roosevelt* (Garden City, N.Y., 1957), 34–35, 161–62, 204–205, 228–30, 275–76.

32. *Congressional Record*, 75th Cong., lst Sess., 968–69, 2nd Sess., 1724–25.

33. Tugwell, *The Democratic Roosevelt*, 160, 204–205, 276, 455–56; Bilbo to W. L. Williams, April 3, 1939, in Bilbo Papers.

focused on burgeoning surpluses as the culprit that beat commodity prices steadily downward. Congress under Hoover had established the Federal Farm Board as a vehicle to stabilize prices by entering declining markets to buy up surplus crops with the intention of selling them when prices recovered. Instead, by the end of Hoover's term, the board had spent over $350 million and come to possess mountains of commodities whose value continued to decline.[34]

Roosevelt and his agricultural experts came to Washington convinced that only when the actual production, rather than marketing, of farm goods came under control would prices rise. Overproduction was the disease and crop control was the cure. The particular medicine favored was a variation of M. L. Wilson's domestic-allotment plan, which, along with other remedies, was embodied in the 1933 AAA. The idea was to allot specific acreages of the basic crops—right down to the individual farmer's share—and somehow induce him to limit planting to the allotment. By referendum growers of each of seven basic commodities could sanction a control plan, whereupon the secretary of agriculture was authorized to negotiate voluntary individual contracts with the farmers themselves to rent a specified acreage. In effect the government decided how many acres of a specific crop each farmer should plant and then rented from him those acres beyond the allotment that he would normally have planted in that commodity. To offset the producer's financial loss from a reduced crop, the government would issue him rental payments for the unplanted acreage.[35]

The payments were designed to create that mystical and arcane panacea called parity. In simplistic terms parity meant a rough equality of purchasing power between the farmer's earnings from his crops and comparable nonfarmers' earnings. The actual numbers were derived by choosing a base period when farm prices actually had earned parity, 1909–1914, and computing what current agricultural prices would have to be to produce the same purchasing power. The funds for payments came from a tax on the processing of farm goods; participation in the control program, and therefore rental benefits, was voluntary. The AAA came too late to control cotton planting on the 1933 crop, so the USDA decided on a plow-up campaign to reduce the volume of that year's crop. Growers received payments for destroying the acres already planted beyond what would have been allotted. Local committees of

34. Gilbert C. Fite, *George N. Peek and the Fight for Farm Parity* (Norman, Okla., 1954), 3–12, 224–26; Richard S. Kirkendall, "The New Deal and Agriculture," in Braeman, Bremner, and Brody (eds.), *The New Deal: The National Level*, 85.

35. Perkins, *Crisis in Agriculture*, 27–28.

farmers and businessmen supervised the program and determined each farmer's allotment and verified compliance.[36]

The program reduced the 1933 crop by three or four million bales and helped secure ten cents a pound for cotton, which had been selling at less than five cents two years earlier. Cotton supplies, however, remained large. The carry-over of unsold cotton from previous seasons was reduced by 1.5 million bales, but it was still 11 million. Moreover, a delay in payments coupled with a midsummer price slump stirred enough farmer agitation to provoke the administration to further action. In September, Roosevelt announced a loan program for cotton farmers and established a Commodity Credit Corporation under the Reconstruction Finance Corporation to lend money to individual farmers who offered their crops as collateral. The loans were nonrecourse: if the farmer failed to repay, the only government recourse was to take title to the cotton as full settlement of the debt. The loan created an effective floor for cotton prices. If prices fell below the loan rate (ten cents a pound at 4 percent interest in 1933), the farmer simply defaulted and let the CCC claim his collateral, in effect selling his crop to the government at ten cents a pound. If the price rose, he could sell his crop, pay off the loan, and pocket the difference.[37]

The loan was undoubtedly a boon to the cotton farmer. Had he been forced to sell in the early fall, he would have missed whatever price rise the control program stimulated. When prices did rise to twelve cents by mid-February, 1934, many cotton farmers, being constitutionally speculative anyway, held out for further price increases. By August only half the loans had been repaid, and the government was carrying three million bales on loans. Although there was no outcry comparable to that of the previous year, the administration, facing a possible textile strike and significant reduction in domestic and foreign demand, announced a twelve-cent loan for the 1934 crop. Prices, which had risen to more than thirteen cents, fell back in early 1935 to the loan rate or below, and by August, 1935, the government held over six million bales.[38]

The administration had created its own monster. Having given life to loan expectations in time of good prices, it could hardly tame them when prices were moving in the other direction. There was lively demand for another twelve-cent loan in 1935, but the AAA opposed it. The administration realized that the 1934 loan had helped shrink ex-

36. Fite, *George N. Peek*, 8, 38, 60; Perkins, *Crisis in Agriculture*, 101–105.

37. Perkins, *Crisis in Agriculture*, 168–73; Henry I. Richards, *Cotton and the AAA* (Washington, D.C., 1936), 212–16.

38. Benedict, *Farm Policies of the U.S.*, 333; Mitchell, *Depression Decade*, 194.

ports and had bloated government holdings. Wallace granted a compromise, a ten-cent loan plus a guarantee to pay additional benefits of up to two cents a pound to offset any price decrease below twelve cents. As a result prices moved ahead of the loan rate, so very few farmers took loans, and those who did repaid them. The government distributed almost forty million dollars in price-adjustment payments and reduced its holdings to fewer than 4.5 million bales by 1936.[39]

In the Bankhead Cotton Control Act of 1934, Congress had made the control program mandatory by placing a prohibitive gin tax on every bale above allotment. Farmers received exemption certificates for their assigned quotas but had to pay the tax on every additional bale. In 1936 the Supreme Court threatened the entire control program when it struck down the processing-tax provision of the AAA. Congress hurriedly passed the Soil Conservation and Domestic Allotment Act, under which the government paid farmers to shift acreage from "soil depleting" commodities to "soil enriching" grasses and legumes. This time the money came directly from Treasury appropriations. But plantings, which increased by several million acres, and an outstanding weather year were combining to produce a tremendous crop, so it became obvious that there would have to be another farm act.[40]

In February, Wallace convened a conference of farm leaders to draft a bill. What emerged was largely the work of Department of Agriculture experts and Edward O'Neal's Farm Bureau staff. The fracas over court packing monopolized the session and shoved the bill farther down the Senate calendar, ruffling the feathers of several cotton-state senators who had heretofore followed White House leadership. Their opposition to a farm bill could have been disastrous. Especially troublesome was Smith, who had become thoroughly annoyed with the administration and who showed his displeasure in the committee hearings. As the session dragged on and nerves became frayed over the court bill, Bilbo suggested that the Agriculture Committee take its hearings out of the capital. Rather than have farm leaders paraded to Washington, he recommended that the committee meet at various sites throughout the farm states to hear from the farmers themselves. The committee agreed and held hearings around the country in an "exhaustive study of the situation."[41]

39. Richards, *Cotton and the AAA*, 212–25; Edwin G. Nourse, Joseph S. Davis, and John D. Black, *Three Years of the Agricultural Adjustment Administration* (Washington, D.C., 1937), 163–71.

40. Mitchell, *Depression Decade*, 192, 206; Benedict, *Farm Policies of the U.S.*, 350–51; Carl T. Schmidt, *American Farmers in the World Crisis* (New York, 1941), 146–47.

41. Grant McConnell, *The Decline of Agrarian Democracy* (Berkeley, 1953), 78;

By August some of the southern senators were growing bold after dismantling the president's court reform plan. They demonstrated little, if any, willingness to cooperate on the farm bill, whose future began to look bleak, particularly during that session. Roosevelt had one last whip, and he decided to use it. With cotton prices down and a bumper crop almost ready to pick, cotton congressmen were clamoring for another twelve-cent loan. When a delegation called at the White House to urge him to authorize a loan, he politely refused. On August 3, Bilbo led a second delegation of cotton, corn, and wheat senators back to the White House only to find the president resolute: no crop control, no loan. Bilbo returned to the Capitol, where he and Hugo Black immediately introduced two resolutions, one instructing the CCC to make the loan and the other committing the Congress to make a farm bill the first order of business at the next session. Both measures went to the Agriculture Committee. Bilbo and Black, who believed Congress was purposely dragging its feet on farm legislation, carried the president's fight in the Senate despite immense constituent pressure for an immediate loan.[42]

Two days later the two senators circulated a petition ordering the congressional committees to report and Congress to consider a farm bill by October 15. That would necessitate a special session in the fall. The paper reached Pat Harrison's desk with forty signatures already on it, but Pat was not sure that he wanted to sign. He took the floor to explain. Still smarting from Roosevelt's sabotage of his candidacy for majority leader in July, he was already ingratiating himself with newfound friends among the administration opponents, in this case Chairman Smith, who argued that there was not enough time to pass a bill in the current session. Accepting the chairman's assessment, Harrison declared that he would not sign and then volunteered some pointed comments about cliques in the Senate trying to conduct business

---

Edward L. Schapsmeier and Frederick H. Schapsmeier, *Henry A. Wallace of Iowa: The Agrarian Years, 1910–1940* (Ames, Iowa, 1968), 241–42; *Congressional Record*, 75th Cong., lst Sess., 8270; U.S. Congress, Senate, Committee on Agriculture and Forestry, *Hearings Before a Subcommittee of the Committee on Agriculture and Forestry Pursuant to S. Res. 158, a Resolution to Provide for an Investigation of Agricultural Commodity Prices, of an Ever-normal Granary for Major Agricultural Commodities, and of the Conservation of National Soil Resources, Part 6: Cotton, Tobacco, and Rice*, 75th Cong., 1st Sess., 684–85.

42. *Congressional Record*, 75th Cong., lst Sess., 8096; New York *Times*, August 4, 1937, pp. 1, 12; Hugo Black to E. A. O'Neal, July 6, 1937, Black to Yancey Quinn, August 10, 1937, both in Senatorial File, Agricultural Legislation, Hugo Black Papers, Library of Congress; Bilbo to Chuck Trotter, August 5, 1937, in Bilbo Papers.

by petition. Pat was obviously not going to help the president on this one.[43]

Smith himself was "utterly astonished" by the petition. It was a slap at his committee, he said, implying to the public that they were not being faithful to the farmers, and he resented it. The leadership had assured Roosevelt that Congress would take up the farm bill in January and insisted that the president ought to instruct the CCC to do its duty and issue the loan without all these petitions and resolutions. Bilbo and Black rushed to FDR's defense. It would not be fair, said Black, to expect the CCC to lend money against collateral that would depreciate in the face of a huge surplus that was sure to come without a control bill. Bilbo scolded his colleagues for not enacting farm legislation and vowed his willingness to stay in session until Christmas, if necessary, to help the farmers. He was afraid, he said, that the small farmers who were already beginning to harvest their crops would have to sell at current low prices, allowing speculators to "walk off with the golden shekels" when the price increased later. An immediate loan announcement would stop the price slide and keep the farmers from being "robbed of . . . hundreds of millions of dollars."[44]

On August 12, Wallace met with the Agriculture Committee in executive session and agreed to a loan like that of 1935, with benefit payments on top of the loan to make up the difference between the selling price and twelve cents a pound. The next day Bilbo led a subcommittee to the White House, where Roosevelt agreed to make such a loan if the farm-bill resolution passed. The same day, Bilbo presented the committee's unanimous report in favor of the resolution to the full Senate and secured unanimous consent to have it considered immediately. It passed on a voice vote. In its final form Senate Joint Resolution 207 called for Congress, at its next session, regular or special, to consider as its first order of business crop control *and* a system of support loans to protect prices and to enact a permanent farm program based on these principles as soon as possible.[45]

After the House approved the resolution and Roosevelt signed it, some cotton senators tried to revive the second Bilbo-Black resolution, which would have directed the CCC to issue a crop loan immediately. Tom Connally of Texas wanted to place the Senate on record in support of a ten-cent loan (and two-cent benefit payment) instead of the nine-

43. *Congressional Record*, 75th Cong., lst Sess., 8270.

44. *Ibid*., 8271–78; Black to Quinn, August 10, 1937, in Black Papers; New Orleans *Times Picayune*, August 4, 1937, pp. 1, 13.

45. *Congressional Record*, 75th Cong., lst Sess., 8794, 8835–36; Memphis *Commercial Appeal*, August 13, 1937, p. 1, August 14, 1937, p. 1.

cent loan (and three-cent payment) that Wallace favored. Bilbo's subcommittee had promised the secretary and the president that no mandatory legislation would be necessary if the administration would agree to guarantee a twelve-cent total. In the teeth of biting criticism from Connally and others, Bilbo objected to consideration of his own resolution. Connally, a key Democratic member of the Judiciary Committee, was one of those who had bitterly resented the president's assault on the Supreme Court. Having so recently whipped Roosevelt on that issue, he surely must have viewed the loan resolution as a safe refuge from which to hurl another vengeful bolt or two. Bilbo made himself the president's senatorial lightning rod on agriculture, much to the dismay of many of his increasingly disgruntled colleagues from the South.[46]

Bilbo knew he was out on a limb with the cotton farmers, and privately he fought hard for the ten-cent loan. Three days after the Senate passed Resolution 207, he wrote Wallace and Roosevelt to explain the advantage of the higher loan, accurately predicting that the market price would follow the loan value of cotton and settle somewhere near it. If that were nine cents, he argued, the mills and export merchants could get market cotton a penny cheaper, and the government would pick up the tab in the form of an extra penny in price adjustments. There was no need, he insisted, for "the Administration to be charged with imposing an additional seventy-five million dollars" on the taxpayers for the benefit of agricultural speculators. Having served Wallace and Roosevelt well during the entire session, Bilbo must have felt that he could speak forcefully. "I must insist upon a ten-cent instead of a nine-cent loan," he declared. It was to no avail, for on August 30, the CCC announced a nine-cent loan. Two days later Roosevelt wrote Bilbo to explain. With foreign cotton production so high, he said, a propped-up American price would simply benefit foreign growers, who could sell slightly under the price of American cotton, threatening American exports. That is exactly what happened anyway, and it got worse in 1938, when American cotton exports fell to a sixty-year low. Wallace correctly blamed the loan.[47]

At any rate, Roosevelt eventually got his farm bill thanks in some measure to Bilbo's efforts in 1937. It did not come easily, however. The president called Congress back into special session in the fall of 1937,

46. *Congressional Record*, 75th Cong., lst Sess., 9571–77.

47. Bilbo to H. A. Covington, August 21, 1937, Bilbo to Wallace, August 16, 1937, Bilbo to Roosevelt, August 16, 1937, Roosevelt to Bilbo, September 3, 1937, all in OF 258, Roosevelt Papers; Schmidt, *American Farmers in the World Crisis*, 155–56.

but it adjourned after squabbling for two months without enacting anything. Finally, in February of 1938, after months of bickering and despite the petty obstructionism by administration opponents like Smith, the second AAA became law. The new program incorporated the production control of the first AAA, the market quotas of the Bankhead Cotton Control Act, the price-support system of nonrecourse loans, and the parity principle. Loans on any commodity were contingent on market quotas that had to be approved by two-thirds of the growers voting in a referendum. Only those growers who stayed within their quotas were eligible for loans, and those who did not faced prohibitive marketing taxes. Loans were mandatory when prices reached a certain level, though the secretary of agriculture retained power to set the loan value anywhere between 52 percent and 75 percent of parity. He could also issue parity payments to cooperating farmers to make up the difference between market prices and parity prices.[48]

The new law consolidated all the previous New Deal efforts into a unified program, and its enactment was facilitated by the compromise that Bilbo negotiated with the administration in the late summer of 1937. Bilbo always considered himself one of those who "fought, bled, and died for . . . this legislation," and considered his part in the lengthy drama among his finest hours as a lawmaker.[49]

To Bilbo the underlying farm problem was not so much one of overproduction or prices or exports, but one involving people, the millions of America's farmers. He hinted as much when he reminded Roosevelt in August of 1937 that a ten-cent loan would still be seven cents below parity. Bilbo believed that the government ought to insure that somehow men and women who worked so long and hard on American farms would receive an honest livelihood from that labor. For him parity became the paramount issue, beside which the problem of exports paled in significance. "What glory is there to the American cotton farmer to meet foreign competition," he asked, "when he does not get enough for his cotton to pay for the cost of production? . . . Ninety percent of the people who are actually engaged in the production of cotton—I mean those who are doing the work—are so 'damned' poor that they are sleeping on shucks and hay. This world market stuff has put him to bed on shucks and hay instead of a comfortable cotton mat-

48. Altman, "Second and Third Sessions of 75th Congress," 1079; Christiana Campbell, *The Farm Bureau and the New Deal: A Study in the Making of National Farm Policy, 1933–1940* (Urbana, 1962), 113–15.

49. Bilbo to MacIntyre, February 16, 1938, PPF 2184, in Roosevelt Papers.

tress after a hard day's labor in the cotton fields of the South. 'To hell' with holding the world market when we can not get enough for it to pay the poor devil who has to produce it."[50]

Bilbo's commitment to parity was more than talk. In 1939, when the economy bloc was brandishing the budget meat ax, urban liberals came to the farmer's rescue. Although enough conservative senators chose political expediency over economic dogma to get $225 million worth of parity payments in the farm bill, the House promptly cut them out completely. A conference committee restored the payments at a higher level, $255 million, but House concurrence came only after several urban congressmen changed their votes. Bilbo's solid record in support of New Deal welfare and labor legislation certainly helped the credibility of rural lawmakers in soliciting that kind of aid from urban progressives.[51]

The following year Bilbo and Josh Lee of Oklahoma presented an amendment to the Agriculture Department's 1941 appropriation that would have raised parity payments from $212 million to $607 million, from 68 percent to full parity. How could farmers buy finished goods without purchasing power, Bilbo asked, and how could they have purchasing power without parity? Between 1931 and 1935, the average annual income of cotton farmers was $95. "How in the name of high heaven," he pleaded, "can people have any purchasing power when they receive an annual income of only $95 each?" The amendment met a thumping defeat, but Bilbo gathered an interesting array of supporters—southern liberals Lister Hill and Pepper, old progressives La Follette, Norris, and Wheeler, and northern New Dealers like Sherman Minton.[52]

Roosevelt himself talked a great deal about restoring the purchasing power of farmers. As Paul Conkin has suggested, "The market penalized farmers for being farmers and . . . by low income and by providing a nation's food supply at very low cost they subsidized the living standards of everyone . . . with worry, hard work, and increasing bitterness." Conkin suggests that deficit spending or progressive taxation would have stimulated the investment necessary for recovery. Bilbo would have backed either vigorously. If, as Conkin further suggests, men like Tugwell were more interested in moral than in economic ends, their goals did not differ substantially from Bilbo's. It would take an enormous mental leap to call Bilbo "first of all a moral philoso-

50. Bilbo to Roosevelt, August 16, 1937, OF 258, in Roosevelt Papers; Bilbo to Walter Parker, March 13, 1939, in Bilbo Papers.

51. Patterson, *Congressional Conservatism and the New Deal*, 308–309.

52. *Congressional Record*, 76th Cong., 3rd. Sess., 3176.

pher," as Conkin deems Tugwell. But if the practical implications were that Tugwell was more concerned with justice and fairness than with economic indices, he was not far distant from Bilbo in principle. That is by no means to equate the two men ideologically but rather to stress that Bilbo was much closer in his thinking and voting to Tugwell than he was to Edward O'Neal of the Farm Bureau or colleagues like Byrnes and Harrison.[53]

That fact underscores a persistent and intriguing paradox. Sophisticated and academic liberals tended to abhor Bilbo. Russell Lord of the Agriculture Department thought he was "the scum of the earth," and Gardner "Pat" Jackson called him "really about the lowest political animal that I've experienced any time anywhere." Tugwell himself thought the deal that originally brought Bilbo to Washington as "Pastemaster General" was a "humiliating—even an immoral—arrangement."[54]

Jackson's perception of Bilbo was almost a caricature of the propensity for moral high-mindedness among such liberals when confronted with an aberration like Bilbo. In Jackson's case it produced a self-inflicted myopia. He was one of Frederic Howe's bright young lawyers in the Consumers' Counsel office of the Department of Agriculture. With their counterparts in Jerome Frank's Office of the General Counsel, they became the vanguard of urban liberalism in the department. Sharing, says Arthur Schlesinger, "a city background . . . and a passionate liberalism," these crusaders saw the depression crisis as a chance to attack the real evils in American agriculture: the degradation of tenants, sharecroppers, and farm laborers, and the exorbitant profits and "restrictive marketing practices of the processors and distributors." Jackson and his comrades found Bilbo's manners and vocabulary sufficiently revolting to turn him into an object of crude intellectual sport, a kind of cosmopolitan "coon on a log." Believing that Bilbo "was filled with . . . foul language about the Negroes and sharecroppers that we were concerned with," they began to bait him. "It was an institution within our group," said Jackson, "that we would invent an incredible episode before we went in to see him."[55]

The more likely story is that the baiters were being baited. Had they

53. Conkin, *The New Deal*, 40–44.

54. "Reminiscences of Wallace," 275; "The Reminiscences of Gardner Jackson," 1955, COHC, 514; Tugwell, *In Search of Roosevelt*, 275–76.

55. Arthur M. Schlesinger, Jr., *The Coming of the New Deal* (Boston, 1958), 50–52, 74–80. Vol. II of Schlesinger, *The Age of Roosevelt*, 3 vols. to date; David E. Conrad, *Forgotten Farmers: The Story of Sharecroppers in the New Deal* (Urbana, 1969), 112–13; "Reminiscences of Jackson," 513.

realized that they were dealing with one who had made a career of cultivating enmity where he deemed it profitable, they might have taken more care to probe behind the calculated crudity to find a potential though unattractive ally. Other, more modest liberals did so. Two were Frank Tannenbaum and Dr. Will Alexander, both of whom were deeply interested in eradicating cotton tenancy in the South and were significant contributors to the enactment of the Bankhead-Jones Act of 1937, the New Deal's only legislative effort to deal with the problem.

Tannenbaum, who had studied similar problems in Latin America, undertook a survey of rural southern poverty in 1934. Appalled after only a few days in the field, he became convinced that the existing system must end and outlined appropriate legislation. When a bill was finally drafted, he suggested that Bilbo, who was, Tannenbaum observed, "a real friend of the people," be asked to introduce it. Alexander concurred, noting that the idea was a tribute to Tannenbaum's discernment, for "in spite of Bilbo's buffoonery, he was consistently always for the under-dog and every vote he ever cast was on that side." Eventually John Bankhead of Alabama introduced the bill, probably because Bilbo had only recently come to the Senate. Nonetheless, the junior senator from Mississippi became a tireless defender of the bill and fought valiantly in its behalf.[56]

Three separate streams of events converged to create the legislation: the FERA's experience with rural relief, criticism of the AAA's impact on tenants, and the efforts of men like Alexander and Tannenbaum. Relief workers in rural areas, especially in the cotton belt, found themselves adrift in an ocean of poverty. Lorena Hickock reported to Harry Hopkins in 1934 that many farmers lived better on relief than they had ever lived on any kind of agricultural work. The FERA reached the startling conclusion that any real effort to deal with sharecroppers and laborers would take every bit of relief money, leaving nothing for those specifically displaced by the depression, the unemployed. The result was a stopgap program of rural rehabilitation that centered in a system of supervised credit. The agency lent money to farmers for subsistence needs and offered guidance concerning farming methods, living habits, and general self-sufficiency.[57]

56. "The Reminiscences of Will Winton Alexander," 1952, COHC, 376–79; U.S. Congress, Senate, Committee on Agriculture and Forestry, *Hearings Before a Subcommittee of the Senate Committee on Agriculture and Forestry on S. 1800, a Bill to Create the Farm Tenant Homes Corporation* (hereinafter cited as *Hearings on Tenancy*), 74th Cong., lst Sess., 46–47; Jackson *Daily News*, July 4, 1935, p. 1.

57. Paul E. Mertz, *New Deal Policy and Southern Rural Poverty* (Baton Rouge, 1978), 56–67; Baldwin, *Poverty and Politics*, 63–66; Harry Hopkins, *Spending to Save: The Complete Story of Relief* (New York, 1936), 142–50.

Meanwhile there was a growing complaint that the AAA was unfair to tenants and croppers. Some landowners withheld parity payments from their tenants or applied their government checks to debts; others simply evicted their tenants—in violation of AAA regulations. Many tenants were thrown onto government relief, which the landowners opposed because it "spoiled" tenants if and when they were to be needed again. Those interested in the plight of tenants capitalized on the criticisms of AAA.[58]

In 1933 Charles S. Johnson of Fisk University, Edwin Embree, and Will Alexander began a survey of the New Deal's impact on blacks. What emerged was an exhaustive study of the whole tenancy problem, which concluded that the problem was not one of race, though any effort to reform the system became enmeshed with the race issue. The research revealed some startling facts. Sixty percent of cotton-belt farmers were tenants, and five of every eight tenants were white, a proportion that was increasing. More than a third of all tenants owed more than one year's debts. In a study of two thousand families in four states, the average income was $1.75 a month per person, and few of the farmers studied had cleared any money since 1921. The tenant, according to the report, was trapped. The shiftlessness, laziness, ignorance, and mobility for which he was condemned were results, not causes, of his condition: "Tenancy demands complete dependence; it requires no education and demands no initiative." But the landlords wanted to retain the system because it provided cheap labor. What was needed, concluded the report, was "some new distribution of land ownership."[59]

From this study came Tannenbaum's trip and the drafting of the Bankhead-Jones Act. In 1935 neither Roosevelt, Tugwell, nor Wallace was very interested in the bill. The fight was left to Alexander's group and friends in the Congress like Bankhead and Bilbo. The plan that evolved was for the government to buy land from banks, insurance companies, and the like, retire submarginal acres, parcel the rest into family-sized plots, and sell them to tenants on generous terms. On April 11, the Senate Agriculture Committee favorably reported what Bilbo called "the greatest piece of legislation that's been introduced in the American Congress in fifty years." Meanwhile, on the authority granted by amendment to a relief bill, Roosevelt was already establishing an agency to make tenant loans. Tugwell would head this new Re-

58. Mertz, *New Deal Policy and Southern Rural Poverty*, 25–28; F. Ray Marshall, *Labor in the South* (Cambridge, 1967), 158–60.

59. Charles S. Johnson, Edwin Embree, and Will Alexander, *The Collapse of Cotton Tenancy* (Chapel Hill, 1935), 4–22, 49–67.

settlement Administration (RA), which would absorb, among other things, rural rehabilitation and the landownership program envisioned by the pending legislation.[60]

On April 24, the same day that Roosevelt announced the makeup of the new agency, disaster struck the Bankhead bill. Several formerly friendly liberal senators joined an effort to recommit the bill for further study. Tannenbaum believed that the group had been "misled by leftists," including Gardner Jackson, who wanted more emphasis on cooperative and communal enterprises than on family farms. By the time the bill was brought back up and approved, there was too little time left to have it considered by the House, where it died in committee.[61]

While Congress moved toward the end of the Second Hundred Days, Bilbo pleaded for passage. As Roosevelt entered a last-minute strategy conference with congressional leaders, Bilbo urged him to give the bill "first place . . . before Congress adjourns." It would deserve even a special message if that were necessary. "I beg for this legislation," he said, "because I know what it will mean. I know the conditions and I know the good and the effect." He wired similar pleas to Harrison and Byrnes and Majority Leader Robinson, all in vain. It was, according to Paul Mertz, "the great lost opportunity of the Second Hundred Days."[62]

Meanwhile, Tugwell did what he could with the RA. He had hoped to make land reform the agency's primary objective, but by the fall of 1935 rural rehabilitation had become dominant. By mid-1936 the agency had lent ninety-five million dollars, more than half its budget, to over half a million families (8 percent of the farm population). That figure included emergency subsistence grants, seed loans, and debt-adjustment loans. But rural rehabilitation had incurred the wrath of much of the agricultural establishment: the extension service, the land-grant colleges, and the Farm Bureau Federation. In early 1936 congressional sympathizers, including Bilbo, barely deflected a conservative effort to embarrass the RA by publicizing a damaging report on its performance.[63]

It was obvious that the RA was vulnerable without congressional sanction, and progress began only when Roosevelt took the reins him-

60. Mertz, *New Deal Policy and Southern Rural Poverty*, 93–127; Bilbo to Adrian Randall, March 29, 1935, in Bilbo Papers; Baldwin, *Poverty and Politics*, 92–96.

61. Mertz, *New Deal Policy and Southern Rural Poverty*, 138–51.

62. Bilbo to Roosevelt, August 18, 1935, Bilbo to Harrison, August 18, 1935, Bilbo to Byrnes, August 18, 1935, Bilbo to Robinson, August 18, 1935, all in Bilbo Papers; Mertz, *New Deal Policy and Southern Rural Poverty*, 259.

63. Baldwin, *Politics and Poverty*, 104–15.

self in late 1935. When the scramble to replace the AAA delayed matters early the next year, Tugwell sought refuge for the RA in the Department of Agriculture. Wallace, however, was reluctant. Finally, in the fall Tugwell and Alexander persuaded him at least to get out and see the work they were doing. What the secretary saw on that brief November jaunt across the backside of the cotton South left him "visibly shaken." "Two thousand miles of Tobacco Road," one reporter called it. "I have never seen among the peasantry of Europe," Wallace declared, "poverty so abject. . . . The city people of the United States should be thoroughly ashamed." On the last day of 1936 Roosevelt transferred the RA to the Department of Agriculture.[64]

Meanwhile, the new Bankhead-Jones bill gained momentum. The president had established a tenancy commission in the fall of 1936, and its report of February 16 became the basis for the new legislation. "I am very much in favor of the pending bill," Bilbo announced when it came to the floor. Undoubtedly Bilbo's sympathies were more in line with Wallace's faith in the family farm than with Tugwell's socialized paternalism. As Bilbo envisioned the tenancy program, "the government would grub-stake, nurse and supervise purchaser-farmers for five years, and then let them start paying for the lands." During floor debate he argued that if after the Civil War the freedmen had been given land of their own, "something to which they would have tied . . . today there would not be a Harlem in New York, or a 'black belt' in Chicago." Bilbo recognized, much as Alexander, Embree, and Johnson had, that the tenant's way of life followed from his status, not the reverse. He is, said Bilbo, "nomadic in his habits, migratory in his character. . . . There is nothing to tie him up with the church community or the school community. His children naturally absorb the same indifferent spirit about the things that mean so much in the making of a good citizen." Landownership, Bilbo believed, would do much to correct that.[65]

The Bankhead-Jones Act, which Congress finally passed in 1937, was a much more timid effort than the 1935 bill. Under it the RA became the Farm Security Administration (FSA), headed now by Alexander, and continued rural rehabilitation and an enlarged purchase program and also began a system of labor camps for migratory workers. As an instrument of land reform, the FSA proved disappointing. Run

64. Lord, *The Wallaces of Iowa*, 459–62; Baldwin, *Politics and Poverty*, 122, 162–64.

65. *Congressional Record*, 75th Cong., lst Sess., 6757–60; Press release by Kenneth Toler, February 20, 1936, in Case Files, "Bilbo," Ross Collins Papers, Library of Congress.

more as a banking venture than anything else, its restrictive qualifications excluded all laborers and most sharecroppers. Before its demise in 1946, the FSA helped secure land for 44,300 tenants, 70 percent of them in the South. That hardly stirred a ripple in the tenant problem. The deficiency was, as Bilbo would later argue, not with the law itself or the agency, but with Congress, which refused to fund it adequately. "It is the best program we have got," he said; it just did not have enough money to do the job. The FSA continued to spend the bulk of its energy on rural rehabilitation, which was more of a welfare effort than anything else, lending and granting money for tools, seed, animals, debts, and often bare subsistence.[66]

Of course, Bilbo never divorced liberal ideology from political reality, and the tenancy program's patronage potential was not lost on him. "There are over thirteen thousand Resettlement clients in Mississippi," he wrote Roosevelt in 1938. "With their wives and friends this means between thirty and forty thousand votes." Bilbo tried constantly to control RA and FSA appointments but with little more success than he enjoyed with the WPA. Nevertheless, he steadfastly supported the program, even after 1940, when conservative opposition increased. By 1942 the American Farm Bureau Federation was openly hostile, as were most other farm organizations and many key southern leaders. Perhaps the reason was the FSA's scrupulously fair treatment of blacks. Bilbo, however, remained friendly.[67]

In 1942 he found himself having to beat back the race issue, which was ironically such a frequent instrument in the hands of his enemies. Bilbo and Congressman Wall Doxey had faithfully supported the FSA despite its unpopularity among the Delta establishment, who suspected that it was being "too friendly to the Negro tenants." After Harrison died, Doxey entered the 1942 race for his vacant Senate post, and Bilbo declared for him "against the world, the flesh, and the devil." Doxey's opponent, James O. Eastland, attacked Doxey and Bilbo for supporting the FSA. Doxey appealed to Henry Wallace, noting that he and Bilbo were being martyred for the agency and the administration, but the secretary reminded them that the president had promised to stay out of Democratic primary fights. Roosevelt's silence

66. Baldwin, *Politics and Poverty*, 187–202, Mertz, *New Deal Policy and Southern Rural Poverty*, 179–201; U.S. Congress, Senate, Committee on Agriculture and Forestry, *Hearings Before a Subcommittee of the Senate Committee on Agriculture and Forestry, on H.R. 3800 to Amend Soil Conservation Act*, 76th Cong., 3rd Sess., 101.

67. Bilbo to Roosevelt, September 19, 1938, in Bilbo Papers; Donald F. Holley, *Uncle Sam's Farmers: The New Deal Communities in the Lower Mississippi Valley* (Urbana, 1975), 245–56.

sealed Doxey's doom, and Eastland became Bilbo's colleague in 1943.[68]

The Man's main interest was always the small white farmer. During the Agriculture Committee's consideration of the 1938 farm bill, he secured an amendment raising the minimum allotment per farm from five to seven and a half acres. Bankhead, who handled the cotton section of the bill, had no objection and allowed the changes, but he doubted if other cotton senators would go along. He was right. The amendments met stiff opposition on the floor from senators like Kenneth McKellar of Tennessee, who thought that it would take acreage away from other growers. Bilbo argued that the earlier acreage allotments had been unfair to the small farmer and warned that the new law would institutionalize the injustice if it based the new allotments on the old ones. Many of the small farmers in the hill sections of his state and others, he said, who had been growing four, five, or six acres before crop control began, were allowed only one, two, or three under the AAA. Although they had dutifully cooperated then, now they were being denied again.[69]

Bilbo was able to get at least a compromise, extending the bases for acreage allotment back to the year before crop control began. But the individual allotment increase would be useless without increases in county allotments in the poor hill sections, where less cotton was produced. Again he met resistance. "I am not willing to rob the one-horse farmer," he declared, "the man with a wife and five or six or seven children, who is trying to make a living on the farm. I am not willing to deny him the opportunity to grow enough cotton to be able to buy shoes and clothes for his children simply for the sake of some insurance company in the East or some English syndicate which handles a great amount of Delta land." The commercial landowners, Bilbo charged, prepared their crops with machines and then at picking time hired relief workers whom the government kept alive the rest of the year. The big farmers were trying to make money; the "poor devils in the hills are trying to make a living."[70]

Despite support from northern liberals like La Follette and Minton and cotton senators Allen Ellender of Louisiana, Walter George of Georgia, and even Harrison, Bilbo's committee amendment was replaced. He did, however, secure another compromise allowing the secretary of agriculture to use up to 5 percent of any state's quota to ad-

68. Saucier, "The Public Career of Bilbo," 186–87, 195–98; John Morton Blum (ed.), *The Price of Vision: The Diary of Henry A. Wallace* (Boston, 1973), 83.

69. *Congressional Record*, 75th Cong., 2nd Sess., 1085–88.

70. *Ibid.*, 1548–58.

just discrimination against particular counties. When the bill went to conference, he again begged Bankhead and the other Senate conferees to retain the seven-and-a-half-acre provision. However, the committee reduced the state adjustment acreage from 5 percent to 2 percent and changed the minimum back to five acres or the highest number of acres planted in cotton in the last three years plus the number of acres diverted under previous reduction programs. It was not what he had hoped for, but it was better than the small farmer would have received without his efforts.[71]

In the general flow of New Deal lawmaking, Bilbo may have been just a quiet tributary, dutifully dumping his small but dependable trickle of votes into the legislative flood. But in the politics of New Deal agriculture, he was in the mainstream. Devoted to the interests of his farmer constituents, he was vigilant and unflinching when he believed those interests were at stake. He was diligent, studious in his ploddingly ordinary way, and persistent to the point of doggedness. Supporting Roosevelt when he could, he was not unwilling to dig in his heels when he felt he had to buck the administration. By no means original in his thinking about farm issues, he remained what he had always been, a politician. But he was a farmer's politician, and the very commonness of his mind enabled him to translate the rarefied notions of the agricultural Brain Trust into terms that the man in brogans and overalls could lay hold of. The compromise over the 1937 cotton loan suggested what an ideal salesman he could be for the administration. As one Mississippian explained to him, "All that 'high-falutin' talk about economic theories does not always 'soak in' with us ordinary folks, but we can understand getting 12c for our cotton."[72]

Henry Wallace recognized the core of sincerity beneath the web of boorish antics and political bombast that Bilbo spun around his public personality. He was not, said Wallace, "such a bad fellow as he's been painted. As a matter of fact, I think those who got acquainted with him rather liked him." Other Washington liberals did not always appreciate Bilbo's usefulness or his commitment to the same objectives that they themselves pursued. Their concerns for the southern poor were sincere enough, but, as one historian has noted, few of them had ever seen a sharecropper.[73]

71. *Ibid.*, 1560, 1764–65; Bilbo to John Bankhead, December 17, 1937, in Bilbo Papers; *House Reports*, 75th Cong., 3rd Sess., No. 1767, p. 29.

72. Hugh Wall to Bilbo, December 10, 1937, in Bilbo Papers.

73. "Reminiscences of Wallace," 275; Conrad, *Forgotten Farmers*, 110–11.

So why could Will Alexander and Henry Wallace find in Bilbo what Tugwell and Pat Jackson could never bring themselves to see? Perhaps it was because, as Alexander's biographer explains, the ideals that Alexander came to cherish through "sympathetic involvement," others like Tugwell acquired by "cerebration." Like Alexander, Bilbo acquired his liberalism experientially rather than theoretically, but his concern for the underdog, especially Mississippi's farming poor, was indisputable. Within the limits of his own personality and the realities of politics, he represented his constituency's interests fairly faithfully. His own words best summarize his efforts on their behalf: "My ideal, my dream, is so to shape my action on the floor of the Senate . . . that when I shall have finished my term of service here the farmer's compensation may be somewhere in the neighborhood of the compensation of those who work in industry when it comes to payment for honest and hard toil in the cotton fields of the South."[74]

74. Wilma Dykeman and James Stokely, *Seeds of Southern Change: The Life of Will Alexander* (New York, 1962), 217–18; *Congressional Record*, 75th Cong., lst Sess., 8097.

Chapter Ten

The Potentate of Mississippi Politics

As the end of his first term approached, Bilbo was confident that he would win reelection. Roosevelt and the New Deal were immensely popular in Mississippi, and Bilbo had been the state's most loyal congressional advocate of both. He had served his constituency well, he thought, and he expected the voters to reward him with a second term. Although he had recently been able to neutralize his enemies' control of federal patronage somewhat, one matter still troubled him: the administration of state government was in the hands of a hostile faction. After the Holmes controversy split the senatorial alliance that had helped put Hugh White in office, the governor aligned himself with Harrison, even though it was Bilbo who had carried the load in the 1935 campaign. White's control of state patronage and Harrison's dominance of federal jobs enabled the anti-Bilbo faction to dominate the Democratic party in Mississippi.

Nineteen thirty-nine was statewide election year, and Bilbo desperately needed a friend in the governor's chair. The only realistic possibility was a man who had been his political antagonist for two decades and to whom he had just denied the governorship in the last election, Paul Johnson. But political musical chairs was not new to Bilbo. He had just played a round of it (with disastrous results) in 1936 with Mike Conner and Pat Harrison. He was perfectly willing to try again should Johnson prove amenable. Ideologically Bilbo and Johnson had much in common, both catering to the same poor-farmer constituency. Their long-standing political enmity stemmed largely from the quirks of one-party factionalism and the 1918 congressional race, in which Johnson had thrashed Bilbo. Now Johnson, still smarting from Harrison's unfriendliness in 1935 and more determined than ever to win executive office, was willing to hold his nose and join forces with Bilbo. By the end of 1938, The Man was working feverishly for his new political ally.

The senator hoped to head off other potential candidates, especially

Conner. Johnson feared that the former governor was determined to run, but Bilbo, who was still on good terms with Conner, seemed less concerned. To pacify Johnson, Bilbo offered to help Conner secure an appointment as president of the Federal Land Bank, but Mike politely declined. White and Harrison also frowned upon a Conner candidacy. Their primary concern was the 1940 election, in which they hoped to unseat Bilbo and send an uncommitted delegation to the national convention. A Johnson victory would wreck those hopes, so White and Harrison sought a candidate who was both viable and willing to work with them. Conner's prospects were as good as any, but his race against Harrison in 1936 made for an awkward alliance now. State Representative Tom Bailey of Meridian was much more to their liking, and he had politely bowed out in Conner's favor in 1931. Bailey's chances of defeating Johnson, however, were questionable.[1]

In September, 1938, a frantic Johnson wrote Bilbo that Conner and Harrison had met recently at a Gulfport hotel where Mike had agreed to step aside in 1939 in return for Bailey-Harrison support in 1940 against Bilbo. Johnson was uneasy and urged his friend to impress upon Roosevelt the implications that such an alliance could have on the makeup of the 1940 Mississippi delegation. If the president wanted Mississippi's support for a third term, Johnson insisted, he would have to stand up for his friends and stop pampering his enemies. "They are hell bent on destroying you," he warned Bilbo, "and they are willing to destroy me to get to you." The senator did his best to calm his ally with assurances that Conner would ruin himself by joining with Harrison and surely had better sense. Johnson remained but little comforted.[2]

Meanwhile another political gathering was causing consternation in Mississippi. Late in 1937 Dennis Murphree had been summoned to the executive mansion, where Governor White and Harrison assured him of their support for governor in 1939. Murphree, who believed that he could win with their support, became irritated later when rumors surfaced that his putative benefactors were now courting Bailey. White assured him that there had been no commitment to Bailey, but Murphree could sense hands being laid on the rug beneath him and began marshaling his forces in case someone should give a tug. He finally decided to run for lieutenant governor, convinced that a first-primary victory would give him a decisive voice in the runoff for

1. Swain, *Pat Harrison*, 207; Bilbo to Conner, January 23, 1938, Murphree to Friends (copy), August 31, 1938, both in Bilbo Papers.

2. Johnson to Bilbo, September 16, 1938, Bilbo to Johnson, September 18, 1938, both in Bilbo Papers.

governor. Bilbo and Johnson seized upon Murphree's disenchantment with White.[3]

The governor and the senior senator seemed to be placing bets all over the table, encouraging any and all candidates who might erode Johnson's first-primary support. The two apparently provided money as well as encouragement to Lester Franklin, who announced quickly and captured early headlines. In a letter that was leaked to the press, Pat advised friends that he found "no fault with the candidacy" of Franklin. Soon afterward Harrison and White, while still openly neutral, held a two-hour conference at the governor's mansion with Bailey, who then threw his hat into the ring. If the behavior of White and Harrison indicated any strategy at all, it was to let their four friends in the race—Bailey, Conner, Franklin, and Lieutenant Governor Billy Snider—fight it out in the first primary, and then unite behind whoever made the runoff with Johnson.[4]

Meanwhile, Bilbo was busy selling his man to the president. He tried to persuade Roosevelt to have Attorney General Cummings appoint Johnson as a consultant to Thurman Arnold's antitrust division of the Justice Department as an expert on the cottonseed trust. It seemed that Harrison's recent coolness toward the New Deal was finally opening some doors for Bilbo within the administration. Near the end of 1938, The Man emerged from a conference with Harold Ickes to announce a three-million-dollar federal grant for Mississippi highways. Harrison, who had not been informed, was incensed as Bilbo appeared to bask in the warmth of presidential favor.[5]

Bilbo was delighted at the publicity but more than a little concerned over who would control the new highway jobs. Conner was unlikely to benefit because of his long-standing feud with the highway commission. Southern District Commissioner Hiram Patterson had managed White's 1935 campaign, and Bilbo feared that the governor and Harrison would put great pressure on him and the other commissioners, S. T. Roebuck and Abe Linker. Early in 1939, Bilbo met with Patterson, Roebuck, and Highway Director Doug Kenna in Washington and afterward assured Johnson that the highway department would be no trouble in the governor's race. Patterson was especially grateful that

3. Murphree to Friends (copy), August 31, 1938, Bilbo to Johnson, January 7, 1939, both in Bilbo Papers.

4. Bilbo to Conner, January 23, 1938, in Bilbo Papers; Memphis *Commercial Appeal*, April 9, 1939, Sec. 5, p. 4, April 23, 1939, Sec. 4, p. 5.

5. Bilbo to Johnson, September 29, 1938, in Bilbo Papers; Woodward to Hopkins, August 11, 1938, in Woodward Papers; New York *Times*, October 13, 1938, p. 22.

Johnson had helped discourage possible opposition for his own commission seat. Bilbo breathed easier, but he remained concerned about the highway commission's influence.[6]

The other patronage package that plagued the campaign was, of course, WPA, and it took on titanic proportions in Johnson's mind. He bombarded Bilbo with a steady stream of ominous reports and dire warnings, but the senator assured him that with Hopkins, Aubrey Williams, and Ellen Woodward all gone from the agency, its political power could at least be neutralized. "We have a hard-boiled West Point Military man at the head of it," he said, "and I am still hopeful that everything will work out all right in the end."[7]

But Johnson remained concerned over the psychological effect of Bilbo's apparent impotence in patronage matters. In March, when the state FHA directorate went to W. T. Pate, a Harrison man, Johnson told Bilbo that it was the worst setback the campaign had yet suffered. Bilbo leaders were disheartened, Johnson warned: "They say they are following an empty basket. Pat's crowd taunt them and tell them you have no influence." He urged Bilbo to do whatever necessary to wrest the WPA from Harrison. Even if it had no substantive effect at all, it would reverse the psychological slide. Everywhere he went, Johnson said, people spoke of the WPA and their fear of it. Bilbo tried to soothe his partner's apprehensions. "The mess is a liability to start with," he said, because those without jobs were angry at whoever controlled it. Nonetheless, he carried the complaint to Roosevelt, arguing that such appointments as Pate's were hurting the administration's interest as well as Bilbo's. Harrison's friends, who already controlled almost all federal jobs in Mississippi, were the New Deal's most vocal critics in the state. The FHA, Bilbo warned, would be just another weapon in the fight against Bilbo *and* Roosevelt.[8]

About the time that Bilbo was making his appeal, the WPA bomb exploded. Wall, who had actually been running the agency as assistant director, was formally promoted to the top post. The impact on the WPA was nil because Wall had been de facto director for three years anyway. The effect on voters, however, was profound. Johnson called it a "tremendous jolt" and pleaded with the senator for anything, some

6. Bilbo to Johnson, September 12, 1938, Bilbo to Johnson, January 25, 1939, both in Bilbo Papers.

7. Johnson to Bilbo, January 9, 1939, Bilbo to Johnson, January 12, 1939, both in Bilbo Papers.

8. Johnson to Bilbo, March 11, 1939, Johnson to Bilbo, March 18, 1939, Bilbo to Johnson, March 27, 1939, Bilbo to Roosevelt, March 22, 1939, all in Bilbo Papers.

significant appointment to something to show his supporters that Bilbo had some influence somewhere. Despite Bilbo's assurances that Wall's appointment was probationary, Johnson complained that there was as much politics as ever in the agency. He warned that Harrison's and Wall's henchmen scoffed at the affidavits forswearing politics that Harrington forced them to sign. Johnson was convinced that his enemies intended to use the WPA in the governor's race.[9]

Bilbo decided to do something about Wall, and it was then that he persuaded Roosevelt to remove the director at least until after the primary. Wall and his assistant, George Parker, were replaced in late June by an outsider, Marvin Porter, who would run the Mississippi agency for sixty days. The change prompted much speculation, despite Harrington's insistence that there was no evidence of any political activity by Wall and Parker. The action was merely a precautionary measure to defuse a volatile situation, Harrington declared. But the news surely heartened the Bilbo troops with at least a prospect of patronage and bolstered the Johnson campaign at its weakest point.[10]

Meanwhile the campaign itself was taking shape. Bilbo sent Johnson a new and extensive list of campaign workers covering over a thousand precincts. He reviewed Johnson's platform and made several suggestions, including two of significance. One was a modification of Johnson's commitment to government retrenchment so as to guarantee that spending reductions would not be at the expense of schools, hospitals, or institutions for the poor. The change was aimed at Conner, whose retrenchment as governor, Bilbo charged, "starved the schools . . . and let the poor and indigent sick die on the doorsteps of the hospitals," which lacked the funds to treat them.[11]

Bilbo's other recommendation concerned the old-age pension for which he was desperately battling at that moment in Congress. Johnson brought the fight to Mississippi and made the issue a central one in his campaign. He scorned the existing state pension system. "To get the old-age pension," the candidate told a Hattiesburg rally, "you must swear you are a pauper and no 'count and that your folks are no 'count." He proposed a direct thirty-dollar pension to all over sixty-five regardless of income, an idea that drew fire from Fred Sullens, who

9. Johnson to Bilbo, April 1, 1939, Johnson to Bilbo, May 8, 1939, Bilbo to Johnson, April 4, 1939, all in Bilbo Papers.

10. Bilbo to R. M. Newton, July 1, 1939, Johnson to Bilbo, June 30, 1939, both in Bilbo Papers; Memphis *Commercial Appeal*, July 2, 1939, Sec. 4, p. 5.

11. Johnson to Bilbo, March 18, 1939, Bilbo to Johnson, March 20, 1939, both in Bilbo Papers.

argued that it would bankrupt the treasury. The editor warned that if the federal government put up any money, it would require payment to blacks as well as whites—with disastrous results. "Every Negro in Mississippi" would instantly become sixty-five, he said, and inadequate black birth records would make it impossible to prevent abuse. Older blacks would then quit work, and every living relative, by blood or in-law, would move in to share the newfound affluence, causing a "complete demoralization of labor conditions." Sullens painted a gruesome picture: deserted dwellings, fields gone to seed, white families without maids, white women doing their own laundry, idle factories, and "general demoralization of business." It was a striking piece of journalism for a self-confessed novice in the school of race-baiting.[12]

Of all his recommendations to Johnson, Bilbo most stressed the importance of absolute silence regarding the other candidates. With Harrison and White officially uncommitted, it made no sense to antagonize any opponent before the second primary. The losers would surely resent the refusal by the governor and senior senator to declare themselves openly. Johnson agreed to be nice, especially to Bailey, whose every vote would come at Conner's expense.[13]

The aura of mystery surrounding the doings of White and Harrison was about all that kept the political news columns from daily starvation. It was manna in a wilderness of election tedium. The early attention focused on Franklin and Bailey. Harrison's rumored interest in Franklin seemed illogical except as a means of ballot padding to hurt Johnson, but it worried Johnson enough. He worried about losing votes to Franklin in northeast Mississippi; he worried about the patronage crumbs with which Harrison seemed to be luring Bilbo's people to Franklin; he worried about the money that Franklin was spending in abundance. "Pat is supporting him," Johnson assured Bilbo. "You need not discount that." Harrison's leaders were indeed helping Franklin, who was visiting WPA camps boasting of the patronage that the senior senator was funneling his way. And, Johnson fretted, "he is getting plenty of money somewhere." The White forces, on the other hand, seemed to be working for Bailey, which prompted cries of "dictator" from many who resented any effort by an incumbent governor to handpick a successor. Bilbo believed that with every passing day White

12. Bilbo to Johnson, March 20, 1939, in Bilbo Papers; Hattiesburg *American*, June 21, 1939, p. 3; Jackson *Daily News*, August 22, 1939, p. 1.

13. Bilbo to Johnson, March 20, 1939, Johnson to Bilbo, April 1, 1939, both in Bilbo Papers.

was unwittingly drawing votes to Johnson. "Just leave him alone," The Man advised, "like you would an ordinary idiot." [14]

Johnson and almost all of Mississippi were sure that White and Harrison would back Conner if he made the runoff, but Bilbo stubbornly refused to believe it. They would lead Conner so far into the water that he could not turn back and then "crucify poor Mike," Bilbo said. White and Pat would never "take him in the end," he insisted, and waited for the endorsement of Bailey. It never came. However much Harrison and the governor preferred Bailey, they knew that he could never win; and however much they mistrusted Conner, they knew that he would be in the runoff. By early June, Harrison and White leaders were surfacing in the Conner camp. Eugene Fly broke a long-standing custom when he appeared at a Conner rally, accompanied by Louis Jiggitts and Harrison's old friend Mayor Joe Milner of Gulfport. It was obvious that the governor and senator were hedging their bets.[15]

About the same time, Bilbo learned that pressure on the highway commission was about to end their neutrality. Should a majority of the three members win in the first primary, White and Harrison would surely press them to throw their patronage and energy into the runoff for governor. Bilbo was tempted to prod some opponents into the highway commissioner races to occupy the incumbents with second-primary fights of their own. But that risked antagonizing the commissioners unnecessarily, since they might be able to resist the governor's pressure after all. Bilbo nonetheless urged John Burkett to try to convince Johnson and campaign manager Charlie Cameron to get at least two more candidates into the highway races in the middle and southern districts. "Everything may be all right," he said, "but there is nothing like playing safe." [16]

By the end of June the commission races were hot, especially Patterson's, and it looked as if all three commissioners might face a runoff. Then, within a week of the vote, Bilbo learned that the pressure on the highway department had become enormous. Instructing Ed Terry, his secretary, to convey the news to Johnson in Jackson, he cautioned that it would perhaps be better if the source of the information remained unknown. Johnson should "pass the word down the line and throw Patterson into a second primary if he is not already in it." It would

14. Johnson to Bilbo, March 18, 1939, Johnson to Bilbo, April 17, 1939, Johnson to Bilbo, May 1, 1939, Bilbo to Johnson, April 15, 1939, all in Bilbo Papers.

15. Bilbo to Johnson, March 9, 1939, Bilbo to Johnson, March 13, 1939, both in Bilbo Papers; Memphis *Commercial Appeal*, June 11, 1939, Sec. 4, p. 4.

16. Bilbo to Burkett, June 6, 1939, in Bilbo Papers.

have to be done with reliable people "and handled after the sun went down." It might even be best to by-pass Cameron and let Johnson decide whether to enlighten his campaign manager. It would be disastrous to let Patterson find out and then fail to force a runoff: "In other words, an attempt followed by failure would be damn bad politics."[17]

Whatever attempt was made failed, because Patterson won in the first primary. Whether he ever discovered his friend's duplicity is a mystery. Roebuck likewise won without a runoff, but Linker lost a second-primary vote. Bilbo need not have worried, because Highway Director Doug Kenna was determined to see Conner defeated. Despite his long-standing friendship with White and Harrison, the director could not afford to see the highway department's chief antagonist elected governor. Kenna's estimate that his organization controlled fifty thousand votes was probably exaggerated, but a goodly portion of Johnson's twenty-five-thousand-vote lead in the first primary was no doubt attributable to the influence of highway patronage. When White and Harrison promptly endorsed Conner for the runoff, Kenna sent Patterson and Roebuck into hiding. As the director held the highway forces in line for Johnson, Conner's backers were irate but helpless. Bailey was the only defeated candidate to join the former governor, as Bilbo's strategy worked almost to perfection: Franklin, Snider, and Dennis Murphree, who won his own race without a runoff, all joined the Johnson campaign.[18]

Two of Johnson's liabilities were his health and his temperament. The first primary had been grueling for him, and he nearly collapsed at the kickoff rally for the second. He recovered, however, and finished the race with apparently renewed vigor. His bad heart condition was aggravated by his difficulty in dissociating political assault from personal attack. Johnson could carry a grudge to extravagance, and his fits of temper were notorious. Conner picked at the sore: "Paul Johnson is the Donald Duck of Mississippi politics—he gets so mad that he bites his friends and then he bites himself to death." Such a man was "temperamentally unfitted" to be governor, said Conner. But Johnson knew his weakness and opened his campaign with a promise to "show them I can take it and they can't make me mad."[19]

17. Ed Terry to Bilbo, July 17, 1939, Bilbo to Terry, August 1, 1939, both in Bilbo papers.

18. *Mississippi Blue Book, 1939–1941*, pp. 251–59; interview with E. D. Kenna, MOHP, Vol. CCXLVI, 11–13; Jackson *Daily News*, August 10, 1939, p. 1, August 11, 1939, p. 1, August 12, 1939, p. 1, August 14, 1939, p. 1.

19. Jackson *Daily News*, August 13, 1939, p. 1; Hattiesburg *American*, August 24, 1939, p. 1, June 21, 1939, p. 1.

The only significant issue in the runoff was the New Deal, which gave the campaign national import. In the race to catch the Roosevelt train, Conner was burdened by his own record and that of his backers, chiefly Harrison. Conner's every charge that Johnson was anti–New Deal echoed back his own equivocal role in the 1932 convention and his own basic conservatism. Johnson was not about to be out-Roosevelted. "They say Johnson's for Roosevelt and they are going to beat me; they say Johnson's for the New Deal and they are going to defeat me. I'm for Roosevelt," he thundered. Moreover, Harrison was equivocal, at best, regarding a third term for the president, and the conservative press, which backed Conner, constantly carped at New Deal policies. Meanwhile, in Bilbo, Johnson had the support of Mississippi's "original third-termer" and a senator whose New Deal record was virtually unblemished. When Johnson captured a twenty-eight-thousand-vote majority in the second primary, the New York *Times* declared: BILBO AND NEW DEAL VICTORIOUS OVER HARRISON. The outcome diminished Pat's chances for a favorite-son candidacy and gave Johnson and Bilbo a substantial voice in Mississippi's 1940 national Democratic delegation. "The good people of the State of Mississippi have spoken," said a pleased Roosevelt, "and how!"[20]

As 1940 opened, Bilbo hoped that his position was strong enough to frighten away any serious opposition to his own reelection, but he could take no chances. Much depended on the Johnson administration. A successful program by the governor would strengthen Bilbo's hand, though any personal involvement in the legislative battles risked unduly antagonizing potential allies in the Senate race. It was a delicate situation.[21]

While The Man offered Johnson free and full advice on legislative strategy, wealthy Picayune lumberman L. O. Crosby led an effort by conservatives to wean Bilbo away from the governor. Most observers agreed that if anyone challenged the senator in 1940, it would be Hugh White. Crosby volunteered to try to convince his good friend and fellow lumberman not to make the race. Many of his business acquaintances, Crosby said, had never supported Bilbo before, but were now

20. Jackson *Daily News*, August 13, 1939, p. 18; John Ray Skates, "From Enchantment to Disillusionment: A Southern Editor Views the New Deal," *Southern Quarterly*, V (1967), 377–79; New York *Times*, August 30, 1939, p. 14; Bernard F. Donahoe, *Private Plans and Public Dangers* (Notre Dame, 1965), 152; Washington *Daily News*, August 31, 1939, clipping in Reference File, Mississippi, 1938–39, Clapper Papers; Roosevelt to Bilbo, August 31, 1939, in Bilbo Papers.

21. H. L. Simmons to Bilbo, March 26, 1940, Lester Franklin to Bilbo, April 5, 1940, both in Bilbo Papers.

willing to see him return to the Senate without opposition. He hinted, however, that Bilbo's intervention in the current legislative session would surely produce "appeals . . . for an opponent." Crosby and his friends were willing to squeeze White if Bilbo would cut Johnson adrift.[22]

The senator played his hand close to the vest. He welcomed Crosby's gesture but made no commitments. "I am depending on you to keep White out of the race," he wrote, but he backed Johnson to the hilt, imploring his faction in the legislature to support the governor. "I want to urge you to go all the way with him," he wired an old friend. "I am . . . pleading with you to stand with Governor Johnson." In fact, after the first week of the 1940 session, one lawmaker complained that there was "too damned much Bilbo" in the legislature. A few weeks later Sullens charged in a front-page editorial that Bilbo, not Johnson, was trying to dominate the statehouse. "The hand is the hand of Esau," said Sullens, "but the voice is the voice of Jacob." Indeed, Johnson's program for "the average man" was very much a Bilbo platform. The 1940 legislature produced the nearest thing to a "little New Deal" that Mississippi would see. The governor's inaugural address called for free textbooks and increased school appropriations, pensions for teachers and the elderly, hospital care for the poor, aid to dependent children, new state departments of labor and conservation, exemption of necessities from sales taxes, repeal of the poll tax, severance taxes on timber and oil, and a state tenancy program patterned after the federal FSA. It was an ambitious platform encompassing a record forty-four-million-dollar budget, but conservatives, particularly the Delta faction, mauled it considerably before the session ended. The legislative struggle, however, did make the ideological lines of Mississippi politics fairly distinct, and Johnson and Bilbo emerged as the undisputed champions of the New Deal in the state. The junior senator clearly tied his reelection hopes to the popularity of New Deal liberalism.[23]

At the last minute Hugh White entered the senatorial race after all, though Crosby assured Bilbo that he had done everything possible to dissuade him. It is impossible to tell how much pressure Crosby and his friends truly placed on the former governor, but once White de-

22. Bilbo to Johnson, October 16, 1939, L. O. Crosby to Newton (copy), April 3, 1940, Crosby to Bilbo, April 16, 1940, Crosby to Bilbo, April 29, 1940, all in Bilbo Papers.

23. Bilbo to Crosby, April 10, 1940, Bilbo to Dr. J. P. Conn, March 26, 1940, both in Bilbo Papers; Jackson *Daily News*, January 7, 1940, p. 6, February 1, 1940, p. 1, January 16, 1940, p. 1; Jackson *Daily Clarion Ledger*, May 12, 1940, p. 6.

clared his candidacy, Crosby declined to support Bilbo financially or otherwise. White never posed a serious threat to Bilbo, but his very presence in the race proved a nuisance. It was especially troublesome for Bilbo to have to raise funds for a campaign. Friends warned the senator that White would amass a huge war chest and that it would take considerable money to combat his propaganda. Much of Bilbo's time and energy was spent on fund raising in 1940.[24]

The most volatile issue in the campaign was the state poll tax. As early as 1935 Bilbo had begun to press for repeal of the two-dollar annual levy that Mississippians had to pay to vote. "I have never believed that the people ought to have to pay a tax to vote," he said. It was a "relic of feudalism," which disfranchised poor people, most of whom in Mississippi were his supporters. In 1940 he urged Johnson to make repeal a major plank in his platform and volunteered to address a joint session of the legislature himself on the issue. Despite early enthusiasm Johnson retreated from the poll-tax debate, unwilling to endanger the rest of his platform for this controversial piece of legislation.[25]

It was controversial because it inevitably became tangled with the race issue. White accused Bilbo of wanting to open the door for black voting. Repeal, he charged, "would amount to turning the state back into the hands of carpet-baggers." The worst assault came from Fred Sullens, who claimed that Bilbo had "won thousands of ardent admirers among the equality-seeking negroes of the North" and such civil rights advocates as John L. Lewis and the NAACP. Repeal, said the editor, would "bring negroes swarming to the polls throughout the South."[26]

Even Bilbo's friends urged him to drop the issue, but he would not be scared away. The poll tax had nothing to do with white supremacy, he insisted, because other provisions of the state constitution would preclude black voting. The notion that Bilbo could be soft on the race issue was more than a little incredible, since he had only recently gained

24. Newton to Bilbo, July 6, 1940, Terry to Newton, August 8, 1940, H. L. Simmons to Bilbo, May 13, 1940, Bilbo to Newton, July 31, 1940, all in Bilbo Papers.

25. Bilbo to Heber Ladner, February 4, 1936; Bilbo to Kelley Hammond, September 10, 1938, Bilbo to Johnson, February 14, 1940, Charles G. Hamilton to Bilbo, April 9, 1940, all in Bilbo Papers.

26. Jackson *Daily Clarion Ledger*, August 24, 1940, p. 1; Jackson *Daily News*, May 23, 1940, p. 6. When officials of the Mississippi AF of L reminded Bilbo that he had once called Lewis "the biggest man in America," the senator recalled that he had once referred to the CIO chief as "at heart a friend of labor" but insisted that he would "feel differently now." Holt Ross to Bilbo, July 10, 1940, Bilbo to Ross, July 31, 1940, both in Bilbo Papers.

national notoriety for advocating a rather eccentric scheme to preserve white supremacy—"repatriation" of American blacks who wished to emigrate to Africa.[27]

Bilbo's relationship to the race issue had been an interesting one. He certainly believed blacks to be inferior, but he did not seem to consider white supremacy to be a political issue. His career prior to 1940 was sufficiently bereft of race-baiting that he could declare on the Senate floor, with some justification, that in thirty years of politics, almost twenty of them in public office, he had "never sought to win an election by trying to arouse or appealing to race prejudice. . . . I did not try to ride into public office on the Negro question." In fact, Bilbo always proudly claimed that he was the very first Mississippi governor after Reconstruction who had not used the race issue to get elected. As for the "back to Africa" idea, he had shunned just such a scheme in 1923 because he thought it impractical though desirable.[28]

Two things changed his mind by 1938. One was the effort by some northern congressmen to pass a federal antilynching law. Like most of his southern colleagues, Bilbo condemned lynching but feared that federal intervention would threaten white supremacy. He despised murder as much as anyone in the Congress, he said, and as governor had commuted death sentences whenever he could, sparing "many human beings, both black and white."[29] Some things, however, were not negotiable, he insisted, and white supremacy was one of them. He vowed to fight the antilynching bill "till hell freezes over." The other cause of his renewed interest in repatriation was the conviction that the idea had gained enough support among blacks that it could be passed off as something more than mere southern white racism.[30]

Sullens took a dimmer view of the repatriation scheme. Bilbo had "made a consummate chump of himself," said the feisty editor, and as "the laughing stock of the nation" was hardly fit to be returned to the

27. Simmons to Bilbo, May 10, 1940, in Bilbo Papers, Jackson *Daily Clarion Ledger*, August 20, 1940, pp. 1–2; Saucier, "The Public Career of Bilbo," 127.

28. Doler, "Bilbo's Rhetoric of Racial Relations," 77; *Congressional Record*, 75th Cong., 3rd Sess., 881; Tony Martin, *Race First: The Ideological and Organizational Struggles of Marcus Garvey and the Universal Negro Improvement Association* (Westport, Conn., 1976), 349.

29. Bilbo opposed capital punishment and considered it "judicial murder." He commuted death sentences, he said, wherever he "could find a shadow of doubt to justify [it] . . . under law." Bilbo to Ethel Hearn, February 20, 1940, in Bilbo Papers.

30. *Congressional Record*. 75th Cong., 3rd Sess., 874. For Mississippi and the antilynching bill see Robert Dubay, "Mississippi and the Proposed Federal Anti-Lynching Bill of 1937–38," *Southern Quarterly*, VII (1968), 73–89. For Bilbo and repatriation, see Epilogue.

Senate. It was true that few Mississippians took the Greater Liberia bill very seriously, but it surely blunted Sullens' charge that Bilbo was soft on white supremacy. It is significant, however, that the attacks by White and Sullens forced Bilbo neither to back down on the poll tax nor to grab the race issue and run with it. He simply praised the New Deal and pointed to his consistent support of Roosevelt's policies.[31]

In fact, throughout 1940, race became a favorite weapon in the hands, not of the redneck leaders Bilbo and Johnson, but of their enemies. Not only did enlightened Delta conservatives cry "nigger" on old-age pensions and poll-tax repeal, but some even opposed free textbooks as a threat to white supremacy. Black-county lawmakers amended Johnson's textbook bill to forbid the teaching of democratic rights and duties in civics books used by blacks and even to provide for separate storage facilities for texts used by the two races so that "books used by negro children will not be distributed among white children." The amendments were removed in conference committee by the Bilbo-Johnson leaders over the vehement objections of conservatives. When the conference report came before the senate, Albert Lake of Greenville, after chivalrously warning women to leave the galleries, read excerpts from letters reputedly written to the author of one of the amendments by northern blacks, representatives of the American Civil Liberties Union, the Congress of Industrial Organizations, and other civil rights advocates. These "obscene and abusive letters," said one reporter, left the senators "trembling with emotions" in a frenzy of indignation aroused not by the spokesmen of benighted poor whites, but by representatives of sophisticated Delta paternalism. After the administration forces turned back efforts to reinstate the racial amendments, the Jackson *Daily Clarion Ledger* congratulated the lawmakers for having foiled "a sordid attempt to 'lynch' the . . . free textbook bill on a gibbet of race prejudice." The scene vividly depicted the real dynamics of the race issue in internal Mississippi politics, with the forces of poor-white "demagoguery" standing firm for progressive legislation in the face of impassioned appeals to racial solidarity on the part of their social betters, refusing even "to proclaim to the world that there shall be no personal contact between the races in Mississippi."[32]

Race was not the only issue on which Sullens attacked Bilbo. Strangely enough, Bilbo and the irascible editor seemed to get along quite well on a personal basis despite their bitter political antagonism.

31. Jackson *Daily News*, May 23, 1940, p. 6; Doler, "Bilbo's Rhetoric of Racial Relations," 108.

32. Jackson *Daily Clarion Ledger*, February 8, 1940, p. 1, February 9, 1940, p. 3, February 15, 1940, p. 9, February 16, 1940, pp. 1, 9, February 17, 1940, p. 3.

Over coffee at the Mayflower Cafe in Jackson, Sullens told Bilbo in November, 1939, "I have decided to defeat you next year by giving you my hearty support." But castigating The Man in print had become part of the editor's nature, and when a *Look* magazine poll declared that only Rush Holt of West Virginia was less esteemed than Bilbo in the Senate, Sullens pronounced Bilbo the Second Most Useless Senator and thereafter affixed the title SMUS to every mention of the senator's name. Sullens took delight in baiting Bilbo but found him "impervious to the most penetrating adjectives." When the rumor surfaced that Mrs. Bilbo might make the race against her husband in 1940, Bilbo denied it and decided it was "just more of Fred Sullens' 'son-of-bitchery.'"[33]

The growing international crisis in 1940 made it difficult for Bilbo to leave the capital to campaign, so he directed matters as best he could from Washington. But by early August his secretary warned, "You had better come down to Mississippi or Hugh White's money is going to make it hard for us on August 27." Bilbo quickly responded by challenging White to a series of public debates, and when White declined as expected, the senator decided to take the stump.[34]

In the final two weeks of the campaign, The Man delivered more than fifty speeches over the state. He was sixty-two years old now, but he seemed to have lost little, if any, of his durability or effectiveness on the stump. When the votes were in, he carried sixty-nine of eighty-two counties, with almost 60 percent of the vote. It was the peak of his political success and a vindication of his first term in the Senate. A high official in the Roosevelt administration wrote, "I was delighted to learn of your splendid victory . . . assuring six years more of a real friend of liberal government."[35]

It was a fitting congratulation. Bilbo had come to the Senate in 1935 committed to the New Deal, and for six years he had remained faithful, even as Roosevelt led the Democratic party from old-style progressivism to welfare liberalism. Although the administration often seemed bent on rewarding its enemies rather than its friends in Mississippi, Bilbo supported the president with loyalty and enthusiasm. He expected that loyalty to pay dividends with the voters, if not with the bureaucrats, and it did. Most Mississippians, Bilbo believed, were

33. Sullens to Bilbo, November 16, 1939, in Bilbo Papers; John Ray Skates, "Journalist vs. Politician: Fred Sullens and Theodore G. Bilbo," *Southern Quarterly*, VIII (1970), 285; Bilbo to Newton, April 2, 1940, in Bilbo Papers.

34. Terry to Bilbo, August 4, 1940, in Bilbo Papers; Saucier, "The Public Career of Bilbo," 177–78.

35. Saucier, "The Public Career of Bilbo," 177–78; Joseph D. Kennan to Bilbo, August 28, 1940, in Bilbo Papers.

"100 percent for Roosevelt . . . and the New Deal," and by that standard no candidate in 1940 could enter a more credible claim for electoral endorsement than could he.[36]

As if to vindicate further his credentials as a New Dealer, The Man offered the party his services as a speaker in the fall campaign. Other northern Democrats perhaps shared Senator Joseph Guffey's trepidation about "how he would please" Yankee voters. But after accompanying him on a speaking tour, the Pennsylvania New Dealer reported that Bilbo "received tremendous ovations everywhere he spoke . . . and convinced thousands of my constituents of the prime necessity" of a third term for Roosevelt. The Young Democrats of New York invited Bilbo to deliver the keynote address for the group's campaign kickoff in September. Thereafter, he spoke almost a hundred times in Missouri, Kansas, Ohio, Indiana, Pennsylvania, and Tennessee. "Can't thank you enough for what you did in Missouri," Truman wrote him after the campaign. A Democratic county chairman in Tennessee declared that the party there doubled its vote over the 1936 total "entirely due to your masterful speech."[37]

As he campaigned in the Midwest, Bilbo issued an appeal to the voters back home to "make the fight of their lives . . . for our great President, Franklin D. Roosevelt, the best friend the South ever had in the White House." His personal and political admiration for the president seemed as genuine as that of his poor Mississippi constituents, many of whose ramshackle dwellings were graced with yellowing photographs of FDR clipped from newspapers and reverently but clumsily tacked upon unpainted walls. Such people did not need to be reminded, as they were by Bilbo, that with the New Deal, Roosevelt had:

fed and clothed our destitute . . . educated and trained . . . our underprivileged . . . given us . . . roads . . . hospitals for our sick . . . modern school houses . . . parks . . . useful public buildings; trained and cared for our blind and crippled . . . increased wages per hour and shortened the hours of labor . . . provided loans for our cotton . . . paid our farmers . . . parity payments, financed the crops of our poor farmers and tenants when the banks, loan companies, and merchants could not help them . . . loaned money to our distressed industries and business people; saved thousand of homes . . . dis-

36. Press release for October 29, 1940, in Bilbo Papers.

37. Press release for September 21, 1940, R. Mahon to Bilbo, November 5, 1940, Harry S. Truman to Bilbo, November 8, 1940, all in Bilbo Papers. Guffey's praise was especially interesting, since he was one of those urban Democrats who had politically "harnessed . . . negroes and labor unions," much to the dismay of his fellow Democrats from the South. James T. Patterson, "The Failure of Party Realignment in the South, 1937–1939," *Journal of Politics*, XXVII (1965), 604.

tributed trainloads of commodities to the poor . . . provided pensions for the old . . . compensation to the unemployed; retirement funds for the laborers . . . enacted laws . . . to protect our people from the manipulators and "slickers" of Wall Street.

That litany of federal reforms perhaps more than anything else explains The Man's success in Mississippi and Roosevelt's in the nation in 1940. "Glory, glory, hallelujah," Bilbo wired the president after the November triumph, "God has blessed America."[38]

38. Press release for October 29, 1940, Bilbo to Roosevelt, November 6, 1940, both in Bilbo Papers.

Chapter Eleven

Still Redneck, Still Liberal

Two things stand out clearly about Theodore Bilbo's first term in the United States Senate. First, he remained what he always had been, a man for whom politics was a consuming passion. Nothing he did in those six years was completely divorced from his determination to be the undisputed potentate of Mississippi politics. That had been the quest of his adult life, and by 1940 he was close to achieving it. Yet somehow, attaining the goal seemed less fulfilling than pursuing it, for he simply reveled in the rough and tumble of stump campaigning. When a reporter once asked him the population of Mississippi, he replied spryly, "Votin' or eatin'?"[1]

No one was ever more suited to a vocation than was Bilbo to redneck politics. For the hordes of the state's poor whites, the summer primary campaigns did more than determine who would hold office; they provided a taste of rustic culture. For these weary, unmannered sons of the soil, here was their only source of drama and comedy, of heroes and villains. Here was their philosophy and rhetoric, however crude, their elocution and wit, however coarse. Above all else, here was a flash of entertainment amidst an abundance of drudgery. And Bilbo was, if anything, a consummate entertainer.

He knew these people because he was one of them. He knew how to make them laugh and weep, how to soothe them and to rouse their fury. Most of all, he knew how to win their trust—and votes. Politics was for him a game, not because he was cynical—for as V. O. Key says, "to a high degree he kept faith" with the rednecks—but because he understood that rural politics in the South, for good or ill, was more cultural than rational, that what one did to gain office was distinct, if not unrelated, to what one did in public office.[2]

1. Saucier, "The Public Career of Bilbo," 294.
2. Key, *Southern Politics*, 367.

None played the game better, perhaps because none was so well equipped physically and temperamentally. Bilbo's vitality and stamina were legendary. In the 1934 campaign, it was said, he began every day at 4 A.M., spoke up to eight times a day and fifty times a week, drove his Ford twenty-five thousand miles, subsisted on sardines and crackers, and finished the race ten pounds heavier than he started it. He was a master of factional politics, knowing that because alliances come and go, one had to be nimble to survive. "You know some people take their politics to heart," he once confided to a friend, "and they never forgive nor forget. I have never entertained that feeling or spirit. I fight my enemies in a campaign by asking no quarter and giving no quarter, but after the battle is over, I am at peace with the world. Life is too short to carry hatred." Bilbo claimed even Fred Sullens as a personal friend. "He always comes to see me in Washington," The Man said, declaring that he had once entered his Senate office to discover the editor "friend" pecking out an anti-Bilbo diatribe on the senator's own typewriter.[3]

Indeed, in the brief period from 1935 to 1940, Bilbo worked both with and against every other significant political figure in Mississippi in one major campaign or another. Conner, Harrison, White, and Johnson all received the kiss of his blessing and the sting of his curse sometime during those six years. Once, in the Conner-Johnson senatorial race of 1936, he let petty spite and jealousy overrule his political sense, and then it cost him dearly, not just in the election but in his status in Washington. In every other instance he backed a winner.

Having made his bed, he was usually content to lie in it. He once admonished a supporter for being unable to choose among competing friends. "You have too many personal friends in . . . politics," Bilbo said. "Cut out this pambly-wambly maudlin attitude. Get on one horse, sink or swim, ride him to the finish. Be for your man and tell all the rest of the world to go straight to Hell. Stay with your crowd; and either win together or go down together. When you try to scatter yourself over so much territory you get so damn thin in places until you do not amount to anything anywhere. Be a positive force. Have an opinion, announce it, and stand by it." Bilbo rarely violated his own advice; no one ever accused him of being pambly-wambly.[4]

The second distinctive feature of Bilbo's first term was his consistent and vigorous support for New Deal liberalism. But this second aspect

3. Saucier, "The Public Career of Bilbo," 119; Bilbo to J. S. Love, July 1, 1935, in Bilbo Papers; Skates, "Journalist vs. Politician," 285.

4. Bilbo to J. L. Denson, March 31, 1938, in Bilbo Papers.

of his early Senate career has largely been swallowed up by the first. What he did to get elected, his rambunctious campaigning, diverted almost all attention away from what he did once in office. Much of that was his own doing. An essential aspect of his appeal to the masses was his cultivation of the enmity of the respectable establishment, including the press. The calculated buffoonery, the petty vulgarity, the excessive rhetoric all combined to create an image that endeared him to the rednecks but dissuaded others from looking beyond the image to the record itself.[5]

Those who did, especially many liberals, found themselves exceedingly uncomfortable in the knowledge of Bilbo's consistent support of the New Deal welfare state, so much so that they often felt compelled to qualify, excuse, or explain away his substantive achievement. Thus there has been the ironic spectacle of liberals apologizing for the indubitable liberalism of this unmistakable ideological kinsman. He became the New Deal's unwanted stepchild.

Most solved the dilemma by simply writing Bilbo off as another demagogue. In fact, no southerner has been more universally accorded that designation by either the academic community or the public at large. There is hardly an anthology of demagoguery that does not mention him or an analysis of him that does not mention demagoguery. His name has become almost symbolic of the image of the southern demagogue.[6]

But the term and the image are elusive. As George Mowry notes, the label *demagogue* is often used to refer to a successful political leader of the masses whose objectives one opposes and whose methods are "not considered cricket by one's own associates." While Bilbo was certainly no statesman—few successful politicians are—was he a demagogue according to the common notion of the term? Most analyses of southern demagoguery focus on at least three essential elements that define the demagogue's style: race-baiting, flamboyant campaigning methods, and cynical appeals to economic and social discontent. How do these standards apply to Bilbo the New Dealer?[7]

Race, said Wilma Dykeman, is "the fundamental cause by which to explain Southern demagoguery." The classical presentation of the case

5. Doler, "Bilbo's Rhetoric of Racial Relations," 258–63.

6. See Michie and Ryhlick, *Dixie Demagogues*; Reinhard H. Luthin, *American Demagogues: Twentieth Century* (Boston, 1954); Raymond Gram Swing, *Forerunners of American Fascism* (New York, 1935); Cal M. Logue and Howard Dorgan (eds.), *The Oratory of Southern Demagogues* (Baton Rouge, 1981).

7. Mowry, *Another Look at the Twentieth-Century South*, 21–22; Logue and Dorgan, "The Demagogue," in Logue and Dorgan (eds.), *Oratory of Southern Demagogues*, 3–6; Williams, *Huey Long*, 432–35.

came from Wilbur Cash in *The Mind of the South*. When he wrote in 1940, Cash was deeply troubled by the amazing dearth of political realism that he found in the South, the failure of the mass of poor farmers and mill workers to embrace a liberal philosophy that would address the social and economic problems that held them captive. He blamed this void of class awareness on a "Proto Dorian convention," which pacified the poorer whites in the economic and social status quo. Like "the Doric knight of ancient Sparta," the abused redneck—by virtue of his race—shared extended membership in the dominant class. Whatever the system denied him economically and socially—and that was a great deal—it guaranteed that he would always stand superior to the black man, so he willingly yielded the political independence that might have won him economic relief, in exchange for this vicarious and illusory fellowship in the ruling class. "The South was *en route*," said Cash, "to the savage ideal . . . whereunder dissent and variety are completely suppressed and men become in all their attitudes, professions, and actions, virtual replicas of one another."[8]

As a result the "captains of Reconstruction," the leaders of the planter-business elite, governed relatively unchallenged until the 1890s, when the People's party first sought to shatter the rigid conformity with the battering ram of class politics. The effort failed, but by injecting economic and social issues into white politics, Populism paved the way for the demagogues. These flamboyant opportunists replaced the Populists as champions of the lower class, but while they railed against the Bourbons who governed in the interests of "the rich," they really only coveted the political power and offices that conservatives monopolized. Having gained that, "those demagogues . . . not only never had any concrete program to offer the commons but never tried to do anything real for them once they were in office." More basic, says Cash, they failed to subordinate race to economics and brought "nigger-baiting straight down to the levels of the more brutal sort," stirring the poor white to resentment against his poverty and degradation "without ever losing sight of the paramount question of race."[9]

Bilbo was by all standards a racist, a defender of white supremacy, and a believer in black inferiority. When he finally turned to race as a political issue, he brought to the debate the same rhetorical excess that he had for years brandished in the battle over economic and social issues. But that did not come until the mid-1940s, when a substantial segment of the Democratic party began openly to advocate civil rights

8. Wilma Dykeman, "The Southern Demagogue," *Virginia Quarterly Review*, XXXIII (1957), 566; Cash, *The Mind of the South*, 40, 93–94.

9. Cash, *The Mind of the South*, 252–59.

for blacks. Bilbo's verbal intemperance was such, however, that in those final four or five years of his life, he earned a national infamy for racial bigotry that overshadowed the rest of his career and distorted public perception of three decades of public life.[10]

Most accounts of southern politics, scholarly and popular alike, project that brief but violent obsession with the race issue back over an entire political career and assume that Bilbo was a race-baiter from the beginning. In 1972, William Havard blamed the enduring weakness of economically oriented politics in Mississippi on "demagogues like Bilbo, whose apparently liberal attitude on economic questions tended to dissolve into inaction under the thick haze of his verbal race-baiting." In 1978 Jerry A. Hendrix asserted that race "ultimately became the central theme of his political career." Even in 1982, a Memphis newspaper declared that Bilbo "made a career out of using race to hide the real issue."[11]

Such was simply not the case. In his study "Theodore G. Bilbo's Rhetoric of Racial Relations," Thurston Doler emphasizes that Bilbo was virtually silent "on racial matters in his political campaigning" before the 1940s. Even the early interest in repatriation could hardly be classed as race-baiting, since so few whites, even in Mississippi, took much interest in it and most of Bilbo's support came from black nationalist groups. Not only did he shun race as a campaign tactic for most of his career, he refused to be frightened away from liberal issues by his enemies' frequent charges that his agitation undermined white supremacy. In the 1938 debate on antilynching legislation, Bilbo ridiculed the notion that its passage would provoke his constituents to "desert the Democratic Party. We are not Democrats because we live in the South," he declared. "We are not Democrats because of the race question. We are Democrats through conviction." Indeed, a few months earlier, Bilbo had been convinced that the bill would pass and seemed relatively undisturbed.[12]

10. Saucier, "The Public Career of Bilbo," 295–96.

11. William C. Havard (ed.), *The Changing Politics of the South* (Baton Rouge, 1972), 698–99; Jerry A. Hendrix, "Theodore G. Bilbo: Evangelist of Racial Purity," in Logue and Dorgan (eds.) *Oratory of Southern Demagogues*, 151; Memphis *Commercial Appeal*, September 13, 1982, p. 5.

12. Doler, "Bilbo's Rhetoric of Racial Relations," 85, 108; *Congressional Record*, 75th Cong., 3rd Sess., 873; Bilbo to Bidwell Adam, November 17, 1937, in Bilbo Papers. When the Democratic party adopted a civil-rights platform in 1948 and Mississippi joined the Dixiecrat movement, the "loyal Democrats," the only group in the state who supported Truman and Barkley, were led by former Bilbo people and headquartered in the same hotel suite in Jackson where Bilbo's own headquarters had been. That was only natural, said loyalist secretary-treasurer John W. Scott, since Bilbo had been "a party

The point is neither to excuse nor to minimize Bilbo's racism. It is rather to correct the false impression that he used race during the New Deal years to divert attention from social and economic issues.[13]

In 1937, writing about men like Bilbo and Huey Long, Daniel Robison warned of the danger of allowing the assessments of a politician's enemies to "be taken for the final judgement of history," and few—journalists, political analysts, and historians alike—have dared to approach Bilbo without hatchet in hand. Harvard Sitkoff typifies the penchant of many liberal historians for letting the convenience and delight of pummeling symbolic whipping boys like Bilbo run roughshod over factual analysis and objective judgment. Sitkoff brings forth Bilbo as an example of the southern politician who resorted to race as a useful means to oppose the New Deal. The "leadership elites in Dixie," said Sitkoff, "looked askance at new federal programs that reduced dependency and paternalism in their domains, raised wages, aided the labor movement, skirted local government, and extended the New Deal to those indigents previously unassisted. . . . To fight back, they cried 'Nigger'" so that by 1940 "racism and economic reaction had become interwoven." What Sitkoff studiously leaves undiscovered is that his prime specimen of this union of racism and conservatism had been a vigorous supporter of every liberal program that supposedly provoked the entire conspiracy: slum clearance and public housing, fair labor standards, and increased relief appropriations. Even those who had earlier seemed fairly friendly to the New Deal were driven into opposition by the fight over the poll tax and antilynching. Bilbo, according to Sitkoff, "began an oratorical rampage that would last until his reelection in 1940. . . . [He] pulled out all the stops in arousing the racial prejudice of his discontented, poor, rural 'redneck' constituency." But the provocative statement against repeal of the poll tax that Sitkoff quotes was uttered by Bilbo in 1944, not 1940. In fact, in 1940 Bilbo was himself trying desperately to get the poll tax repealed, not by Congress but by the Mississippi legislature, and not to produce racial justice but to increase the poor-white vote. It was not Bilbo but his opponent, Hugh White, who cried "nigger" in 1940.[14]

---

man, a Roosevelt Democrat, and a close political and personal friend of Senator Barkley." Key, *Southern Politics*, 340.

13. Bilbo was even bold enough to ridicule the traditional southern assertion that blacks were satisfied with their lot. He acknowledged that blacks were discriminated against and were discontented, but his solution was, of course, repatriation. *Congressional Record*, 75th Cong., 3rd Sess., 1342–43; Bilbo to Mrs. Rebecca Delaney, June 30, 1945, in Bilbo Papers.

14. Robison, "From Tillman to Long," 291–92; Harvard Sitkoff, *A New Deal for*

Yet Bilboism becomes, for Sitkoff, the perfect label to describe the kind of antilabor, anti-Communist, anti-Semitic, and anti–New Deal intolerance that often accompanied virulent racism. It was the mentality personified in the House by Martin Dies, who, having supported the early New Deal, by 1937 considered the economic crisis over and demanded an end to social experimentation and free-spending welfare programs. But to equate the New Deal sentiments of Bilbo and Dies is historical nonsense, as is the suggestion that Bilbo's bigotry extended to other, nonblack minorities. In fact, Bilbo prided himself on his open-mindedness. He had pleaded for toleration as well as votes for Catholic Al Smith in 1928. As a senator he labored diligently in the interests of Mississippi's Choctaw Indians. Most intriguing of all was his attitude toward Jews, which was based on much more than the fact that several of his most loyal Mississippi supporters and friends were Jewish, including his 1940 campaign manager. Bilbo was an early and enthusiastic supporter of Zionism and vowed to do all in his power for "this great Race of people that have done so much for the world and for American civilization." In 1938, he urged Secretary of State Cordell Hull that "the whole world, with possibly few exceptions, will agree that Palestine should be kept open as a place of refuge for the Jews who are being oppressed in so many parts of the world at this time." When the Jewish War Veterans adopted "Tolerance" as the theme of their annual convention in 1937, Bilbo volunteered his hearty endorsement and declared that laws aimed at social justice and economic security "cannot be written except in the language of Tolerance." Nonetheless, Bilbo's later attacks on those Jews who supported black equality were so typically intemperate and offensive as to earn him a questionable reputation as a Jew-baiter, including an infamous reference in *Gentlemen's Agreement*, a late-1940s movie attacking anti-Semitism. There is, however, a difference between racism and political race-baiting, and while Bilbo was certainly guilty of the former throughout his life, there is little evidence before the 1940s to convict him of the latter.[15]

As for the charge of flamboyance, the Man was guilty almost beyond comprehension. In fact, "flamboyant" hardly does justice to his antics. Two classic illustrations of the Bilbonic style should suffice. In 1938 he received a postcard from a Massachusetts opponent of Roosevelt's ex-

Blacks: The Emergence of Civil Rights as a National Issue, Volume I: The Depression Decade (New York, 1978), 102–17.

15. Sitkoff, *New Deal for Blacks*, 118–19; Bilbo to Ross Collins, May 17, 1938, Bilbo to Marvin MacIntyre, June 24, 1938, Bilbo to Roosevelt, June 29, 1938, Bilbo to Charles Schwager, August 8, 1937, Bilbo to Cordell Hull, October 14, 1938, Bilbo to Major Arthur W. Hofmann, August 11, 1937, all in Bilbo Papers.

ecutive reorganization bill, probably a form correspondence sent to all who had supported the measure. Most lawmakers would simply have ignored it. Bilbo chose to respond.

I have just received your postal card—a damn cheap way for a citizen of the Republic to write a United States Senator—in which you say "you should be ashamed to face the people from your own state after the way you shamefully betrayed them last Monday."

Now, in reply to your audacious and impudent postal card, please permit me to say to you that I think that you are a consummate, pusillanimous, premeditated, naturally-born monumental jackass. Your ignorance of what my vote on last Monday really meant is distressing and really it disturbs me to think that such ignorant asses of your kind may have the right of franchise in our Republican form of Government.

I am betting you dollars to doughnuts that you have never read the Reorganization Bill, for which I voted last Monday. You are so void of conceptions of our scheme of Government that you could not even catch a faint glimpse of what it is all about.

You are one of the thousands of puerile, unthinking, unanalyzing, intellectual bankrupts that becomes an easy prey to the propagandists of the money power and Republican manipulators. You know nothing except what you read in the newspapers and you do not have enough of discretionary power to select the papers that are disseminated among the people by the million, some good and some bad.

If I should judge you finally by your cheap, puny, tawdry, insulting post card, I would be forced to conclude that you need a guardian to provide not only your diet for physical maintenance but the materials that you should be permitted to read because you are so sterile in intellectuality that you do not possess the powers of discrimination that would make it safe for you to read all of the piffle that is being printed and disseminated to the American people in these hectic days when the propagandists are trying to influence the Government in the interest of the favored few.

I am your friend and I am sorry that your breadth of vision is not able to appreciate it.[16]

The other incident occurred early in Bilbo's tenure as "pastemaster general" when a Jackson publication printed a story that he had been jailed briefly in Washington. He responded with a letter.

Any person, Jew or Gentile, male or female, black or white, that intimates, insinuates, alleges or charges, circulates or disseminates, by direction or indirection, or by innuendo, that I, Theodore G. Bilbo, Sr., have been in jail in Washington or the District of Columbia, U.S.A., at any time on any charge whatsoever, is a dirty, vicious, fiendish, depraved, malignant, spiteful, deliberate, contemptible, pusillanimous, demoniacal, diabolical, hellacious, pre-

16. Bilbo to M. M. Balleu, April 1, 1938, in Bilbo Papers.

meditated, unmitigated, self-made, black-hearted, bench-legged, low-down, cock-eyed, flea-scratching, skunk-smelling, gol-darned, damnable liar whose mother howls in the night time and whose father sits on his hind legs and tail when he gazes at the moon. In fact, the only way in which I can account for the creation of such a miserable, inhuman misfit is to believe that when the good Lord had created all the other liars, murderers, thieves, midnight assassins, libertines, and hypocrites, that he gathered up the scraps and ran them through the dog molds and pinched the tail off and said, "Here is the creature that said Bilbo had been in jail in Washington."[17]

As others have pointed out, however, such manners revealed more about the circumstances in which "demagogues" like Bilbo functioned and the obstacles that they had to surmount than about the men themselves. Spokesmen for the poor farmers had to use such methods, according to Robison, to be heard above the conservative din of "the molders of public opinion"—the press, the bar, the clergy, and the Democratic party—all of which were almost universally hostile. Or as Benjamin Tillman explained when a reporter asked why he "raised so much hell" on the stump, "If I didn't the damn fools wouldn't vote for me." Bilbo, as a peerless practitioner of the art, would have understood.[18]

Finally, there is the question of ideological sincerity, and as Wilma Dykeman argues, it is easier smugly to dismiss the demagogues altogether than "to distinguish between their boorish manners and their basic appeal." Was Bilbo's progressive social and economic stance mere cynical political posturing, or was he genuinely liberal in the New Deal sense of the term? The only access to a man's inner convictions is through the external record of his words and actions, and nowhere—in his public pronouncements, private correspondence, or certainly in his voting record—is there anything to indicate that Bilbo's support for the New Deal was anything but genuine.[19]

What is arresting is that such a notion seems so extraordinary. Gerald Johnson lamented in 1936 that so many people believed Huey Long's appeal to the masses was attributable to his "ruffianly" behavior rather than to his achievements. All the demagogues who succeeded did so, Johnson argued, not by playing on the "passions and prejudices of the poor white trash . . . but by actually delivering some of the goods promised."[20]

17. Bilbo to C. E. Downing, October 25, 1933, in Bilbo Papers.

18. Williams, *Huey Long*, 439–40; Robison, "From Tillman to Long," 297.

19. Dykeman, "The Southern Demagogue," 563.

20. Gerald W. Johnson, "Live Demagogue or Dead Gentleman?" *Virginia Quarterly Review*, XII (1936), 12.

One suspects that the shrewder among the rednecks laughed up their sleeves at aristocrats like Percy who justified claims on the poor man's allegiance by ridiculing his heroes' manners. Bilbo was, after all, a redneck himself. His manners—earthy, crude, sometimes vulgar, and always volatile—were their manners, and his enemies were their enemies—all the more reason to believe that their cause was his cause. And the peckerwoods voted accordingly, inflicting on their social betters one whose very excess of commonness veritably flaunted the demise of political deference, like Faulkner's Ab Snopes wiping his manure-smeared boot on Major de Spain's rug.

The Bilbo-Harrison relationship accurately reflected the New Deal's impact on the continuing "battle," as Key described it, "between the delta planters and the rednecks." The two senators functioned in Washington as perfect symbols, almost caricatures, of the essence of Mississippi politics: the one urbane, respectable, "nearly the quintessential conservative," Martha Swain called him; the other crude, boisterous, the demigod of the "runt pigs." The New Deal provided the ideal backdrop to bring their contrasting careers into focus.[21]

In *Another Look at the Twentieth-Century South*, George Mowry suggests that Harrison, with others like Byrnes, Robinson, and Garner, were the congressional spokesmen for "the powerful politicians and the propertied establishment" of their region, "the Southern power elite." Their legislative records suggest that their ultimate principle was not the Democratic party, ideological conservatism, or states' rights. These rather served as "instruments to secure and maintain the existing socio-economic society at home in the South," a society with perhaps the greatest gulf between rich and poor of any in America at the time. The political *raison d'être* for men like Harrison, Mowry concludes, was "to maintain this disparity, to see that the proper people were in their proper place on top, the masses of the poorer whites were near the bottom, and the Negro held in virtual poverty." The race issue became a prime weapon in their war to preserve the status quo. Since any real threat to white supremacy necessitated white unity—almost always at the political expense of the poor whites—"a certain amount of racial animosity worked to the benefit of the owning classes."[22]

Gerald Johnson captured the tradition in an image. Reconstruction had stamped all white southerners, he said, with a sense of the desperate

21. Bobby Wade Saucier, "Pat Harrison: Conservative New Dealer" (Master's thesis, Mississippi State University, 1960), 38.

22. Mowry, *Another Look at the Twentieth-Century South*, 60–74, 81.

need to protect white supremacy from northern interference. L. Q. C. Lamar, who led the "Revolution of 1875" ending carpetbag rule in Mississippi, epitomized the "ideal statesman" as Horatius at the bridge. "But that was a long time ago," said Johnson. "The way is clear again; nevertheless, the South has ever since been afflicted with politicians who aspire to be Lamar and who think that the way to do it is to defend the bridge. They have defended it with prodigious success; but unfortunately, instead of halting the ranks of Tuscany, they have been holding up traffic." By 1937 many New Dealers considered Harrison among those blocking the road.[23]

In contrast was Bilbo's unfeigned enthusiasm for the entire array of New Deal welfare measures: relief, social security, progressive taxes, public power, public housing, and fair labor standards. Yet his credentials as a liberal were never above suspicion in some quarters. Frances Perkins, Roosevelt's secretary of labor, regarded him as "the lowest type of cracker," much like Georgia's violently anti–New Deal governor, Eugene Talmadge. Harrison, on the other hand, she considered a true "humanitarian," despite his resistance to the later New Deal. Harrison balked at welfare legislation, she believed, because he did not really understand the depths of poverty in America. "Poverty didn't seem so hard" to him. She suspected that had he seen the extremes of deprivation that someone like Al Smith had seen, had he been exposed to urban poverty, he might have felt differently.[24]

But one surely did not have to leave Mississippi to find want and degradation in the 1930s. In fact, it seems astounding that anyone who was at all familiar with the rural South could entertain romantic notions about poverty. Harrison's Mississippi colleague certainly did not. It was the sophisticated "humanitarian" who torpedoed the 1937 tax bill, helped emasculate the wages-and-hours law, and joined the economy bloc to slash relief appropriations; and it was the vile "cracker" who consistently backed the liberal administration and at times even tried to nudge it beyond its economic timidity.

Here was the distinction between Harrison and Bilbo and between the constituencies they represented. The distinction centered on eco-

23. Johnson, "Live Demagogue or Dead Gentleman?" 7–9.

24. "Reminiscences of Frances Perkins," 1955, COHC, Book II, 55–62. Henry Wallace offered a different view. While he liked Harrison personally and believed him an honest man, he thought Pat's "game was always purely political." Like many southern politicians, Harrison had found that politics was the shortest route to advancement. Once in office he discovered that "further advancement depended on playing ball with certain very wealthy Northern interests. That was the way Pat played the game." "Reminiscences of Wallace," 1444–45.

nomics, not on race; all white politicians agreed on the place of the black man.[25] When V. O. Key said that the beginning and end of Mississippi politics was race, he was correct in a sense. But the popular notion of how race functioned within white politics has often been distorted. That distortion was articulated as recently as September, 1982, in a Memphis newspaper article that suggested that Bilbo "was hated by many planters and businessmen," particularly in the Delta, "who objected to his race-baiting at a time when they were working to improve education for blacks."[26]

In truth the only time that Bilbo ever ran well in the Delta was in 1946 when race was the only issue in the campaign. It was the only campaign he ever ran as a white supremacist rather than an economic liberal. More often it was the opposition who dragged the race issue into Bilbo's campaigns to discredit his liberal proposals: the free textbooks he advocated would mean too much white money spent on black students; the old-age pension he demanded would swell the ranks of the black freeloaders; the poll-tax repeal he favored would undermine white supremacy. Almost always it was his enemies who cried "nigger," not Bilbo.[27]

Gerald Johnson asserted that Huey Long was the only man who brought realism to politics in the South, because he convinced millions that the issues of the 1930s were different from those of the 1860s. T. Harry Williams agrees but adds that Long stood apart from other "demagogues" in that he sought to overthrow the conservative power structure and replace it rather than bring it to terms. It was for those very excesses of power that he has been roundly condemned by many liberals. But Long was not the only southern politician of his day who subordinated race to economics. In that sense Bilbo was every bit as realistic as his Louisiana neighbor. The difference was that Bilbo sought the solution within the normal political processes, convinced that a liberalized Democratic party under Franklin Roosevelt was the

25. During the antilynching debate, even Claude Pepper participated in the southern filibuster, declaring that despite government action, "the colored race will not vote, because in doing so under the present circumstances they endanger the supremacy of a race to which God has committed the destiny of a continent, perhaps of a world." Alexander Rudolph Stoesen, "The Senatorial Career of Claude D. Pepper" (Ph.D. dissertation, University of North Carolina, 1964), 76–79.

26. Key, *Southern Politics*, 229; Memphis *Commercial Appeal*, September 13, 1982, p. 5.

27. William D. McCain, "Theodore Gilmore Bilbo and the Mississippi Delta," *Journal of Mississippi History*, XXXI (1969), 22–24; Greenville *Delta Democrat Times*, July 5, 1946, p. 4.

best hope of the rural South. It is notable that Bilbo supported the New Deal most vigorously on those very issues that Cash considered fundamental to southern progress: unemployment, tenancy, a rational farm policy, and the extension of political democracy. Bilbo's continued and seemingly genuine admiration for the president was all the more remarkable in light of his personal frustration over the patronage squabble. Yet there is not a trace of bitter criticism of Roosevelt in The Man's public statements or his private correspondence, and his record on the New Deal speaks for itself.[28]

The real key to Bilbo's achievements and his frustrations in New Deal Washington was his identification with his constituents. The essential substantive element that should have earned him acceptance among fellow New Dealers, his commitment to welfare liberalism, was overshadowed by the style that endeared him to the rednecks he championed. Unlike Long, who was "the remote great leader," belonging to the people but "not like them or of them," Bilbo was a redneck at heart, above the masses in shrewdness, energy, and ability, but deep down one of them yet.[29]

It is not clear that the hordes of poor farmers and mill hands followed Bilbo because of any reasoned intellectual commitment to the New Deal, unless one counts simple appreciation of the fact that federal programs made life marginally more tolerable and encouraged hopes of even better times to come. Similar poor-white constituencies did, after all, rally around New Deal opponents like Long and Eugene Talmadge. Or as William Leuchtenburg explains, "ideological issues that seemed clear in Washington blurred" in southern primaries where "local loyalties" prevailed.[30]

Some, like James Holt and Alan Brinkley, have argued that Long's popularity reflected an abiding American tradition of antistatist localism that runs counter to the principles of the New Deal's emerging welfare democracy. But even Brinkley acknowledges that Long raised "economic issues of genuine importance" and spoke much of collectivism and government activism, however circumscribed. Moreover, the continued popularity of Roosevelt himself raises the question of whether Long's attraction, among the rednecks at least, was rooted in ideological opposition to bureaucratic centralism or simply the potency of the Kingfish's political style and the perception that he was prescribing the same medicine as Dr. New Deal, only in larger doses.

28. Johnson, "Live Demagogue or Dead Gentleman?" 9–12; Williams, *Huey Long*, 435; Cash, *The Mind of the South*, 435–39.

29. Williams, *Huey Long*, 440.

30. *Ibid.*; Leuchtenburg, *Roosevelt and the New Deal*, 435–39.

Brinkley simply errs when he suggests that Long's popularity cowed Bilbo into a timid silence that was broken only after the Kingfish's death. In 1935 Bilbo virtually dared Long to intervene in the Mississippi governor's race. "I'm going down to New Orleans," he told Heber Ladner, "put up there at the hotel, and issue a challenge to Huey to come in person to campaign for his candidate." A skeptical Ladner warned that the Kingfish had just helped Hattie Caraway to a big victory in Arkansas. "Why bring all that pressure on yourself?" he asked his friend. "We don't need him to cross that river." "I want him to cross the river," The Man shot back, "just to see who's who." Bilbo turned the race into a referendum on FDR versus Long, with results that must have encouraged New Dealers throughout the South. Likewise in Georgia, Talmadge's resistance to the president's programs did not seem to diminish Roosevelt's appeal with that state's poor whites. In fact, the Talmadge forces in 1936 suffered a crushing defeat at the hands of administration supporters who soon fashioned a little New Deal for Georgia.[31]

Opposition to Roosevelt by Long and Talmadge simply accentuates Bilbo's loyalty by contrast, making his success as a New Deal missionary to Mississippi's poor whites all the more remarkable. The administration failed to crack the power of Democratic conservatism in the South precisely because so few leaders of the rednecks, the New Deal's most natural constituency in the region, were, like Bilbo, willing to embrace Roosevelt's brand of liberalism. Even in the case of Mississippi, administration forces failed to capitalize fully because so many New Dealers, like Hopkins, were unwilling to endure redneck style in order to sustain liberal substance. Often New Deal bureaucrats wanted to remake the southern poor after their own image, with their own brand of intellectual and social paternalism. What the redneck wanted, however, was simply a better standard of living, a lessening of the drudgery and misery of day-to-day existence. The contempt in which men like Hopkins held Bilbo was implicitly a contempt for those whom Bilbo represented, an attitude not totally unlike that of the Delta Bourbons, with whom sophisticated New Dealers often found themselves much more comfortable despite their ideological differences. Most of Bilbo's fellow senators, including New Dealers, considered him rather

31. James Holt, "The New Deal and the American Anti-Statist Tradition," in Braeman, Bremner, and Brody (eds.), *The New Deal: The National Level*, 27–47; Alan Brinkley, *Voices of Protest: Huey Long, Father Coughlin, and the Great Depression* (New York, 1982), ix–xii, 218–22; Heber Ladner, personal interview with the author, August 26, 1983; William Anderson, *The Wild Man from Sugar Creek: The Political Career of Eugene Talmadge* (Baton Rouge, 1975), 164–67, 215.

common and kept their distance accordingly. The academics of the Brain Trust and the bureaucracy preferred southerners like Hugo Black "who spoke with the polish of a Bourbon but with the sentiments of a Populist."[32]

But the peckerwoods had had their fill of Bourbon polish. The Percys and their like had provided urbane wit and gentlemanly enlightenment and with it grinding poverty, poor health, and illiteracy. In the thirties the poor whites opted for barnyard humor, bastard King Jamesian orotundities, and gaudy diamond horseshoe stickpins. Their link with the New Deal was not intellectual conviction but poverty, and as Will Alexander observed, they had no better friend in Congress than Bilbo. Wilma Dykeman notes that "the people who so revolted Percy might have been ignorant, but they were also shrewd; they might have lacked delicacy and grace but they possessed a groping sort of sensitivity." Percy underestimated both their shrewdness and their sensitivity when he assumed that such people were "not aware of his scorn and revulsion, and the patronizing concern of his father." Bilbo was hardly a paragon of delicacy and grace. In fact, he was in many ways a despicable and unsavory character, but politically he kept faith with those who were themselves disdained by respectable society. Redneck *and* liberal, he was their man.[33]

32. Hamilton, "Senate Career of Hugo Black," 122.
33. Dykeman, "The Southern Demagogue," 565–66.

Epilogue

It is ironic that one whose career had for so long been remarkably devoid of racist rhetoric should be remembered as the nation's vilest purveyor of white-supremacy twaddle. But the reputation is justified. From about 1942 until his death in 1947, Bilbo waged a relentless and often vicious battle against the incipient crusade for black equality in America. The decline of the New Deal, the impact of the Second World War, the resurgence of the Republican party, and the growing voice of blacks within the Democratic party all combined to make the political environment of the 1940s substantially different from that of the previous decade. The economic-welfare issues that had divided Americans into liberal and conservative camps in the thirties dimmed as Roosevelt sought to unify a nation fighting a desperate war against totalitarianism. For the first time in his career, Bilbo found himself in a political context in which class politics was largely out of place. And he was lost. Periods of national unity and consensus deprived him of his political lifeblood, righteous war against the forces of privilege. Outside of the conflict between "the masses and the classes," Bilbo was a political nonentity. The worst campaign defeat he ever suffered came in the midst of the First World War, when the spirit of national unity submerged issues of social and economic justice.[1]

As the advocates of black civil rights became more vocal and more bold, Bilbo's pronouncements on white supremacy became more frequent and more virulent. The virulence was by no means surprising; Bilbo was no more truculent on the race issue than on any other. Rhetorical savagery was simply his standard mode of operation. What was surprising was that he became so obsessed with the race issue in the first place. Some date the beginnings of Bilbo's personal crusade against black civil rights from the introduction of his repatriation proposal. There is reason, however, to distinguish between Bilbo's first-term efforts in behalf of repatriation and his later rantings in defense of segregation. Although the whole Greater Liberia scheme was rooted in

1. Green, *The Man Bilbo*, 98–105.

The Man's racist convictions and was at first a response to antilynching legislation, much of the initial momentum for the plan was sustained by black-nationalist groups. As early as 1933, the Peace Movement of Ethiopia (PME), led by Middie Maud Lena Gordon of Chicago, had petitioned Roosevelt for federal assistance for black repatriation to Liberia. The PME was one of several black-nationalist organizations derived from the remnants of Marcus Garvey's Universal Negro Improvement Association (UNIA). Gordon and others argued that a government-subsidized program of voluntary African repatriation would be cheaper than the public relief upon which so many American blacks depended for survival during the depression.[2]

Through the PME's leading white advocate, Earnest Sevier Cox of Richmond, Gordon solicited Bilbo's aid in getting the proposal before the Congress. By early 1938, the senator was cooperating with Gordon and Cox on behalf of the repatriation idea, which he had spurned earlier. In May he offered an amendment to a work-relief bill that would have empowered the president and the WPA director to divert as much of the relief appropriation "as in their judgement seems adequate, proper, and just" to transport and colonize any who volunteered to emigrate. By that time Cox and Gordon claimed to have almost two million signatures of blacks who wanted to participate. Lacking any support from other senators, however, Bilbo decided to withdraw the amendment and introduce a Greater Liberia bill the following year. Gordon was bitterly disappointed but acquiesced and began to marshal black support for the coming battle.[3]

Garvey himself, who had been deported in 1927 and now resided in London, was persuaded to support the Bilbo bill. The international convention of the UNIA endorsed the proposal unanimously, and Garvey sent a lobbying committee to Washington to work for its passage. Bilbo even tried to obtain a permit to allow Garvey to reenter the country in 1938. The following April the senator met with representatives of all the supporting black groups to discuss strategy before introducing the bill, and hundreds of black supporters thronged the galleries when Bilbo presented the bill on the floor with a three-hour speech.[4]

2. Martin, *Race First*, 349; Arna Bontemps and Jack Conroy, *Anyplace but Here* (New York, 1966), 208–209; Ethel Wolfskill Hedlin, "Earnest Cox and Colonization: A White Racist's Response to Black Repatriation, 1923–1966" (Ph.D. dissertation, Duke University, 1974), 112–17.

3. Hedlin, "Earnest Cox and Colonization," 117–39; *Congressional Record*, 75th Cong., 3rd Sess., 7240–41, 7370.

4. Marcus Garvey to Earnest Sevier Cox, December 9, 1938, in Earnest Sevier Cox

Since the proposal required dealings with foreign powers, it was referred to the Foreign Relations Committee, where, for all practical purposes, it died. But Gordon continued to believe that in Bilbo she had "found a Moses to lead us thru the Senate and that our work will become an accomplished fact." She continued to express "the greatest confidence" in Bilbo's sincerity, despite having to ask Cox to persuade him to soften his offensive references to black inferiority. Racist fears of black equality surely outweighed any sense of enlightened benevolence in Bilbo's motives for sponsoring the legislation. Nonetheless, before the mid-1940s Gordon supplied as much if not more of the driving force behind the measure.[5]

By 1944, however, Bilbo had become a vicious opponent of the emerging civil rights movement. His positions on congressional efforts to establish a Fair Employment Practices Commission (FEPC), to outlaw the poll tax, and to end lynching in the South were basically no different from those of most southerners. He was simply, as usual, louder, cruder, and more offensive in his opposition, earning for himself the passionate revulsion of respectable people around the nation. It was the same kind of passionate revulsion that similar tactics in defense of economic liberalism had provoked among respectable conservatives throughout his career. Ironically, his crude and savage defense of southern racial customs now caused many of those same respectable Mississippians to rally to his new cause.[6]

Why Bilbo resorted to racial politics in the 1940s is beyond the scope of this book, but it is an intriguing question. The most obvious answer is that he was simply responding, as were almost all white southerners, to a growing commitment by the nation, particularly the Democratic party, to racial equality. Despite the excess and offensiveness of his style, Bilbo's defense of white supremacy was basically no different from that of his fellow white southerners. It is not so surprising that he finally embraced the politics of race; what is surprising is that he eschewed it for so long. Moreover, by the 1940s race had became in some sense a legitimate issue, because white supremacy was

---

Papers, Perkins Library, Duke University, Durham; Thomas Hervey to Bilbo, February 8, 1938, Bilbo to Frances Perkins, February 9, 1938, Bilbo to Raymond Martinez, May 2, 1939, all in Bilbo Papers; "Memoirs of Carl Loeffler, Secretary of the U.S. Senate, 1947–49" (MS in Senate Historical Office, Washington, D.C.), 166.

5. Bilbo to Martinez, May 2, 1939, in Bilbo Papers; Mrs. M. M. L. Gordon to Cox, June 29, 1938, Gordon to Cox, September 9, 1939, Cox to Bilbo, May 29, 1938, all in Cox Papers.

6. Saucier, "The Public Career of Bilbo," 202–16; Key, *Southern Politics*, 244.

indeed under attack. Howard Odum's *Race and Rumors of Race* clearly depicts the rampant fears that swept the South during the war: fear of miscegenation, of riots, and of outside agitation. However exaggerated and unjustified those fears might have been, they were real. Again, bigotry and demagoguery are not synonymous. Bilbo was certainly a bigot; that he was a demagogue is open to question. He certainly used the race issue politically in the forties; that his actions were cynical or insincere is open to question. Ironically, as he lay dying in a New Orleans hospital, he granted his last press interview to Leon L. Lewis of *Negro South*, to whom he said, "I am honestly against the social intermingling of negroes and whites. But, I hold nothing personal against negroes as a race. God made them as they are and they should be proud of that God-given heritage as I am of mine."[7]

None of this diminishes or excuses Bilbo's racism. His infamy as the "archangel of white supremacy" was richly deserved. He did almost single-handedly talk the FEPC to death with filibuster. He did publish a volatile defense of white supremacy, *Take Your Choice: Separation or Mongrelization*. He did run a race-oriented campaign for reelection in 1946 in which he said, among other things, that "the way to keep the nigger from the polls is to see him the night before." He did make outrageous ethnic references to individual Italians, Jews, and others who supported civil rights. Such behavior, combined with charges that he engaged in questionable dealings with war contractors, became the basis for an effort to deny him his senatorial seat in 1947, and probably only his imminent death from cancer spared him that final humiliation.[8]

Paradoxically, Bilbo's most inglorious hour as a public figure earned him the most widespread support and popularity that he ever knew among white Mississippians. In 1946, he won a first-primary victory over four opponents, carrying seventy-six of the state's eighty-two counties, including all but one in the Delta. He was again the martyr; only now he was the faithful southerner suffering under Yankee persecution. Bilbo ran his 1946 campaign against "the Drew Pearsons,

7. Howard W. Odum, *Race and Rumors of Race: Challenge to American Crisis* (Chapel Hill, 1943); Charles Pope Smith, "Theodore G. Bilbo's Senatorial Career: The Final Years, 1941–1947" (Ph.D. dissertation, University of Southern Mississippi, 1983), 177.

8. Robert J. Bailey, "Theodore G. Bilbo and the Fair Employment Practices Controversy: A Southern Senator's Reaction to a Changing World," *Journal of Mississippi History*, XLII (1980), 27–42; Theodore G. Bilbo, *Take Your Choice: Separation or Mongrelization* (Poplarville, Miss., 1947); Saucier, "The Public Career of Bilbo," 241–49, 207–13; Green, *The Man Bilbo*, 106–19.

the Walter Winchells . . . old Lady Roosevelt, Harold Ickes and Hank Wallace, together with all the negroes, communists, negro lovers and advocates of social equality who poured out their slime and money in Mississippi."[9]

It was probably real life's choicest example of the dictum voiced by Mark Twain's Abner Dilworthy. "Persecution is the one thing needful," said the novelist's fictional senator. "Give us newspaper persecution enough, and we are safe . . . It scares off some of the weak supporters, true, but it soon turns strong ones into stubborn ones. And then, presently, it changes the tide of public opinion. The great public is weak-minded; the great public is sentimental . . . in a word, the great putty-hearted public loves to 'gush,' and there is no such darling opportunity to gush as a case of persecution affords." But Bilbo did not need Twain's tutelage, because he had learned the same lesson forty years earlier from an old one-armed Baptist preacher who had shown him the flesh-and-blood power of a sympathy vote. The Man had now discovered a different empty sleeve, but he dangled it before the putty-hearted public with the same old genius. Instead of suffering for economic justice, he was now a martyr for racial injustice.[10]

Bilbo had finally succumbed to the union of white supremacy and economic conservatism that, according to Harvard Sitkoff, southern enemies of the New Deal had fashioned with such skill. By weaving together "racism and economic reaction," the conservatives had transformed New Deal policies, in the mind of southerners, "into issues of Negro rights." But if, as some have argued, the race issue finally killed Bilbo's liberalism, it seemed to die hard. He did, after 1945, oppose the full-employment bill, an unemployment-compensation measure, and a minimum-wage law. But his growing coolness toward such labor issues was no doubt related to the growing power of the CIO, which openly espoused racial equality and which placed Bilbo on its "purge list" in 1946. Moreover, in 1942 Bilbo had opposed suspension of the forty-hour work week in defense plants, arguing that labor was "still getting the hot end of the poker." He supported the G.I. Bill of Rights, rural electrification, participation in the United Nations, and almost all of the administration's wartime spending requests. Even as chairman of the Senate District of Columbia Committee, and therefore de facto mayor of Washington, he called for slum clearance, construction of a medical center, additional parks, and a modern transit system, though

9. Saucier, "The Public Career of Bilbo," 249–50.

10. Mark Twain and Charles Dudley Warner, *The Gilded Age: A Tale of Today* (New York, 1873), 392–93.

these progressive proposals were overshadowed by his opposition to home rule and black voting. In 1945, unlike most southerners, Bilbo supported Henry Wallace's nomination as secretary of commerce. Wallace, he said, represented "the ideals and policies of President Roosevelt, the world's greatest humanitarian and Democrat." As late as 1946, Bilbo supported the National School Lunch Act, which, he argued, "adds much to the health and welfare of the school children of America, especially the poor classes." If Bilbo had indeed turned conservative, it was a half-hearted conversion.[11]

Alan Brinkley argues that "neither the Depression nor the New Deal" seemed to have inspired "any significant changes in the . . . internal political organization or in the nature of . . . political leadership" in the South. After some effort to explain the region's ability to resist such changes, Brinkley concludes that the New Deal did, after all, pave the way for "a series of profound transformations . . . in southern social, economic, and political life." While the New Deal did not accomplish this "Second Reconstruction," it did lay the groundwork for it in two ways. The first occurred within the South, as New Deal programs, often unintentionally, reshaped the region's social and economic structure. The second and more significant occurred outside the South, as Roosevelt transformed the Democratic party into a powerful and effective liberal coalition that could succeed even in the face of southern opposition. It was this newfound Democratic liberation from the shackles of the Solid South that made possible the civil rights movement and the consequent revolution in southern politics.[12]

Bilbo's entire career was fraught with paradox, but nowhere more than with his relationship to this transformation. His very dates are almost symbolic: born the year that the last federal troops were withdrawn from the South, he died on the eve of his party's formal adoption of black civil rights. The two Reconstructions bracket Bilbo's life. He in some sense epitomized the political essence of his own era, an era of struggle between the Delta and the hills, in which poor whites fought to reshape the political and social institutions of the region along more democratic lines, though it was democracy for whites only. That struggle culminated in the sweeping reform of the New Deal, and very few southerners followed the course of reform as far and as consistently as did Bilbo.

11. Sitkoff, *A New Deal for Blacks*, 103–13; Smith, "Bilbo's Senatorial Career," 88–131.

12. Alan Brinkley, "The New Deal and Southern Politics," in James C. Cobb and Michael V. Namorato (eds.), *The New Deal and the South* (Jackson, Miss., 1984), 98, 112–14.

At the end he realized what others had seen earlier, that his own cherished liberalism had become the greatest threat to the one southern institution that he did not want to change, white supremacy. In a crowning irony Bilbo's belated conversion to racist politics only speeded the very change that he had compromised his liberalism to avoid. The excessiveness of his own war against racial equality helped to solidify the determination of those who hated what he now symbolized. But Bilbo, as much as anyone else, had helped to create the instrument that would destroy white supremacy. His conservative enemies in Mississippi saw the paradox quite clearly. "Many anti-Bilbo Mississippians," concluded an opposition newspaper, "see in him the only force strong enough to hold back the tide of communism which is sweeping the country largely (at present) through the race question. People who recognize in him the same man who helped Franklin Roosevelt and his New Dealers lay the groundwork for this troubled era see in him the only hope of Mississippi retaining sovereignty, already toppling because of Franklin Roosevelt's New Deal Supreme Court of injustice. It is in bitterness of soul that they see it—but see it they do."[13]

13. Saucier, "The Public Career of Bilbo," 216; Summit (Miss.) *Sun*, June 27, 1946, as quoted in Saucier, "The Public Career of Bilbo," 248.

Bibliography

Manuscripts

Bailey, Josiah W. Papers. Perkins Library, Duke University, Durham.

Bilbo, Theodore G. Papers. McCain Library, University of Southern Mississippi, Hattiesburg.

Black, Hugo L. Papers. Library of Congress, Washington, D.C.

Clapper, Raymond. Papers. Library of Congress, Washington, D.C.

Collins, Ross. Papers. Library of Congress, Washington, D.C.

Colmer, William. Papers. McCain Library, University of Southern Mississippi, Hattiesburg.

Cox, Earnest Sevier. Papers. Perkins Library, Duke University, Durham.

Drago, Laurie. "The Second Bilbo Administration, 1928–1932." MS in possession of the author.

Farley, James A. Papers. Library of Congress, Washington, D.C.

Federal Emergency Relief Administration. Central Files. Records of the Work Projects Administration, Record Group 69, National Archives, Washington, D.C.

Green, A. Wigfall. Papers. Williams Library, University of Mississippi, Oxford.

Halsey, Edwin. Papers. Senate Historical Office, Washington, D.C.

Harrison, Pat. Papers. Mitchell Library, Mississippi State University, Starkville.

———. Papers. Williams Library, University of Mississippi, Oxford.

Henry, Marion. Papers. Mitchell Library, Mississippi State University, Starkville.

Hopkins, Harry L. Papers. Franklin D. Roosevelt Library, Hyde Park.

Ickes, Harold. Papers. Library of Congress, Washington, D.C.

Loeffler, Carl. "Memoirs of Carl Loeffler, Secretary of the U.S. Senate, 1947–49." MS in Senate Historical Office, Washington, D.C.

Morgenthau, Henry M. Diary. Franklin D. Roosevelt Library, Hyde Park.

Murphree, Dennis. Papers. Record Group 27, Mississippi Department of Archives and History, Jackson.

Pittman, Key. Papers. Library of Congress, Washington, D.C.

Robinson, W. D. Papers. Southern Historical Collection, Wilson Library, University of North Carolina, Chapel Hill.

Roosevelt, Franklin D. Papers. Official File. Franklin D. Roosevelt Library, Hyde Park.

Roosevelt, Franklin D. Papers. President's Personal File. Franklin D. Roosevelt Library, Hyde Park.

Roosevelt, James. Papers. Franklin D. Roosevelt Library, Hyde Park.

Toler, Kenneth. Papers. Mitchell Library, Mississippi State University, Starkville.

U.S. Congress. Senate. Papers of the Committee on the Judiciary, 74th Cong. Record Group 46, National Archives, Washington, D.C.

Whittington, Will. Papers. Williams Library, University of Mississippi, Oxford.

Williams, Aubrey W. Papers. Franklin D. Roosevelt Library, Hyde Park.

Woodward, Ellen. Papers. Mississippi Department of Archives and History, Jackson.

Work Projects Administration. Papers. Central Files. Records of the Work Projects Administration, Record Group 69, National Archives, Washington, D.C.

———. Papers. Records of the Division of Investigation. Records of the Work Projects Administration, Record Group 69, National Archives, Washington, D.C.

Government Documents

Congressional Record. 74th Cong.

———. 75th Cong.

———. 76th Cong.

House Reports. 75th Cong., lst Sess., No. 1570.

———. 75th Cong., 3rd Sess., No. 1767.

Investigation by the Senate of the State of Mississippi of the Charges of Bribery in the Election of a United States Senator (Nashville, 1910).

Mississippi Blue Book: Biennial Report of the Secretary of State to the Mississippi Legislature, 1935–1937.

———. *1937–1939.*

———. *1939–1941.*

Rowland, Dunbar, comp. *The Official and Statistical Register of the State of Mississippi, Centennial Edition, 1917.* Madison, Wis., 1917.

———. *The Official and Statistical Register of the State of Mississippi, 1924–1928.* New York, 1928.

Senate Reports. 75th Cong., 3rd Sess., No. 1892.

———. 76th Cong., 3rd Sess., No. 1403.

Sixteenth Census, 1940: Agriculture.

U.S. Congress. Senate. Committee on Agriculture and Forestry. *Hearings Before a Subcommittee of the Committee on Agriculture and Forestry, U.S. Senate, on H.R. 3800, to Amend Soil Conservation Act.* 76th Cong., 3rd Sess., 1940.

———. Senate. Committee on Agriculture and Forestry. *Hearings Before a Subcommittee of the Committee on Agriculture and Forestry Pursuant to S. Res. 158, a Resolution to Provide for an Investigation of Agricultural Commodity Prices, of an Ever-Normal Granary for Major Agricultural Commodities and of the Conservation of National Soil Resources.* 75th Cong., 1st Sess., 1937.

———. Senate. Committee on Agriculture and Forestry. *Hearings Before a Subcommittee of the Senate Committee on Agriculture and Forestry on S. 1228, a Bill to Provide for the Use of Net Weights in Interstate or Foreign Commerce Transactions in Cotton and for Other Purposes.* 76th Cong., 1st Sess., 1939.

———. Senate. Committee on Agriculture and Forestry. *Hearings Before a Subcommittee of the Senate Committee on Agriculture and Forestry on S. 1800, a Bill to Create the Farm Tenant Homes Corporation.* 74th Cong., 1st Sess., 1935.

———. Senate. Committee on Commerce. *Hearings Before the Committee on Commerce on H.R. 6732, an Act Authorizing the Construction, Repair and Preservation of Certain Public Works on Rivers and Harbors and for Other Purposes.* 75th Cong., 1st Sess., 1935.

———. Senate. Committee on the Judiciary. *Hearings Before a Subcommittee of the Committee on the Judiciary, U.S. Senate, on the Nomination of Judge Edwin R. Holmes for Judge of the United States Circuit Court of Appeals for the Fifth District.* 74th Cong., 2nd Sess., 1936.

Interviews

Adam, Bidwell. Mississippi Oral History Program, Vol. XXXIV, McCain Library, University of Southern Mississippi, Hattiesburg.

Adam, Mr. and Mrs. Bidwell. Personal interview, May 30, 1979.

Alexander, Will Winton. "The Reminiscences of Will Winton Alexander," 1952, Columbia University Oral History Collection.

Brady, Thomas P. Mississippi Oral History Program, Vol. II, McCain Library, University of Southern Mississippi, Hattiesburg.

Buckley, Wilburn. John C. Stennis Collection, Mitchell Library, Mississippi State University, Starkville.

Conner, Dudley F. Personal interview, June 8, 1982.

Davis, Chester C. "The Reminiscences of Chester Charles Davis," 1953, Columbia University Oral History Collection.

Emmerich, John Oliver. Mississippi Oral History Program, Vol. XVI, McCain Library, University of Southern Mississippi, Hattiesburg.

Hamilton, Charles G. Personal interview, March 3, 1983.

Hewitt, Purser. Mississippi Oral History Program, Vol. X, McCain Library, University of Southern Mississippi, Hattiesburg.

Jackson, Gardner. "The Reminiscences of Gardner Jackson," 1955, Columbia University Oral History Collection.

Jones, Marvin. "The Reminiscences of Marvin Jones," 1953, Columbia University Oral History Collection.

Kenna, E. D. Personal interview, June 3, 1979.

———. Mississippi Oral History Program, Vol. CCXLVI, McCain Library, University of Southern Mississippi, Hattiesburg.

Ladner, Heber. Mississippi Oral History Program, Vol. XXX, McCain Library, University of Southern Mississippi, Hattiesburg.

———. Personal interview, August 26, 1983.

Perkins, Frances. "The Reminiscences of Frances Perkins," 1955, Columbia University Oral History Collection.

Reyer, Alma M. Mississippi Oral History Program, Vol. LXXXIX, McCain Library, University of Southern Mississippi, Hattiesburg.

Wallace, Henry Agard. "The Reminiscences of Henry Agard Wallace," 1951, Columbia University Oral History Collection.

Books

Abney, Francis Glenn. *Mississippi Election Statistics, 1900–1967.* Oxford, Miss., 1968.

Allen, George E. *Presidents Who Have Known Me.* New York, 1950.

Alsop, Joseph, and Stewart Alsop. *The Reporter's Trade.* New York, 1946.

Alsop, Joseph, and Turner Catledge. *The 168 Days.* Garden City, N.Y., 1938.

Altmeyer, Arthur J. *The Formative Years of Social Security.* Madison, Wis., 1966.

Anderson, William. *The Wild Man from Sugar Creek: The Political Career of Eugene Talmadge.* Baton Rouge, 1979.

Baker, Bill R. *Catch the Vision: The Life of Henry L. Whitfield of Mississippi.* Jackson, Miss., 1974.

Baldwin, Sidney. *Poverty and Politics: The Rise and Decline of the Farm Security Administration.* Chapel Hill, 1968.

Benedict, Murray R. *Farm Policies of the United States, 1790–1950.* New York, 1953.

Benedict, Murray R., and Oscar C. Stine. *The Agriculture Commodity Programs: Two Decades of Experience.* New York, 1956.

Bettersworth, John K. *People's College: A History of Mississippi State.* Tuscaloosa, 1953.

Bilbo, Theodore G. *Take Your Choice: Separation or Mongrelization.* Poplarville, Miss., 1947.

Blaisdell, Donald C. *Government and Agriculture: The Growth of Federal Farm Aid.* New York, 1940.

Blum, John Morton, ed. *From the Morgenthau Diaries: Years of Crisis, 1928–1938*. Boston, 1959.

———, ed. *The Price of Vision: The Diary of Henry A. Wallace*. Boston, 1973.

Bond, Willard F. *I Had a Friend*. Kansas City, Mo., 1958.

Bontemps, Arna, and Jack Conroy. *Anyplace but Here*. New York, 1966.

Braeman, John, Robert H. Bremner, and David Brody, eds. *The New Deal*. 2 vols. Columbus, Ohio, 1975.

Brinkley, Alan. "The New Deal and Southern Politics." In *The New Deal and the South*, edited by James C. Cobb and Michael V. Namorato. Jackson, Miss., 1984.

———. *Voices of Protest: Huey Long, Father Coughlin, and the Great Depression*. New York, 1982.

Brown, Josephine Chapin. *Public Relief: 1929–1937*. New York, 1940.

Burns, James MacGregor. *Deadlock of Democracy: Four Party Politics in America*. Englewood Cliffs, N.J., 1963.

———. *Roosevelt: The Lion and the Fox*. New York, 1956.

Byrnes, James F. *All in One Lifetime*. New York, 1958.

Cabaniss, Allen. *The University of Mississippi: Its First Hundred Years*. Hattiesburg, 1971.

Campbell, Christiana. *The Farm Bureau and the New Deal: A Study in the Making of National Farm Policy, 1933–1940*. Urbana, 1962.

Carter, Hodding. *Where Main Street Meets the River*. New York, 1952.

Cash, Wilbur J. *The Mind of the South*. New York, 1941.

Chafe, William H. *Civility and Civil Rights: Greensboro, North Carolina, and the Black Struggle for Freedom*. New York, 1980.

Charles, Searle F. *Minister of Relief: Harry Hopkins and the Depression*. Syracuse, 1963.

Cobb, James C. *The Selling of the South: The Southern Crusade for Industrial Development, 1936–1980*. Baton Rouge, 1982.

Cohn, David L. *God Shakes Creation*. New York, 1935.

Conkin, Paul K. *The New Deal*. New York, 1967.

———. *Tomorrow a New World: The New Deal Community Programs*. Ithaca, N.Y., 1959.

Connally, Tom, as told to Alfred Steinberg. *My Name is Tom Connally*. New York, 1954.

Conrad, David E. *Forgotten Farmers: The Story of Sharecroppers in the New Deal*. Urbana, 1965.

Dabney, Virginius. *Liberalism in the South*. Chapel Hill, 1932.

Donahoe, Bernard F. *Private Plans and Public Dangers*. Notre Dame, 1965.

Douglas, Paul H. *Social Security in the United States*. New York, 1936.

Dykeman, Wilma, and James Stokely. *Seeds of Southern Change: The Life of Will Alexander*. New York, 1962.

Emmerich, John Oliver. *Two Faces of Janus: The Saga of Deep South Change*. Jackson, Miss., 1973.

Farley, James A. *Jim Farley's Story: The Roosevelt Years*. New York, 1948.

Faulkner, William. *Go Down Moses and Other Stories*. New York, 1942.

Fite, Gilbert C. *George N. Peek and the Fight for Farm Parity*. Norman, Okla., 1954.

Flynt, J. Wayne. *Dixie's Forgotten People: The South's Poor Whites*. Bloomington, 1979.

Freidel, Frank. *F. D. R. and the South*. Baton Rouge, 1965.

Graham, Otis L., Jr. *An Encore for Reform: The Old Progressives and the New Deal*. New York, 1967.

Grantham, Dewey W., Jr. *The Democratic South*. New York, 1963.

Green, A. Wigfall. *The Man Bilbo*. Baton Rouge, 1963.

Hackney, Sheldon. *Populism to Progressivism in Alabama*. Princeton, 1969.

Hale, William J. *Farmward March: Chemurgy Takes Command*. New York, 1939.

Hamilton, Charles G. *Mississippi, Mirror of the 1920s*. Aberdeen, Miss., 1979.

———. *Progressive Mississippi*. Aberdeen, Miss., 1978.

Havard, William C., ed. *The Changing Politics of the South*. Baton Rouge, 1972.

Hickman, Nollie W. *Mississippi Harvest: Lumbering in the Longleaf Pine Belt, 1840–1915*. Oxford, Miss., 1962.

Hobbs, George A. *Bilbo, Brewer, and Bribery in Mississippi Politics*. Nashville, 1917.

Holley, Donald F. *Uncle Sam's Farmers: The New Deal Communities in the Lower Mississippi Valley*. Urbana, 1975.

Holmes, Michael S. *The New Deal in Georgia: An Administrative History*. Westport, Conn., 1975.

Holmes, William F. *The White Chief: James Kimble Vardaman*. Baton Rouge, 1970.

Holtzman, Abraham. *The Townsend Movement: A Political Study*. New York, 1963.

Hopkins, Harry L. *Spending to Save: The Complete Story of Relief*. New York, 1936.

Howard, Donald S. *The WPA and Federal Relief Policy*. New York, 1943.

Ickes, Harold. *The Inside Struggle, 1936–1939*. New York, 1954. Vol. II of *The Secret Diary of Harold Ickes*. 3 vols.

Johnson, Charles S., Edwin Embree, and Will Alexander. *The Collapse of Cotton Tenancy*. Chapel Hill, 1935.

Key, V. O., Jr. *Southern Politics: In State and Nation*. New York, 1949.

Kirby, Jack Temple. *Darkness at Dawning: Race and Reform in the Progressive South*. Philadelphia, 1972.

Kirwan, Albert D. *Revolt of the Rednecks: Mississippi Politics, 1876–1925*. Lexington, Ky., 1951.

Kousser, J. Morgan. *The Shaping of Southern Politics: Suffrage Restriction and the Establishment of the One-Party South, 1880–1910*. New Haven, 1974.

Leuchtenburg, William E. *Franklin D. Roosevelt and the New Deal, 1932–1940*. New York, 1963.

Logue, Cal M., and Howard Dorgan, eds. *The Oratory of Southern Demagogues*. Baton Rouge, 1981.

Long, Huey P. *Every Man a King: The Autobiography of Huey P. Long*. New Orleans, 1933.

Lord, Russell. *The Wallaces of Iowa*. Boston, 1947.

Luthin, Reinhard H. *American Demagogues: Twentieth Century*. Boston, 1954.

Lytle, Andrew Nelson. "The Hind Tit." In *I'll Take My Stand: The South and the Agrarian Tradition*. New York, 1930.

McConnell, Grant. *The Decline of Agrarian Democracy*. Berkeley, 1953.

McDonnell, Timothy L. *The Wagner Housing Act: A Case Study of the Legislative Process*. Chicago, 1957.

McLemore, Richard Aubrey, ed. *A History of Mississippi*. 2 vols. Hattiesburg, 1973.

MacMahan, Arthur W., John D. Millett, and Gladys Ogden. *The Administration of Federal Work Relief*. Chicago, 1941.

McMillan, Wheeler. *New Riches from the Soil: The Progress of Chemurgy*. New York, 1946.

Maney, Patrick J. *"Young Bob" La Follette: A Biography of Robert M. La Follette, Jr., 1895–1953*. Columbia, Mo., 1978.

Marshall, F. Ray. *Labor in the South*. Cambridge, 1967.

Martin, Tony. *Race First: The Ideological and Organizational Struggles of Marcus Garvey and the Universal Negro Improvement Association*. Westport, Conn., 1976.

Mertz, Paul E. *New Deal Policy and Southern Rural Poverty*. Baton Rouge, 1978.

Michie, Allan A., and Frank Ryhlick. *Dixie Demagogues*. New York, 1939.

Mississippi Power and Light Company, Economic Research Department. *Mississippi Statistical Summary of Population*. Jackson, Miss., 1983.

Mitchell, Broadus. *Depression Decade: From New Era Through New Deal, 1929–1941*. New York, 1947.

Moley, Raymond. *After Seven Years*. New York, 1939.

Mowry, George E. *Another Look at the Twentieth-Century South*. Baton Rouge, 1973.

Mulder, Ronald. *The Insurgent Progressives in the United States Senate and the New Deal, 1933–1939*. New York, 1979.

Nourse, Edwin G., Joseph S. Davis, and John D. Black. *Three Years of the Agricultural Adjustment Administration*. Washington, D.C., 1937.

Odum, Howard W. *Race and Rumors of Race: Challenge to American Crisis*. Chapel Hill, 1943.

Patterson, James T. *Congressional Conservatism and the New Deal: The Growth of the Conservative Coalition in Congress, 1933–1939*. Lexington, Ky., 1967.

———. *The New Deal and the States: Federalism in Transition*. Princeton, 1969.

Percy, William Alexander. *Lanterns on the Levee: Recollections of a Planter's Son*. New York, 1941.

Perkins, Dexter. *The New Age of Franklin Roosevelt, 1932–1945*. Chicago, 1957.

Perkins, Van L. *Crisis in Agriculture: The Agricultural Adjustment Administration and the New Deal, 1933*. Berkeley, 1969.

Pope, Robert Dean. "Of the Man at the Center: Biographies of Southern Politicians from the Age of Segregation." In *Region, Race, and Reconstruction: Essays in Honor of C. Vann Woodward*, edited by J. Morgan Kousser and James M. McPherson. New York, 1982.

Porter, David L. *Congress and the Waning of the New Deal*. Port Washington, N.Y., 1980.

Pulley, Raymond H. *Old Virginia Restored: An Interpretation of the Progressive Impulse, 1870–1930*. Charlottesville, 1968.

Richards, Henry I. *Cotton and the AAA*. Washington, D.C., 1936.

Roebuck, Julian B., and Mark Hickson III. *The Southern Redneck: A Phenomenological Class Study*. New York, 1982.

Rosenman, Samuel I. *Working with Roosevelt*. New York, 1952.

Schapsmeier, Edward L., and Frederick H. Schapsmeier. *Henry A. Wallace of Iowa: The Agrarian Years, 1910–1940*. Ames, Iowa, 1968.

Schlesinger, Arthur M., Jr. *The Coming of the New Deal*. Boston, 1958. Vol. II of Schlesinger, *The Age of Roosevelt*, 3 vols. to date.

———. *The Politics of Upheaval*. Boston, 1960. Vol. III of Schlesinger, *The Age of Roosevelt*, 3 vols. to date.

Schmidt, Carl T. *American Farmers in World Crisis*. New York, 1941.

Schwarz, Jordan A. *The Speculator: Bernard M. Baruch in Washington, 1917–1965*. Chapel Hill, 1981.

Sherwood, Robert E. *Roosevelt and Hopkins: An Intimate History*. New York, 1948.

Sitkoff, Harvard. *A New Deal for Blacks: The Emergence of Civil Rights as a National Issue, Volume I: The Depression Decade*. 3 vols. projected. New York, 1978.

Skates, John Ray. *Mississippi: A Bicentennial History*. New York, 1979.

Swain, Martha H. *Pat Harrison: The New Deal Years*. Jackson, Miss., 1978.

Swing, Raymond Gram. *Forerunners of American Fascism*. New York, 1935.

Timmons, Bascom N. *Jessie H. Jones: The Man and the Statesman*. New York, 1956.

Tindall, George B. *The Emergence of the New South, 1913–1945*. Baton Rouge, 1967.

Tugwell, Rexford G. *The Brains Trust*. New York, 1968.

———. *The Democratic Roosevelt: A Biography of Franklin D. Roosevelt*. Garden City, N.Y., 1957.

———. *In Search of Roosevelt*. Cambridge, 1972.

Twain, Mark, and Charles Dudley Warner. *The Gilded Age: A Tale of Today*. New York, 1873.

Warren, Robert Penn. *All the King's Men*. New York, 1946.

Wharton, Vernon L. *The Negro in Mississippi, 1865–1890*. Chapel Hill, 1947.

Williams, T. Harry. *Huey Long*. New York, 1969.

———. *Romance and Realism in Southern Politics*. Athens, Ga., 1961.

Woodward, C. Vann. *The Origins of the New South, 1877–1913*. Baton Rouge, 1951.

Zorn, Roman J. "Theodore G. Bilbo: Shibboleths for Statesmanship." In *Public Men: In and Out of Office*, edited by J. D. Salter. Chapel Hill, 1946.

Articles

Altman, O. R. "First Session of the 75th Congress." *American Political Science Review*, XXXI (1937), 1071–94.

———. "Second and Third Sessions of the 75th Congress." *American Political Science Review*, XXXII (1938), 1099–1122.

———. "Second Session of the 74th Congress." *American Political Science Review*, XXX (1936), 1086–1107.

Bailey, Robert J. "Theodore G. Bilbo and the Fair Employment Practices Controversy: A Southern Senator's Reaction to a Changing World." *Journal of Mississippi History*, XLII (1980), 27–42.

Beatty, Jerome. "Mississippi Pearl." *American Magazine*, February, 1935, pp. 31, 94–97.

"Bilbo: Ex-Pastemaster General Turns on Man Who Got Him Job." *Newsweek*, February 1, 1936, pp. 16–17.

"Bilbo: Mississippi's Mighty Atom Explodes in Huey's Face." *Newsweek*, August 24, 1935, pp. 10–11.

"Bilbo v. Bilbo." *Time*, September 2, 1935, p. 14.

"Broom or Bilbo." *Time*, August 24, 1936, pp. 22–23.

Carleton, William G. "Why Call the South Conservative?" *Harper's*, July, 1947, pp. 61–68.

Clapper, Raymond. "Politics in the WPA." *Review of Reviews*, April, 1936, pp. 35–36, 69–71.

Davenport, Walter. "Brethren and Sisters." *Collier's*, March 16, 1935, pp. 19, 53–55.

Dubay, Robert W. "Mississippi and the Proposed Federal Anti-Lynching Bill of 1937–38." *Southern Quarterly*, VII (1968), 73–89.

Dykeman, Wilma. "The Southern Demagogue." *Virginia Quarterly Review*, XXXIII (1957), 558–68.

Edmondson, Ben G. "Pat Harrison and Mississippi in the Presidential Elections of 1924 and 1928." *Journal of Mississippi History*, XXXIII (1971), 333–50.

Erdman, H. E. "An Appraisal of the Movement to Increase Industrial Uses of Farm Products." *Scientific Agriculture*, XX (1939), 20–28.

Flynt, J. Wayne. "A Vignette of Southern Labor Politics—The 1936 Mississippi Senatorial Primary." *Mississippi Quarterly*, XXVI (1972–73), 89–99.

Fraser, Hugh Russell. "Bilbo: Mississippi's Mouthpiece." *American Mercury*, XXXVIII (1936), 424–32.

Giroux, Vincent A., Jr. "The Rise of Theodore G. Bilbo (1908–1932)." *Journal of Mississippi History*, XLIII (1981), 180–209.

Halsell, Willie D. "The Bourbon Period in Mississippi Politics, 1875–1890." *Journal of Southern History*, XI (1945), 519–37.

———. "Democratic Dissensions in Mississippi, 1878–1882." *Journal of Mississippi History*, II (1940), 123–36.

———. "James R. Chalmers and 'Mahoneism' in Mississippi." *Journal of Southern History*, X (1944), 37–58.

———. "Republican Factionalism in Mississippi, 1882–1884." *Journal of Southern History*, VII (1941), 84–101.

Hamilton, Charles G. "The Turning Point: The Legislative Session of 1908." *Journal of Mississippi History*, XXV (1963), 93–111.

Herring, E. Pendleton. "First Session of the 74th Congress." *American Political Science Review*, XXIX (1935), 985-1005.

Hickman, Nollie W. "The Lumber Industry in South Mississippi, 1890–1915." *Journal of Mississippi History*, XX (1958), 211–23.

Hudson, John B. "The Spoils System Enters College: Governor Bilbo and Higher Education in Mississippi." *New Republic*, September 17, 1930, pp. 123–25.

Johnson, Gerald W. "Live Demagogue or Dead Gentleman?" *Virginia Quarterly Review*, XII (1936), 1–14.

Koeniger, A. Cash. "The New Deal and the States: Roosevelt Versus the Byrd Organization in Virginia." *Journal of American History*, LXVIII (1982), 876–96.

Link, Arthur S. "The Progressive Movement in the South, 1870–1914." *North Carolina Historical Review*, XXIII (1946), 172–95.

McCain, William D. "The Life and Labor of Dennis Murphree." *Journal of Mississippi History*, XII (1969), 183–91.

———. "Theodore Gilmore Bilbo and the Mississippi Delta." *Journal of Mississippi History*, XXXI (1969), 1–27.

Meek, Edwin E. "Eugene Octave Sykes, Member and Chairman of Federal Communications Commission and Federal Radio Commission, 1927–1939." *Journal of Mississippi History*, XXXVI (1974), 377–86.

"Mississippi's Two Edged Sword." *Literary Digest*, September 7, 1935, p. 4.

Patterson, James T. "The Failure of Party Realignment in the South, 1937–1939." *Journal of Politics*, XXVII (1965), 602–17.

"Primary: Pat Overwhelms Mike as Mud Flies over Mississippi." *Newsweek*, September 5, 1936, pp. 9–10.

Riddick, Floyd M. "First Session of the 76th Congress." *American Political Science Review*, XXXIII (1939), 1022–43.

Robison, Daniel M. "From Tillman to Long: Some Striking Leaders of the Rural South." *Journal of Southern History*, III (1937), 289–310.

Rutledge, Wilmuth Saunders. "The John J. Henry–Theodore G. Bilbo Encounter, 1911." *Journal of Mississippi History*, XXXIV (1972), 357–72.

Skates, John Ray. "From Enchantment to Disillusionment: A Southern Editor Views the New Deal." *Southern Quarterly*, V (1967), 363–80.

———. "Journalist vs. Politician: Fred Sullens and Theodore G. Bilbo." *Southern Quarterly*, VIII (1970), 273–85.

"Taxmaster." *Time*, June 1, 1936, pp. 10–12.

Tindall, George B. "Business Progressivism: Southern Politics in the Twenties." *South Atlantic Quarterly*, LXII (1963), 92–106.

T. R. B. "Washington Notes." *New Republic*, August 18, 1937, p. 45.

Whatley, Larry F. "The Works Progress Administration in Mississippi." *Journal of Mississippi History*, XXX (1968), 35–50.

Witte, Edwin E. "Old-Age Security in the Social Security Act." *Journal of Political Economy*, XLV (1937), 1–44.

Newspapers

Bay St. Louis *Sea Coast Echo*, August 21, 1936.

Biloxi *Daily Herald*, August 28, 1936.

Gloster *Record*, January 20, 1922.

Greenville *Delta Democrat Times*, July 5, 1946.

Hattiesburg *American*, 1939.

Jackson *Daily Clarion Ledger*, 1934–1940.

Jackson *Daily News*, February 16, 1908, 1935–1940.

Memphis *Commercial Appeal*, 1935–1939, 1982.

New Orleans *Times Picayune*, 1935–1937.

New York *Times*, 1935–1939.

Picayune *Item*, March 12, 1964.
Poplarville *Free Press*, May 16, 1907, October 25, 1917.

Theses and Dissertations

Bailey, Robert J. "Theodore G. Bilbo: Prelude to a Senate Career, 1932–1934." Master's thesis, University of Southern Mississippi, 1971.

Balsamo, Larry T. "Theodore G. Bilbo and Mississippi Politics, 1877–1932." Ph.D. dissertation, University of Missouri, 1967.

Blackwelder, Lynda Lawrence. "Theodore Gilmore Bilbo: The *Mississippi Free Lance* Years, 1923–1927." Master's thesis, University of Southern Mississippi, 1975.

Doler, Thurston E. "Theodore G. Bilbo's Rhetoric of Racial Relations." Ph.D. dissertation, University of Oregon, 1968.

Ethridge, Richard C. "Mississippi and the 1928 Presidential Campaign." Master's thesis, Mississippi State University, 1961.

Graham, Hardy P. "Bilbo and the University of Mississippi, 1928–1932." Master's thesis, University of Mississippi, 1965.

Hamilton, Charles G. "Mississippi Politics in the Progressive Era." Ph.D. dissertation, Vanderbilt University, 1958.

Hamilton, Virginia Van der Veer. "The Senate Career of Hugo L. Black." Ph.D. dissertation, University of Alabama, 1968.

Hanlon, Edward Francis. "Urban-Rural Cooperation and Conflict in the Congress: The Breakdown of the New Deal Coalition, 1933–1938." Ph.D. dissertation, Georgetown University, 1967.

Hartwig, Lynn Cook. "The Mississippi Highway Program, 1932–1945." Honors thesis, University of Southern Mississippi, 1969.

Hedlin, Ethel Wolfskill. "Earnest Cox and Colonization: A White Racist's Response to Black Repatriation, 1923–1966." Ph.D. dissertation, Duke University, 1974.

Kinsella, Dorothy C. "Southern Apologists: A Liberal Image." Ph.D. dissertation, St. Louis University, 1971.

Lewis, Jon Richard. "Progressivism Revisited: A Reevaluation of Mississippi Politics, 1920–1930." Master's thesis, University of Southern Mississippi, 1977.

Lucas, Aubrey Keith. "The Mississippi Legislature and Mississippi Public Higher Education: 1890–1960." Ph.D. dissertation, Florida State University, 1966.

McCain, William D. "The Populist Party in Mississippi." Master's thesis, University of Mississippi, 1931.

Marcello, Ronald. "The North Carolina Works Progress Administration and the Politics of Relief." Ph.D. dissertation, Duke University, 1968.

Saucier, Bobby Wade. "Pat Harrison: Conservative New Dealer." Master's thesis, Mississippi State University, 1960.

———. "The Public Career of Theodore G. Bilbo." Ph.D. dissertation, Tulane University, 1971.

Smith, Charles Pope. "Theodore G. Bilbo's Senatorial Career: The Final Years, 1941–1947." Ph.D. dissertation, University of Southern Mississippi, 1983.

Stoesen, Alexander Rudolph. "The Senatorial Career of Claude D. Pepper." Ph.D. dissertation, University of North Carolina, 1964.

Wallace, Frank. "A History of the Conner Administration." Master's thesis, Mississippi College, 1960.

Whatley, Larry F. "The New Deal Public Works Program in Mississippi." Master's thesis, Mississippi State University, 1965.

Index

Agricultural Adjustment Act: 1933, pp. 69, 161, 163, 165, 192, 198, 199, 201; 1938, pp. 180, 188, 195, 202–203, 204–205
Agricultural Adjustment Administration: 63, 64, 200, 208–209
Agricultural laboratory, 169, 188–94
Agriculture: 26, 198; Bilbo's interest in, 180–81; legislation, 187–206, 208–14
Alexander, Will, 208, 209, 211, 215
Alliston, Wayne, 81, 83, 84, 134–38, 140, 141, 143, 145
American Chemical Foundation, 189
American Farm Bureau Federation, 125, 188, 212
American Federation of Labor, 71, 125, 173
Army Corps of Engineers, 175

Bailey, Thomas, 19, 217–18, 221, 222, 223
Balance Agriculture With Industry program, 22–23, 141, 141*n*, 173
Bankhead Cotton Control Act, 201, 205
Bankhead, John, 179, 191, 208, 213, 214
Bankhead-Jones Act of 1935, p. 190
Bankhead-Jones Act of 1937, pp. 153, 208–12
Bankhead, William, 191, 192
Barkley, Alben, 167–69, 175, 179, 180
Baruch, Bernard, 129, 130, 171, 177
Bell, Daniel, 189–90
Bell, Percy, 40
Bilbo, Linda Gaddy Bedgood, 27, 60–61, 100, 229
Bilbo, Theodore G.: Baptist church, 27; birth, 26, 252; brick speech, 41; conservatism, 251, 252; constituency, 19, 38, 40–41, 48, 49–50, 53, 81, 84, 99–100, 104, 117–18, 119, 120, 130, 158, 172, 187, 197, 215, 216, 232, 234, 237, 242, 244; death, 247, 250, 252; demagoguery, 13, 234–41; Dream House, 58, 105–106; early career, 27, 28, 30–33, 36; education, 27, 28, 31; family, 26, 27, 58, 60–62, 82, 100, 186; farmer, 39, 186; federal job, 63–64, 118; financial problems, 27, 29, 58–60, 103, 113–14; as governor, 16, 19, 37–39, 42–46; jailed, 40, 107, 110, 111; liberal, 2–4, 16, 23, 25, 30–31, 37, 39, 46–50, 66, 70–71, 72–75, 77, 86, 104, 156–61, 169–78, 180–85, 185*n*, 197, 206–207, 229–30, 233–34, 236–37, 240, 242–44, 246, 251–53; morality and ethics, 28–29, 32–33, 34, 36, 37, 186, 250; patronage, 98, 117, 124–25, 129, 131–60, 169, 212, 219; politician, 3, 46, 62, 159, 212, 214, 232–34, 247; populist heritage, 174; relationship with the press, 46, 57, 64, 234; public opinion, 1, 5, 46–47, 49, 57, 65, 131, 148–49, 185*n*, 193–94, 229, 234, 236–38, 250; race, 47–50, 66, 100–101, 226–27, 235–38, 247–53; redneck, 2–4, 25, 48, 53, 99–100, 241, 244, 246; as senator, 25, 57, 59, 64–66, 116, 232–34, 241–46; style, 2, 3, 35, 48, 50, 52, 53, 57, 114–15, 122–23, 159, 233–34, 238–40, 244, 249, 250; as symbol, 241, 252
—Campaigns: early, 27–30, 33–36, 37, 38–39, 39–40, 40–42, 50, 53, 104; Senate, 1934, pp. 46, 62–63, 64, 70–71, 104, 118, 132; Senate 1940, pp. 153, 224–26, 228–29; Senate 1946, pp. 250–51
—as New Dealer: 3, 4, 23, 57, 64, 66, 70–77, 86, 99, 105, 116, 154, 156–60, 171–78, 180–85, 185*n*, 187, 188, 197–99, 201–204, 206, 210–12, 214, 229–31, 233–34, 236–38,

237*n*, 240, 242–45, 252–53; agriculture, 180, 186–94, 197–98, 201–206, 210–15; farm policy, 154; food stamps, 180–81; labor, 76, 173–74; parity, 198, 205–206; public housing, 176; relief, 72, 180–81; social security, 73–74, 182–84; tax, 75–76, 176–77
Birkhead, Frances, 40, 40*n*, 107, 111
Black counties. *See* Bourbons; Conservatives; Planters
Black, Hugo, 42, 70, 76, 166, 169–70, 173, 176, 202
Blacks, 8–11, 13, 15–16, 51, 73. *See also* Race issue; Race relations
Bond, Willard F., 28
Borah, William E., 68, 176, 187
Bourbons, 2, 8, 10, 12, 17–19, 42, 50–52, 245–46. *See also* Conservatives; Planters; Redeemers
Brandeis, Louis, 74
Braun, Charles, 80–81, 124, 137
Brewer, Earl, 16, 36–37
Bribery scandal of 1910, pp. 32–33, 36–37
Broom, Stewart C., 110, 125–26
Bruce, Blanche K., 8
Bryan, Nathan P., 107, 110
Burkett, John, 85, 110, 135, 137, 138, 140, 222
Bush, B. A., 139, 143, 146, 148–49
Business, 74–75, 76
Byrd, Harry, 71, 176, 183
Byrnes, James F., 66, 68, 69, 162–64, 167, 168, 170, 172, 176, 177, 180, 207, 210

Capt, J. C., 145–46, 149–50
Carter, Hodding, 98, 102
Cash, Wilbur J., 2, 13, 29, 234–35
Catledge, Turner, 172–73
Cattle Dipping Law, 38–39, 197
Civil rights, 3, 66, 247, 249–53. *See also* Race issue; Race relations
Cohen, Ben, 74, 165
College Board. *See* Education
Collins, Ross, 20, 64
Colmer, William, 191
Commodity Credit Corporation, 187, 200, 202, 203, 204
Congress of Industrial Organizations, 163, 251
Congressional Record, 175
Connally, Tom, 164, 182–84, 203, 204
Conner, Martin Sennett: and Bilbo, 104, 119, 132; career of, 21, 104; Highway Commission, 21–22, 78–79, 134; patronage, 80–81, 84, 97, 98, 134, 136, 140; political activity, 40–42, 78, 80–81, 83, 84, 97–99, 104, 105, 116–30, 139, 144, 146, 152, 153, 216, 217, 220–24 *passim*; Roosevelt, 98; mentioned, 135, 139, 233
Conner, Oscar Weir, 21
Conservatism, 46–49, 159–60, 245
Conservatives: Mississippi government, 8, 11, 13, 35–36, 41–43, 225, 228; New Deal, 66, 68–70, 162–64, 171, 173, 176–80, 182, 184, 212; race, 49–50, 228
Constitution of 1890, pp. 10, 11, 12, 78
Copeland, E. A., 79
Corcoran, Tom, 74, 165
Corrupt Practices Act, 130
Cotton, 187–97, 199–205, 208–12, 213–14, 225
Cotton Textile Institute, 196
Court reform plan, 202, 204
Cox, Earnest Sevier, 248, 249
Crop control, 188, 198–203
Crosby, L. O., 224–26
Cummings, Homer, 107–109, 163, 218

Daniels, Josephus, 47, 158
Demagoguery, 13, 48–50, 86, 158, 234–41, 250
Democratic National Convention, 1940, pp. 147, 152, 153, 217, 224
Democratic party: civil rights, 235–36, 236*n*, 249; liberalization, 134, 179, 184, 243, 252; Mississippi, 9, 10, 13, 62, 105, 146–47, 216; New Deal, 67–69, 161, 162, 164, 170, 177, 178
Depression, 46, 197–99
Disabled American Veterans, 125
Disfranchisement. *See* Rednecks; Blacks
Doxey, Wall, 192, 212–13
Dulaney, L. C., 32–33, 34
Dunn, Aubert, 128

Eastland, James O., 212–13
Economic conditions: America, 180–82, 197–99; Mississippi, 23, 26, 43–44, 57, 83, 132, 157, 159, 174, 183; politics of, 49–52; the South, 172–73, 190, 200, 202, 204, 205–206, 208, 213
Education, 44–46
Emergency Relief Appropriations Act, 71, 72, 81, 124, 133, 134
Executive reorganization plan, 177, 178

Fair Employment Practices Commission, 249
Farley, James, 128, 129, 134, 148–49
Farmers Home Administration, 219
Farm Security Administration, 211–12
Favre, "Red," 124
Federal Emergency Relief Act, 69
Federal Emergency Relief Administration, 80, 84, 98, 134, 153, 208
Federal Farm Board, 199
Federal Surplus Commodities Corporation. *See* Food stamp program
Flood control, 175
Fly, Eugene, 140, 143, 144, 222
Food stamp program, 180–81, 187
Ford, Henry and Edsel, 189
Frankfurter, Felix, 74
Franklin, Lester, 20, 40, 79, 96, 97, 120, 218, 221, 223

Garner, John Nance, 66, 68, 69, 163, 164, 170, 177, 179
Garvey, Marcus, 248
George, J. Z., 7, 11, 14, 19
Gibbs, Washington, 34
Gladney, T. G., 147, 149
Glass, Carter, 47, 165, 166, 171
Gordon, Middie Maud Lena, 248–49
Governorship—Mississippi, 104
Governor's race: 1903, pp. 14–15, 50; 1923, p. 104; 1931, p. 99; 1935, pp. 77–106, 108, 113, 119, 135–38, 245; 1939, pp. 103, 131, 152–53, 216–24 *passim*
Greater Liberia Bill. *See* Repatriation
Green, William, 71–72, 125
Guffey, Joseph, 175, 180, 230, 230*n*
Gulf & Ship Island Railroad, 26, 30–31, 173

Hammond *Daily Courier*, 98
Hall, Toxey, 119
Harrington, Francis G., 149–52, 180, 220
Harrison, Byron Patton: and Bilbo, 62–66, 86, 105, 107–109, 112–21, 123, 131–33, 138–40, 168–69, 207, 241–43; conservatism, 167, 241–43, 242*n*; constituency, 117–18, 130, 146, 152, 163–64, 242; death, 153; financial problems, 112–13; early career, 38; Hopkins, 155–56; New Deal—con, 66, 68, 69, 75–76, 116, 131, 146–47, 152, 155, 157, 164, 176–77, 179, 202, 210, 242; New Deal—pro, 64, 127–29, 172–73, 213; patronage, 117–34, 138–49, 151–56, 169, 216; political activity, 42, 80, 81, 84, 98, 105, 108–109, 110, 117–31, 147, 167–69, 178, 216–24; political influence, 107–108, 116, 127–29, 131, 133, 155–56, 170; mentioned, 47, 233
Hederman, R. M. and T. M., 121
Henry, J. J., 34
Highway Commission, 21–22, 43, 78–79, 130, 134, 218–19, 222–23
Hobbs, George, 36
Holmes, Edwin, 40, 107–15, 126, 139, 140, 216
Hoover, Herbert, 42–43, 199
Hopkins, Harry, 72, 80–81, 84, 124, 134, 137, 140, 142–45, 147–51, 153–56, 159–60, 187, 208, 219, 245
Housing, public, 170, 176, 185
Hughes, Charles Evans, 164
Hume, Alfred, 44–46
Hunter, Howard, 142, 152

Ickes, Harold, 77, 117, 155, 169, 189, 218
Industrialization, 18, 22–23
Inman, Cecil, 82

Jackson *Daily Clarion Ledger*, 34, 45, 121, 228
Jackson *Daily News*, 31, 85, 98, 100, 101–102, 135
Jackson, Gardner, 207, 210, 215
Jews, 238
Jiggitts, Louis, 129, 222
Johnson, Paul B.: Bilbo, 104, 216; career, 20, 224–26; political activity, 38–39, 78, 80–85 *passim*, 96–98, 100–105 *passim*, 119–21, 131, 136–38, 152, 153, 216–24 *passim*; mentioned, 158, 223, 233
Johnstone, Alan, 140–44
Judicial Reform Bill. *See* United States Supreme Court
Juniper Grove, 26, 58, 60, 65

Kenna, Doug, 218, 223
Knox, Rush, 82
Kramer, X. A., 59, 168
Ku Klux Klan, 42, 43

Labor law, 69–72, 76, 150, 163, 166, 170–74, 178, 185, 251
Ladner, Heber, 122, 130, 143–44, 193, 245
La Follette, Robert, 3, 38, 68, 71, 166,

171, 176, 177, 180, 181, 206, 213
Lamar, L. Q. C., 7, 8, 19, 169, 242
Landon, Alf, 161
Legislature, Mississippi, 10, 18–19, 30–33, 36, 42, 43, 45, 52, 62, 104, 130, 225, 226, 228
Lewis, John L., 226
Liberalism, 3, 25, 158
Liberals: Bilbo, 25, 49, 57, 159–60, 207–208, 214–15, 234, 236–38, 242, 244–46; and conservatives, 159–60, 245–46; New Deal, 69, 70, 162, 164, 170–71, 184, 206–208
Linker, Abe, 218, 223
Literacy test, 11, 12
Long, Huey: Bilbo, 86, 96, 99–100, 103–105, 243–45; constituency, 135, 244–45; death, 103, 139; demagoguery, 240, 243–44; New Deal, 75, 86, 99, 244–45; political activity, 80, 86, 96–100, 102–105; mentioned, 69, 108, 109, 114, 119, 129
Lumbering, 26, 174
Lynching, 227, 236, 237, 243*n*, 248, 249

McGehee, Dan, 148, 174
McLaurin, Anselm J., 31
Memphis *Commercial Appeal*, 121, 127, 141
Miller, Malcolm J., 80, 140, 143, 144, 147, 149, 151, 154, 155
Mississippi Agricultural and Mechanical College, 45
Mississippi Bar Association, 109, 115
Mississippi Emergency Relief Administration, 134, 136, 137, 140
Mississippi Farm Bureau Federation, 196
Mississippi Federation of Labor, 72, 125
Mississippi *Free Lance*, 40–41, 47–48
Mississippi State College for Women, 45
Mississippi Supreme Court, 109
Mississippi's image, 1
Mitchell, W. W., 27
Money, H. D., 14
Morgenthau, Henry, 127, 128
Murphree, Dennis, 21, 41–42, 78–80, 82–84, 97, 98, 120, 217–18, 223
Myers, George, 42

National Association for the Advancement of Colored People, 226
National Farm Chemurgic Council, 189
National Grange, 196
National Industrial Recovery Act of 1933, pp. 69, 70, 180
National Labor Relations Act of 1935, pp. 76, 163, 173
National Labor Relations Board, 173
National Recovery Administration, 70, 163, 172
National School Lunch Act, 252
New Deal: 23, 67–70, 159–62, 170–71, 178, 244; coalition, 161, 162, 164, 170–71, 184, 252; Congress, 170, 177–78; Mississippi, 146–47, 159–60, 216; Second Hundred Days, 66, 70–76, 170–71; second term, 170–85; the South, 173, 252
New South Creed, 17
New York *Herald Tribune*, 142
New York *Times*, 172–73, 183, 224
Newsweek, 122
Norris, George, 38, 171, 180, 187, 206

O'Neal, Edward, 125, 188, 201, 207

Parity, 177, 198–99, 205–206
Patman, Wright, 77, 123
Patronage: federal, 72, 80–84, 98, 109, 116–18, 121, 123–25, 127, 129–60, 169, 212, 216, 218–21, 244; state, 45, 80, 117, 119, 134–35, 216, 222, 223
Patterson, Hiram, 81, 82, 85, 218, 222–23
Peace Movement of Ethiopia, 248
Pensions, 220–21. *See* Social security
Pepper, Claude, 156–57, 159, 173, 174, 179, 180, 193, 206, 243*n*
Percy, LeRoy, 32, 33–35, 50
Percy, William Alexander, 5, 9, 11, 24–25, 32, 41, 51, 246
Planters, 5, 7, 10. *See also* Bourbons; Conservatives; Redeemers
Politics—Mississippi: 6–8, 14, 104, 241–43; Bilbo, 116, 121, 122, 216–18; 1911 election, 35; violence in, 101–102
Politics—National, 42–43, 154–60
Poll tax, 11–13, 130, 226, 228, 237, 249
Poor whites. *See* Rednecks
Poplarville *Free Press*, 145
Populism, 8, 12, 14, 15, 26, 27, 174, 235
Porter, Marvin, 152–53, 220
Presidential elections: 1936, p. 161; 1940, pp. 230–31
Primary law, open, 10, 12–15, 51
Prison system, Mississippi, 36
Progressivism: in Mississippi, 6, 7, 16, 17, 19–23, 35–36, 38, 49–50, 78, 101, 103–104; New Deal, 67–71,

74–77, 158, 164, 171, 177; in the South, 46–50
Prohibition, 42
Public Works Administration, 117

Race issue, 9, 11, 12, 15, 42–43, 47–52, 62, 66, 73, 100, 160, 171, 209, 212, 221, 226–28, 234–38, 241–43, 247–53
Race relations, 1, 2
Railroads, 26
Rankin, John, 148, 173
Reapportionment—congressional, 62
Reconstruction, 9
Reconstruction Finance Corporation, 132, 200
Redeemers, 6, 7, 9–15 *passim*, 17–18, 19, 51–52
Rednecks: 2, 5, 6, 10–12, 35, 232, 240–41, 245, 246; Bilbo, 19, 25, 29, 33, 35, 38–39, 53, 57, 65, 99, 117, 119, 120, 130, 139, 157, 159, 234, 244–46; economic conditions, 7–8, 14, 49, 99, 174; Long, 135; New Deal, 228, 244–45; politics, 10–14, 20, 25, 51; progressivism, 17, 18, 41; race, 51–52, 237; Vardaman, 50–52, 53
Relief, 72–73, 132–34, 157, 159, 170, 178–81, 184, 187, 208
Repatriation, 227–28, 236, 237*n*, 247–49
Republican party, 9, 164, 178
Resettlement Administration, 209–11
Revenue Act of 1935, p. 75
Revenue system, Mississippi, 37
Robinson, Joseph, 66, 68, 69, 127, 156, 162, 166–68, 170, 172, 179, 210
Roebuck, S. T., 218, 223
Roosevelt, Franklin D.: Bilbo, 64, 73, 86, 99, 102, 105, 115–16, 131, 146–49, 151–53, 218, 224, 229–31, 243, 244, 252; agriculture, 188–91, 194, 209–11; judiciary, 107–109, 162–67, 169, 170, 172, 202, 204; patronage, 98, 117, 138, 145; political influence, 105, 127–29, 146–47, 155, 177, 178, 212, 217–20, 224; public opinion, 99, 154, 159, 162, 171, 216, 244–45; race issue, 3, 49; veterans' bonus, 123; mentioned, 23, 134
Roosevelt, James, 146–47, 169, 185*n*
Rotarianism. *See* Progressivism
Rural Rehabilitation Administration, 98, 208, 210, 212
Russell, Lee, 16, 39–40, 40*n*, 107, 111

Sales tax, 21, 42, 43, 130
Sawmills. *See* Lumbering
Secret caucus of 1910, pp. 32–33, 35, 52
Segregation. *See* Race issue
Sharecroppers. *See* Cotton; Rednecks
Shipman, W. S., 79
Sledge, Norfleet, 120, 127, 144
Smith, Al, 42–43, 238, 242
Smith, E. D., 172, 177, 189, 197, 201–203
Smith, Lamar, 82, 126
Snider, J. B., 102, 120, 218, 223
Social conditions, 23, 159, 211
Social security, 73–74, 127, 163, 178, 181–85
Soil erosion, 161, 175, 201
South, the, 46–50, 66
Southern Association of Colleges and Secondary Schools, 44–45
Southern Commissioners of Agriculture, 196
State Tax Commission, 37
State Teachers College, 45
Stephens, Hubert, 39, 62–64, 97, 109, 128, 132–33
Sullens, Fred: 31, 34, 35, 37, 40, 45, 64, 80, 97–98, 100, 101, 135, 194, 220–21, 225, 226–28; and Bilbo, 103, 228–29, 233
Sykes, Eugene, 109, 118

Talmadge, Eugene, 242, 244–45
Tannenbaum, Frank, 208, 209, 210
Taxation, 37, 75–76, 176–77
Tenants. *See* Cotton; Rednecks
Tennessee Valley Authority, 129, 174–75
Texas tick fever, 38–39
Textbook printing plant issue, 42, 43
Townsend, Francis, 69, 182, 182–83
Truman, Harry, 175, 180
Tugwell, Rexford, 197, 198, 206, 207, 209–11, 215

United States Congress: elections, 62, 69, 161, 177–78; House elections, 104, 216; Senate, 108, 110–15, 127, 167–69
—Senate elections: 1907, p. 50; 1910, pp. 31–33; 1911, pp. 50, 52–53, 57; 1918, pp. 38, 117; 1922, pp. 38, 39; 1934, pp. 104, 118, 132, 133; 1936, pp. 80, 81, 116–31, 135, 139, 140, 144–45, 233; 1940, pp. 153, 169, 217, 224–26, 228–29; 1946, pp. 250–51

United States Fifth Circuit Court of Appeals, 107–16
United States Supreme Court, 62, 70, 161, 162, 167, 169–70, 172, 177, 178
Universal Negro Improvement Association, 248
University of Mississippi, 44–46

Vardaman, James K.: 3, 13–16 *passim*, 38, 50; and Bilbo, 19, 24–25, 35, 39, 50–53, 57; campaigns, 14, 15, 31–32, 34–35, 38, 39, 50, 52–53, 57, 117; constituency, 38, 40–41, 49–50, 53; progressivism, 19, 24–25; race, 49–50, 51–52
Veterans' bonus issue, 70, 76–77, 123, 125, 135, 161

Wages and hours debate. *See* Labor law
Wagner Act, 76, 163, 173
Wagner, Robert, 76, 157, 176
Wall, Roland, 124–25, 135, 139–40, 143–53 *passim*, 155, 173, 219–20
Wallace, Henry, 63, 181, 185*n*, 188, 189, 191, 193, 194, 196, 201, 204, 209, 212, 214–15, 252
Walthall, E. C., 7, 8, 14, 19
Washington *Daily News*, 152
Welfare, 70–74, 158, 171, 178
Westbrook, Lawrence, 153–54
Wheeler, Burton K., 68, 74, 164, 177, 206
White, Edward Douglass, 169
White, Hugh L.: career, 22–23; Bilbo, 102–105, 165, 191; campaigns, 78, 79–80, 82–85, 97–102 *passim*, 104, 105, 107, 108, 113, 136–39, 224–26, 228–29; political activity, 120–21, 147, 216–18, 221–23; race, 237; mentioned, 21, 117, 119, 131, 135, 152, 233
White, John James, 22
White supremacy. *See* Race issue
Whitfield, Henry L., 18, 19, 40, 41, 44
Whittington, Will, 62, 148
Williams, Aubrey, 136, 140, 146, 147, 149, 150, 155, 159, 160, 219
Williams, John Sharp, 38, 39, 47, 50
Wilson, Woodrow, 38
Woodward, Ellen, 125, 139, 152, 155, 219
Works Progress Administration: 81, 83, 98, 116, 181; finance, 177, 178–79, 180; patronage, 117, 119, 121, 124–25, 131, 132, 134–60, 219–21; "vocational schools," 141–43, 149–50, 173